THE ASSURANCE
OF FAITH

Conscience in the
Theology of Martin Luther and John Calvin

THE ASSURANCE
OF FAITH

RANDALL C. ZACHMAN

FORTRESS PRESS   **MINNEAPOLIS**

THE ASSURANCE OF FAITH
Conscience in the Theology of Martin Luther and John Calvin

Scripture quotations unless otherwise noted are from the New Revised Standard Version Bible, copyright © 1989 by the Division of Christian Education of the National Council of the Churches of Christ in the United States.

Excerpts from *Calvin's New Testament Commentaries*, ed. David W. Torrance and Thomas F. Torrance, are copyright © 1959-1972 William B. Eerdmans Publishing Co., Grand Rapids, MI. Used by permission.

Excerpts from *Calvin: Institutes of the Christian Religion*, ed. John T. McNeill and trans. Ford Lewis Battles (Volume XX and XXI: The Library of Christian Classics), are copyright © MCMLX W. L. Jenkins. Used by permission of Westminster/John Knox Press.

Interior design: Publishers' WorkGroup
Cover design: Patricia Boman
Cover art: Rogier van der Weyden, The Magdalen Reading (detail). Reproduced by courtesy of the Trustees, The National Gallery, London.

Library of Congress Cataloging-in-Publication Data

Zachman, Randall C., 1953–
   The assurance of faith : conscience in the theology of Martin Luther and John Calvin / Randall C. Zachman.
      p.   cm.
   Includes bibliographical references and index.
   ISBN 0-8006-2574-9 (alk. paper)
      1. Luther, Martin, 1483–1546.   2. Calvin, Jean, 1509–1564.
3. Conscience—Religious aspects—Christianity—History of
doctrines—16th century.   4. Assurance (Theology)—History of
doctrines—16th century.   I. Title.
BR333.2.Z33   1992
241'.1'0922—dc20   92–12726
                                                                    CIP

The paper used in this publication meets the minimum requirements of American National Standard for Information Sciences—Permanence of Paper for Printed Library Materials, ANSI Z329.48-1984.   ∞™

Manufactured in the U.S.A.   AF 1-2574
97   96   95   94   93   1   2   3   4   5   6   7   8   9   10

CONTENTS

PREFACE

The thesis of my book can be stated briefly: Even though Luther and Calvin do have different emphases and motifs in their theology, they agree fundamentally that the foundation of the assurance of faith lies in the grace and mercy of God toward us in Jesus Christ crucified, revealed to us in the gospel. The testimony of a good conscience confirms, but does not ground, this assurance of faith by attesting that our faith in Christ is sincere and not feigned. Given the axiom, however, that both theologians follow—that God is only gracious to those who sincerely believe in Jesus Christ—the distinction they make between the foundation and confirmation of assurance is not as stable as they hoped, leaving open the possibility that the relation between the two might in fact be reversed.

Such a thesis owes it inception to two questions posed to me by my teachers of theology. The first question emerged during an independent study that I and two others took with George Lindbeck, Yale Divinity School. During our reading of Luther's *Lectures on Galatians*, Lindbeck asked me, "Why do you think Luther speaks about the peace and assurance of conscience so often?" My inability to answer that question haunted me from then on. The next quarter I studied Calvin's theology with David Kelsey. During my reading of the *Institutes*, I found to my surprise that Luther and Calvin were not as different as the common wisdom surrounding them had suggested, but were rather in fundamental agreement concerning the foundation of the assurance of faith. I knew then that my dissertation would argue a thesis about this fundamental agreement between the two reformers not only to clarify their theological relationship to one another but also to advance ecumenical understanding and reconciliation between the two traditions.

The second question was posed to me by B. A. Gerrish during a conversation at the University of Chicago Divinity School regarding my thesis about Luther and Calvin. After concurring with me that the two were in fundamental agreement about the assurance of faith, Gerrish asked me, "Then why is it that they *sound* so different?" That question proved to be most difficult but also most fruitful to answer, because it forced me to understand the inner dynamic at work in the theology of Luther and Calvin that would account for their different emphases. During this time my studies of Schleiermacher and Barth with Langdon Gilkey and James Gustafson convinced me that testimony was a central issue for the thesis: namely, the relationship of the testimony of God to us, and the testimony of our conscience to ourselves. Indeed, as my committee pointed out to me during my oral review, Karl Barth lurks behind the thesis as the hidden theologian (*theologus absconditus*). Undoubtedly the kinds of questions he raised concerning the theology of Schleiermacher and the Reformers have shaped my theological thinking in general, and the thesis of this book in particular, although this thesis is by no means intended as a defense or vindication of Barth's theology or his reading of Luther and Calvin.

I am profoundly grateful to my teachers for the discipline and critical openness they fostered in me, especially for encouraging me to understand sympathetically those with whom I disagree and to think critically about those with whom I agree. I also am grateful to my students, past and present, for their provocative questions and for all the insights they have shared with me. I give special thanks to the many people who have carefully read and criticized previous drafts of this manuscript, especially B. A. Gerrish, James M. Gustafson, Langdon Gilkey, and Dr. Heiko Obermann. They have all kept me from making obvious mistakes and have sharpened my reading of Luther and Calvin with their questions, especially in those places where our interpretations finally differed.

The translations used in this book are taken from the standard English translations of the works of Luther and Calvin and have been checked against the originals in every instance. Many of the footnotes include reference to a larger passage in the original from which the quote has been taken.

This book is dedicated to my wife, Gina. We met and were married during my first year at the University of Chicago. She has not only brought genuine joy into my life, but has also encouraged me throughout the preparation of this manuscript to keep putting one foot down before the other, even when there seemed to be no end in sight. For her love, and for the love of our son, John Alex, I give thanks to God. I dedicate this work to her in gratitude.

ABBREVIATIONS

C.N.T.C.	*Calvin's New Testament Commentaries*. Edited by David W. Torrance and Thomas F. Torrance. 12 vols. Grand Rapids, Mich.: Wm. B. Eerdmans, 1959–1972.
C.O.	*Ioannis Calvini opera quae supersunt omnia*. Edited by Wilhelm Baum, Edward Cunitz, and Edward Reuss. 59 vols. *Corpus Reformatorum* vols. 29–87. Brunsvigae: A. Schwetschke and Son (M. Bruhn), 1863–1900.
C.T.S.	*The Commentaries of John Calvin on the Old Testament*. 30 vols. Edinburgh: Calvin Translation Society, 1843–1848.
Inst.	John Calvin, *Institutio Christianae religionis 1559*. Cited by book, chapter, and section, from O.S. III–V, followed in parentheses by volume and page references to: *Calvin: Institutes of the Christian Religion*. Edited by John T. McNeill and translated by Ford Lewis Battles. 2 vols. Philadelphia: Westminster Press, 1960.
L.W.	*Luther's Works*. American edition. Edited by Jaroslav Pelikan and Helmut T. Lehman. 54 vols. St. Louis: Concordia Publishing House; Philadelphia: Fortress Press, 1955–1967.
O.S.	*Ioannis Calvini opera selecta*. Edited by Peter Barth, Wilhelm Niesel, and Dora Scheuner. 5 vols. Munich: Chr. Kaiser, 1926–1952.
Psalms	*Luther's Commentary on the First Twenty-two Psalms*. Edited by John Nicholas Lenker. Vol. 1. Sunbury, Pa.: Lutherans in All Lands, 1903.
Sermons	*Sermons of Martin Luther*. Edited by John Nicholas Lenker. 8 vols. Grand Rapids, Mich.: Baker Book House, 1983.

St. L.   *Dr. Martin Luthers Saemmtliche Schriften*. Edited
                    by Johann Georg Walch. 23 vols. Saint Louis:
                    Concordia, 1881–1910.

Tracts   John Calvin. *Tracts and Treatises*. Translated by
                    Henry Beveridge. 3 vols. Grand Rapids, Mich.:
                    Wm. B. Eerdmans, 1958.

Treatises   *Calvin: Theological Treatises*. Edited by J. K. S.
                    Reid. Philadelphia: Westminster Press, 1954.

W. A.   *D. Martin Luthers Werke: Kritische
                    Gesamtausgabe*. Weimar: Hermann Boehlau, 1883–
                    1983.

W. A. D. B.   *Die Deutsche Bibel*

THE ASSURANCE
OF FAITH

INTRODUCTION

HOW CAN WE BE ASSURED
THAT GOD IS MERCIFUL
TO US?

Who is God, and what is the will of God toward humanity? Is the will of God one of grace and love toward us? If so, how do we know this? Do we know this on the basis of what God has done *for* us once for all in Jesus Christ, revealed to us in the gospel through the Holy Spirit? Or do we know this on the basis of what God is doing *in* us through the sanctifying power of the Holy Spirit? If the former, can our faith in the work of God for us be strengthened or confirmed by the testimony of our conscience regarding the work of God in us? In other words, is our knowledge of the grace of God derived solely from the testimony of the Father in Jesus Christ through the Holy Spirit, or can we also testify to ourselves, via the good conscience, of the grace of God toward us?

These questions have been central to the theological tradition of the West since the time of Augustine, gaining a special urgency at the time of the Reformation, especially in the theology of Luther and Calvin. Although Luther and Calvin must be understood within the continuum of the Augustinian tradition, they introduced into that tradition a new primary definition of grace, and therefore a new understanding of how we come to an assured knowledge of that grace. In the previous Augustinian tradition, grace was primarily understood as the gift of infusion by the Holy Spirit: "God's love has been poured into our hearts through the Holy Spirit that has been given to us" (Rom. 5:5). Justification by grace thus meant the making right of the will; for grace frees the will from sinful bondage to self-love and concupiscence and gives it both the volition and the ability to love God and neighbor. According to Augustine, we know of the gracious will of God toward us primarily on the basis of what God has done and is doing within us. "Or shall anything restore us to hope, unless it be your known mercy, since you have begun to change us?"[1]

For Luther and Calvin, on the other hand, the word "grace" refers primarily to the work of God for us in the death and resurrection of Jesus Christ. "For

---

1. *The Confessions of Augustine*, trans. John K. Ryan (Garden City, N.Y.: Image Books, 1960), Book X, chap. 36, p. 266.

1

our sake he made him to be sin who knew no sin, so that in him we might become the righteousness of God" (2 Cor. 5:21). Justification by faith occurs through faith in this happy and wonderful exchange, wherein Christ takes our sin, death, and the wrath of God upon himself and freely gives us his own righteousness, life, and grace, which alone can stand before the judgment seat of God. Those who are justified also receive the gift of the Holy Spirit, which sanctifies the intellect and will along lines similar to Augustine's; however, the basis of our knowledge and assurance that God is gracious to us is the work of God for us in Jesus Christ, revealed to us by the gospel and the Holy Spirit. The knowledge of our renewal confirms our assurance of God's mercy, but it can never be the foundation of that assurance.

The new definition of grace given by Luther and Calvin brought about a corresponding shift in the particular anthropological locus toward which the grace of God is directed. The locus is no longer primarily the will, as it was for Augustine, but the conscience. The conscience is that power of the soul that judges what the person does on the basis of what the person should do, thereby rendering the person either condemned or acquitted—that is, justified—before God. Apart from the grace of Christ, the conscience only finds grounds for condemnation before God, no matter how hard it tries to overcome such condemnation by the performance of good works. The grace of Jesus Christ frees the conscience from its attempt to justify itself before God by trusting in its own works, and places the trust of the conscience in the righteousness and forgiveness of Christ alone.

In other words, the testimony that renders the conscience—and hence the person—acquitted and justified before God cannot come from the conscience, but rather must be given to the conscience by the Word of the gospel. The conscience that believes the testimony of the gospel receives peace and consolation, for its sins are forgiven and it need no longer fear the judgment of God. The conscience also finds certainty, for the testimony on which it relies is the Word of God, and God cannot and will not lie. The faithful conscience acquires freedom as well, for it is freed by grace from the futile attempt to justify itself before God on the basis of works.

Is it actually the case that Luther and Calvin agree on the relation of the grace of Christ and the testimony of the gospel to the conscience? The evidence of much of the secondary literature, as well as much theological and historical common wisdom, suggests that they do not. Luther is often described as being preeminently concerned with consoling terrified consciences by directing them away from the law and toward the certainty of divine mercy found in Jesus Christ alone. His theological concern to comfort terrified consciences is usually seen to be an outgrowth of his own religious struggles in the monastery, where he experienced the futility as well as the terror of seeking to justify himself before God on the basis of works. His theology is often termed "existential"; his biographical development is used as a way of charting his theological development, as can be seen in the massive amount of scholarly material produced concerning the date and nature of Luther's so-called tower experience.

Calvin, in contrast, is often characterized (especially among Lutheran scholars) as subverting the heart of Luther's Reformation theology. Calvin's emphasis on the importance of sanctification in the Christian life, made most apparent in the third use of the law, is described as an attempt to turn the consciences of believers away from trust in the mercy of Christ so that they seek to ascertain their status before God on the basis of works. Calvin's doctrine of election only compounds the problem, it is said, by rendering consciences uncertain as to whether the promise of forgiveness revealed in Christ applies to them, thereby turning them even more anxiously to works in an effort to gain assurance of election—and hence of forgiveness—from the evidences of a sanctified life. Finally, Calvin's emphasis on church discipline and excommunication and his formulation of church polity are seen as subjecting the consciences of believers to a new kind of legalism and illegitimate coercion.

To make matters worse, Calvin's theology is subjected to the same biographical and existential test as that administered to Luther's. Not surprisingly, Calvin is seen as a cold, austere, and arrogant man (qualities revealed with chilling clarity in the trial and execution of Servetus), and these personality traits are automatically and uncritically read back into Calvin's theology. Hence Calvin's doctrine of God is seen to be cold, remote, and austere, as contrasted to Luther's God of love. Calvin's God predestines some to salvation and most to damnation in God's hidden and majestic will, whereas Luther's God dies for the forgiveness of sinners according to God's revealed will.

Such a comparison of Luther and Calvin gained wide acceptance at the beginning of this century. Reinhold Seeberg, for instance, in his *The History of Doctrines*, attempts to show significant and fundamental similarities between Luther and Calvin, especially with regard to the doctrine of justification and the assurance of faith. However, he concludes his treatment of the theology of Calvin with a comparison between Luther and Calvin along the lines laid down above: "The God of Calvin is the omnipotent Will, ruling throughout the world; the God of Luther is the omnipotent energy of Love manifest in Christ."[2]

Similar comparisons are to be found in the work of Max Weber. Indeed, Weber makes his contrast between Luther and Calvin central to the thesis of his book *The Protestant Ethic and the Spirit of Capitalism*. "The Father in heaven of the New Testament . . . is gone. His place has been taken by a transcendental being . . . who with His quite incomprehensible decrees has decided the fate of every individual . . . from eternity."[3] Weber combines this apparent change in the doctrine of God with the corresponding attempt to

2. Reinhold Seeberg, *The History of Doctrines*, 2 vols. (Grand Rapids, Mich.: Baker Book House, 1977), vol. 2, p. 416.

3. Max Weber, *The Protestant Ethic and the Spirit of Capitalism*, trans. Talcott Parsons (New York: Charles Scribners' Sons, 1958), pp. 103–4.

gain certainty of salvation not through faith in the mercy of Christ, but through the consciousness of sanctified obedience.[4]

Finally, Ernst Troeltsch, in his *The Social Teaching of the Christian Churches*, follows the lines laid down by Seeberg and especially Weber: a shift in the doctrine of God brings about a corresponding shift in the understanding of faith. "Instead of the characteristic of happiness in the grace of God which forgives sins, we find the certainty of belonging to the elect, and a spirit of active energy."[5] The pattern again is clear. Luther's doctrine of God emphasizes mercy and forgiveness, whereas Calvin's emphasizes predestination and majesty. Luther understood faith as trust in mercy, whereas Calvin understood faith as the confidence and certainty of election through the awareness of sanctified obedience.

This kind of contrast between Luther and Calvin lives on in contemporary scholarship. Jaroslav Pelikan, in his *Reformation of Church and Dogma (1300–1700)*, asks this question of Calvin's doctrine of predestination: "Yet the gravest of all objections was the question of consolation, hope and the certainty of election—not, of course, its objective certainty, which, being grounded totally in the will of God, was an absolute and unchangeable decree; but its subjective certainty in the conscience of the anxious believer."[6] Pelikan rightly points out that Calvin spoke of Christ as being the mirror in which our election may be safely contemplated; yet he seems to understand that to mean that Christ is an example of an elect person.[7] It is hard to see how such a mirror could give certainty in the conscience of the anxious believer; for true certainty and assurance are to be found in Christ as the object of faith and hence of election, not in Christ as the example of the elect person. It should be noted, however, that Pelikan does not state that Calvin taught believers to seek certainty of election in their works, and thus he represents an advance in the interpretation of Calvin when compared to Seeberg, Weber, and Troeltsch.

Such is not the case, however, in the work of Steven Ozment. In his book, *The Age of Reform, 1250–1550*, Ozment presents the same kind of comparison between Luther and Calvin as was found in the work of Seeberg, Weber, and Troeltsch. "For Luther, works might attest a strong faith, but they resolved no man's anxiety over his final destiny; only faith in God's promise did that. . . . On the other hand, Calvin's teaching, like his conduct of the Genevan church, once again made good works and moral behavior the center of religious life and reintroduced religious anxiety over them."[8] Ozment, therefore, represents a classical passage *(locus classicus)* of the kind of comparison between

---

4. Ibid., pp. 114–15.
5. Ernst Troeltsch, *The Social Teaching of the Christian Churches*, 2 vols., trans. Olive Wyon (Chicago and London: University of Chicago Press, 1981), vol. 2, p. 584.
6. Jaroslav Pelikan, *Reformation of Church and Dogma (1300–1700)* (Chicago and London: University of Chicago Press, 1984), p. 229.
7. Ibid., p. 231.
8. Steven Ozment, *The Age of Reform, 1250–1550* (New Haven and London: Yale University Press, 1980), p. 379.

Luther and Calvin described above. Luther makes faith in the promise central to the gospel, whereas Calvin, through his doctrine of election, makes good works the foundation of the certainty of faith. This disparity with Luther is confirmed biographically and existentially in Calvin's conduct of the Genevan church. Indeed, one of the most recent biographies of Calvin examines his theology as an attempt to address his fundamental religious anxieties.[9]

At the heart of these contrasts between Luther and Calvin lies the claim that Calvin seeks to ground the assurance and certainty of the conscience in God's sight (*coram Deo*) in the testimony of the good conscience of the believer to itself concerning its good works, whereas Luther insisted that certainty and assurance of conscience were attained only when the conscience believed the testimony of the forgiveness of sins spoken to the conscience by the Word of God in the gospel. What is surprising about the near-ubiquity of this kind of contrast between the theologies of Luther and Calvin is that it takes place in the absence of any thorough comparative studies of their theologies. The time is long overdue for a study that would test the accuracy of this kind of contrast between Luther and Calvin.

The following chapters will look carefully and extensively at the ways in which Luther and Calvin define and describe the conscience and the ways in which they relate the conscience to grace. In particular, the relationship between the testimony of the Word and Spirit and the testimony of the conscience will be held in focus. The argument will begin by establishing Luther's position on the concept of the conscience and its use in his theology. Attention will be paid to the theological claim that undergirds and directs the whole of Luther's theology: that God alone is true and all persons are liars. The conscience can never testify to itself concerning God's attitude toward the person, but must always believe and trust in the testimony of the Word of God to the conscience.[10]

Luther's position will then be used as a basis of comparison for presenting the ways in which Calvin relates the testimony of the Word and Spirit to the testimony of the conscience. In the comparison, several questions will be addressed "from" Luther "to" Calvin concerning the relationship of the conscience to the gospel: (1) Does Calvin understand the theological use of the law in the same way that Luther does, that is, as driving the terrified conscience to the mercy of Christ? (2) Does Calvin's emphasis on sanctification differ fundamentally from Luther's? Does such an emphasis undermine the assurance of the conscience in the mercy of Christ alone? (3) Does Calvin's claim that election is confirmed by the testimony of a good conscience to its obedience undermine the foundation of the conscience's assurance in the love of God toward us (*pro nobis*), either by giving the conscience two foundations of

9. "Calvin was a singularly anxious man, and, as a reformer, fearful and troubled." William J. Bouwsma, *John Calvin: A Sixteenth Century Portrait* (Oxford & New York: Oxford University Press, 1988), p. 32.

10. *Vorlesung ueber den Hebraerbrief*, 1518. W.A. 57-3.169; L.W. 29:171–72.

assurance, or by making the testimony of the good conscience the foundation of assurance? (4) Does Calvin's doctrine of election per se necessarily place consciences in doubt as to whether God is indeed gracious to them? (5) Does Calvin's third use of the law encourage consciences to find security in their own works rather than in the promise of forgiveness? (6) Does Calvin's emphasis on church polity, and especially on church discipline, place consciences under human rules rather than under the Word of God?

In order to test the adequacy of interpretations of Luther, several questions will also be addressed "from" Calvin "to" Luther. (1) Does Luther also allow for the possibility, or even the necessity, of the testimony of the good conscience regarding its sincere obedience to the will of God? (2) Does Luther ever norm the testimony of the Word, especially of the commands of God, by his understanding of the testimony of the conscience? (3) Does Luther's doctrine of election differ significantly from Calvin's? (4) Does Luther also speak of confirming our faith and election by the testimony of good works? Just as a comparison with Luther will highlight aspects of Calvin's theology that are often neglected, so also a comparison with Calvin will illuminate several themes in Luther's theology that are too often ignored.

I will argue the thesis that although Luther and Calvin do have different emphases in their theological treatment of the conscience, they fundamentally agree that the foundation of the peace, assurance, and certainty of the conscience lies in the grace of God *pro nobis*, as revealed to the conscience both by the external witness of the Word of God and the internal witness of the Holy Spirit. Both Luther and Calvin insist that the conscience—whether of the infidel or of the believer—cannot testify to itself as to God's will toward us. Rather, the conscience must always look to the Word of God, in matters of faith as well as in matters of obedience. The testimony of a good conscience has a legitimate place in both Luther's and Calvin's theology; yet such testimony does not tell us about the grace or favor of God toward us, but only about the sincerity of our response to that grace in faith and love. The question that the testimony of a good conscience addresses is not, "Do I have a gracious God?" but rather, "Is my faith in the grace of God sincere or hypocritical?" In other words, the testimony of the good conscience builds on the foundation of God's witness to us in the gospel and cannot replace that foundation.

However, I shall also argue that the distinction that both Luther and Calvin wish to maintain between the foundation of assurance and its confirmation has at its heart an inconsistency that both theologians seem to overlook. By making the distinction between the foundation and confirmation of assurance, both theologians meant to point us away from our works and the testimony of the good conscience, toward the promise of God in Jesus Christ for the foundation of our faith. But by saying that the testimony of the good conscience confirms both our faith and our eternal election, they left the door open for the possibility that the foundation of faith might be reversed, as indeed happened immediately after the death of Calvin in the theology of Beza, with the emergence of the practical syllogism (*syllogismus practicus*) as the foundation of faith and assurance. Because of the Lutherans' neglect of the question of election, as well as their disinterest in sanctification, the same possibility of reversal that appears in Luther's theology does not emerge in later Lutheran theology (with the possible exception of certain forms of Pietism).

Given the fact that both Luther and Calvin had a doctrine of limited election, which restricts the saving efficacy of the reconciliation won in Christ to those who believe in Christ, the possibility of this reversal could not in principle be removed; and this gives rise to a suspicion that their distinction between the "foundation" and "confirmation" of assurance is a distinction without a difference. If we are assured of our faith only by the testimony of Jesus Christ to us (which Luther and Calvin rightly maintained), and yet the testimony of Jesus Christ to us only applies for those whom God's secret will has elected (which both also maintained), how are we to turn from ourselves to Christ with assurance and ignore the question of our own individual election by the God behind and in a real sense distinct from Jesus Christ, a question that can only be answered by the testimony of the individual to him/herself via the *syllogismus practicus*? Either the question of assurance will be asked alone and the question of election will be ignored (the happy inconsistency of the Lutherans), or the question of assurance will be asked directly in the light of the limited election of individuals (the miserable consistency of the Reformed, attaining confessional status at Westminster). It is clear that both Luther and Calvin wished to steer clear of the second alternative, but they did so only by ignoring the dilemma which their theologies had in fact created. As Barth rightly says about Calvin, "A happy inconsistency led him to believe that he could unify the christological beginning and the anthropological conclusion of his thinking."[11]

Thus, I will not only argue that Calvin agrees with Luther in seeking to ground the assurance of faith in the testimony of Jesus Christ alone (a testimony that we must hear and that we cannot say to ourselves); I will also argue that Luther as much as Calvin operates with the assumption that the testimony of the good conscience can, and indeed must, confirm both our faith and hence our election, and that therefore Luther as much as Calvin leaves the door wide open for the reversal that occurred in Reformed theology. The ground of assurance that both theologians seek to establish in Jesus Christ alone is undercut by their doctrines of election, which limit the mercy of Christ to those who believe, and hence by the testimony of the good conscience that confirms faith and election. Within both of their theologies, the possibility exists in principle for the internal testimony to take precedence over the testimony of the Word of God, in spite of their attempts to make such a reversal impossible.

---

11. Karl Barth, *Church Dogmatics* II/2, ed. G. W. Bromiley and T. F. Torrance (Edinburgh: T. & T. Clarke, 1957), p. 338.

This is not to deny that real differences in emphasis exist between Luther and Calvin. One difference is seen most clearly in the kinds of hypocrisy that most bothered the two theologians. For Luther, the most disturbing kind of hypocrisy involved those who feigned to be believers by means of good works and other external matters but who lacked the inward peace and freedom of conscience that could only flow from faith in the forgiveness of sins. Luther was convinced that once the conscience attained peace and certainty in the Word of forgiveness, the external matters—such as love and forms of worship—would spontaneously take care of themselves. He bitterly opposed the efforts of those, such as Karlstadt, who wanted to make the reform of externals part of the central issue of the Reformation. To emphasize externals could only result in the loss of faith and the binding of consciences to human laws. Hence Luther's own method of reform might best be seen in the following, written against Karlstadt: "One is obligated, however, to destroy [images of God] with the Word of God, that is, not with the law in a Karlstadtian manner, but with the gospel. This means to instruct and enlighten the conscience that it is idolatry to worship them, or to trust in them, since one is to trust in Christ alone. Beyond this let the external matters take their course."[12] Only by preaching the Word of God to the consciences of believers, and by letting externals "take their course," would one avoid the hypocrisy of appearing to be a believer while still having an unbelieving conscience. As Luther said of his reform movement, "I simply taught, preached, and wrote God's Word; otherwise I did nothing."[13]

Calvin, in contrast, was most concerned with the kind of hypocrites whose outward behavior did not conform with their inward profession of faith. Calvin agreed with Luther that externals should not be emphasized to the detriment of faith and Christian freedom; yet he did not agree that the gospel alone was to be preached while externals should be allowed to take their course. Rather, worship and obedience should conform to certain God-given forms, and believers must be exhorted to seek after such conformity. The central thrust of Calvin's reform work in Geneva centered on the attainment of such conformity to the will of God in the external life and practice of the church. Thus, in contrast to Luther, Calvin could say of his reform work: "When I first came to this church, I found almost nothing in it. There was preaching and that was all. They would look out for idols it is true, and they burned them. But there was no reformation. Everything was in disorder."[14] Whereas for Luther the preaching of the Word was the reformation, for Calvin there was no reformation where the church was not externally as well as internally conformed to the Word and will of God. The emphasis on regeneration, the third

---

12. *Wider die himmlischen Propheten, von den Bildern und Sacrament,* 1525. W.A. 18.74.6–10; L.W. 40:91.
13. *Invocavit Predigten,* 1522. W.A. 10(III).18.14–15; L.W. 51:77.
14. Dr. Jules Bonnet, ed., *Letters of John Calvin,* trans. Marcus Robert Gilchrist, 4 vols. (New York: Burt Franklin Reprints, 1972), vol. 4, p. 373.

use of the law, the concern for church discipline, the attention given to church polity, and the concern with purifying the external worship of the church (including the removal of images) all attest to Calvin's desire to have the outward life of the church conform to its profession of faith in Christ, without rebinding the faithful conscience to coercive human laws.

What, then, accounts for the difference in emphasis between the theology of Calvin and that of Luther? Although the answer to that question will occupy the remainder of this book, it is possible to give a preliminary answer here. The primary difference between Luther and Calvin lies in the overall framework in which the two set their soteriology. For Luther, that framework is provided by the theology of the cross (*theologia crucis*): "the theology of the cross alone is our theology!"[15] The *theologia crucis* means that when God reveals himself, God does so under an appearance that contradicts the revealed truth.[16]

In the context of *theologia crucis*, faith means believing with certainty that God's Word is true even when the whole world, the heart of the believer, and even God himself contradict the truth that is revealed in the Word, particularly the Word of promise. Thus, when God begins to show mercy, God does so by first revealing wrath (in the law); when God makes alive, God does so by slaying. The same contradictions apply especially to those who have already come to faith. God promises to protect the church, and yet it is persecuted by the world; God promises the forgiveness of sins, yet our conscience feels nothing but sin and wrath; God promises life, yet we see nothing but death. Faith, therefore, is the art of believing the Word while experiencing, seeing, and feeling the opposite. We believe that Christ is the Son of God, even though we see an abandoned man on the cross; we believe that God cares for the church, even though we see nothing but a church persecuted by the world and apparently abandoned by God; we believe in eternal life, even though we see and feel nothing but death.

However, the primary locus of the theology of the cross is the experience of trial or tribulation (*Anfechtung*), when the very heart and conscience of the believer sense that God's promise of grace and forgiveness is a lie. The believer must regard the promise of forgiveness as true and certain even though the conscience testifies to the contrary.

> But under the cross which we experience, eternal life lies hidden. . . . We, too, experience the cross, and death appears to us, if not in fact, yet in our conscience through Satan. Death and sin appear, but I announce life and faith, but in hope. Therefore, if you want to be saved, you must battle against your feelings. Hope means to expect life in the midst of death, and righteousness in the midst of sins.[17]

15. *Operationes in Psalmos*, 1519–1521. W.A. 5.176.31; *Psalms*, p. 289. See Walter von Loewenich, *Luther's theologia crucis*, 5th ed. (Witten: Luther-Verlag, 1967); Alister E. McGrath, *Luther's Theology of the Cross* (Oxford: Basil Blackwell, 1985).

16. Pelikan, *Reformation of Church and Dogma*, p. 165.

17. *Vorlesung ueber die Briefe an Titus und Philemon*, 1527. W.A. 25.12.2–3, 12–16; L.W. 29:10–11.

This is the very meaning of being simultaneously righteous and a sinner (*simul iustus et peccator*): to believe that we are righteous *coram Deo* even though we feel like condemned sinners.

Within the context of the theology of the cross, the grace of sanctification and its attestation in the testimony of a good conscience would necessarily be subordinated to the grace of justification and the promise of the forgiveness of sins. This is because the testimony of the good conscience confirms one's faith in the promise, whereas the theology of the cross emphasizes that testimony of the conscience that contradicts faith in the promise; that is, *Anfechtung*. Therefore, although Luther continually insisted upon the necessity of sanctification and of the testimony of the good conscience, within the framework of *theologia crucis* he could not help but consistently subordinate the grace of sanctification to that of justification.

Luther's concentration on the theology of the cross also accounts for his refusal to involve the Reformation directly in the external reform of the church. The Word of God does not deal with external, temporal things, but rather with invisible, eternal things; and such invisible things are revealed under an external appearance that contradicts what is being revealed.[18] The theology of glory, in contrast—such as Luther found in the papacy—emphasizes externals to the point of neglecting the invisible truths revealed by the Word: indeed, to the point of calling God's Word a lie. Thus, those in the Reformation who would reintroduce concern for externals—such as Karlstadt with his rejection of idols and the papal mass—misunderstand the whole nature of the Word of the cross, and divert the attention of believers from the invisible, eternal things of God's promises to the visible, temporal things of human reason and senses. Yet it is precisely reason and the senses that must be mortified if we are to believe that the Word of the cross is true.[19]

Luther's *theologia crucis* also explains his suspicion of those, such as the Anabaptists, who emphasized the external holiness and moral behavior of the church. If the Word of the cross reveals the truth of God under a contrary appearance, then one would expect the true church not to look like the church at all, but rather to look like God-forsaken sinners. The "synagogue of Satan," on the other hand, with its theology of glory, would look like the true church of God and would demonstrate a superior holiness externally—as in the monks and friars—but inwardly it would be rejected by God. The theology of the cross would therefore lead one not to stress the conformity of the appearance of the church with its faith, but rather to stress the ways in which the appearance of the church denies its claim to be the people of God. The church looks like a gathering of sinners rejected by God and the world, whereas it is in truth the beloved people of God. The church cannot be judged by its

---

18. *Vorlesung ueber 1. Mose von 1535–1545.* W.A. 43.567.36–39; L.W. 5:201–2.
19. Ibid. W.A. 43.555.20–23; L.W. 5:184.

appearance, but only by whether it has the Word of Christ crucified. Hence the primary task of the church is to preach the Word of God, while letting externals take their course.

Calvin, on the other hand, sets his discussion of salvation within the context of the Fatherhood of God.[20] Our salvation takes place when we can claim with certainty and assurance that God is our Father, and that God regards us as God's children. It is only in Jesus Christ, the Son of God, that God reveals himself to sinners not as a wrathful judge but as a Father, the fountain of every good thing. We are adopted as children of God by our incorporation into Jesus Christ, who is the Son of God by nature. It is faith, created in us by the Holy Spirit, that incorporates us into Christ and makes us one with him. The assurance of faith is therefore founded on Jesus Christ himself, the image of the invisible God, who is set forth by the Father as the fountain of every good thing that the Father wishes to give sinners. By means of our participation in Christ (*participatio Christi*), we receive the twofold grace of Christ (*duplex gratia Christi*), justification and sanctification. The grace of justification is the foundation and basis of our adoption by God; for God can only regard us as God's children if God forgives us our sins and reckons us as righteous. However, the grace of sanctification is the purpose and goal of our adoption, for God adopts us so that we might actually become God's gratefully obedient children.

Thus, with regard to the basis of our adoption, Calvin is in complete agreement with Luther: God can only regard us as God's children on the basis of the forgiveness of sins. In this context, the grace of sanctification is necessarily subordinated to the grace of justification. However, given Calvin's emphasis on adoption over and above the theology of the cross (which is also found in his theology), Calvin can also speak of the necessary subordination of justification to sanctification when he speaks of the purpose of our adoption, something that Luther's emphasis on *theologia crucis* would not allow him to do. Hence Calvin could place his discussion of regeneration before his discussion of justification in the 1559 *Institutes*, while insisting that the doctrine of justification is the "main hinge on which our religion turns." Calvin's understanding of Jesus Christ as the fountain of every good also gives faith an additional foundation in Christ that is not found in Luther. The basis of assurance is Jesus Christ himself, followed by the assurance of free forgiveness and justification in Christ alone, and confirmed a posteriori by the testimony of a good conscience to our sanctification.

Within the context of adoption, Calvin can give equal weight not only to the testimony of the conscience that contradicts the Word that reveals God as our Father—that is, the conscience that feels its sins and the wrath of God,

---

20. Benjamin B. Warfield, *Calvin and Augustine* (Philadelphia: Presbyterian and Reformed Publishing Co., 1956), p. 176. See also Garret Wilterdink, *Tyrant or Father? A Study of Calvin's Doctrine of God*, 2 vols. (Bristol, Ind.: Wyndam Hall Press, 1985).

and therefore feels that God is not a Father but a wrathful judge—but also to the testimony of the conscience that confirms our faith in God as our Father—that is, the good conscience that testifies we are living as God's children and our lives correspond to the goal of our adoption. With regard to the basis of our adoption, the testimony of the good conscience can never replace the foundation of assurance that the conscience has in the mercy of God. We are certain God is our Father only because God forgives our sins for the sake of Christ the Son. However, with regard to the purpose and goal of adoption, the assurance of the conscience in the forgiveness of sins does not excuse believers from seeking to confirm their adoption by the testimony of a good conscience. "For these two things are always joined: the faith which apprehends the free love of Christ; and a good conscience and newness of life."[21]

The context of adoption also accounts for the emphasis Calvin placed on the external reformation of the church, that is, on the reform of polity and church discipline. Calvin agreed with Luther that externals should not be binding on the conscience, as they were under the papacy. However, whereas Luther's *theologia crucis* led him to stress the disharmony between the inward faith and the external appearance and behavior of the church, Calvin's doctrine of adoption led him to seek conformity and harmony between inward faith and the external behavior of believers.[22] The third use of the law involves exhorting believers to manifest in their lives their adoption as children of God by living in conformity with the will of God. Those who do not show such conformity, but rather live in outward and unrepentant wickedness, are to be excommunicated from the church, so that the good might not be corrupted by bad examples and so that the wicked may be brought to repentance.[23]

Even the polity of the church, while not binding on the conscience as under the papacy, is to exhibit such conformity to the will of God as revealed in the Word. Thus, those elements of the papacy that are against the will of God, such as images and the mass, are not only to be removed from the conscience by the preaching of the Word, but are also to be externally removed from the churches.

This, as we shall see, constitutes the one area of genuine disagreement between Luther and Calvin. Luther refused to categorically reject images in Christian worship, while Calvin categorically rejects them on the grounds that they contradict God's infinite, spiritual essence, and also because they contradict Jesus Christ alone as the image of the invisible God. Calvin did not believe that external compliance should be withheld out of concern for offending the weak, as did Luther; in Calvin's view the weak are offended more by the presence of the mass and images than by their removal. "Hence it

21. Comm. John 15:10, C.O. 47:342–43; C.N.T.C. 5:97–98.
22. *Inst*. III.vi.1; O.S. IV.146.14–17 (1:684).
23. *Inst*. IV.xii.5; O.S. V.215–16 (2:1232–33).

happens, that while they all profess to be withheld by fear of giving offense, but are, in fact, afraid of exciting indignation against themselves, no one begins to be distinguished from others by the sincerity and purity of his conduct."[24] The church, including (if not especially) the weak in faith, is edified and strengthened when its conduct does not contradict but rather conforms with its profession to be the children and people of God. The faith of the conscience must be manifested by external behavior: it cannot remain hidden.

Previous comparisons of the theologies of Luther and Calvin have paid insufficient attention to the overall structure and character of their theologies and have thus distorted the nature of the differences between the two. Luther's *theologia crucis* has blinded many of his interpreters to the rather strong statements he makes about sanctification and about the necessity for the testimony of a good conscience in all believers. Similarly, Calvin's ability to subordinate the doctrine of justification to sanctification with regard to the *goal* of our adoption has led his interpreters to miss the corresponding subordination of sanctification to justification with regard to the *basis* of our adoption, and to neglect the ultimate foundation of assurance and faith, which is Jesus Christ himself as the fountain of every good offered to sinners in the gospel. We have certain assurance that God is our Father only because God has mercy on us and forgives us our sins in Jesus Christ. In the following chapters, Luther's *theologia crucis* and Calvin's trinitarian doctrine of the Fatherhood of God will be the frameworks for a comparison of the ways in which these two theologians understand the assurance of faith in the mercy of God.

A final note is necessary with regard to the methodological procedure of the book. This is a work of historical theology. By that I mean that I am not using Luther and Calvin as a way of developing my own theological proposal concerning the assurance of faith. Rather, I am trying to understand Luther and Calvin on their own terms, with no judgment as to who is right and who is wrong, in order to compare them as fairly as possible. However, the presentation and argument will be more systematic than historical. No attempt will be made to show the development of Luther's concept of the conscience and its relationship to previous understandings of the conscience. Luther's understanding of the conscience stabilizes around the year 1518, and I am taking his use of the conscience from that date onward as my material for Luther.[25] Nor am I seeking to show any influence of Luther on the theology of Calvin, as though Luther were the root and Calvin the branch, or as though Calvin completed what was incomplete in Luther's thought. Although the theology of Luther was an undoubted influence on Calvin, the book will treat

---

24. *De fugiendis impiorum illicitis sacris, et puritate Christianae religionis observanda.* C.O. 5:273; *Tracts* 3:405–6.

25. I am thus focusing on Luther's theology after his transition from the theology of humility to the happy exchange, which occurs around 1518–1519. See Martin Brecht, *Martin Luther: His Road to Reformation, 1483–1521* (Philadelphia: Fortress Press, 1985), pp. 128–44, 221–37.

the theologies of Luther and Calvin as systematic wholes to be compared as such, and not as two stages in the development of the notion of the conscience. The order of presentation does begin with Luther, but it could just as easily have begun with Calvin.

I am aware that the question of systematic wholeness is particularly acute with regard to the theology of Luther. He never wrote a comprehensive theological work like Calvin's *Institutes*, and many of Luther's interpreters have insisted that his theology cannot be systematized. I have read as widely as possible in both theologians, including scriptural commentaries, treatises, sermons, and letters, in order to gain as accurate a picture as possible of the nature of their theologies. On the basis of the evidence, I am convinced it is possible to show that the *theologia crucis* is the governing motif of Luther's theology, and that the Fatherhood of God in the Son through the Holy Spirit is the guiding doctrine of Calvin's theology.

The relationship of the conscience to the testimony of the Word and Spirit raises other systematic questions that are of contemporary interest, especially in light of Barth's disagreement with Schleiermacher regarding the role of subjectivity in theology, and the debate between Barth and Brunner concerning the possibility of a point of contact (*Anknuepfungspunkt*) in the person toward whom the preached Word is directed. To take up these questions directly would be the task of a whole book in itself. However, to ignore them would be to slight the theological concerns of Luther and Calvin.

Both theologians were intensely interested in the question of revelation, and both raised the question as to whether there was something in the person that made the reception of revelation possible. On the one hand, Luther and Calvin rejected Roman theologies that claimed that the natural person could in any way prepare for the reception of grace. On the other hand, both Luther and Calvin insisted that faith was possible only for those whose consciences had been terrified by the law: "The sinner will never be capable [*capax*] of pardon until he learns to tremble from consciousness of his guilt."[26] The theologies of both Luther and Calvin will be discussed here in light of the question of whether the conscience is a point of contact for the preaching either of the law or of the gospel or of both. The test by which such a point of contact will be discerned is whether the hearing of the revealed Word is only possible by the inward testimony of the Holy Spirit to the conscience, or whether the conscience itself has the natural capacity to hear the Word.

The question of the role of subjectivity and religious experience in theology is also directly pertinent to the interpretation of Luther and Calvin. Both speak of the sole authority of the Word of God as attested in Scripture (*sola Scriptura*), and yet both make the certainty and consolation of consciences a criterion for distinguishing the true Word of God from human falsehood. "Heavenly light and truth has this nature, that it lifts up the conscience,

---

26. Comm. Exod. 19:17, C.O. 24:202; C.T.S. 3:327–28.

comforts the heart, and creates a free spirit; just as on the other hand the teaching of men naturally oppresses the conscience, tortures the heart, and quenches the spirit."[27] The question must be asked whether Luther and Calvin have introduced a second, subjective criterion for theology along with the objective criterion of Scripture, or whether the objective criterion of Scripture in effect collapses into the subjective criterion of the certainty and consolation of conscience. What is the relationship between the testimony of Scripture and the testimony of the experience of the conscience as authorities both in theology and in the life of faith?

In sum, although these two systematic questions cannot be made the central theses of this book, an adequate interpretation of Luther and Calvin on the assurance of faith must at least address these questions in the course of its presentation. By doing so in the chapters that follow, I hope to make the theology of Luther and Calvin of more than historical concern to the present theology of the church.

27. *Kirchenpostille*, 1522. W.A. 10(I).1.555–58; *Sermons* 1:442.

PART ONE

LUTHER—LET GOD BE TRUE AND ALL OTHERS BE LIARS

1

THE IDOLATROUS RELIGION
OF CONSCIENCE

The heart of Luther's theology is the theology of the cross (*theologia crucis*). The testimony of the Word to the conscience comes under an appearance that contradicts the truth revealed in the Word: thus God's mercy is hidden under wrath, God's power is made manifest in weakness, God's life is hidden under death, God's blessing is hidden under a curse.[1] Luther contrasted the theology of the cross with the theology of glory (*theologia gloriae*). Whereas the theology of the cross comes to the knowledge of God through the indirect and hidden way of the cross, the theology of glory attempts to know God directly through what is apparent in the world. "That person does not deserve to be called a theologian who looks upon the invisible things of God as though they were clearly perceptible in those things which have actually happened. He deserves to be called a theologian, however, who comprehends the visible and manifest things of God seen through suffering and the cross."[2] The theology of glory finds a direct continuity between what it sees and feels and what it believes about God, whereas the theology of the cross finds a contradiction between what it sees and feels and what it believes. "Nature wants to feel and be certain before she believes, grace believes before she perceives."[3]

In order to understand the role of the conscience in the theology of the cross, it is advisable first to understand the role of the conscience in the theology of glory. If the *theologia crucis* must be understood as the testimony of the Word to the conscience that contradicts what the conscience sees and feels, then the *theologia gloriae* must be understood as the testimony of the conscience to itself about God that is made on the basis of what is apparent and perceptible to the conscience, that is, works of the law. "That wisdom which sees the invisible things of God *in works as perceived by man* is completely puffed up, blinded, and hardened."[4]

---

1. *Praelectio in psalmum 45*, 1532. W.A. 40(II).482.15–18; L.W. 12:204. Alister E. McGrath, *Luther's Theology of the Cross* (Oxford: Basil Blackwell, 1985), p. 169.
2. *Disputatio Heidelbergae habita*, 1518. W.A. 1.354.17–20; L.W. 31:40.
3. *Kirchenpostille*, 1522. St.L. XIX.334; *Sermons*, 1:362.
4. W.A. 1.354.23–24; L.W. 31:40–41, my emphasis.

This chapter examines the testimony of the conscience to itself about the nature and will of God as an aspect of the false knowledge of God that Luther called the *theologia gloriae*. First, Luther's definition of the conscience will be examined as well as the place it has in his anthropology. Second, the way in which the conscience comes to its judgments and the kind of guilt or acquittal that the conscience can render on its own (that is, the knowledge of humanity [*cognitio hominis*] of the *theologia gloriae*) will be delineated. Third, the way in which the conscience makes a direct inference about the status of the person in God's sight (*coram Deo*) on the basis of its judgment of the works of the person will be set forth. By definition, the judgment of the conscience makes us stand either accused or saved before God. Of special interest is the god before whom the conscience thinks it stands, because that god turns out to be a portrayal of the conscience to itself and not the God who reveals himself in God's Word. Knowing that there is a god who is to be worshiped, but not knowing *who* this god is or *how* this god is to be worshiped, the conscience portrays a god to itself and invents its own way of worshiping: namely, it sees God as a righteous judge who hates sin but who delights in works of the law. Thus, at the heart of all false knowledge of God—which Luther calls either *theologia gloriae*, general knowledge (*cognitio generalis*), or legal knowledge (*cognitio legalis*)—is the conscience's attempt to testify to itself about God and its status before God on the basis of what it sees and feels, that is, works of the law.

The Power That Judges Works

Although the conscience played a central role in his theology,[5] Luther rarely turned his attention directly to the conscience as a locus of theological inquiry. In order to come to a coherent picture of the nature and function of the conscience, the unsystematic references that Luther makes to the conscience need to be pieced together in some sort of systematic way. The danger inherent in such an undertaking is that one may read into the analysis many inferences that Luther did not intend. Fortunately, Luther did leave us with one rather complete definition of the conscience in the *Judgment of Martin Luther on Monastic Vows* (1521). In order to avoid imposing an alien structure or meaning on Luther's depiction of the conscience, this definition will be used as the organizing principle for this chapter and as the material norm by which to assess the various functions ascribed by Luther to the conscience.

> For the conscience is not the power of acting but the power of judging which judges about works. Its proper work (as Paul says in Romans 2) is to accuse or

5. Karl Holl, *Gesammelte Aufsaetze zur Kirchengeschichte*, vol. 1 (Tuebingen: J. C. B. Mohr [Paul Siebeck], 1948), pp. 1–110; Guenter Jacob, *Der Gewissensbegriff in der Theologie Luthers, Bertraege zur historischen Theologie* (Nendeln, Liechtenstein: Kraus, 1966); Yrjo J. E. Alanen, *Das Gewissen bei Luther*, Annales Academiae Scientiarum Fennicae, Series B., Vol. 29/2 (Helsinki, 1934); Emanuel Hirsch, *Lutherstudien*, vol. 1: *Drei Kapitel zu Luthers Lehre von Gewissen* (Gutersloh: C. Bertelsmann, 1954); Michael G. Baylor, *Action and Person. Conscience in Late Scholasticism and the Young Luther* (Leiden: E. J. Brill, 1977).

to excuse, to cause one to stand accused or absolved, terrified or secure. Its purpose is not to do, but to speak about what has been done and what should be done, and this judgment makes us stand accused or saved before God.[6]

The order of presentation for the rest of this chapter will follow the order of ideas set forth in this definition. First, the conscience as a power (*virtus*) of the flesh will be considered and placed in relation to the other powers of the flesh, especially those of the intellect and the will. Second, the way in which the conscience comes to its judgments concerning what has been done and what should be done will be analyzed. Third, the kind of guilt and acquittal to which the conscience can come by its own testimony and judgment will be considered. Finally, the relationship between the judgment of the conscience and our status *coram Deo* will be examined, with special emphasis on the idea of the god before whom the conscience imagines it stands.

Luther states that the conscience is the power to judge works. This means that the conscience is one of the powers of the person, or of the flesh.[7] For Luther, the flesh is oriented toward sensible and visible things.[8] Luther is quite clear that the conscience is part of humanity as flesh. He links the conscience with the wisdom of the flesh and with the thoughts of the flesh.[9] As a power of the flesh, therefore, the conscience has a strongly empirical orientation: it is oriented toward present, temporal things that are sensible and visible.[10] The particular objects the conscience "sees and feels" are works, which it judges, and the law, which is the norm by which it makes its judgments.

It is important to see the conscience as a power of the flesh in order to understand its role in Luther's theology. As a part of the person's fleshly nature, the conscience cannot be seen as a highest consciousness (*apex mentis*) that has direct contact with the divine. Nor is the conscience a form of higher consciousness (above the empirical senses) that has an immediate awareness of God. Although the conscience does make inferences about the attitude of God toward us, it does so on the basis of what it can see and feel—that is, works of the law—and not on the basis of some form of consciousness that transcends the temporal, sensible world. For Luther, the conscience is as worldly and fleshly as any other power of the soul. It has as its object human works.[11]

What, then, is the relationship between the conscience and the other powers of the flesh? In his definition, Luther explicitly distinguishes the power of the

---

6. *De votis monasticis Martini Lutheri iudicium*, 1521. W.A. 8.606.32–37; L.W. 44:298.
7. *In epistolam S. Pauli ad Galatas Commentarius*, 1535. W.A. 40(I).244.17–18; L.W. 26:139. Baylor, *Action and Person*, pp. 206–8.
8. *Enarratio Psalmi II*, 1532. W.A. 40(II).224.14–15; L.W. 12:27.
9. Ibid. W.A. 40(II).211.32–33, 212.15–17; L.W. 12:17.
10. St.L. XI.334.
11. W.A. 1.354.23; Baylor, *Action and Person*, pp. 234–35.

conscience from the power of the will.[12] The will is the power to act (*virtus operandi*), whereas the conscience is the power to judge (*virtus iudicandi*). Thus the will provides the conscience with its objects of judgment—that is, works. In spite of the close relationship between the conscience and the will, the conscience must be a power independent from the will, inasmuch as it judges the works of the will. The judgment of the conscience has both an antecedent and a consequent function: it judges both what the will should do and what the will has done.[13]

However, the conscience also shares in certain activities that are usually associated with the will or the heart. In particular, the conscience can both generate and experience a large range of affectivity, such as joy, terror, fear, despair, tranquility, and anxiety. Such affectivity is included in the definition of conscience that is explicated here.[14] Luther also speaks of the ability of the conscience to trust, which is one of the functions of the will and heart. Indeed, Luther indicates the close relationship between the conscience and the will by using the term "heart" (*cor*) as a synonym for the conscience on some occasions, while at other times he restricts the term "heart" to the will and its affections. Yet in spite of the affective capabilities of the conscience, it cannot be collapsed into the will; for the will is the power to do works, whereas the conscience is the power to judge works.

What, then, is the relationship of the conscience to the intellect? Luther indicates that the conscience is a power independent from that of the intellect. As such, it not only has the ability to judge the works of the will, but can also judge the activity of the intellect. When Luther accuses his opponents of holding a theological position "against their consciences," he gives the conscience the ability to judge the intellectual activity of the person.[15] A position is held against the conscience when the person says or writes something that contradicts or hides what the person actually thinks is true. Those who so contradict their conscience in theological matters are by definition heretics.[16]

Luther used this definition of heresy implicitly in his defense before the Diet of Worms. On the one hand, he did not want to be forced to deny a position he was certain was true; but on the other hand he was willing to be instructed as to where he was in error. "Unless I am convinced by the testimony of the Scriptures or by clear reason, I am bound by the Scriptures I have quoted and my conscience is captive to the Word of God. I cannot and I will not retract anything, since it is neither safe nor right to go against conscience."[17] Ironically, it was the papists themselves whom Luther accused of heresy, especially after the Diet of Augsburg, because the papists admitted that the

12. W.A. 8.606.32.
13. W.A. 8.606.35–36.
14. W.A. 8.606.34–35; Baylor, *Action and Person*, pp. 207–8.
15. *Wider die himmlischen Propheten*, 1525. W.A. 18.191.14–17; L.W. 40:201.
16. *Von den Konziliis und Kirchen*, 1539. W.A. 50.545.3–5; L.W. 41:50.
17. *Verhandlungen mit D. Martin Luther auf dem Reichstage zu Worms*, 1521. W.A. 7.838.4–8; L.W. 32:112.

teaching of the Lutherans was in agreement with Scripture, but they still insisted that it be refuted as heresy.[18]

The conscience does not have the ability to judge the truth or falsehood of the positions themselves; otherwise Luther's appeal at Worms to be further instructed would be meaningless. Rather, the conscience judges the contradiction between one's public position and what one acknowledges to be true. Since the intellect has truth as its object,[19] it is clear that the conscience can judge the activity of the intellect as much as the activity of the will. Hence the conscience must be a power independent from both intellect and will.

Nevertheless, Luther sometimes describes the work of the conscience in ways analogous to the activity of the intellect. The conscience, like the intellect, has truth as its object, of which the conscience must be certain.[20] Indeed, the question of truth is crucial for the conscience, for God has willed that our conscience be certain in all it does. "God wants our conscience to be certain and sure that it is pleasing to Him."[21] This explains Luther's appeal to the Word of God alone for the truth of which the conscience can be certain: it is axiomatic that God is true and cannot lie. However, the truth of which the conscience must be certain concerns God's promises and commands, both of which are revealed in God's Word, and both of which have to do with the particular judgments of the conscience. The promises of God tell us of our status *coram Deo* and of God's will toward us, and the commands of God tell us what we should do and hence involve the antecedent judgments of the conscience. Thus, although the conscience, like the intellect, has truth as its object, the truth that is directed to the conscience has to do with the specific functions of the conscience and not with the activity of the intellect as a whole.

At times Luther seems to make the conscience one of the functions of the intellect, along the lines of practical reason. "It [*mens*] refers to the mind or the spirit, the cognitive power [*vis cognitiva*] in man, which accepts instruction. Their thinking, mind, and opinion are corrupt; therefore an impure conscience also follows, because as the mind judges, so the conscience dictates."[22] The conscience can be seen by Luther as one moment in the process of practical reason and not as an independent power in its own right. The conscience works in conjunction with the mind in drawing conclusions about the antecedent and consequent works of the will. As the mind judges, so the conscience dictates. Because both the conscience and the mind have the ability to judge, it makes sense that their activities should be closely related. Luther, however, can also ascribe directly to the conscience the activity that he here

18. *Vorlesung ueber 1. Mose von 1535–1545*. W.A. 43.293.22–24, 295.23–26; L.W. 4:220, 222–23.

19. *Galatas Commentarius*, 1535. W.A. 40(II).26.13, 21.

20. *Die ander Epistel S. Petri und eine S. Judas gepredigt und ausgelegt*, 1523/24. W.A. 14.28.31–32, 29.1–2; L.W. 30:164.

21. *Deuteronomon Mosi cum annotationibus*, 1525. W.A. 14.644.22–23; L.W. 9:123.

22. *Vorlesung ueber die Briefe an Titus*, 1527. W.A. 25.39.13–16; L.W. 29:47; Baylor, *Action and Person*, p. 252.

ascribes to the mind, particularly the ability to receive and be shaped by instruction. "From the conscience comes every doctrine according to the way in which the conscience is influenced. It lives according to what it teaches. . . . Every doctrine creates a conscience."[23] The conscience is therefore closely related to the cognitive power of the flesh, but it is not identical with it.

The conscience can at times perform in ways similar to both the intellect and the will. However, as a distinct power of the flesh, the conscience's proper work is to judge the activity of the whole person: the works of the will as well as the thoughts of the intellect. Thus, when Luther describes the way in which original sin has affected the whole of human nature, he explicitly distinguishes the conscience from both the intellect and the will.[24] The conscience is similar to the intellect in that it also has the knowledge of God as its object; and the conscience is similar to the will in that it also can trust in the mercy of God and can also fear God. However, as will be seen more fully below, the proper domain of the conscience lies in placing the person before the judgment seat of God on the basis of works, and of giving forth a judgment that makes us either accused or saved before God.

The Syllogism of Practical Reason

How does the conscience perform its work of judgment? "The proper work of the conscience (as Paul says in Romans 2) is to accuse or to excuse, to cause one to stand accused or absolved, terrified or secure." How does the conscience go about its proper work? The previous section noted how Luther could describe the conscience as a moment of practical reason. Along the same lines, Luther frequently uses the model of the practical syllogism to describe how the conscience comes to its judgments. "As the mind judges, so the conscience dictates. The conscience always draws the conclusion, but the mind sets forth the minor premise. . . . The major premise is always true, because it does not contradict the common sense of all men. If the minor premise is upheld, the conclusion follows."[25] Within this model, the conscience gives the conclusion of the syllogism, common sense provides the major premise, and the mind provides the minor premise.

The syllogism may be set up in the following way:

Major premise: All sin is to be avoided (common sense)
Minor premise: X is a sin (mind)
Conclusion: To do/to have done X is a sin (conscience)

---

23. *Vorlesung ueber den 1. Timotheusbrief*, 1528. W.A. 26.69.14–16, 20–21; L.W. 28:311.
24. W.A. 42.86.18–25; L.W. 1:114.
25. W.A. 25.39.16, 25–26; L.W. 29:47.

Common sense also provides the major premise that "Everything good is to be done," in which case the syllogism would be:

Major premise: Everything good is to be done (common sense)
Minor premise: Y is good (mind)
Conclusion: To do/have done Y is good (conscience)

It should be noted that both major premises provided by common sense are always true, yet both are formal injunctions devoid of material content. They say that all good is to be done and all sin is to be avoided, but they do not say *what* is good and *what* is a sin. It is the minor premises that give specificity and content to "good" and "sin." However, the minor premises are not always true. Nonetheless, "If the minor premise is upheld, the conclusion follows." The quotation from Titus is one of the few places where Luther describes three different aspects of reason coming together to arrive at the conclusion of the conscience. Usually Luther includes all three moments of the syllogism in the operation of the conscience per se, rather than ascribing them to common sense (*communis sensus*) and mind (*mens*). The passage from Titus is helpful, however, in clearly setting forth the syllogistic reasoning by which the conscience arrives at its judgments. Luther frequently uses this syllogistic model when speaking about the conscience, as will be seen below. Although he does not always attribute the major premise to common sense, Luther insists that the major premises of the conscience are always true.

The minor premise, therefore, is the crucial term in the syllogism, for it tells us what renders us guilty or acquitted. Luther does not claim that the minor premises are always true. Where, then, do the minor premises come from? Luther's initial answer follows the lines laid down by Paul in Rom. 2:15: "They show that what the law requires is written on their hearts, to which their own conscience also bears witness." In an answer that is prescriptive as well as descriptive, Luther states that the minor premises are provided in the natural law written on the hearts of all people.[26] Although the same minor premises are given in the law of Moses and of Christ, the latter teachings only set forth more clearly what is already known in the natural law. Therefore, all people should be able to arrive at judgments of conscience along these lines:

Major Premise: All sin is to be avoided
Minor Premise: Adultery is a sin (natural law)
Conclusion: To commit/to have committed adultery is a sin

The Ten Commandments, particularly those of the second table, are at least in principle given in the natural law, and thus should form the minor premises in the syllogism of the conscience.

26. W.A. 18.80.28–33, 37–38; L.W. 40:97.

The natural law formed the basis of the moral codes of the pagans and guided their understanding of proper civic behavior. Indeed, the civil law of the pagans is empirical evidence that the minor premises of the Mosaic law were known among the Gentiles.[27] The use of the natural law in governing the temporal affairs of humans was not only of historical interest to Luther, but also had application to the government of his day. Indeed, Luther thought that the natural law was a better norm for governing the temporal domain than were written laws.[28] The commandment to love one's neighbor as oneself is known to all persons, even the pagans, and should be used as the norm from which to derive the minor premises of the practical syllogism, from which the conscience draws its conclusions about actions. The scope of such judgments of conscience is the temporal realm, which underscores what was stated at the beginning of this chapter: the conscience, like reason, is oriented toward present, temporal reality.

Given the presence of the natural law in the hearts of all persons, does the conscience always derive its major premises from the love commandment? Luther's affirmative answer is both descriptive and prescriptive. The conscience should be bound by the minor premises contained in the natural law, and in the case of the pagan philosophers, the conscience actually was so bound. However, Luther insisted that although the natural law is present in all hearts, Satan obscures the natural law so that people are no longer aware of it or no longer follow it.[29]

In a sense Luther could say that this hiding of the natural law from the knowledge of most people was divinely ordained. Although the natural law is the source of all human law, not every person has the acute knowledge of the natural law that is necessary to govern properly.[30] Knowledge of the natural law is a rare gift, and those who have it are ordained by God to rule over those who do not. "If the natural law and reason were inherent in all heads that resemble human heads, then fools and children and women would be just as capable of ruling and waging war as David, Augustus, and Hannibal. . . . But God has created things in such a way that men are not all alike and that one should rule while the other should obey him."[31] Those who have insight into the natural law rule over those who do not and teach others the content of the natural law. "These heathen, godless prophets and kings taught and directed the people about how to preserve the secular kingdom."[32] The natural law may be written on the hearts of all persons, but many know the content of the natural law only by being taught it by those with more wisdom and insight, whom God raises up among the people.[33]

27. W.A. 26.667.13–19; L.W. 22:150.
28. *Von weltlicher Oberkeit*, 1523. W.A. 11.279.30–34; L.W. 45:128.
29. W.A. 40(II).66.34–39, 67.13–14; L.W. 27:53.
30. W.A. 40(II).66.34–39, 67.13–14; L.W. 27:53.
31. *Auslegung des 101. Psalms*, 1534–1535. W.A. 51.212.14–16, 19–20; L.W. 13:161.
32. Ibid. W.A. 51.243.12–16, 19–22; L.W. 13:199.
33. W.A. 42.374.11–16; L.W. 2:160. See F. Edward Cranz, *An Essay on the Development of Luther's Thought on Justice, Law, and Society* (Cambridge, Mass.: Harvard University Press, 1959), p. 109.

The malice of Satan enters in when the people who are taught the law do not find and feel the law within themselves, even though they have the law written on their hearts.[34] The law can only become a matter of conscience when the heart feels inwardly what the law teaches outwardly. Given the presence of the natural law in the hearts of all persons, the heart should be able to feel the law in itself. However, through the malice of Satan, the heart can be so blinded that it does not do so, and hence the conscience is left without a law to govern its minor premises and conclusions.[35] The blindness of the heart and conscience to the teaching of the law will have a direct bearing on the relationship of the conscience to the theological use of the law. For now, it should simply be noted that the conscience has the ability, through the power of Satan, to reject the very commandments that should in principle form the minor premises of its practical syllogism. The result of such rejection would be lawlessness.

The second way in which the natural law is hidden from the conscience is through false teaching. The conscience not only has the ability to reject the true teaching of the law; it also has the ability to invent, teach, and receive false laws. Such laws almost always have nothing to do with the rule of love, but rather concern themselves with external behavior and ceremonies.[36] The minor premises of the syllogism of the conscience come from the mind, which is "the cognitive power in man, which accepts instruction."[37] However, the conscience not only has the ability to deny the teaching of truly good works, but it also has the ability to invent and receive the teaching of childish and ostentatious works that obscure or even contradict the rule of love.

False teaching creates a false conscience. "It is the nature of all hypocrites and false prophets to create a conscience where there is none, and to cause conscience to disappear where it does exist."[38] Such a false conscience will neglect truly important works, such as the second table of the Ten Commandments, and will pay strict attention to childish works that are of no consequence. It will be terrified by sins that are in fact illusory, and it will not even be aware of transgressions that are in fact mortal.[39] The false teaching that creates a false conscience stems from a strongly religious motivation, usually associated with the worship of God that the conscience invents (*excogitatio*) for itself. The false worship of God will be explored more fully in a later section of this chapter. For now it should be noted that the conscience has the capacity not only to reject true teaching but also to accept and embrace false teaching. In both ways, the minor premises of the natural law are excluded from the syllogism of the conscience.

34. W.A. 18.80.35–38, 81.1; L.W. 40:97.
35. W.A. 40(II).66.38–39, 67.13–14; L.W. 27:53.
36. W.A. 40(II).67.14–17; L.W. 27:53.
37. W.A. 25.39.14.
38. W.A. 26.69.11–12; L.W. 28:311.
39. *Sermon von dreierlei Gutem Leben, das Gewissen zu unterrichten,* 1521. W.A. 7.795.29, 796.1, 6–10; L.W. 44:236.

In sum, even though Luther insists that the natural law is written in the hearts of all people, he does not emphasize those minor premises that all consciences should be able to generate of themselves, but rather focuses on those laws that the conscience is taught. Even without the interference of Satan, God has ordained that not all persons have equal insight into the natural law. Those who have such insight are to govern and to teach those who lack it. However, through the malice of Satan, the conscience can both ignore true teaching and be bound by false teaching; thus the conscience is not a fit criterion by which to judge true versus false laws. In other words, Luther describes the conscience more as a power to receive instruction than as a power of autonomous self-legislation. The conscience is a capacity for judging good and evil but is not of itself an infallible source for knowing what is good and what is evil. One can have a true conscience only if one follows true teaching, not if one follows the feeling of the conscience. For Luther, such true teaching is found only in the Word of God. "God wants our conscience to be certain and sure that it is pleasing to Him. This cannot be done if the conscience is led by its own feelings, but only if it relies on the Word of God."[40] The Word of God is the sole criterion by which to judge the true teaching of the law.

The Self-Knowledge of Sinners

Thus far the conscience has been treated as the power to judge works. The conscience arrives at its judgments about works along the lines of a practical syllogism. The major premises of the syllogism—do good and avoid evil— are always true. The minor premises may or may not be true, given the capacity of the conscience to accept false teaching as well as to ignore true teaching. The conclusions that the conscience reaches on the basis of the minor premises determine whether the work was a good work or a sin.

However, the conscience does not stop at works, but moves on to judge the whole person on the basis of works. This judgment is directly involved in the proper work of the conscience. "Its proper work (as Paul says in Romans 2) is to accuse or to excuse, to cause one to stand accused or absolved, terrified, or secure."[41] The conscience therefore comes to a knowledge of the person (*cognitio hominis*) on the basis of its assessment of the person's works. The person is either accused or absolved by the conclusion the conscience reaches about the person's works. But what is the extent of the accusation or absolution that the conscience can attain through its own testimony to itself? What is the knowledge of the self that the conscience attains through its judgments and conclusions? How much sin and guilt is it capable of acknowledging, and what kind of absolution does it pronounce or recognize?

It is clear from what has been said so far that the conscience has the ability to recognize sins—that is, works that are contrary to what the conscience feels

---

40. W.A. 14.644.22–24; L.W. 9:123.
41. W.A. 8.606.34–35; Baylor, *Action and Person*, p. 228.

is good. It thus knows the person as one who can be accused on the basis of sins, of discrete actions contrary to the law as the conscience perceives it. When the conscience is following true teaching, it is aware that disobeying parents and government, murdering, lying, stealing, and committing adultery are all sins. When the conscience is following false teaching, the conscience makes it a graver sin to eat meat on Friday than to commit adultery; but it still regards sins as discrete, external works that are contrary to its false law.[42]

Such an understanding of sin would seem to follow from the proper work of the conscience in judging works. Given this focus on external works, the conscience would regard as morally indifferent the sinfulness or goodness of inward dispositions and intentions (such as concupiscence). Indeed, because it judges on the basis of what it can see and feel, the conscience can only conclude that such inclinations are natural—it sees and feels them in all persons. "Besides, reason does not know either that the evil inclination of the flesh, and hatred of enemies, is sin. Because it observes and feels that all men are so inclined, it holds that these things are natural and right."[43] The scope of the judgment of conscience does not include the attitudes and inclinations of the heart, but only the works of the will.

Yet the conscience not only accuses, makes guilty, and terrifies on the basis of works; it also has the ability, by definition, to render the person acquitted, excused, and secure on the basis of works. As a consequence, the conscience will not acknowledge its sin to be of such a magnitude that it cannot be overcome by works of the law. If the conscience can accuse the person on the basis of works, then it can also acquit the person through works of the law.[44] Thus the conscience is limited in its knowledge of sin to those acts of the will that violate the dictates of the law (whether that law is true or false) and that can be remedied by works of the law. "Although hypocrites, who do not know Christ, may feel sorry for sin, they still suppose that they can get rid of it easily by their works and merits."[45] No matter how grievous the sin or how hopeless the predicament, no matter how much the conscience may be stung, it will not sense in sins an evil so great that it cannot be surmounted by works. "Although it [sin] brings with it the sting and remorse of conscience, still we suppose that it has so little weight and force that some little work or merit of ours will remove it."[46] The conscience, as noted in the first section of this chapter, is a power of the flesh and thus judges on the basis of what it sees and feels. If it sees and feels that it has sinned, then it also sees and feels no other remedy for sin than in the works of the law.[47]

42. W.A. 7.796.17–22; L.W. 44:236.

43. *Vorrede zum Alten Testament*, 1523. W.A., D.B. 8.11–31; L.W. 35:252.

44. *Auslegung des dritten und vierten kapitels Johannis in Predigten*, 1538–1540. W.A. 47.169.30–35; L.W. 22:456.

45. W.A. 40(I).86.23–26; L.W. 26:34.

46. W.A. 40(I).84.17–19; L.W. 26:33.

47. W.A. 40(I).115.21–24; L.W. 26:55.

In sum, the *cognitio hominis* that the conscience can attain by means of what it sees and feels is of one who has the ability to be both accused by transgressions of the law as well as acquitted by works of the law. It knows the sinner as one who sins, but not as one who is a sinner. Thus it not only sees the law as the remedy of sin, but also feels that it has the ability—that is, free will (*liberum arbitrium*)—to do works of the law. "Accordingly, it is Satan's work to prevent men from recognizing their plight and to keep them presuming that they can do everything that they are told."[48] If the conscience can accuse the person on the basis of works, it can also excuse the person on the basis of works. Therefore, when the conscience feels sins, it senses only one way of redemption: to do works of the law until the feeling of sin is overcome by the approving testimony of the conscience, which renders the person excused, acquitted, and secure.

The False Portrait of God the Judge

The next aspect of the judgment of the conscience not only renders the person guilty or acquitted in his or her own eyes, but also in the eyes of God. "Its purpose is not to do, but to pass judgment on what has been done and what should be done, and this judgment makes us stand accused or saved in God's sight [*coram Deo*]."[49] The judgment rendered by the conscience on the basis of works refers us to our status before God. But who is the God before whom the conscience places the person, and how does the conscience have knowledge of this God?

If the conscience by definition comes to judgments about works that make us stand either accused or saved before God, then it follows that the conscience must have some kind of knowledge of God. Luther calls such knowledge either general knowledge (*cognitio generalis*) or legal knowledge (*cognitio legalis*) of God.[50] "Reason can arrive at a 'legal knowledge' of God. It is conversant with God's Commandments and can distinguish between right and wrong."[51] The source of the legal knowledge of God is the law that is either written in the hearts of all or that is given to Israel by Moses. As seen above, the natural law has special reference to the conscience. Thus far the natural law has been treated as providing the conscience with the major and minor premises of the practical syllogism from which the conscience draws its conclusions about actions in the temporal realm. All of those premises should be derived from the commandment to love our neighbor as ourself, and thus have to do with our lives before humanity (*coram hominibus*). Yet the natural law also provides us with commandments that deal with our life *coram Deo*, and these commands in particular form the basis of our legal knowledge of God.

---

48. *De servo arbitrio*, 1525. W.A. 18.679.31–33; L.W. 33:130.
49. W.A. 8.606.35–37.
50. W.A. 40(I).607.20; W.A. 46.668.9–10.
51. *Auslegung des ersten und zweiten kapitels Johannis in Predigten*, 1537–1538. W.A. 46.668.9–13; L.W. 22:151.

The natural law provides the conscience with two related major premises that are always true: All sin is to be avoided, and everything good ought to be done.[52] These premises have to do with our temporal lives. In a similar way, the natural law provides the conscience with major premises that have to do with our life before God, and these form the basis of the legal knowledge of God. All of the major premises revolve around and can be derived from the command to worship God that is given in the law of nature. "God is One who promises, and He is truthful, that is, He makes promises to all men in the law of nature, which says: 'Call upon God, or worship Him.' "[53]

From this commandment to worship God, several things about the nature of God may be directly inferred, according to Luther. The first is that God exists, and that God is the Creator of all that exists besides God. "All men have the general knowledge, namely, that God is [quod Deus sit], that He created heaven and earth."[54] From the existence of God the Creator, both the omnipotence and omniscience of God can be inferred.[55] Thus the first thing that can be known about God on the basis of the natural law—when properly expounded—is that God exists, that God created heaven and earth, and that God is omnipotent and omniscient.

The second thing the conscience knows about God is to be inferred from the command to call upon God. If God commands that we call upon God, then it must follow that God is the source of all good and the refuge from every distress. "Accordingly, the knowledge that the afflicted should have their refuge in God has been implanted in the minds of all men."[56] Even though the Epicureans and the Sadducees may call this knowledge of God into doubt with their lips, they cannot extinguish this knowledge from their consciences. "There are, to be sure, some people, for instance, the Epicureans, Pliny, and the like, who deny this with their lips. . . . However, they do not succeed in this, their conscience tells them otherwise."[57] The conscience knows that all good is to be expected from God, and that God's help and protection are to be sought in every distress. One is reminded of Luther's definition of God in the Large Catechism: "What is God? Answer: A god is that to which we look for all good and in which we find refuge in every time of need."[58]

The third thing that can be known from the natural law is that God is a righteous judge; the conscience knows that it is God who commands that God be worshiped. "All men have the general knowledge, namely, that God is, that He has created heaven and earth, that He is just, and that He punishes the wicked, etc."[59] The knowledge of God as a righteous judge is given directly

52. W.A. 25.39.18–19, 26; L.W. 29:47–48.
53. W.A. 44.84.22–23; L.W. 6:113.
54. W.A. 40(I).607.29–30; L.W. 26:399.
55. W.A. 18.719.22–26, 33–35; L.W. 33:191.
56. W.A. 44.549.20–22; L.W. 7:336.
57. Der Prophet Jona ausgelegt, 1526. W.A. 19.205.34, 206.1–3, 5; L.W. 19:53–54.
58. The Book of Concord, ed. Theodore Tappert (Philadelphia: Fortress Press, 1959), p. 365.
59. W.A. 40(I).607.29–30; L.W. 26:399.

to the conscience, for the judgment of the conscience itself renders us either guilty or saved before God. "All Turks, Jews, papists, Tartars, and heathen concede the existence of a God, who, as they say, makes life contingent on our observation of His commandments and prohibitions."[60] The conscience knows God as a judge who saves those who fulfill the works of the law and who condemns those who sin. Therefore, if the conscience accuses and condemns the person on account of sins against the law, it can only conclude that God also condemns and accuses the person. In other words, God's attitude toward us may be inferred directly from the feeling and judgment of the conscience: if the conscience accuses, so does God; if the conscience acquits, so does God. In this way, the conscience comes to know "the invisible things of God," that is, God's will toward us, "in works as perceived by man."[61] The conscience's knowledge that God is a judge is fundamental to the *theologia gloriae*.

In sum, the legal or general knowledge of God is derived from the awareness that God is an omnipotent and omniscient Creator and judge who commands us to worship and to call upon God in our distress. The knowledge of God as Creator, judge, and refuge is derived from several major premises given to the conscience in the natural law. However, it is critical to note that the conscience is provided only with the major premises regarding the existence and nature of God and has no idea what the minor premises might be. The conscience knows that God exists, but it does not know who that God is; it knows that God is to be worshiped, but it is in the dark as to how. "They call God a helper, kind, and forgiving, even though afterwards they are in error as to who that God is and how He wants to be worshipped."[62] In the same way, the conscience knows that God is a refuge, but it does not know for whom God is a refuge, nor who this God is.[63] The major premises of the natural law to worship and call upon God raise the question of the existence and nature of God and of God's worship, but no minor premises are given from which the conscience might come to conclusions about the nature and will of God. Unlike the natural law that is given to govern the affairs of men *coram hominibus*, the natural law regarding our life *coram Deo* is only formal and not material.

We must not imagine, however, that the conscience is satisfied with this rather abstract and formal knowledge about God, or that it would wait patiently until God revealed himself more fully to the conscience in the Word. If God does not tell us who God is and how God is to be worshiped, the conscience will tell itself who God is and how God is to be worshiped. If the natural law

---

60. W.A. 46.669.22–26; L.W. 22:153.
61. W.A. 1.354.23.
62. W.A. 42.631.40–42; L.W. 3:117.
63. W.A. 19.206.13–16, 31–33; L.W. 19:54–55. See Fredrik Brosche, "Luther on Predestination: The Antinomy and Unity Between Love and Wrath in Luther's Concept of God" (doctoral diss., Uppsala University, 1978), pp. 30–47.

will not provide us with the minor premises with regard to the identity and worship of God, then the conscience will invent these for itself.

In other words, on the basis of the major premises given to the conscience concerning God, the conscience imagines, portrays, and pictures to itself both the nature of God and God's will for us. "But because men had this natural knowledge about God, they conceived vain and wicked thoughts about God apart from and contrary to the Word; they embraced these as the very truth, and on the basis of these they imagined God [*Deum finxerunt*] otherwise than He is by nature."[64] Even though the conscience is ignorant of the nature and will of God, the ungodly do not admit their ignorance, nor do they await instruction from God as to who God is. Rather, they go ahead and imagine God and God's will for themselves on the basis of what seems right to the conscience. "But while retaining the name of the true God without the true knowledge of God (which flesh and man cannot have of themselves), they thought about God what seemed right to them."[65]

What, then, is the picture of God and God's worship that the conscience imagines? On the one hand, the conscience knows from the natural law that God is to be worshiped, but it has no minor premises to tell it who God is or how God wants to be worshiped. On the other hand, the conscience is given both major and minor premises from the natural law with regard to the governance of temporal life. The conscience portrays God to itself by combining the major premises regarding God with the minor premises regarding temporal works. Thus the conscience arrives at the following portrait of God: "God is a righteous Judge who is pleased with works of the law and who hates sin. Those who do good works have a gracious God; those who sin have an angry and wrathful God."[66] The conscience therefore takes the major premise that God is to be worshiped and combines it with the minor premises from the temporal sphere—that we should not disobey parents, murder, steal, lie, and so on—and concludes that God is to be worshiped, and we are to be saved, by works of the law.

Although all pictures of God that the conscience portrays to itself have the same basic idea, different people imagine different things about God. "The Jews imagine that it is the will of God that they should worship God according to the commandment of the Law of Moses; the Turks, that they should observe the Koran; the monk, that he should do as he has learned to do."[67] Not only do different pictures of God form different religious traditions, but even the same tradition can have different pictures of God within it, and hence different gods. Such was the case with the papacy, for instance. "A monk makes a God who sits on high and thinks: 'Whoever observes the rule of St. Francis, I will

64. W.A. 40(I).608.25–30; L.W. 26:400.
65. W.A. 14.588.10–12; L.W. 9:53.
66. W.A. 40(I).603.20–22, 26–29; L.W. 26:396.
67. W.A. 40(I).608.15–21; L.W. 26:400.

save.' A nun imagines: 'If I am a virgin, God is my bridegroom.' A priest: 'God gives heaven to everyone who offers Mass and prays his hours.' "[68]

On the basis of these different notions and pictures of God, Luther says that whatever notion one has about God and God's worship *is* one's God. Each idea of conscience is a different God, and from these ideas come all the external trappings and forms of idolatry. "Strange gods are not only an external idol but much more an erring notion of conscience devised about the true God. For as the conscience is, so is God."[69] Each erring notion of the conscience gives one a different god. However, as noted above, all of these pictures have one thing in common: they all see God as one who is pleased by our own opinions and works and who delights in what we can do by our own power.[70] According to the testimony of the conscience to itself, God is gracious to those who do the works of the law, but wrathful and angry with those who sin.

Within the self-invented worship of the conscience, however, Luther discerns a kind of hierarchy. As was observed in the second section of this chapter, the conscience may be bound either by the minor premises of the natural law, which are in significant agreement with the law of Moses, or by human traditions that the conscience is taught, which obscure or contradict the natural law. Although all religions of conscience agree that God is a righteous judge who is to be worshiped by works of the law, not all such religions are in agreement as to which works constitute proper worship. For Luther, the best forms of such religions are those that worship God either according to the natural law or according to the law of Moses; at least they are performing works that God has commanded, either by teaching us in our hearts or by raising up teachers who would instruct us. "Those who would be the most pious argue: 'I will honor father and mother, offend or murder no one, will not defraud anyone or rob him of his wife, child, property, and good name; if I conduct myself in this way, I shall be saved.' "[71] Even though the worship of God through these works is imaginary, at least the works themselves are of benefit to other people in the temporal realm.

However, many pious consciences do not stop with these works of the natural law. They reason that if God is pleased with works, then the holier our works, the more God will be pleased. Thus the conscience invents laws and works for itself on the basis of what appears to be the most holy. "To illustrate, let us take a monk. He depicts God to himself as enthroned in His heaven, tailoring cowls, shaving heads, and manufacturing ropes, coarse shirts, and wooden shoes. And then he imagines that whoever clothes himself in these not only merits heaven for himself but also helps others get into heaven."[72] Such self-invented worship is on the same level as the heathen

68. *Das schoene Confitemini, an der Zahl der 118 Psalm*, 1530. W.A. 31(I).175.12–13, 18–23; L.W. 14:99.
69. W.A. 14.648.12–17; L.W. 9:130.
70. W.A. 14.588.28–29, 32–35; L.W. 9:54.
71. W.A. 46.668.16–18; L.W. 22:151–52.
72. W.A. 46.668.18–25; L.W. 22:152.

worship of oxen and calves; it is much blinder than the worship of heathens who followed the natural law, or of the Jews who obeyed the law of Moses. Self-invented works of piety have no other foundation or authorization than the opinion of human beings; and they do not help but rather hinder the rule of love in the temporal realm.[73] The more the conscience is guided by its feelings of piety, the more it falls from works that are good in themselves to works that seem to be good and holy but are in fact worthless and even harmful.

Luther was convinced that by means of the persistent teaching of fictitious human traditions in the papacy, the legal knowledge of God derived from the natural law had wholly perished.[74] Left to itself and its own piety, the conscience will not only invent a god for itself on the basis of the law, but it will also invent works of the law that are "more pious" than the works of the natural law. If we judge the worship of God according to the feeling of the conscience, we will be led away from even the natural law to our own fabricated works.

All of the pictures of God and God's worship that the conscience portrays to itself have one basic idea in common: that God is a righteous judge who is pleased by works and who hates sin. In order to have a gracious God, one must do works of the law and avoid sin. Therefore, if the conscience accuses the person of sin, the conscience can only conclude that God also accuses the person. The judgment of God may be known directly through the judgment of the conscience, as is clear from the definition of the conscience.[75] Since God is righteous, those who feel sins in their conscience cannot approach or implore God. God is gracious only to those who have an approving testimony of conscience. "All men judge this way: 'You are a sinner, but God is righteous. Therefore He hates you, therefore He inflicts punishment upon you, therefore He does not hear you.' Nothing in our nature can deny this conclusion."[76] According to the religion of the conscience, the righteous God means the God who hates sinners. Nothing in our nature will allow us to understand God's righteousness, including the "righteous God" in Scripture, in any other way.[77]

The portrayal by the conscience of God as a righteous judge is one that Luther himself had before his evangelical breakthrough. Luther judged his status before God directly through the judgment and feeling of his conscience. Because he felt he was a sinner, he could only conclude that God hated him. "Though I lived as a monk without reproach, I felt that I was a sinner before God with an extremely disturbed conscience. I did not love, yes, I hated the righteous God who punishes sinners."[78] The conscience, given its relationship

73. W.A. 46.671.7–8, 10–15; L.W. 22:155.
74. W.A. 46.671.22–25; L.W. 22:155.
75. W.A. 8.606.35–37.
76. *Enarratio Psalmi LI*, 1532. W.A. 40(II).331.16–24; L.W. 12:313.
77. Ibid. W.A. 40(II).331.24–28; L.W. 12:313.
78. *Praefatio*, 1545. W.A. 54.185–86; L.W. 34:336–37.

to the law, and its judgment that renders us either condemned or acquitted *coram Deo*, simply cannot picture God in any other way than as a righteous judge who hates sinners but who rewards those who are righteous according to works of the law.

The religion of the conscience, therefore, is fundamentally a theology of glory. The attitude of God toward us may be known directly through the judgment of the conscience: if the conscience condemns, so does God; if the conscience acquits, so does God. In this way, the conscience comes to know "the invisible things of God"—that is, God's will toward us—"in works as perceived by man."[79] The religion of conscience is also a religion of the flesh, for, as a power of the flesh, conscience judges according to what it feels: "I felt that I was a sinner before God with an extremely disturbed conscience."[80]

So long as the conscience feels its sins, it cannot help but conclude that it has a wrathful God: "human sense or reason talks this way: 'I feel that I have sinned. Therefore I have a wrathful God. Therefore all grace is gone.' "[81] In order to have a gracious God, the person must do works that bring about an approving testimony of the conscience, a judgment that makes one saved before God. "In short, human reason would like to present to God an imitation and counterfeit sinner, who is afraid of nothing and has no sense of sin."[82] One can only believe that one has a gracious God when one does not sense any sin in the conscience. If the conscience does feel sin, then one has an angry God who sentences one to death and to eternal damnation. "For where there is sin, there the conscience soon declares: 'You have sinned; therefore God is angry with you. If He is angry, He will kill you and damn you eternally.' "[83]

Those who feel sin in their conscience cannot pray to God for mercy in their distress, for God is wrathful toward sinners. Those who wish to pray to God must first try to find in themselves some good work upon which the conscience can rely, so that it can approach God. In the attempt to overcome the sense of sin in the conscience, the person will turn not only to works of the law of Moses or of nature, but also to self-invented works, which, because they concentrate on externals, have a greater chance of overcoming the sense of sin.[84] The religious motivation behind self-invented works is the need of the conscience to find some worthiness on which to stand before God. It was just this motivation that Luther saw behind the Roman system of satisfactions associated with the penitential system.

However, the attempt to attain a saving judgment of the conscience through the law has a snowballing effect, for no law fully succeeds in putting the conscience at peace with God. One law therefore breeds ten more, until the

79. W.A. 1.354.23.
80. W.A. 54.185.
81. W.A. 40(II).459.23–24; L.W. 12:404.
82. W.A. 40(I).86.29–32; L.W. 26:34.
83. W.A. 40(I).260.17–24; L.W. 26:150.
84. W.A. 40(II).332.29–37; L.W. 12:314.

conscience is buried in laws. "In fact, they only pile laws upon laws, by which they torture themselves and others and make their consciences so miserable that many of them die before their time because of excessive anguish of heart."[85] The conscience can never wholly eradicate the sense of sin from itself through works of the law, and hence can never produce of itself a judgment of conscience that declares with certainty that the person is saved *coram Deo*. No matter how many good works the person may do, the conscience always has at least a scruple that the person has not done all that was required; that scruple is enough to place the person before an angry God. "Even if I lived and worked to eternity, my conscience would never be assured and certain how much it ought to do to satisfy God."[86] It is part of the definition of the conscience that it causes the person to stand either terrified or assured. However, works of the law can never make the conscience assured and safe, but can only leave it in uncertainty.

The religion of conscience, with its *theologia gloriae*, cannot succeed in its undertaking. It cannot place the person before a gracious God; it cannot attain the certain and final judgment of conscience that makes the person saved before God. Indeed, the religion of conscience does not lead toward faith in a gracious God, but rather further and further away from it. The *theologia gloriae* leads not to confidence in God's mercy, but rather to indifference, presumption, or despair.

The religion of conscience leads to indifference and antinomianism in those people who look about and observe that the wicked flourish while the good languish. "They infer that there is no God who punishes sin, and accordingly they follow the crowd bent on sin."[87] The indifferent sinners test the claim of the conscience that God is the judge of the world against empirical evidence. Since they see that the wicked are not punished but rather prosper in this life, and that the righteous have no reward other than affliction, they infer that there is no such God who judges and punishes sinners.[88] The theology of glory can thus lead to the denial of the existence of a judging God, especially if the visible things of the world do not support such a claim.

The presumptuous, on the other hand, are fully convinced of the existence of God and of God's nature as a righteous judge. They willingly take the yoke of the law upon themselves, full of confidence in their ability to fulfill the law and thereby to stand saved before God. However, such people do not obey the law from the heart. They do not love God, but rather fear God as an angry judge whom they wish to placate with their works. Thus they put on an outward show of holiness while their hearts remain far from God. "When the members of the first class hear the message of the law, they assume that they can keep it by their own power and strength: they grow presumptuous and

85. W.A. 40(I).616.24–29; L.W. 26:406.
86. W.A. 18.783.24–27; L.W. 33:288–89.
87. W.A. 46.688.13–16; L.W. 22:151–52.
88. St.L. XI.334.

proud, lapse into hypocrisy, [and] become pseudo-saints."[89] The presumptuous therefore do not trust in the mercy of God, but in their own strength and works. They do not give glory to God; rather, they want God to give glory to them.

For those hearts and consciences that cannot drown the sense of sin with outward, hypocritical works, the religion of conscience leads to despair. The more the despairing labor to comfort their consciences with works of the law, the more they find their conscience burdened with a sense of sin. "They expend their strength on the Law, toiling, disciplining, and tormenting themselves, only to sense in their hearts, that they are unable to keep the law with their deeds."[90] The sense of sin in the conscience leads to greater and greater exertion on the part of the despairing, for they, like the presumptuous, are certain that God is only gracious to those who feel themselves to be righteous. However, the greater their exertion, the greater their sense of sin. Such exertion does not lead them to trust in God, but rather to hate God and flee from God as if from the devil.

Nor does the religion of conscience lead us to believe in God. We believe God when we acknowledge the truth of God's Word to us and deny all that would challenge that truth. It might seem as though the conscience would be receptive to the Word; for, as was seen earlier, the conscience knows only that God is to be worshiped, whereas the Word reveals to the conscience both who God is and how God wants to be worshiped. However, as already noted, the conscience portrays God and God's will to itself, and thus is certain that it already knows who God is and how God is to be worshiped; it portrays to itself a God who is pleased by works of the law. When the Word tells the conscience that God wishes to be worshiped by faith alone and not by works, reason and conscience reject the Word as an outright lie and falsehood. "See, this is the virtue of the light of nature, that it raves against the true light, is constantly boasting of piety, piety, and is always crying 'Good works!' 'Good works!' but it cannot and will not be taught what piety is and what good works are; it insists that what it thinks and proposes must be right and good."[91]

The conscience not only raises the question of the existence and nature of God, but it also answers that question with finality and certainty. Since it is certain that it knows the truth about God, it refuses to be instructed by anyone else. The conscience is certain that what it imagines about God is the surest truth.[92] Hence the Word of God, which contradicts the testimony of the conscience to itself, must be heresy. Thus the religion of conscience is the greatest obstacle to faith in God's Word. The conscience does not open the person up to either the possibility of revelation or the need for it; rather,

89. W.A. 46.659.25–33; L.W. 22:141.
90. W.A. 46.660.15–25; L.W. 22:142.
91. W.A. 10(I)1.205.17–25; 206.1–6; L.W. 52:59.
92. W.A. 40(I).608.27–30, 609.8–11; L.W. 26:400.

it forecloses the question of the need for revelation, because it is certain that it already knows who God is and what God requires.

Even though the god that the conscience portrays to itself is by nature no god, Luther claims that such false gods become real for those who believe in them. God will act toward the person according to what the person believes about God, on the basis of the principle, "As you believe, so you have." "If you believe that God is wrathful, you will certainly have Him to be wrathful and hostile to you."[93] God will be a righteous judge to those who believe God to be a righteous judge, and God will judge on the basis of their works those who seek to stand saved in God's sight on the basis of their works. "For as the conscience is, so is God."[94]

The conscience cannot help but picture God as one who is wrathful to those who feel their sins but merciful to those who are aware of their righteousness. Because the conscience seeks to know the invisible things of God through works as perceived by man, it creates for itself its own *theologia gloriae*. However, the notion that the conscience invents about God is a false and empty one. The truth is that God is only merciful to those who feel and confess their sins, while God is wrathful toward those who attempt to justify themselves on the basis of works. "However, the other thought, that God is gracious to sinners who feel their sins, is simply true and remains so."[95] Such a thought could never arise from the conscience's own testimony to itself concerning the will of God toward it. Indeed, as has been seen throughout this chapter, such a thought is impossible according to the religion of conscience. The trust that God has mercy on those who feel and confess their sins can neither arise from nor be grasped by the testimony of the conscience. It must be revealed to the conscience by the external testimony of the Word of God and sealed on the conscience by the internal testimony of the Holy Spirit.

93. W.A. 40(II).343.24–25; L.W. 12:322.
94. W.A. 14.648.14.
95. W.A. 40(II).343.19–21; L.W. 12:322.

2

THE CONDEMNATION OF THE LAW LEADING SINNERS TO PARDON

This chapter will examine the revelation of God in God's Word, and the theology of the cross (*theologia crucis*) to which the Word gives rise. The revelation of God in the Word comes under the form of the cross, for the truth that God reveals contradicts what can be known about God on the basis of what we see and feel: God's mercy is given to sinners, God's strength is revealed in weakness, God's life is disclosed in death, God's grace is hidden under the feeling of wrath. Three aspects of the Word of God as presented in Luther's theology will be considered: the Word as law, the Word as gospel, and the Word as command.

In all three forms of the Word, Luther emphasizes the contradiction between what the conscience is told by the Word and what the conscience tells itself on the basis of its own feeling and judgment. The cross emerges in the Word as law in the fact that God condemns those whom God would acquit and slays those whom God would make alive. The Word as gospel contradicts the feeling of the conscience by telling us that we are to believe we are righteous and forgiven for the sake of Christ even though we feel in our conscience that we are sinful and condemned. The Word as command is a Word of the cross by telling us that God is pleased with those works and forms of life that appear to be insignificant and even defiled when compared to the works that the conscience chooses for itself to please God. In all three forms of the Word, Luther is most interested in the contradiction between the testimony of the Word and the testimony of the conscience with regard to the nature and will of God. At the heart of the theology of the cross, however, lies the central claim of the gospel that most contradicts the theology of glory of the conscience: that God is merciful to those who feel and acknowledge their sins. "The proper subject of theology is man guilty of sin and condemned, and God the Justifier and Savior of man the sinner."[1]

---

1. *Enarratio Psalmi LI*, 1532. W.A. 40(II).328.17–18; L.W. 12:311.

The revelation of the gospel under the form of the cross reveals two kinds of knowledge to the believer, and both kinds must always be kept together: first, that all men and women are sinners; second, that God is merciful to those who feel and confess themselves to be sinners. The knowledge of sin without the knowledge of mercy results in despair and hatred of God, while the knowledge of mercy without the knowledge of human sinfulness breeds presumption and self-righteousness. When God reveals God's truth in the gospel, both the knowledge of sin and the knowledge that God is merciful to those who confess their sins are revealed. We would misunderstand Luther if we thought that these two aspects of revelation were separable. The evangelical knowledge of God, which stands in direct contrast to the legal knowledge of God, reveals both sin and mercy.[2]

Although this discussion of the testimony of the Word of God to the conscience begins with the Word as law, it should be remembered that the revelation of human sinfulness and the wrath of God on sin is already part of the evangelical knowledge of God. The awareness of sin and wrath is the beginning of God's gracious revelation. In other words, the revelation of the gospel comes under the form of the cross. Our knowledge of God's mercy is not direct, for that would be another form of the theology of glory (*theologia gloriae*); it is indirect, concealed under its opposite: "it is necessary that everything which is believed should be hidden. It cannot, however, be more deeply hidden than under an object, perception, or experience which is contrary to it."[3] The knowledge of God's mercy is hidden under the appearance of wrath; the knowledge of God's justification and acquittal is hidden under the condemning judgment of the conscience and the law.

God's revelation thus goes directly against the way in which the conscience attempts to know God. According to the conscience's own testimony about God, we can only know the acquittal of God through the acquittal of the conscience; thus we must do the works of the law until we arrive at an approving testimony of conscience. According to God's own self-revelation in the Word, however, the acquittal of God is offered only to those who are condemned before God in their own consciences; and the law is preached not so that we might attain an approving testimony of conscience through works, but so that the conscience might stand condemned before God on the basis of its own works. The self-revelation of God thus directly contradicts the testimony of the conscience to itself about God. "But God first of all terrifies the conscience, then, however, he consoles us with the promises of the Gospel which endure forever."[4] God does not justify those who acquit themselves in their conscience, but justifies those who condemn themselves in their conscience. The Word as law is given in order to bring about this condemning judgment of conscience before God.

2. *Auslegung des Johannis in Predigten*, 1537–1538. W.A. 46.669.1–9; L.W. 22:152–53.
3. *De servo arbitrio*, 1525. W.A. 18.663.8–12; L.W. 33:62.
4. *Fastenpostille*, 1525. St.L. XI.477; *Sermons* 2:69.

The beginning of the knowledge of God's mercy is therefore the knowledge of God's wrath on human sin; and the beginning of the knowledge of God's justification is the awareness of our condemnation. God's wrath and our sin are revealed through God's Word as law in its spiritual or theological use. The natural person and the conscience have no knowledge of the theological or proper use of the law, for by nature all think that the law is given to us so that we might stand justified before God on the basis of works. It is only the gospel that reveals to us that the law has as its goal not the person's justification but the person's condemnation.[5] It may now be better understood why the knowledge of the law in its spiritual use is already part of the evangelical knowledge of God: for it is only from the gospel that we learn that the proper use of the law is not to justify the conscience but to condemn it.[6] Only the gospel, and not the feeling of the conscience, gives the proper interpretation of the law. Therefore the revelation of the spiritual use of the law must be seen as inseparable from the revelation of the gospel.

With this necessary relationship between the gospel and the law established, however, it must be stated that Luther clearly insisted that there was an irreversible order in God's revelation. Even though the revelation of the law is part of the revelation of the gospel, Luther claimed that the revelation of the law and the disclosure of human sin precede the revelation of God's mercy on sinful humanity. The law must first make us feel and acknowledge our sinfulness, then the gospel can proclaim God's mercy on those who feel and acknowledge their sin. "For this must also be observed, that just as the voice of the law is not raised except over those who do not feel or acknowledge their sin, . . . so the Word of grace does not come except to those who feel their sin and are troubled and tempted to despair."[7] The order of revelation is thus clear and irreversible for Luther. God first reveals sin through the law, and then reveals God's mercy on those who feel and acknowledge their sins through the gospel. Luther clearly rejects those who attempt to reverse the order—that is, the antinomians.[8]

This chapter will first examine how the law reveals that we are sinners for whom it is impossible to perform any good work, with special emphasis on the condemnation by the law of the religion of the conscience. Second, the chapter will look at the relationship between the conscience and the revealed Word of the law. Does the conscience have of itself the ability to hear the law and to justify God in the Word? In other words, is the conscience a point of contact (*Anknuepfungspunkt*) for the law, or is the inner working of God also necessary so that the law may be heard effectively? The third point to be examined will be the way in which the law is said to be a preparation for justification. Can the law itself impel us to Christ? Or does the law only have

---

5. Ibid., *Sermons* 2:67–68.
6. *Galatas Commentarius*, 1535. W.A. 40(I).504.28–33; L.W. 26:326.
7. W.A. 18.684.3–7; L.W. 33:137.
8. W.A.40(I).223.29–36, 224:15–25; L.W. 26:126.

its proper effect in us when we apprehend God's mercy at the same time that we apprehend God's wrath? Is there an inconsistency, of which Luther was aware, behind the model of "first Law, then Gospel"?

Finally, behind all of these questions is the larger question of the ultimate source of our knowledge of human sin and the wrath of God. Is not the passion of Christ the full and complete revelation of both human sin and the wrath of God on human sin, while at the same time being the revelation of God's mercy? And is not the terrified conscience itself the fruit of Christ's passion working within us?

In order to answer these questions, it will be necessary to look at Luther's controversy with the antinomians and his rejection of some forms of preaching that emphasized the knowledge of human sin through the testimony to Christ's passion alone.

The Revelation of Sin and Wrath

Chapter 1 showed how the conscience could of itself be aware of sins as discrete works against the law, but only such sins as could be overcome with good works, thus leaving intact within the person the ability to do the law, especially the power of free will. The whole form of worship with which the conscience hopes to please God is predicated upon the ability to do good works according to the law.

The law of God, however, reveals both the extent of human sin, including our inability to do anything but sin, and the wrath of God that lies over the sinner. "So the law reveals a twofold evil, [one] inward and [the other] outward. The first, which we inflict on ourselves, is sin, and the corruption of nature; the second, which God inflicts, is wrath, death, and being accursed."[9] As opposed to the knowledge of sin that the conscience may have of itself, the knowledge of sin and wrath that the law reveals is not partial, dealing only with selected works, but total, extending over the whole person. "Contrition, according to the Scriptures, is not partial, . . . but it extends over the whole person with all its life and being, yes, over your whole nature, and shows that you are an object of God's wrath and condemned to hell."[10]

The law therefore reveals the inward corruption of the person that renders the person's works liable to judgment. The conscience judges external works, not internal attitudes or inclinations. The law reveals to the conscience the sinfulness of those attitudes and desires that the conscience thought were natural and harmless.[11] However, even these sinful desires are but the fruit of the corruption of our nature resulting from original sin; and it is the revelation of original sin that shows us we are unable to do any good work. The knowledge of original sin cannot come from the conscience or reason, but can only be known through the Word of God. "We need the Word of God from heaven

9. *Rationis Latomianae confutatio*, 1521. W.A. 8.104.22–24; LW.32:224.
10. *Sommerpostille*, 1526. St.L. XI.709; *Sermons* 2:335.
11. *Vorrede zum Alten Testament*, 1523. W.A.D.B. 8.11–31; L.W. 25:242.

to reveal this uncleanness or fault of our nature."[12] The law reveals to sinners not only the sinfulness of their works and inclinations, but more importantly the inward corruption of our nature that makes it impossible for us to do any good work.

The law also reveals to the conscience the worship and service that God requires of us, of which the conscience is otherwise ignorant. God does not wish to be worshiped through works of the law, as the conscience told itself, but by faith and trust in God alone.[13] The religion of conscience, as stated above, leads neither to trust nor belief in God, but rather to presumption, despair, or indifference. The conscience cannot trust God, for it either flees from God as from an angry judge or trusts in its own works instead of in God. It does not believe God, for it thinks it knows well enough who God is and how God wishes to be worshiped.

At the center of the law's revelation of sin stands the condemnation of the conscience's testimony to itself about God. The whole of the religion of conscience stands under the wrath of God. Indeed, the more pious the person tries to become, the more wrath the person finds on him/herself. "Therefore the piety of man is sheer blasphemy of God and the greatest sin a man commits."[14] The religion of conscience is condemned on two counts. First, given the corruption of our nature by original sin, we are unable to do anything other than sin. Thus the attempt to worship God according to works only heaps sin upon sin before God.[15] Second, the self-invented worship of the conscience is not even required by God, but is instead idolatry. What God does require—trust and belief in God—the conscience is utterly unable to provide. "This is the greatest idolatry that has been practiced up to now, and it is still prevalent in the world. . . . It concerns only that conscience which seeks help, comfort, and salvation in its own works, and presumes to wrest God from heaven."[16] By revealing to the conscience the true worship that God requires, the law condemns the whole piety of the conscience and shows that its worship angers God more than any other sin. Were it not for the Word of the law, the conscience would be wholly ignorant of the sinfulness of its own piety.[17] "For idolatry is recognized only through the Word of God."[18]

The central task of the law, therefore, is to show the sinfulness of our life both before others and before God. The Word reveals to us that God requires faith toward God and love toward our neighbor, including the enemy; the conscience finds neither of these things in its works. The law thus reveals the failure and futility of the imagined worship of the conscience. "When human nature, then, catches on to this, it must be frightened, for it certainly finds

12. W.A. 40(II).385.22–27; L.W. 12:351.
13. W.A.D.B. 11–31; L.W. 35:242.
14. *Epistel S. Petri gepredigt und ausgelegt*, 1523. W.A. 12.292.1–3; L.W. 30:37.
15. W.A. 40(I).223.35–36, 224.15; L.W. 26:126.
16. *The Book of Concord*, ed. Theodore Tappert (Philadelphia: Fortress Press, 1959), p. 367.
17. St.L. XI.712; *Sermons* 2:339.
18. *Vorlesung ueber 1. Mose von 1535–1545*. W.A. 42.440.11–14; L.W. 2:250.

neither trust nor faith, neither fear nor love to God, and neither love nor purity towards one's neighbor."[19] The proper use and purpose of the law is exactly the opposite of the use the conscience imagined for it. Rather than being the way in which God wishes to be worshiped and pleased, the law is the revelation of God's wrath at the human presumption that lies behind all self-invented piety and worship. Only God, in the Word, has the authority to tell us who God is and how God wishes to be worshiped. But before we can know who God is, God must slay the presumption of conscience that seeks to attain a gracious God through works of the law.[20]

The revelation of the law is necessary not only for the presumptuous, who imagine that they can keep the law, but also for the despairing; for even though the latter cannot pacify their consciences by means of their works, they still imagine that the law can be kept, and that God demands such worship and obedience.[21] The despairing as well as the presumptuous are convinced that the purpose of the law is to justify us before God. The Word of God reveals the true use of the law to both kinds of persons, showing them their inability to do anything other than sin.

With the revelation of human sinfulness, especially the sinfulness of the religion of conscience, comes the revelation of the wrath of God. This awareness seems to come from two sources for Luther: from the Word of the law and from the inference of the conscience. The law threatens transgressors with wrath and death; the conscience infers the wrath of God from the sense of sin. "For just as the Law reveals sin, so it strikes the wrath of God into a man and threatens him with death. Immediately his conscience draws the inference: 'You have not observed the Commandments; therefore God is offended and is angry with you.' "[22] The law reveals only sin and inability where the conscience thought there were righteousness and ability. However, once such sin and inability have been revealed to the conscience, the conscience itself immediately draws the inference that God is wrathful and condemns the person to eternal death, thereby echoing the condemnation of sinners handed down by God in the revealed law.[23]

The revelation of sin through the spiritual use of the law results in an agreement between what God declares to be true about us in the Word and what our own consciences declare about us. Without the revelation of sin in the Word, the conscience could never arrive at the conclusion that we are helpless sinners who deserve only the wrath of God. "If it depended on us, sin would very likely remain dormant forever. But God is able to awaken it

19. W.A.D.B. 8.11–31; L.W.35:242–43.

20. W.A. 40(I).482.26–28, 483.11–13; L.W. 26:310.

21. St.L. XI.475–76; *Sermons* 2:68.

22. W.A. 40(I).260.15–22; L.W. 26:150. Michael G. Baylor, *Action and Person. Conscience in Late Scholasticism and the Young Luther* (Leiden: E. J. Brill, 1977), p. 228.

23. *Das 15 Kapitel S. Pauli an die Korinther*, 1532. W.A. 36.691.36–37, 692.18–20; L.W. 28:210.

effectively through the Law."[24] Once sin has been revealed by the law, however, the testimony of our conscience confirms it. The conscience thus acknowledges the truth of the law and thereby justifies God in the Word.[25] This agreement between the testimony of the Word of God and the testimony of our conscience is the purpose of the revelation and preaching of the law, whereby we know and confess ourselves to be guilty of sin and condemned to eternal wrath and damnation.

Given the fact that the terrified conscience agrees with the testimony of the revealed Word as law, the question now arises as to whether the conscience is a point of contact for the reception of the revealed law. There is no doubt that the law is revealed, for it shows to the conscience several things of which the conscience is otherwise entirely ignorant: that it is in bondage to concupiscence and original sin and is thus unable to obey the law, and that God wishes to be worshiped by faith and trust, not by works of the law. However, once the law of God reveals sin, the testimony of the conscience comes into agreement with the testimony of the Word in acknowledging the person as a sinner subject to the wrath of God. Is the conscience therefore the subjective condition that makes possible the hearing of the Word of the law? Or does God need not only to reveal the law to the conscience, but also to move the conscience inwardly so that it can hear and acknowledge what the law reveals?

The evidence at first sight would seem to support the thesis that the conscience makes possible the hearing of the revealed law. After all, the conscience has an essential relationship to law, inasmuch as it judges the works of the person by the law, be it natural, human, or divine. Also, the conscience has the ability to accept instruction of both a true and false nature. Because the Word of God is true teaching, it would seem the conscience could receive it as well, even though the Word reveals to the conscience that which the conscience could not know of itself. Finally, the testimony of the conscience can be brought into harmony with the revealed law of God, so that it justifies God in the Word and confesses the sinner to be worthy of wrath and damnation. The conscience would thus appear to be in essential agreement with the revealed law, and thus a point of contact for the preaching of the law.

However, Luther makes it clear not only that the law must be revealed to the conscience by the Word of God, but also that God must move the conscience inwardly so that it acknowledges the truth of the Word. If the conscience were a sufficient point of contact for the law, it would follow that the majority of humanity would be able to accept and acknowledge the preaching of the law, since all persons are endowed with a conscience. Yet Luther claims that only a small number of people justify God in God's Word of judgment, while the majority call God a liar when God tells them they are sinners. "The

24. Ibid. W.A. 36.689.27–29; L.W. 28:209.
25. W.A. 40(I).224.15–19; L.W. 26:126.

greater part of the world belongs to this latter group, condemning and per-
secuting the Word by which sins are denounced."[26] Hence something more
than the conscience must be needed for the subjective appropriation of the
law.

Luther gives two reasons why the conscience per se cannot accept the
revealed law. The first is that Satan blinds the hearts and consciences of
unbelievers so that they cannot feel inwardly what the law tells them outwardly,
even though in principle it would seem as though the conscience should agree
with the Word of the law.[27] "Accordingly, it is Satan's work to prevent men
from recognizing their plight and to keep them presuming that they can do
everything they are told."[28] God must therefore enlighten the conscience so
that it feels what the Word proclaims to it and thereby justifies God in the
Word.

The second reason the conscience cannot accept the revealed Word of the
law is that the Word transcends the insight and ability of the natural person.
"For no man's reason and no lawyer will say that I am a sinner and an object
of God's wrath and condemnation if I do not steal, rob, commit adultery, and
the like, but am a pious, respectable man."[29] Even if the devil did not blind
the hearts of humans, the revelation of the law would outstrip the ability of
carnal beings to recognize its truth. The conscience can recognize sins, but
it cannot of itself, even under the external revelation of the law, acknowledge
the person as a sinner. The subjective ability to feel oneself a sinner and to
sense the wrath of God on sinners is thus a gift of God, and not an ability of
the conscience.[30] The acknowledgment of ourselves as sinners is not something
the flesh can see and feel by itself, even when the Word reveals this to us.
That we are sinners is a hidden truth not acknowledged by the natural mind
but only disclosed by the gift of the Holy Spirit.[31]

In sum, because of the limitations of the natural mind, compounded by the
blindness inflicted by Satan, the conscience is not capable of hearing the Word
of the law and acknowledging its truth. Unless God works inwardly in the
heart and conscience, the Word will be rejected as a lie.[32] "Therefore one
must preach the law and impress it on the minds of the people till God assists
and enlightens them, so that they feel in their hearts what the Word says."[33]

Luther further specifies the inner working of God that allows the conscience
to acknowledge the truth of the law as being the effect of the cross of Christ
within us. At the beginning of this section it was noted how the *theologia
crucis* manifests itself in Luther's understanding of the Word as law: when

26. W.A. 40(II).371.34–40; L.W. 12:341.
27. *Wider die himmlischen Propheten*, 1525. W.A. 18.80.38–39, 81.1–3; L.W. 40:97.
28. W.A. 18.679.31–33; L.W. 33:130.
29. St.L. XI.712; *Sermons* 2:339.
30. *Auslegung des 90. Psalms*, 1534. W.A. 40(III).575.26–29; L.W. 13:130.
31. W.A. 40(II).391.33–36; L.W. 12:356.
32. *Die sieben Busspsalmen*, 1525. W.A. 18.492.27–29; L.W. 14:156–57.
33. W.A. 18.81.1–3; L.W. 40.97.

God makes alive, God does so by slaying; when God justifies, God first makes us guilty. However, it becomes clear that for Luther the confounding of the conscience by the revelation of the law is not only *like* the crucifixion of Christ, it is actually the work of the cross of Christ within us.[34] The law and the gospel are thus as inseparable as the cross and resurrection. The terrified conscience that results from the revelation of the law is the work of the cross within us, and the consoled conscience that comes from the gospel is the work of the resurrection within us.[35]

The benefit of Christ's sufferings on the cross is realized by those who come to know themselves as sinners through the revelation of the law and who are thereby slain in their conscience because of sin just as Christ was slain on the cross for their sins. "The benefit of Christ's sufferings depends almost entirely upon a man coming to a true knowledge of himself, and becoming terror-stricken and slain before himself."[36] The ability to acknowledge the truth of the law and to be terrified in one's conscience because of sin and wrath is not something the conscience has of itself, but is rather the beneficial effect of Christ's passion and death.

If the knowledge of sin and wrath, and the terrified conscience that such knowledge brings, are the benefits of Christ's passion, then one would expect Luther to point to the passion of Christ as the fullest revelation of the Word as law.[37] The suffering and death of the Son of God are the clearest and fullest revelation both of our sin and of the wrath of God that falls on our sin. Indeed, the cross of Christ reveals our utter inability to fulfill the law and please God by our works. "Certainly the greatness of the ransom—namely, the blood of the Son of God—makes it sufficiently clear that we can neither make satisfaction for our sin nor prevail over it."[38] The death of Christ on the cross puts an end to any discussion of the existence of a human power, such as free will, that could fulfill the law in some way. "To sum up: If we believe that Christ has redeemed men by his blood, we are bound to confess that the whole man was lost."[39] The passion of Christ also reveals the greatness of God's wrath toward sin and sinners.[40]

In sum, the cross of Christ is the clearest revelation both of human sin and of the wrath of God, and is therefore the most concrete presentation of the law in its spiritual use. The cross thus gives specificity and content to Luther's statements about the revelation of the law, which at times sound rather abstract: "They meditate on the Passion of Christ aright who so view Christ that they become terror-stricken in heart at the sight, and their conscience at once sinks

---

34. *Operationes in Psalmos*, 1519–1521. W.A. 5.216.32–34, 217.37–38; *Psalms*, p. 361.
35. *Deutsche Auslegung des 67. (68.) Psalmes*, 1521. W.A. 8.8.35–36, 9.1–10; L.W. 13:7–8.
36. St.L. XI.577–78; *Sermons* 2:186.
37. W.A. 40(I).224.21–23; L.W. 26:126.
38. W.A. 40(I).84.13–16; L.W. 26:33.
39. W.A. 18.786.17–18; L.W. 33:293.
40. *Unterricht der Visitatoren an die Pfarrhern*, 1528. W.A. 26.217.1–6; L.W. 40:292.

in despair."[41] The cross as law also makes it apparent that the hearing of the law is not an achievement of nature or the conscience, but is rather a gift of grace and the fruit of Christ's passion. "For it is impossible for us profoundly to meditate upon the sufferings of Christ of ourselves, unless God sinks them into our hearts."[42]

However, although the cross is the fullest revelation of the Word of the law, it is not the only revelation of the law; and thus Luther resisted the attempts of the antinomians to preach the cross alone in order to bring about repentance. "No, one must preach in all sorts of ways—God's threats, His promises, His punishments, His help, and anything else—in order that we may be brought to repentance."[43] The danger Luther saw in preaching the law via the cross of Christ alone was that the judgment of God on our sin, and the terror of conscience that judgment brings, might be lost and only the consolation of the cross left. The cross must be preached so that it is clear that Christ died for our sins, and that the wrath of God that fell on Christ should have fallen on us.[44] Therefore, so long as the cross is both preached and heard first as the revelation of human sin and of God's eternal wrath on sin, Luther is willing to concede that the death of Christ is the fullest and clearest revelation of the Word of the law. "For in the Son of God I behold the wrath of God in action, while the law of God shows it to me with words and with lesser deeds."[45] The Word of the law is thus a word of the cross: just as Christ suffered and died on the cross for our sins, so we also must suffer in our consciences on account of our sins, so that we might know and confess as our own the sins for which Christ died.

Driving the Conscience to Christ

Luther insisted throughout his life that the revelation and preaching of the law preceded the revelation of the gospel. Although the spiritual use of the law is part of the evangelical knowledge of God, the revelation of sin and wrath that comes through the law, and the confounding of the conscience that results, must come before the revelation of God's mercy on sinners.[46] The truth about the nature and will of God is that God has mercy on those who acknowledge their sin. Both the law and the gospel are revealed to make known this truth about God, which contradicts the knowledge of God that the conscience has of itself. However, Luther insisted that the acknowledgment of sin was necessary before the disclosure of God's mercy could be heard. We must first know and confess ourselves to be those sinners on whom God bestows mercy before God will actually show us mercy. "Accordingly, I followed this

41. St.L. XI.576; *Sermons* 2:185.
42. St.L. XI.579–80; *Sermons* 2:187–88.
43. *Wider die Antinomer*, 1539. W.A. 50.472.14–25; L.W. 47:111–12.
44. Ibid. W.A. 50.473.13–19; L.W. 47:112–13.
45. Ibid. W.A. 50.473.20–25; L.W. 47:113.
46. *In Esaiam Prophetam D. Doc. Martini Lutheri Enarraciones*, 1527. W.A. 31(II).263.2–5; L.W. 17:5.

example and comforted only those who were first contrite and despairing, whom the law had thoroughly frightened."[47]

Luther even describes the acknowledgment of sin brought about by the law as a necessary preparation for grace that makes us capable of receiving the gospel. "Only those who are afflicted have comfort and are capable of it, because comfort means nothing unless there is a malady."[48] God is not a God of the righteous who feel no sin, as the conscience imagined, but is instead a God of the afflicted sinners who feel their sin. In order to know this God, we must first become God's people; and we become God's people through the revelation and hearing of the law. "Therefore the Law is a minister and preparation for grace. For God is the God of the humble, the miserable, the afflicted, the oppressed, the desperate, and of those who have been brought down to nothing at all."[49]

On the one hand, therefore, God only gives grace to those who feel their sin, affliction, and emptiness. On the other hand, the grace of God is only received by those who seek after it and thirst for it. The law of God is revealed to disclose our own need and distress so that we long for and seek after the grace that God has revealed in Christ.[50] In this way, Luther can say that the law prepares us for grace, or drives us to Christ: "Therefore the Law only shows sin, terrifies, and humbles; thus it prepares us for justification and drives us to Christ."[51] The law terrifies the conscience by showing that there is no salvation, only damnation, in the worship the conscience invented for itself. Such terror of conscience is the proper thirst that leads us to seek the grace of God in Christ.[52]

Therefore, although the law is part of the evangelical knowledge of God, the revelation of God's wrath in the law is distinct from and prior to the revelation of God's mercy in the gospel.[53] The revelation of God's wrath brings about the feeling and acknowledgment of sin, which is the necessary condition for the revelation of God's mercy. "Where there is no acknowledgment, there is no remission. For the remission of sins is preached to those who feel sin and seek the grace of God."[54] Even the cross of Christ must first be seen as the revelation of the wrath of God, which alone brings about the necessary acknowledgment of sin.

This order of revelation—first law, then gospel—is one of the most familiar aspects of Luther's theology. However, at the very heart of this model is a problem, of which Luther himself was aware. The problem, which arises

---

47. W.A. 43.171.28–31; L.W. 4:50–51.
48. W.A. 31(II).261.27–30; L.W. 17:3.
49. W.A. 40(I).488.13–19; L.W. 26:314–15.
50. W.A.D.B. 8.11–31; L.W. 35:224.
51. W.A. 40(I).224.23–25; L.W. 26:126.
52. *Auslegung des 6, 7, und 8. kapitels Johannis in Predigten*, 1530–1532. W.A. 23.425.40–42, 426.1–6; L.W. 23:267.
53. W.A. 43.32–34; L.W. 5:154.
54. *Vorlesung ueber den 1. Brief des Johannis*, 1527. W.A. 20.797.33–35; L.W. 30:325.

primarily from the nature of the conscience, may be broken down into two distinct yet related questions: (1) How can the revelation of the law lead the conscience to seek after something beyond the law, given the fact that the law is the only form of salvation of which the conscience is aware? (2) Does the person in general, and the conscience in particular, acknowledge sins in the face of God's wrath, or in the light of God's forgiving mercy? Both of these questions challenge Luther's claim that the revelation of the law precedes the revelation of God's mercy. Although Luther was aware of this problem, he was not led to reformulate his "first law, then gospel" model.

The first question may be reformulated as follows: How can the preaching of the law drive us to Christ (*impellit ad Christum*) when Christ has not yet been made known? How can the conscience thirst for something of which it is ignorant? Even though the law reveals the wrath of God on the whole undertaking of works-righteousness, the conscience only sees one way of salvation, and that is by works of the law. It is hard to understand how the preaching of the law per se could lead the conscience to seek something beyond the law. Luther himself describes the problem thus: "The foolishness of the human heart is so great that in its conflict of conscience, when the law performs its function and carries out its true use, the heart not only does not take hold of the doctrine of grace, . . . but it actually looks for more laws to help it out."[55] As this passage indicates, the terrified conscience might not prepare us for grace or drive us to Christ at all, but might rather drive us more anxiously to works of the law. This would be especially true if the law were understood as being distinct from and prior to the preaching of God's grace in Christ.

The second question may pose an even more serious challenge to Luther's sequence of law-gospel. How can the revelation of God's wrath per se bring about the acknowledgment and confession of sin? The law, as has been stated, reveals to the conscience that God is a wrathful judge who damns sinners. Yet this is just the kind of God the conscience imagines for itself. In the face of such a God, the conscience does not acknowledge its sin, for that would involve the damnation of the person. Instead, the conscience conceals its sin until it can rid itself of the feeling of sin; or, short of that, it despairs of God and salvation and thereby accuses God in order to excuse itself. In either case, the revelation of a wrathful God does not bring about the confession of sin, but rather the excusing of sin and the accusing of God.

Luther shows his awareness of this problem most clearly in the narrative in Genesis that describes the fall of Adam and Eve into sin. Even though Adam was properly convicted of sin in his conscience, he did not acknowledge his sin, but rather excused himself and accused God. As Luther states, such is the way of all sinners when they are accused by God. "Thus when man has been accused of sin by God, he does not acknowledge his sin but rather

---

55. W.A. 40(I).489.17–21; L.W. 26:315.

accuses God and transfers his guilt from himself to the Creator."[56] In other words, the disclosure of human sin and the revelation of God's wrath lead the sinner to conceal his or her sin and to accuse God. The law does not lead to the acknowledgment of sin, but to the accusation of God. "But this is amazing, that he still persists in his excuse after his conscience has convicted him and he himself has also heard his sin from God."[57]

The revelation of the law can thus bring about the feeling of sin in the conscience, but it will not allow for its confession. Where the conscience perceives only wrath, it cannot acknowledge its sin. The acknowledgment of sin is thus dependent upon the knowledge of God's desire and will to forgive. "Where there is no promise of forgiveness of sins and no faith, the sinner cannot act otherwise."[58] According to this line of thinking, the acknowledgment of sin is not the necessary condition for the knowledge of forgiveness but is itself dependent upon the knowledge of God's mercy. "But as long as the Law alone rules and stings us, the frightened conscience cannot produce this confession, as the example of Adam and Eve proves."[59] Nor does a terrified conscience impel us to Christ or prepare us for grace. Rather, the terrified conscience will flee from God, for it knows God only as a condemning judge, and the revelation of the law only confirms this knowledge. "Such a conscience is also unmindful of confession and does not admit its sin."[60]

In sum, given the nature and function of the conscience, the revelation of the law alone will not produce the confession of sin, no matter how much sin, inability, and wrath the law reveals. "Such is the nature of conscience. Although it feels sin and the heart is terrified and agitated to the point of damnation, it nevertheless does not confess its transgression."[61]

It is clear that the revelation of the law alone cannot bring about the effects Luther ascribes to it. The acknowledgment of sin is as dependent upon the revelation of God's mercy as it is a necessary condition for it. The knowledge of God's grace is as much the cause of our thirst for grace as it is the cure for that thirst. The revelation of the law cannot, therefore, be separated from the revelation of the gospel even in a temporal sense. "And such is the working of the Law that, when the Law stands alone without the Gospel and the knowledge of grace, it leads to despair and ultimate impenitence."[62]

The acknowledgment of sin that marks the beginning of repentance is as much the result of the promise of forgiveness as it is its necessary condition. "But who can repent gladly and joyfully without having the certain consolation and promise of grace which is not the product of our own mind . . . but must

---

56. W.A. 42.131.9–11; L.W. 1:175. See Gerhard Heintze, *Luthers Predigt von Gesetz und Evangelium* (Munich: Chr. Kaiser Verlag, 1958).

57. W.A. 42.132.13–15; L.W. 1:177.

58. W.A. 42.132.32–39; L.W. 1:178.

59. W.A. 42.133.25–34; L.W. 1:181.

60. *Der Prophet Jona ausgelegt*, 1526. W.A. 19.214.21–35; L.W. 19:63.

61. W.A. 44.501.36–38; L.W. 7:273.

62. W.A. 42.133.22–24; L.W. 1:178.

be offered and presented through a definite promise of God's Word?"[63] Thus Luther not only insists on "first law, then gospel," but also insists on the simultaneity of law and gospel. "But what profit is there in being bruised for sins and not to understand even the faintest spark of God's mercy? . . . This is the source of the shouting and sobbing in perplexities and troubles of the conscience, so that one begins at the same time [simul] to taste eternal life."[64] Such qualifications by Luther should keep us from overreading him along the lines of "first law, then gospel." Although the bulk of his theology does set forth such an order, Luther was aware of the contradiction that resulted from separating law from gospel, a contradiction rooted in the nature of the conscience itself. Luther can speak not only of *simul* law and gospel, but also of the gospel itself as revealing both the condemnation of sin and our redemption from it.[65]

In a real sense, the law and the gospel are but two aspects of the one revelation of God in Jesus Christ. The cross and death of Christ are the law in that they reveal our sin and inability and the extent of God's wrath on sin. The resurrection of Christ is the gospel in that it shows that Christ took our sin, death, and curse upon himself and overcame them, giving us the victory. The passion as law forces us to see the sins for which Christ died as our own. The resurrection as gospel allows us to see our sins as no longer ours but Christ's, and his victory as not only his but also ours. This happy exchange reveals how God can have mercy on those who feel and acknowledge their sins.

63. W.A. 30(II).507.1–7; L.W. 40:377.
64. W.A. 44.469.12–24, 470.1–6; L.W. 7:229–30.
65. *Praelectiones in prophetas minores. Sacharja,* 1525. W.A. 13.640.16–23; L.W. 20:110.

3

THE PARDON OF THE GOSPEL
FOR THOSE WHO CONFESS
THEIR SIN

The first aspect of the self-revelation of God is the revelation of the law, which brings about the feeling and acknowledgment of sin in the sinner, and which condemns the whole religion of conscience. However, the revelation of the law is not an end in itself, but the beginning of the revelation of God's mercy on sinners, although God's mercy is initially hidden under wrath.[1] The disclosure of human sin and the wrath of God is necessary, but only as it leads to the revelation of God's mercy. "Although He is the God of life and salvation and these are His proper works, yet, in order to accomplish this, He kills and destroys. These works are alien to Him, but through them He accomplishes His proper work."[2] The revelation of God's wrath on sin is an alien work of God, because it is God's true nature and will to have mercy on sinners; however, the blindness of human sin to its own predicament makes this wrath necessary.[3] The alien work of God must give way to the proper work of God: the revelation of God's wrath on sin must lead to the knowledge of God's mercy.

Once the law has performed its work, it is time for the revelation of the gospel.[4] The revelation of the law leads not so much to the knowledge of God as to the knowledge of self—that we are lost sinners who have no ability to please God. Only the gospel gives us the true knowledge of God, that it is the nature of God to have mercy on those who acknowledge their sins. The revelation of the law is inseparable from the revelation of the gospel, even though Luther insisted that the law preceded the gospel.

The Happy Exchange in Christ

One way in which to understand both the order and inseparability of law and gospel is to see both as elements of the death and resurrection of Christ. The law was most fully revealed for Luther in the passion and death of Christ.

---

1. *De servo arbitrio*, 1525. W.A. 18.633.9–10; L.W. 33:62.
2. *Operationes in Psalmos*, 1519–1521. W.A. 5.63.33–39, 64.1–2; L.W. 14:355.
3. *Vorlesung ueber 1. Mose von 1535–1545*. W.A. 42.356.21–24; L.W. 2:134.
4. *Galatas Commentarius*, 1535. W.A. 40(I).556.21–27; L.W. 26:364.

The cross discloses both our sin and the wrath of God on our sin, and the knowledge of the cross terrifies the conscience. The resurrection, on the other hand, reveals to us that Christ took our sins upon himself, died for them, and then triumphed over sin, death, and the wrath of God in his resurrection. If the death of Christ revealed sin and wrath to our consciences, the resurrection reveals that our sins no longer lie upon us but have been taken up and vanquished by Christ: "just as the sins flowed out of Christ and we become conscious of them, so should we pour them again upon him and set our conscience free."[5] The death of Christ drives our sins into our consciences so that we acknowledge that it was for our sins, not his own, that Christ died on the cross. The resurrection, however, takes our sins out of our consciences and lays them on Christ, who is the victor over sin and death.[6]

The resurrection reveals to us that Christ has taken our sin, death, and curse upon himself and has given us his victory. Our sins no longer belong to us but to Christ, and his righteousness is not only his but also and especially ours. This, according to Luther, is the meaning of Paul's statement that Christ "was handed over to death for our trespasses and was raised for our justification" (Rom. 4:25).[7] If the cross as law forces us to see our sins in our conscience, so that we both feel and confess them, then the resurrection as gospel allows us to see our sins on Christ and Christ's victory on us.

The mercy of God is revealed in Christ in the form of the happy exchange of our sin for Christ's righteousness, as enacted in his death and resurrection. "By this fortunate exchange [*feliciter commutans*] with us He took upon Himself our sinful person and granted us His innocent and victorious Person. Clothed and dressed in this, we are freed from the curse of the Law, because Christ Himself voluntarily became a curse for us."[8] Although the law of God reveals sin in our conscience, God takes our acknowledged sin from us and places it upon Christ.[9] Therefore, when we feel sin in our conscience, we should transfer it to Christ, for it is God's will that our sin should lie on Christ and not on us. "Therefore beware, as you place your sins in your conscience, that you do not panic, but freely place them on Christ, as the text says, 'He has borne our iniquities.' "[10] At the same time, we should transfer the righteousness and victory of Christ to ourselves, for God has willed that the victory be ours. "Let us learn, therefore, in every temptation to transfer sin, death, the curse, and all the evils that oppress us from ourselves to Christ, and, on the other hand, to transfer righteousness, life, and blessing from Him to us."[11]

The happy exchange has two aspects. On the one hand, there is the exchange of our sin for Christ's victory, which took place objectively in the death and

5. *Fastenpostille*, 1525. St.L. XI.580; *Sermons*, 2:189.
6. Ibid. St.L. XI.580–81; *Sermons* 2:189–90.
7. *Sommerpostille*, 1526. *Sermons* 2:242.
8. W.A. 40(I).443.23–34; L.W. 26:284.
9. *Auslegung des Johannes in Predigten*, 1537–1538. W.A. 46.683.21–23; L.W. 22:169.
10. *In Esaiam*, 1527. W.A. 31(II).433.35–36, 434.1–6; L.W. 17:223.
11. W.A. 40(I).454.30–34; L.W. 26:292.

resurrection of Christ. On the other hand, there is the exchange of our sin for Christ's victory, which takes place when we transfer the sin we feel in our consciences from ourselves to Christ and transfer the victory we see in him to ourselves. Luther makes it clear that the former exchange is not effective without the latter. In other words, the happy exchange benefits only those who have faith in Christ. "Therefore we are justified by faith alone, because faith alone grasps this victory of Christ. To the extent that you believe this, to that extent you have it."[12]

Faith brings about the fruits of the happy exchange for us by making us one with Christ, by cementing our person with his. By our unity with Christ through faith, all that is ours becomes his, and all that is his becomes ours.[13] More specifically, Luther states that faith makes Christ and the conscience into one body. "But here Christ and my conscience must become one body, so that nothing remains in my sight but Christ, crucified and risen."[14] When Christ and the conscience are made into one body by faith, then the sins that the conscience feels are placed upon Christ, while the righteousness that the conscience does not feel is taken from Christ and given to the conscience to console it. In other words, such a conscience sees both its sin and righteousness in Christ alone.[15] "Whenever I feel remorse in my conscience on account of sin, therefore, I look at the bronze serpent, Christ on the cross."[16]

In the happy exchange, God reveals to us that God has mercy on those who feel their sins. In Christ, God has taken away the sins that subjected us to wrath and condemnation, and has given us the righteousness that allows us to stand acquitted in God's sight. The sins we feel are no longer ours, nor are the curse and death that follow from sin. On the basis of the happy exchange, Luther can say: "Therefore where sins are noticed and felt, there they really are not present."[17] Faith in Christ is thus a form of the theology of the cross (*theologia crucis*): we are to believe that we are righteous, innocent, and blessed, even though we feel as though we are sinful, guilty, and damned. "Our feelings must not be considered, but we must constantly insist that death, sin, and hell have been conquered, although I feel that I am still under the power of death, sin, and hell."[18] Christ tells us that our sins are his, and yet we feel them in our consciences. He tells us that his righteousness is ours, and yet we feel none of it within ourselves. Thus our feelings must be ignored, in opposition to the religion of the conscience, and we must believe that we are righteous even though we feel we are sinners. "We believe life, glory, righteousness, and peace, but on the contrary feel death, shame, sin, and trouble."[19]

---

12. W.A. 40(I).443.35–36, 444.12–14; L.W. 26:284.
13. W.A. 40(I).285.24–27, 286.15–16; L.W. 26:168.
14. W.A. 40(I).282.21–22; L.W. 26:166.
15. W.A. 40(I).546.16–21; L.W. 26:357.
16. W.A. 40(I).273.17–18; L.W. 26:159.
17. W.A. 40(I).445.19–22; L.W. 26:285.
18. St.L. XI.627–28; *Sermons* 2:224.
19. W.A. 31(II).71.5–8; L.W. 16:101.

This contrast between what the faithful feel and what they believe becomes constitutive for Luther of the Christian life. "Therefore we define a Christian as follows: A Christian is not someone who has no sin or feels no sin; he is someone to whom, because of his faith in Christ, God does not impute his sin. This doctrine brings firm consolation to troubled consciences amid genuine terrors."[20] Such a contrast between what we feel and what we believe is the manifestation in the conscience of our Christian status before God as simultaneously righteous and a sinner (*simul iustus et peccator*): we feel sin, death, and wrath in our consciences, but we are to believe that Christ has taken our sin and death upon himself. We do not feel righteousness and blessedness in our consciences, but we are to believe that they are ours, for Christ has given them to us.

The Testimony of Christ

The happy exchange, and the mercy of God revealed therein, are not things to which the conscience can testify of itself. The conscience can only conclude that God is wrathful toward those who feel their sins. Thus, the theology of glory (*theologia gloriae*) of the conscience would urge us to do good works until the feeling of sin is eradicated.[21] On the basis of the happy exchange, however, the *theologia crucis* directs those who feel their sins not to good works but to Christ. "Believe in Him. His righteousness is yours; your sin is His."[22]

Faith in Christ thus directly contradicts the testimony of the conscience to itself about God. When the conscience feels its sin, it can only conclude that God is wrathful. Faith in Christ begins with the same feeling of sin but concludes that God is merciful, because the victory of Christ over sin has been bestowed upon it.[23] Faith allows believers to see the condemnation for sin no longer on themselves—as the testimony of the conscience would have it—but on Christ. Instead of condemnation for sin, faith receives the victory of Christ over sin, death, and the wrath of God.

Thus, although both the law and the gospel are revealed to the conscience by the Word of God, there is a difference in the extent of the two kinds of revelation. The law, although revealed by God, fulfills its purpose when it brings the testimony of the conscience into agreement with it. "For the law dins this into your ears and holds the register of your sins before your nose: 'Do you hear? You committed this and you committed that in violation of God's commandment, and you spent your whole life in sin. Your own conscience must attest and affirm that.' "[24] When the law reveals the full extent

20. W.A. 40(I).235.15–17; L.W. 26:133. See F. Edward Cranz, *An Essay on the Development of Luther's Thought on Justice, Law, and Society* (Cambridge, Mass.: Harvard University Press, 1959).

21. W.A. 40(I).368.26–29; L.W. 26:232–33.

22. W.A. 40(I).369.25; L.W. 26:233.

23. *Das 15. Kapitel S. Pauli an der Korinther*, 1532. W.A. 36.693.27–37, 694.23-24; L.W. 28:211–12.

24. Ibid. W.A. 36.689.31–34; L.W. 28:209.

of our sin and impotence, both through the Word and inner working of God, the conscience cannot help but agree with the law that we are sinners subject to death and the wrath of God. The revelation of the gospel, in contrast, can never be brought into agreement with the testimony of the conscience. The conscience cannot help but conclude that God hates those who feel their sin, whereas the gospel declares that God has mercy on them. "For human nature and reason cannot rise above the judgment of the Law, which concludes and says: He that is a sinner is condemned of God. . . . This teaching, in which God offers his grace and mercy to those who feel their sins and God's wrath, God's own Son himself must institute and command to be spread abroad in the world."[25] The testimony of the gospel, in which God offers grace to those who feel their sins and God's wrath, is not something believers can know and understand of themselves, especially in their conscience. It is something to which God must bear witness in the Son.[26] The revelation of the gospel is therefore the Son's own peculiar work. His testimony tells us of the will of the Father to have mercy on sinners, and thus contradicts both the testimony of the conscience and the revelation of the law.

The work of Christ in redeeming us from sin is twofold. First, Christ took our sin upon himself and thus became subject to death and the wrath of God. In his resurrection, he became the Victor over sin, death, and wrath. Second, Christ bore testimony to the meaning of his death and resurrection in his Word—that is, that in his death he has taken upon himself our sin, while in his resurrection he has given us his victory. Without this testimony, we would not be able to know of the salvation that took place in the death and resurrection of Christ. "Human reason cannot say that a man who dies is God, is the redeemer of the world from its sins and who gives eternal life. To be sure God sees this, but not we. Therefore we must have the testimony of the Word to announce this to us."[27] Thus Christ has two offices: the work of redemption, and the testimony about that redemption.[28] Just as no one but Christ could perform the work of redemption, so no one but Christ could testify as to the significance of that work; for the testimony that God wishes to be gracious to sinners is unknown to the heart, mind, and conscience of humanity.

The testimony of Christ stands in direct contrast to the testimony of the conscience to itself about God. The conscience cannot help but invent or imagine a god for itself—a god who is a judge who is pleased with works. The testimony to the conscience concerning the work of Christ, on the other hand, is not our invention but the Word of God. "Nor is it our invention that the Lamb was sacrificed by God and that, in obedience to the Father, this Lamb took upon Himself the sins of the whole world."[29] Nor is the testimony of

---

25. St.L. XI.716; *Sermons* 2:343.
26. *Auslegung in Johannis Predigten*, 1538–1540. W.A. 47.178.4–15; L.W. 22:466.
27. *Vorlesung ueber den 1. Timotheusbrief*, 1528. W.A. 26.41.16–19; L.W. 28:269.
28. Ibid. W.A. 26.40.2–4, 12–16; L.W. 28:267–68.
29. W.A. 46.679.11–16; L.W. 22.164–65.

Christ something that Christ invented. If it were, we would still be uncertain as to whether God has mercy on sinners. Christ bears faithful witness to the will of God toward us (*pro nobis*). "What He preaches is not a fiction or a figment of His imagination; it deals with the things He has seen, for He is God's Son, and He knows the depth of God's will and wisdom and of the Father's counsel. To this He bears witness."[30] In Christ alone do we have the true testimony about God.

The testimony of Christ comes to us in the form of Word and sacrament. "They say: 'Christ completed the redemption with a single work.' Yes, but He distributes it, applies it, and tells it by testimony. He gave it out through the medium of washing in Baptism, through the medium of eating in the Sacrament of the Altar, through the media of comforting the brethren, of reading in the Book, that the fruit of His passion might be spread everywhere."[31] All of these forms of the testimony of Christ set forth the forgiveness of sins that Christ has won for us by his death and resurrection. Therefore, the testimony of the Word is of special use in comforting those consciences that are uncertain of the mercy of God.[32]

These testimonies to the mercy and forgiveness of God are given through human witnesses to Christ. Thus, those who weigh the testimony by the authority of the speaker per se will conclude that the witness is from humans and not from God. "But such is the perversity of human nature that we do not believe that we are hearing the Word of God whenever He speaks through a man."[33] However, Christ continues to bear witness to himself through others, so that whoever hears them hears Christ.[34] The human words that bear witness to Jesus Christ are to be heard as the words of Christ himself, for Christ has promised to speak to us through his witnesses and the testimonies he entrusted to them—preaching, baptism, the Lord's Supper, and brotherly consolation. If Christ did not continue to speak through his witnesses, their testimony to him would have disappeared long ago.[35] Only Christ can bear testimony to us concerning the mercy of God for sinners, even if he does so through the testimony of human beings.

If only Christ can bear witness concerning himself and his work, then it follows that we cannot verify his testimony by what we see and feel. All other forms of human testimony can be verified by empirical testing. "In other books and arts you must study and put all things to the test so that you may hear and understand and grasp what is presented."[36] This is even true of the law of God revealed in his Word: we must find and feel within us that which the law tells us outwardly, even if this feeling is effected by the inner working of

30. W.A. 47.178.40–42, 179.1–4; L.W. 22:467.
31. W.A. 26.40.21–23, 41.4–6; L.W. 28:268–69.
32. *Wider die himmlischen Propheten*, 1525. W.A. 18.204.2–8; L.W. 40:214.
33. W.A. 44.166.23–25; L.W. 6:224.
34. *Praelectiones in prophetas minores. Sacharja*, 1525. W.A. 13.550.5–6, 9–13; L.W. 20:213.
35. *Praedigt ueber den 110. Psalm*, 1535. W.A. 41.196.8–14; L.W. 13:324.
36. W.A. 31(II).57.32–33; L.W. 16:82.

God. The testimony of Christ, however, cannot be verified by what we see and feel, for it speaks of things not revealed anywhere else on earth. "The nature of bearing witness is that it speaks of that which others do not see, know, or feel; but they must believe him that bears testimony."[37] This is especially true of Christ's testimony to the mercy of God toward those who feel their sins and the wrath of God; for such testimony is directly contradicted by the feeling of the conscience. Those who accept the testimony of Christ must ignore what they see and feel, and follow only what Christ tells them. "A Christian, however, is not guided by what he sees or feels; he follows what he does not see or feel. He remains with the testimony of Christ; he listens to His words and follows Him into the darkness."[38] The testimony of Christ cannot be supported or verified by feeling, especially the feeling of the conscience. Rather, the Word of Christ is accepted only by faith, which acknowledges that God is true even when God tells us things that transcend or contradict what we see and feel.

By acknowledging the truth of God's Word, in the face of what we can know of ourselves, faith gives glory to God. Faith reckons God to be true, even though all humans be liars. "The believer thus makes God truthful and himself a liar. For he disbelieves his own mind as something false in order to believe the word of God as the truth, even though it goes against all he thinks in his own mind."[39] Faith gives glory to God by acknowledging the truth of the witness of Christ to the happy exchange, and thus completes the exchange by making it an event in our lives.

Faith as giving glory to God therefore becomes another way in which Luther describes our justification by faith alone, along with the blessed exchange. Faith gives glory to God by reckoning God to be true in the Word. To give glory to God is to render what is due God, and those who do so are righteous.[40] Faith therefore permits God to be God's own truthful witness concerning God's will toward us and refuses to determine of itself what it should think about God. "We are not to determine out of ourselves what we must believe about Him, but to hear and learn it from Him. For this reason it is fitting we honor Him by conceding the truth of what He tells us."[41]

In particular, faith believes God's promise to have mercy on sinners to be true, even though both reason and conscience oppose such a promise. "He takes hold of God the Promisor and turns the whole vision of His heart upon His mercy. He could not do this if he had not taken hold of God the Promisor with the help of the Spirit and known that in God there remained a hope of forgiveness for sinners."[42] Faith trusts in the truth of the testimony of God

---

37. *Kirchenpostille*, 1522. *Sermons* 1:202.
38. W.A. 47.35.6–11; L.W. 22:306.
39. *Roemerbriefvorlesung*, 1515–1516. W.A. 56.296; L.W. 25:283–84.
40. W.A. 40(I).360.21–23, 361.12–16; L.W. 26:227.
41. W.A. 40(I).92.11–15; L.W. 13:237.
42. *Enarratio Psalmi LI*, 1532. W.A. 40(II).344.24–34; L.W. 12:323.

even when it means that the testimony of the believer's own heart and conscience must be a lie.

The consolation of the conscience that is the fruit of faith in the work of Christ and the happy exchange is inseparable from the certainty of conscience that is the fruit of faith in God's Word and testimony. Indeed, we have access to the mercy of God revealed in the death and resurrection of Christ only by means of the testimony of Christ's Word about his own work. Such testimony both contradicts and transcends what we can know about God of ourselves; thus faith has no other knowledge of the mercy of God than what it obtains from the gospel of Christ. "And this is the reason why our theology is certain: it snatches us away from ourselves, so that we do not depend on our own strength, conscience, experience, person or works but depend on that which is outside ourselves, that is, on the promise and truth of God, which cannot deceive."[43] Faith clings to the truth of God's Word—that God offers grace to those who feel their sins—even though our own reason, heart, experience, and conscience tell us that God must be lying. Let God be true, and all humans be liars.

The Witness of the Holy Spirit

Given the opposition between the Word of God and our mind and conscience, it is clear that faith in the Word is not within our power. Human knowledge can only proceed on the basis of what we see and feel; yet faith demands that we ignore what we see and feel and cling only to the testimony of Christ. Faith is therefore not an ability of the person, but is rather the work and gift of the Holy Spirit.[44] Christ not only reveals the mercy of God toward sinners in his testimony, a mercy of which the conscience is totally ignorant; but he also gives us the ability to accept his testimony, for of itself the conscience cannot place the sinner before a merciful God and cannot accept Christ's Word as true. "The conscience cannot pluck out these thorns; it cannot put the sinner before a gracious and forgiving God. This is the gift of the Holy Spirit, not of our free will or strength."[45]

It is the Holy Spirit, and not the conscience, that allows us to acknowledge the truth of the gospel. "For the Holy Spirit must be both the Preacher of this message and the Author who inscribes it in my heart, so that I believe and say: 'I believe in Jesus Christ.' "[46] The external testimony of Christ to the conscience must be combined with the internal witness of the Holy Spirit to the heart and conscience so that we acknowledge the Word as true. "Then, when the Spirit has been received, the heart is certain and has confidence."[47] The Holy Spirit gives us the ability to acknowledge and trust in the truth of

---

43. W.A. 40(I).589.17–28; L.W. 26:387.
44. W.A. 36.493.4–9; L.W. 28:69.
45. W.A. 40(II).346.33–37, 347.1; L.W. 12:324.
46. W.A. 47.14.4–6; L.W. 22:286.
47. *Vorlesung ueber den 1. Brief des Johannes*, 1527. W.A. 20.780.30–33; L.W. 30:315.

the Word, even though we neither see nor feel what the Word proclaims to us.[48]

The Holy Spirit also gives faith the ability to cling to the truth of the Word even when the world and the conscience oppose the Word. "The Holy Spirit does this in order that man may remain alive in the midst of death and may be able to keep a good conscience and God's grace even though he is aware of his sins."[49] Only the Holy Spirit can give us the ability to believe and trust in the gospel, for the gospel is revealed under an appearance or a feeling that contradicts the revealed truth. We believe we are righteous even though we feel only our sinfulness; we believe God is merciful even though all we feel is God's wrath; we believe we have eternal life even though death surrounds us. "For because the awareness of the opposite is so strong in us, that is, because we are more aware of the wrath of God than of His favor toward us, therefore the Holy Spirit is sent into our hearts."[50]

In sum, the witness of the Holy Spirit makes it clear that the gospel of Christ is not something the conscience can ever tell itself, but is rather a testimony the conscience can only receive from God.[51] As Christ alone reveals the mercy of God toward those who feel their sin, so he alone, by the power of his Holy Spirit, can give us the ability to believe his revelation.[52]

The revelation of the gospel through the testimony of the Word and Holy Spirit brings both consolation and certainty to consciences terrified by the law. Whereas the law reveals sin in the conscience along with the wrath of God toward sin, the gospel reveals the forgiveness of sins through Christ and the mercy of God toward sinners. The preaching of the gospel thus consoles terrified consciences by revealing to them that they have a gracious God.[53] The gospel also brings certainty to consciences previously uncertain as to how they stood before God. Unlike the religion of conscience, which imagines for itself both the nature and will of God, the gospel is not the invention of human beings but is the very Word of God and as such is the most certain truth. "We have not invented this ourselves; but we have seen and heard it through the revelation of God, who has commanded us to listen to this Christ."[54] Not only does the conscience have the certain Word of God, but it also receives the gift of the Holy Spirit, through which the conscience is made certain that God's Word is true.[55]

In brief, the gospel consoles the conscience by revealing the mercy of God toward those who feel both their sins and God's wrath; and it makes the

---

48. W.A. 42.452.23–26; L.W. 2:267.
49. W.A. 46.56.11–13; L.W. 24:360.
50. W.A. 40(I).581.12–14; L.W. 26:381.
51. *Vorlesung ueber den Hebraerbrief*, 1518. W.A. 57(III).169; L.W. 29:171–72.
52. *Epistel S. Petri gepredigt und ausgelegt*, 1523. W.A. 12.293.27–30, 294.4–8; L.W. 30:39.
53. W.A. 18.65.14–18; L.W. 40:82.
54. *Die ander Epistel S. Petri und eine S. Judas gepredigt und ausgelegt*, 1523–1524. W.A. 14.26.26–28, 27.1–2; L.W. 30:162–63.
55. *Auslegung des Johannes in Predigten*, 1530–1532. W.A. 23.362.20–30; L.W. 23:229.

conscience certain, because it is the Word of God and not a human invention. "The gospel makes a conscience certain and causes it to have peace."[56]

The Contradiction of Assurance

Even though faith in Christ consoles the conscience, we should not think that the testimony of the gospel and the feeling of the conscience come into some sort of harmony in faith. The conscience of the Christian is as opposed to the gospel as is the conscience of the pagan, for the conscience can only conclude that God is wrathful toward those who feel their sins. In the experience of tribulation (*Anfechtung*), the opposition between the Word of God and the feeling of the conscience is intensified. After God reveals God's grace and mercy to the conscience through the Word and Spirit, God again hides, so that the believer is no longer aware of the mercy of God but only of the wrath. "And it seems to the Christian that God is up there in His heaven, not with us but entirely oblivious of us. For God conceals Himself so thoroughly that all seems to be lost for us, and that there is no more help from Him."[57]

At times Luther ascribes to Satan this concealment of God, for Satan wishes to eradicate our faith in the mercy of God by means of the feelings of sin and wrath that remain in the consciences of believers.[58] The devil tries to get us to believe the feeling of our own conscience instead of the Word of God, so that we might fall from trust in God's mercy.

At other times, however, Luther ascribes the hiddenness of God to God; that is, the God of mercy appears to the conscience as a God of wrath. "Beyond all this is the highest stage of faith, when God punishes the conscience not only with temporal sufferings but with death, hell, and sin, and at the same time refuses grace and mercy, as though he wanted to condemn and show his anger eternally."[59] At such times, God appears to have forgotten his promises and acts as though he had nothing to do with us.[60] "For God keeps His promises and can never be changed. Nevertheless, He confronts us with something that is the very opposite. With this He tries us."[61] In *Anfechtung*, the God who consoled the conscience with the promise of forgiveness now terrifies the conscience with the appearance of wrath. The God who revealed the truth of the Word now acts as though the Word were a lie.

The trial of *Anfechtung*, whether inflicted by Satan or by God, is made possible by the fact that the legal knowledge of God is never eradicated from the conscience. "For the knowledge from the Law suggests itself automatically and very emphatically when one is terror-stricken or in the agony of death."[62]

---

56. *Praelectiones in prophetas minores. Micha*, 1524. W.A.13.329.26; L.W. 18:255.
57. *Auslegung des 14, 15, und 16. kapitels Johannis in Predigten*, 1537. W.A. 45.596.27–34; L.W. 24:148.
58. *Das schoene Confitemeni*, 1530. W.A. 31(I).147.21–28; L.W. 14:84.
59. *Von den Guten Werken*, 1520. W.A. 6.208.34–37; L.W. 44:29.
60. W.A. 44.192.27–28; L.W. 6:259.
61. W.A. 44.637.18–23; L.W. 8:79.
62. W.A. 46.670.6–9; L.W. 22:154.

Even though faith trusts in Christ rather than in its own works, the conscience is never rid of the desire to stand before God on the basis of its works. The devil takes advantage of an inclination already present in the conscience of the believer in order to extinguish faith in the mercy of God.[63] When the conscience of the Christian testifies to itself, it tells itself that it must stand before God on the basis of works. When it is terrified by its feeling of sin, it does not of itself turn to Christ, but rather seeks to eradicate its sin by works.

> Therefore when you feel your sin, when your bad conscience smites you, or when persecution comes, then ask yourself whether you really believe. At such times one is wont to run to saints and helpers in cloisters and in the desert for succor and relief, crying: "O dear man, intercede for me! O dear saint, help me! O let me live! I promise to become pious and do many good works!" That is how a terrified conscience speaks. But tell me, where is faith?[64]

On the basis of its own feeling and testimony, the conscience of the Christian cannot help but portray God as a judge who condemns sinners. "Here nature shrinks back and cannot see the rays of mercy in the clouds of divine wrath."[65]

Although faith believes Christ to be the Lamb of God who takes away the sins of the world, the conscience portrays Christ as a lawgiver and judge. In *Anfechtung*, Satan uses the conscience to try to convince the Christian that Christ is an accusing judge who condemns sinners. "By adulterating the true definition of Christ with his poison he produces this effect, that although we believe that Christ is the Mediator, in fact our troubled conscience feels and judges that He is a tyrant and a tormentor."[66] Even without the deception of Satan, the conscience has a natural inclination to see Christ as a judge. Luther claimed that this is what had happened under the papacy: although Christ was called a mediator, he was portrayed in consciences as a judge.[67]

When the conscience relies on its own feeling and testimony concerning Christ, it is defenseless against the false Christ that the devil sets forth. When the devil presents Christ as a judge in the midst of *Anfechtung*, the conscience will confirm this illusion and will drive the person into despair, even to the point of suicide. "For they have been so demented by the devil that they have been convinced that it is most certainly true that they are being accused and tempted, not by the devil but by Christ Himself."[68] The conscience, even that of the most pious believer, always bears within itself the portrayal of God as a judge. The conscience thus has no criterion with which to reject the false Christ that Satan portrays to the believer.

63. W.A. 40(I).41.27–29, 42.16–21; L.W. 26:5.
64. W.A. 23.113.7–18; L.W. 23.75.
65. W.A. 40(II).335.34–37; L.W. 12:316.
66. W.A. 40(I).94.11–17; L.W. 26:38–39.
67. W.A. 40(I).562.28–30, 563.15–18, 24; L.W. 26:368–69.
68. W.A. 40(I).320.18–24; L.W. 26:195.

The strategy of the devil in *Anfechtung* is to tempt believers into identifying Christ with the feeling of their conscience. The devil usually tries to associate Christ with the conscience's portrayal of him as a Judge. However, it is just as dangerous to associate Christ with the feeling of a consoled and peaceful conscience and to think that Christ has nothing to do with the feeling of sin. According to Luther, the antinomians fell into just such a temptation. They portrayed Christ as nothing but consolation and comfort, and thus identified Christ with the feeling of a secure and quiet conscience. The danger latent in such a picture of Christ lies in the fact that the conscience has an essential relationship to the law, and hence to the feeling of sin and wrath. If Christ is identified with security and peace of conscience, then when the feelings of sin and wrath emerge in the conscience, they can only be taken as a sign that Christ has deserted the believer. "For they have learned to perceive in Christ nothing but sweet security. Therefore such terror must be a sure sign that Christ (whom they understand as sheer sweetness) has rejected and forsaken them. That is what the devil strives for."[69] In sum, the devil tries to have the conscience testify to itself about Christ on the basis of its own feeling, whether of wrath or of security. Once this is done, the conscience has no ability to withstand the *Anfechtung*, and the fall from faith is inevitable.

The other way in which the devil seeks to drive faith from the heart of the believer is by having the believer separate the will of God the Father from the mercy of God revealed in Christ. Even though we see in Christ a merciful mediator, it is difficult for the conscience to believe that the Father is as merciful as the Son, for the conscience always pictures God as wrathful toward sinners. Satan exploits this feeling of conscience by having us doubt the divinity of Christ; if Christ is not God by nature, then the mercy he reveals tells us nothing of God's will. "Now we miserable people are assailed by sins, we fear death, we fear damnation, for this reason alone that our conscience doubts that Christ is the Son of God."[70] Even if the conscience believes that Christ is the Son of God, it is very difficult for it to believe that God the Father is so minded as Christ. Even though we see in Christ mercy toward sinners, we do not see the Father; and the conscience cannot help but portray the Father as a judge, thereby nullifying the mercy revealed in Christ.[71] "Conscience, the devil, hell, the judgment of God, and everything resist, in order that we may not believe that God is love but may believe that God is an Executioner and a Judge."[72]

In *Anfechtung*, Satan builds on the separation that the conscience already effects between Christ and the Father, and attempts to have the conscience ignore the testimony of Christ about the will of the Father toward sinners. Satan even uses the doctrine of predestination to convince believers that God

---

69. *Wider die Antinomer*, 1539. W.A. 50.471.22–37; L.W. 47:110–11.
70. *Enarratio Psalmi II*, 1532. W.A. 40(II).249.28–35; L.W. 12:46.
71. Ibid. W.A. 40(II).254.27–33; L.W. 12:50.
72. W.A. 20.757.19–21; L.W. 30:301.

is not fully revealed in the gospel and that God's hidden will is different from God's revealed will.[73] Satan's ultimate purpose in *Anfechtung* is to get the believer to set aside the testimony of Christ to the mercy of God, so that it might testify to itself concerning the nature and will of God. The conscience of the believer, just like that of the unbeliever, cannot help but portray God as a judge. The believer who gives in to the temptation of Satan must die in despair. In other words, the experience of *Anfechtung* shows the impossibility of the conscience ever testifying to itself about the nature and will of God, for its testimony always contradicts the Word of God as revealed in Christ.

If we are to retain our faith in the midst of *Anfechtung*, we must ignore the feelings of our conscience and cling simply to the naked Word of God, no matter how much our own conscience contradicts that Word. The truth revealed in God's Word is hidden under a contrary appearance and thus cannot be deduced from what we see and feel. "When God says, 'I will help you,' conscience replies, 'I feel someone crushing me.' When God says, 'I will be with you,' it seems to me like, 'Go away, Satan is with me.' "[74] Only the Word of God reveals God's mercy toward those who feel their sin. Without the Word, the conscience can only conclude that the sinner is condemned by God.[75] Against the feelings of the conscience and the temptations of the devil that lead us to think of God as a judge, we must simply hold to the Word of forgiveness, and thereby overcome both the devil and our own conscience. "Just so, the conscience tormented by the Law, by hell, by sin, and by Satan ought to cling to the bare Word. 'Take heart, my son, your sins are forgiven.' "[76]

Although Satan inflicts us with *Anfechtung* in order to compel us to deny God's Word, God allows us to be tempted in order to try us as to whether we judge God according to the Word or according to the testimony of our own conscience.[77] In temptation, it becomes clear whether we are convinced that God is true and all people liars. "But faith wrestled against the flesh and said: 'Flesh and Satan, you are lying; for God has spoken and has made a promise. He will not lie, even if the opposite happens or I die in the meantime.' "[78] Believers are certain that God's Word and testimony is true, even though it is contradicted by all experience. "For it is the wisdom of the saints to believe in the truth in opposition to the lie, the hidden truth in opposition to the manifest truth, in hope in opposition to hope."[79]

We triumph in *Anfechtung* when we acknowledge and trust that what God tells us is true, while also confessing that what we tell ourselves about God is a lie. Indeed, Luther insisted that God's Word was something we could not

---

73. W.A. 43.460.36–42; L.W. 5:46.
74. W.A. 31(II).294.34–35, 295.1–2; L.W. 17:44–45.
75. W.A. 40(II).30.28–34, 31.18–24; L.W. 27:25–26.
76. W.A. 31(II).238.13–15; L.W. 16:321.
77. *Fastenpostille*, 1525. St.L. XI.549; *Sermons* 2:152.
78. W.A. 43.570.7–9; L.W. 5:205.
79. W.A. 43.393.16–18; L.W. 4:357.

tell ourselves but must be told by another—that is, a fellow believer.[80] The truth of God must be sought in the testimonies Christ gave us, the Word and sacraments. A Christian brother or sister who comforts another will emphasize the truth of these testimonies that reveal the mercy of God toward sinners. "He will say: 'God is truthful; He promises to be gracious to you for His Son's sake. Moreover, the Son of God has absolved you from all your sins by His Word, has baptized you, and has promised you eternal life if you believe, that is, if you conclude that His death is your redemption.' "[81]

The believer will also battle against the false portrayal of Christ as set forth by his conscience and Satan with the true picture of Christ as given in the apostolic witness in the Scriptures. "For these texts give us a faithful portrayal of Christ, of His person and of His work."[82] Scripture portrays Christ not as a judge but as the Lamb of God who takes away the sins of the world and who thus has mercy on those who feel their sins. "For Scripture portrays Christ as our Propitiator, Mediator, and Comforter. This is what He always is and remains; He cannot be untrue to His very nature."[83] The scriptural picture of Christ must be set against the false picture of Christ that the conscience imagines: "for here He says: 'Do not picture Me thus, do not regard Me as a judge. . . . Your conscience lies to you when it suggests that you must fear Me as a judge."[84] We are not to depict Christ to ourselves on the basis of the testimony of our conscience, but are rather to believe Christ's self-portrayal through his apostolic witnesses.

In the same way, we are not to separate Christ from the Father, for Christ is the only true witness concerning the Father's heart and will for the world. The Father has the same love toward sinners as Christ does. "Christ Himself refers everywhere to the authority and will of the Father . . . on account of our conscience. . . . It is useful to learn this, lest we think that the Father is disposed toward us otherwise than we hear from the Son, who surely cannot hate us, since He dies for us."[85] Nor are we to allow the conscience to divorce the work of Christ from the will of the Father by means of the doctrine of predestination; for the Father revealed his predestinating will in Christ. If we cling to Christ in faith, we can be certain we are elected by God. "Behold, this is My Son; listen to Him. If you listen to Him, are baptized in His name, and love His Word, then you are surely predestined and certain of your salvation."[86] We must seek the will of the Father, including his predestinating will, in the testimony of Christ, not in the testimony of the conscience: "You

---

80. W.A. 40(I).493.14–16, 19–20, 26-27; L.W. 26:318.
81. W.A. 43.28.13–19; L.W. 3:214.
82. W.A. 46.597.24–30; L.W. 22:71–72.
83. W.A. 40(II).13.15–17; L.W. 27:11.
84. W.A. 23.88.14–16, 25-31; L.W. 23:59–60.
85. W.A. 40(II).255.19–24, 32–34; L.W. 12:50–51.
86. W.A. 43.459.21-33; L.W. 5:44-45. See Fredrik Brosche, "Luther on Predestination: The Antinomy and Unity Between Love and Wrath in Luther's Concept of God" (doctoral diss., Uppsala University, 1978), p. 186.

believe you have a gracious God, since you believe in Christ and have seen Him. God will not act according to your will or your conscience; He will not treat you as your conscience tells and teaches you."[87]

The experience of *Anfechtung* tests believers to see if they believe the testimony of Christ over the testimony and feeling of the conscience. For those who do trust the Word and disbelieve their conscience, *Anfechtung* has two positive effects. First, it helps bring about the mortification of the flesh. "For in this way feeling is killed, and the old man perishes, so that nothing but faith in God's goodness remains, and no feeling."[88] The flesh, including if not especially the conscience, wishes to judge God on the basis of what it sees and feels. However, in *Anfechtung* God is proved to be gracious and true in the Word even though we see and feel that God is wrathful and a liar.[89]

Second, the experience of *Anfechtung* brings with it both the experience of the power of God's Word and the experience of the mercy of God that was previously only believed. If we believe that God is merciful even though we feel only God's wrath, God will again be revealed to be merciful, so that we experience the truth of the Word. "At this point experience must enter in and enable a Christian to say: 'Hitherto I have heard that Christ is my Savior, who conquered sin and death; and I have believed this. Now my experience bears this out. For I was often in the agony of death and in the bonds of the devil, but He rescued me and manifested Himself.' "[90] The experience of the truth of the Word does not lead us to seek to confirm that truth by what we see and feel; rather, the Word itself discloses its truth and its power to us in triumphing over the contradiction of the conscience and Satan. Thus the experience of the truth of the Word leads us to cling more and more to the Word.[91] In sum, both the mortification of the flesh and the experience of the power and truth of the Word lead the believer to disbelieve the testimony of the conscience regarding the will of God, and to believe more and more in the witness of the Word and Spirit. The experience of *Anfechtung* makes it clear that not even the most pious conscience can tell itself about God's will *pro nobis*. God's mercy on those who feel and acknowledge their sin is revealed only in the testimony of Christ through the Holy Spirit.[92]

---

87. W.A. 23.97.22-28; L.W. 23:65-66.
88. St.L. XI.471; *Sermons* 2:63.
89. W.A. 43.555.18-24; L.W. 5:184.
90. W.A. 45.599.6-15; L.W. 24:151.
91. W.A. 31(II).38.8-10; L.W. 16:54.
92. W.A. 40(I).589.25-28; L.W. 26:387.

4

THE EXHORTATION OF THE COMMAND FOR THE JUSTIFIED

The Word of God as gospel reveals to the conscience that which the conscience can never tell itself—that God offers mercy to those who feel their sins and God's wrath. The mercy of God is revealed to the human mind and conscience only by the external testimony of the Word of Christ and the internal witness of the Holy Spirit. The experience of trial (*Anfechtung*) makes it clear that the testimony of the conscience can never be brought into agreement with the gospel, for even the most pious Christian conscience can only conclude that God is angry toward sinners. If the gospel is to be believed, the conscience must be disbelieved. To those who believe God's Word in the face of what they see and feel in their conscience, God again discloses mercy, so that they experience the truth and power of God's Word. In this way, faith is strengthened and confirmed in opposition to the testimony of the conscience. The knowledge of God's mercy is thus the central form of the theology of the cross (*theologia crucis*) for Luther: for the revelation of God's righteousness and mercy is hidden under the feeling of sin and wrath.

Yet God not only speaks a Word of promise to believers, but also a Word of command. God not only offers mercy to sinners, but also enjoins them to conform their wills to God's command.[1] Although the promise is inseparable from the command, Luther insists that God not only promises mercy to believers, but also commands them to follow and obey God's law.[2] In other words, God not only promises to forgive the sins of those who confess and acknowledge that they are sinners; God also commands them to walk no longer in the way of sin but according to God's law and Word.

The command of God can be obeyed by believers because God not only gives them grace but also God's gift. God not only forgives our sins through the grace of Christ, God also heals our sinful hearts and wills through the gift

---

1. *Vorlesung ueber 1. Mose von 1535–1545*. W.A. 42.565.19–23; L.W. 3:23. See Wilfried Joest, *Gesetz und Freiheit*, 2d ed. (Goettingen: Vandenhoeck und Ruprecht, 1961).
2. *Vorlesung ueber 1. Mose*. W.A. 43.575.22–29, 576.18–20; L.W. 5:213–14.

of the Holy Spirit.[3] The grace of Christ alone gives us a gracious God, for the faithful always have enough sin to condemn them before God's judgment seat; yet the gift is also necessary to heal us from sin. "A righteous and faithful man doubtless has both grace and the gift [*gratiam et donum*]. Grace makes him wholly pleasing so that his person is wholly accepted, and there is no place for wrath in him anymore, but the gift heals from sin and from all corruption in his body and soul."[4] Even though it is by grace and not by the gift that we have a gracious God, Luther insists that grace is of no account without the gift. "Grace causes God to be favorably inclined; faith and love cause man to be holy. The first is useless without the second."[5] The same Holy Spirit that creates and preserves faith in the hearts and minds of believers also sanctifies believers so that they walk in obedience to the commands of God.[6]

Perhaps the best way in which to understand the inseparability of grace and the gift, along with their distinct functions, is to look at Luther's description of the fact that "Christ is in us, and we are in him." From the fact that we are in Christ come the forgiveness and justification of the sinner through the fortunate exchange. "For we must first be in Him with all our being, with our sin, our death, and our weakness; we must know that we are liberated from these before God and are redeemed and pronounced blessed through this Christ."[7] From the fact that Christ is in us come our sanctification and renewal, so that we begin to obey the commandments of God. "Now he also manifests Himself in me and says: "Go, preach, comfort, baptize, serve your neighbor, be obedient, be patient. I will be in you and you will do all this."[8] We have a gracious God because we are in Christ; and we obey the commands of God because Christ is in us. We cannot have one without the other. "For there is no such Christ that died for sinners who do not, after the forgiveness of sins, desist from sins and lead a new life."[9]

God does not give grace without also bestowing the gift of the Holy Spirit; and God does not give a promise without also giving a command. As already seen, the promise of God can never be confirmed but only contradicted by the testimony of the conscience. The question now arises whether the same contradiction holds between the conscience and the command of God, or whether the testimony of the conscience in some sense confirms our conformity to the law of God. In other words, does Luther allow for a testimony of the good conscience that confirms us in our faith in Christ, inasmuch as it bears witness that our lives are beginning to conform to the commands of God?

3. *Enarratio Psalmi LI*, 1532. W.A. 40(II).357.35–37, 358.19–23; L.W. 12:331.
4. *Rationis Latomianae confutatio*, 1521. W.A. 8.107.13–16; L.W. 32:229.
5. *Vorlesung ueber den 1. Timotheusbrief*, 1528. W.A. 26.24.16–18; L.W. 28:245.
6. W.A. 40(II).429.23–26; L.W. 12:382.
7. *Auslegung des Johannis in Predigten*, 1537. W.A. 45.591.13–19; L.W. 24:142–43.
8. Ibid. W.A. 45.591.29–36; L.W. 24:143.
9. *Von den Konziliis und Kirchen*, 1539. W.A. 50.599.21–23; L.W. 41:114.

Given Luther's emphasis on the work of the Holy Spirit in the Christian, one would expect the answer to be yes.[10]

As will be seen below, Luther does allow for the confirmation of faith in Christ by the testimony of a good conscience, both before the world and before God. The good conscience confirms the faithful in their innocence and integrity in the face of the persecution and slander of the world. The good conscience also confirms the faithful in God's sight (*coram Deo*), by testifying that their call and election have not been in vain but have brought forth fruit in love of neighbor and good works.

However, Luther qualifies the testimony of the conscience that confirms our faith with the testimony that contradicts it; for in *Anfechtung*, the conscience can only stand against our trust in the mercy of God. Even though the testimony of the good conscience cannot be the foundation of our confidence *coram Deo*, Luther insists that it is a necessary and important confirmation of our faith in the Lamb of God who takes away the sins of the world.[11] As will be seen at the end of this chapter, this claim creates an unavoidable dilemma for Luther: in order to be assured of our salvation, we must not only have faith in the grace of God in Jesus Christ, but we must *know* that we have genuine faith in the grace of God. We must not only receive the testimony of grace, but we must also give to ourselves the testimony of the gift—that is, a good conscience.

The Free Obedience of Christians

It is necessary to begin a discussion of the relation between the Word as command and the conscience by turning first to Luther's understanding of the freedom of the Christian conscience from the law. Just as the Word as command keeps us from reading Luther as an antinomian, so the freedom of the conscience will keep us from making Luther into a legalist. According to Luther, faith in Christ brings three kinds of freedom from the law: freedom from the wrath and condemnation of the law; freedom from coercion from the law; and freedom from the laws and traditions of human beings.

The first and most important freedom that faith in Christ brings to the conscience is freedom from the wrath and condemnation of the law. "This is the freedom with which Christ has set us free, not from some human slavery or tyrannical authority but from the eternal wrath of God. Where? In the conscience."[12] Through the happy exchange, the wrath of God on sin has fallen not on us but on Christ, whereas Christ's victory over sin, death, and wrath are not only his but also ours. Freedom from the wrath of God therefore means freedom from the condemnation of sinners that is revealed in the law.[13]

---

10. *Vorlesung ueber die Brief an Titus und Philemon*, 1527. W.A. 25.65.9–15; L.W. 29:83–84.

11. *Galatas Commentarius*, 1535. W.A. 40(II).155.21–23; L.W. 27:121.

12. Ibid. W.A. 40(II).3.20–24; L.W. 27:4.

13. Ibid. W.A. 40(II).4.13–20; L.W. 27:4–5.

The law does not cease to reveal sin to the conscience, but it cannot pronounce the condemnation of God on sinners, for the victory of Christ has been given to the conscience of the believer.[14] The freedom of the conscience from the law means that the conclusion of the syllogism of the law—that God is wrathful toward sinners—is removed from the conscience. Thus when the law reveals that we are sinners, faith turns the conscience to Christ.[15] Freedom from the law does not mean freedom from the feeling of sin and wrath in the conscience, but rather freedom from the condemnation that the law threatens against those who feel their sins.[16]

Freedom from the law therefore means freedom from the attempt to justify ourselves on the basis of our works. Since our sins have been taken from us and laid upon Christ, and his righteousness has been given to us, our works can neither accuse nor justify us before God. "Thus a good conscience is freed from all works, not only those that ought to be done, but from those that accuse us as well as those that shield us from condemnation."[17] Justification comes through faith in Christ, not through works. Thus the conscience condemns its own works and trusts only in the works of Christ.[18]

Freedom from works means freedom from trust in works before God, not freedom from works altogether. "Christian or evangelical freedom, then, is a freedom of conscience which liberates the conscience from works. Not that no works are done, but no faith is put in them."[19] The testimony of the good conscience cannot be understood as giving the conscience any trust in its works in terms of the justification of the believer, for faith in Christ frees the conscience from such trust.

The second kind of freedom given to the conscience in faith is freedom from the coercion from the law. The voice of the law can only coerce obedience from sinners, for they lack the gift of the Holy Spirit and hence cannot delight in the law. Believers have received the gift of the Spirit and hence love the law of God and willingly obey its commandments. Thus they have no need of coercion or admonition from the law. "For the just man lives as though he had no need of the Law to admonish, urge, and constrain him; but spontaneously, without any legal constraint, he does more than the Law requires."[20]

The coercion and constraint of the law are felt the most by those who seek to justify themselves by works of the law. For such people, obedience cannot be free and spontaneous, for they fear God as a judge and hence fear the condemnation of the law. Believers, on the other hand, are justified by faith alone and hence are certain that God is merciful toward them. Thus their obedience can be free and selfless, for it is the result not of their own anxious

---

14. Ibid. W.A. 40(I).566.25–29; L.W. 26:371.
15. Ibid. W.A. 40(I).275.23–30; L.W. 26:161.
16. Ibid. W.A. 40(I).214.18–21; L.W. 26:120.
17. *De votis monasticis*, 1521. W.A. 8.608.17–22; L.W. 44:301.
18. Ibid. W.A. 8.607.9–10; L.W. 44:299.
19. Ibid. W.A. 8.606.30–32; L.W. 44:298.
20. W.A. 40(II).121.14–16; L.W. 27:96.

effort, but of Christ working through them. "Actually, then, our works are no longer works of the law but of Christ working in us through faith and living in us in everything we do. For that reason these works can no more be omitted than faith itself, nor are they less necessary than faith."[21]

Works are done with a free conscience when they are not performed to improve our relationship with God but are done out of confidence and trust in the mercy of God revealed in Christ. Thus we cannot understand the Word as command in such a way that it imposes a new religious anxiety on the conscience concerning its works. The obedience of the faithful is free and spontaneous and does not have to be forced by threats or ulterior motives. "Of course, conscience lays hold of its own good works too, but declares these works are to be done freely and only for the good of one's neighbor, and to give the body something to do, but in no case acquire righteousness and peace and the satisfaction and remission of sins. For conscience seeks these things only in the works of Christ and finds them in a firm faith."[22] The conscience does lay hold of its own good works, but not in such a way as to seek justification from them; it does them freely, being already justified in Christ.

The third kind of freedom given to the conscience in faith is freedom from human laws and traditions. The legal knowledge of God leads the conscience to invent works and ceremonies it thinks will please God. These self-invented works even obscure the works of the natural law, such as love for neighbor. When the evangelical knowledge of God is revealed to the conscience, however, the conscience is freed from these self-invented works, for it knows that God is not pleased by them but only by faith in Christ. "Everything not specifically commanded by God is abrogated and made a matter of free choice."[23]

Because human laws and traditions are invented with the sole purpose of making us pleasing to God and of justifying us in God's sight, it is faith in Christ alone that frees the conscience from these laws. When the confidence of the conscience is placed in Christ, these laws may be observed or abrogated freely, as the occasion demands.[24] The conscience that is made one with Christ in faith may freely break or observe human laws, as long as it does not violate the commands of God. The only rule governing the conscience's freedom with regard to externals is the law of love: we should use externals to the benefit of our neighbor. "As we have said, therefore, the apostle imposes an obligation on Christians through this law about mutual love in order to keep them from abusing their freedom."[25] In sum, everything not specifically commanded by God is made a matter of freedom. Human laws may be observed or ignored freely, so long as love of neighbor is not violated.

21. W.A. 8.608.24–35; L.W. 44:301.
22. W.A. 8.607.12–16; L.W. 44:299.
23. W.A. 8.613.11–18; L.W. 44:309–10.
24. W.A. 8.609.38–40, 610.1–3; L.W. 44:303–4.
25. W.A. 40(II).62.13–17; L.W. 27:49.

For Luther, freedom of conscience from human law is synonymous with freedom of conscience from externals. Externals include everything from church ceremonies and images to food and clothing. The commandments of God have nothing to do with such matters, according to Luther; therefore they are a matter of freedom for the conscience. This means, however, that we cannot attain such freedom simply by changing our external behavior; we must change our conscience.

Indeed, when our conscience has been freed from externals by faith, we may perform external actions that appear to be in compliance with human law but are in fact free. Conversely, if our conscience has not been set free by faith, then it remains bound even when we perform external actions that appear to be a manifestation of Christian liberty. Thus if our conscience believes the mass is a sacrifice, then it is a sacrifice even if we deny it with our action; and if our conscience does not believe it is a sacrifice, then it is not, even if our external behavior says it is.[26] Once the conscience has been set free from externals by faith, external actions become a matter of complete indifference for Luther. Those who judge Christian freedom on the basis of external works and appearances rather than on the basis of the conscience are strongly condemned by Luther, as is evident from his controversy with Karlstadt.[27]

To make Christian freedom a matter of externals is to keep the conscience bound to externals. If we have such a conscience, then we sin whether we observe human laws or abstain from them. To observe them is to sin against faith, for faith sets us free from such laws. To abstain from such observance is to sin against the conscience, which holds that such laws are still binding.[28] Consciences caught in such bondage to human law can only be set free by the Word of God. The conscience must be made certain that the law is against the will of God or is not commanded by God before the law can be abrogated in deed. In particular, it must be shown that there are clear Scriptural arguments against the human laws that are to be set aside. "For if we are going to change or to do away with customs that are traditional, it is necessary to prove convincingly that these are contrary to the Word of God."[29]

The conscience must take its stand on the Word of God alone if it is to be free of human law, for only then is the conscience certain that it has not sinned against God. Without such certainty, it might despair in the face of *Anfechtung* or at the hour of death. "But who can stand in the presence of Satan and before the judgment seat of God except the man who can stand firmly on solid ground made strong by the most certain warrant of the word of God . . . able to say without hesitation or trembling of heart, 'You, who cannot lie, have said these things?' "[30]

26. *Wider die himmlischen Propheten*, 1525. W.A. 18.122.22–28; L.W. 40:140.
27. Ibid. W.A. 18.122.7–10; L.W. 40:140.
28. *Kirchenpostille*, 1522. St.L. XI.428; *Sermons* 1:454–55.
29. *Von der Widdertauffe an zween Pfarherrn*, 1528. W.A. 26.155.33–37, 156.1–2; L.W. 40:241.
30. W.A. 8.668.35–37, 669.1–4; L.W. 44:399–400.

Where there is no certain Word of God against human custom, we cannot safely and with certainty oppose the custom. Such was the case for Luther with regard to infant baptism: "I did not invent it. It came to me by tradition and I was persuaded by no word of Scripture that it was wrong."[31] The same held true with regard to the removal of images from the church, since Luther was certain only that the Word prohibited the worship, not the presence, of images. "In the face of such uncertainty who would be so bold as to destroy the images?"[32] Without a clear and certain word of God in opposition, human tradition cannot be abrogated but must be accepted as a work of God.[33]

Even when there is a clear and certain Word of God, believers should not act against human law until they are certain in their conscience that they are free from such law. "The task at this point is to sustain oneself by depending mightily on the pure word of God alone, and not for a moment to shrink back from the judgment seat of God, since we know that he is true and cannot deny himself."[34] When the conscience is not certain, one should not act; nor should one be forced to violate human tradition even if free to do so. Weak and uncertain consciences are not made certain of their freedom by being forced to violate their own dictates, but are strengthened by the Word of God alone.[35]

Luther's method of reforming the church involved preaching the Word of God while letting externals take their course. Once consciences have been freed from human laws, their external actions are of no importance. Thus, with regard to the idolatrous use of images in the church, Luther insisted that they be destroyed not by removing them physically but by removing them from the conscience by the Word of God. "This means to instruct and enlighten the conscience that it is idolatry to worship them, or to trust in them, since one is to trust alone in Christ. Beyond this, let externals take their course."[36] The minister can preach the Word of God against such things but cannot compel outward conformity with Christian freedom. "We have the *ius verbi* [right to speak] but not the *executio* [power to accomplish]. We should preach the Word, but the results must be left solely to God's good pleasure."[37]

Indeed, according to Luther, it is best to leave human customs in place even after consciences have been liberated from them, so that the weak who still think the customs are necessary are not offended by their removal. Once the weak have been strengthened by the Word, such customs will fall aside on their own. "This way love will rule with regard to these external works and regulations."[38] The best way in which human law can be abrogated is

31. W.A. 26.166.37–38, 167.1; L.W. 40:254.
32. *Invocavit Predigten*, 1522. W.A. 10(III).27.1–5, 7–8; L.W. 51:82.
33. W.A. 26.167.13–16; L.W. 40:255.
34. W.A. 8.669.5–12; L.W. 44:400.
35. W.A. 25.19.17–23; L.W. 29:20.
36. W.A. 18.74.6–10; L.W. 40:91.
37. W.A. 10(III).15.10–12, 29–31; L.W. 51:76.
38. Br. 17 March 1522. W.A. Br.474.24–28; L.W. 48:402.

therefore in conscience but not in deed; once the conscience is free, the deed is a matter of indifference.[39]

In this sense Luther was even willing to honor the pope in an external way, so long as the pope left Luther's conscience free.[40] So also, when Luther became convinced on the basis of Scripture and the Word of God that his monastic vows violated Christian freedom, he did not immediately manifest his freedom of conscience by setting aside his cowl. "What difference does it make whether I retain or lay aside the cowl and tonsure? . . . My conscience has been freed, and that is the most complete liberation."[41] By remaining under the outward observance even after his conscience had been freed from human law, Luther made it clear that his freedom of conscience came not from the external abrogation of human law but through the preaching of the Word of God alone. "I simply taught, preached, and wrote God's Word; otherwise I did nothing. . . . I did nothing; the Word did everything."[42]

The Certainty Our Works Please God

Not only does the conscience gain freedom from human laws, but it is also certain of the commands of God that are still binding on it through the Word. The source of human law is the conscience that invents for itself works and ceremonies that it imagines will please God. In opposition to such imagined worship and works, the Word of God sets forth the promise of God, so that we might be certain that our *person* is pleasing to God, and the command of God, so that we might be certain that our *works* please God. "But obedience should be certain concerning faith, which does not exist where there is no divine promise. Nor do the works please Him where there is no command of God."[43] The Word of God frees the conscience from bondage to human works and reveals the commands of God, by which the conscience may be certain that its works are pleasing to God. "All this He commands in order that in the worship of God the people may not be carried away by its own feeling, however holy and good, but may be governed by the Word."[44]

The conscience cannot testify to itself about the commands of God any more than it could about the promises of God. We can only be certain of the commands of God on the basis of the Word of God revealed to the conscience. "He wanted to have His will and His counsels delineated for us by His words alone, not by our thoughts or imagination."[45] Therefore, the freedom of the conscience from human laws and traditions means the end of the bondage of the conscience to its self-chosen works, but it does not mean freedom from the commands of God. "So far as the commands of GOD are concerned, man

39. St. L. XI. 427; *Sermons* 1:453–54.
40. W.A. 40(I).177.22–23; L.W. 26:97.
41. W.A. 8.575.24–25, 27–28; L.W. 48:334–35.
42. W.A. 10(III).18.10–15, 19.2–3; L.W. 51:77–78.
43. W.A. 43.224.42, 225.1–5; L.W. 4:124.
44. *Deuteronomon Mosi cum annotationibus*, 1525. W.A. 14.644.19–24; L.W. 9:123.
45. W.A. 14.594.29–35; L.W. 4:124.

is not free; he must obey the voice of God, or he will endure the sentence of death. His freedom pertains to things about which God has given no command, as, for example, outward actions."[46] Making the commands of God a matter of conscience is therefore the positive result of the liberation of the conscience from human laws.[47]

In sum, the Word of God that frees our conscience from self-invented laws also binds our conscience to the Word of God alone: "it gives us liberty and absolves us of all works, efforts, laws, and traditions of men; and it binds our consciences to the Word of God alone."[48]

The conscience errs in its choice of works because it thinks that God is most pleased with works that have the greatest appearance of holiness. In works as well as in faith, when the conscience testifies to itself about the will of God it does so under the form of the theology of glory (*theologia gloriae*), assuming that those works are holy before God that appear to be holy before the world.[49] The world admires such self-invented works as monasticism and virginity, while treating with scorn ordinary works such as marriage and government. The Word of God, on the other hand, reveals the works that truly please God, but these come under the form of the *theologia crucis*: they are outwardly contemptible, lowly, and common, and yet the pleasure of God is in them, for they have been commanded by God's Word.

The Word of God thus battles with the *theologia gloriae* of the conscience both with regard to faith as well as to works. "Therefore we must battle unremittingly not only against the opinions of our own heart, on which by nature we would rather depend in the matter of salvation than on the Word of God, but also against the false front and saintly appearance of self-chosen works."[50] The conscience can be certain of the will of God, and of those works that please God, only if it disregards the appearance of the works and looks solely to the Word of God. "Accordingly, we have to learn to recognize good works from the commandments of God and not from the appearance, size, or number of the works themselves."[51]

The good works of the faithful are therefore hidden under the opposite appearance. Their works seem to be common and worthless, yet the faithful are certain that they are pleasing to God, for they have God's Word and command.[52] Hidden under the common appearance of the works of the faithful is the certainty of conscience that these works are pleasing to God, and this certainty makes all stations of life blessed, no matter how bitter their appearance.

46. W.A. 42.512.21–24; L.W. 2:350.
47. W.A. 14.585.16–17; L.W. 9:50.
48. W.A. 14.646.4–6; L.W. 9:125.
49. *Sermon von dreierlei gutem leben*, 1521. W.A. 7.798.4–10; L.W. 44:238.
50. W.A. 40(II).71.34–36; L.W. 27:57.
51. *Von den guten Werken*, 1520. W.A. 6.204.19–22; L.W. 44:23.
52. *Vom ehelichen Leben*, 1522. W.A. 10(II).295.9–14; L.W. 45:39.

The self-chosen works of humans, by contrast, have a holy and glorious appearance but are inwardly defiled by a conscience that is uncertain whether such works please God. Such uncertainty is inevitable where the works of humans lack the Word of God as warrant. "A conscience is impure when it does not believe that it pleases God in the work of using a creature."[53] A conscience that lacks the Word of God is impure, and thus its works are inwardly defiled, no matter how holy they might appear. Indeed, such an uncertain conscience cannot help but violate itself. "If you do not believe you are pleasing to God, then you have a conscience which tells you the work is not pleasing to God. And so, by your own admission, you are doing against your conscience a work which is not pleasing to God."[54] Thus "whatever does not proceed from faith is sin" (Rom. 14:23), for a conscience that lacks the Word of God does not believe its works please God, and hence it violates itself and all its works are sins. "For as their conscience stands in relation to God and as it believes, so are the works which issue from it."[55] No matter how many works such a conscience performs, it cannot free itself from its own inward contradiction.[56]

The conscience cannot judge the command of God on the basis of what it sees and feels any more than it could judge the promise of God, for both are revealed in the form of the *theologia crucis* and are therefore hidden under a contrary appearance.[57] The glory of the works of the saints comes from the Word of God alone and is hidden under a contrary appearance before the world. "It is a great blessing for one to have God's Word as warrant, so that he can speak right up and say to God, 'See, this Thou hast spoken, it is Thy good pleasure.' What does such a man care if it seems to be displeasing and ridiculous to the whole world?"[58] The command of God alone makes the conscience certain that its works please God.

Life in the Orders of God

The Word of God sets apart three kinds of callings or orders that are pleasing to God. "This life is profitably divided into three orders [*ordines*]: (1) life in the home; (2) life in the state; (3) life in the church."[59] Although pleasing to God, these areas are scorned by humans because of their ordinary appearance and because of the ceaseless trials they inflict on the flesh. Thus the theologians of glory in the papacy advised people to take up a life of holiness in the monastery, set apart from the trials and tribulations of life in the world. God's Word, however, commands us to live in household, state, and/or church, and thus condemns other ways of life. "'But are these ordinary works?' you will

---

53. W.A. 25.38.22–26; L.W. 29:46.
54. W.A. 8.593.21–25; L.W. 44:277.
55. W.A. 6.205.8–9; L.W. 44:24.
56. W.A. 8.593.36–39; L.W. 44:277–78.
57. W.A. 43.477.27–39; L.W. 5:70–71.
58. W.A. 10(II).298.5–8; L.W. 45:42.
59. W.A. 43.30.13–14; L.W. 3:217.

ask. Nevertheless they are commended by Holy Scripture, which bears witness that man was created for the duties of the household and of the state. Hence these ordinary works are God's order."[60] The Word of God bears witness that God is pleased with the common offices of life, and that God wants us to share with others in their hardships rather than fleeing from them.[61]

When those who live in such offices hear that they are ordained by God's Word and hence are pleasing to God, they gain a good conscience in their office. "When they acknowledged that the government is a divine ordinance, they acquired a good conscience and administered their office well."[62] A good conscience is therefore the result of being certain in one's conscience that one's station in life has been commanded by God and is therefore pleasing to God.[63]

The command of God has to do not only with the station of life in which we are called by the Word, but also with the commands of God that are mediated to us by those who have authority over us. "For God speaks with us and deals with us through the ministers of the Word, through parents, and through the government, in order that we may not be carried about with any wind of doctrine."[64] Therefore we can attain a good conscience by obeying those in authority, so long as doing so does not lead us to disobey God. Soldiers, for example, can obey the commands of the emperor with a good conscience, for they know that in obeying him they are also obeying God. "Then everyone can be sure in his conscience that he is obeying the ordinance of God, since we know that the emperor is our true overlord and head and that whoever obeys him in such a case obeys God also."[65] In a case where the emperor commands something that is unjust or contrary to God's Word, then we can maintain a good conscience only by obeying God rather than the emperor. "If you know for sure that he is wrong, then you should fear God rather than men, Acts 4, and you should neither fight nor serve, for you cannot have a good conscience before God."[66]

A good conscience also leads us to perform our office well, for "when conscience has in this way been strengthened through the Word and made sure that God approves a work of the kind it has initiated at God's command, then it dares anything."[67] A good conscience leads rulers to administer their offices well and leads soldiers to fight with courage. "For whoever fights with a good and well-instructed conscience also can fight well. . . . A good conscience fills a man's heart with courage and boldness."[68] Luther himself was strengthened by his good conscience and the command of God. "Once in this position,

---

60. W.A. 43.105.40–41, 106.1–6; L.W. 3:321.
61. W.A. 43.106.26–29; L.W. 3:322.
62. W.A. 25.57.1–11; L.W. 29:72.
63. W.A. 42.343.19–21; L.W. 2:115.
64. W.A. 43.478.8–15; L.W. 5:71.
65. *Vom Kriege wider den Turken*, 1529. W.A. 30(III).107 ff.; L.W. 46:185.
66. *Ob Kriegsleute auch in seligem Stande sein koennen*, 1526. W.A. 19.656.23–25; L.W. 46:130.
67. *Praelectiones in prophetas minores. Haggai*, 1524. W.A. 13.536.28–30; L.W. 18:374.
68. W.A. 19.623.23–25; L.W. 46:93.

I have to stay in it, and cannot give it up or leave it yet with a good conscience, even though both pope and emperor were to put me under the ban for not doing so."[69]

The Confirmation of Assurance

The Word as command gives the believer a good conscience because it carries assurance that what the believer does has been commanded by God and thus is pleasing to God. However, still unanswered is the question set forth earlier in this chapter: Is there a testimony of conscience that confirms our faith because it bears witness to our obedience to God's commands? In order to answer this question in the affirmative, we have to find evidence in Luther for the testimony of a good conscience that is the result not only of what we are commanded to do but also of how we do it. In other words, the good conscience must testify to the sincerity and integrity of our obedience to the commands of God, over and above its certainty that it has been commanded by God. Does Luther allow for this fuller testimony of the good conscience, and does it serve any role in confirming our faith in the mercy of God?

At first glance, the answer appears to be negative. Luther seems to limit the legitimate testimony of the good conscience to the Word of God, and not to our conformity with that Word. "Such works as are done on the basis of the Word are certain and holy. . . . But as far as attitudes are concerned, this boasting is nothing, and therefore we must cry, 'Forgive us our trespasses.' "[70] Luther does not appear to allow for any strengthening of faith on the basis of sincere obedience to God's will, but rather limits positive testimony of the conscience to its certainty that it has been commanded by God's Word. The testimony of the good conscience seems to have nothing to do with confirming our faith *coram Deo*, for such faith is strengthened only by the forgiveness of sins. This issue will be readdressed later in this section.

Although Luther seems to be wary of giving any positive value to the testimony of the good conscience before God, he shows no such reluctance with regard to such testimony before humanity (*coram hominibus*). Christians must not think they can do without the testimony of a good conscience before the world, for such testimony is a necessary effect of faith and love. "For any man who does not pay attention to living his life in such a way that he can put to silence everyone and defend himself and prove before men that he has lived, spoken, and done well, that man is not yet a Christian and has neither a pure heart nor love within him. . . . It is rather love from a pure heart and a good conscience, that no man can blame or accuse him of anything evil."[71] The testimony of the good conscience has its most direct use not before the judgment seat of God—for there we are all sinners—but before the judgment

---

69. *Der 82. Psalm ausgelegt*, 1530. W.A. 31(I).212.13–16; L.W. 13:66.
70. *In Esaiam*, 1527. W.A. 31(II).248.11–27; L.W. 16:334.
71. *Summa des christlichen Lebens, aus S. Paulo 1. Timoth. 1. neulich gepredigt*, 1532. W.A. 36.363.17–24; L.W. 51:273–74.

of the world. We must be able to defend ourselves before the world both on the basis of God's command and on the basis of our innocence of behavior. The good conscience testifies *coram hominibus* not only to our obedience to God's command but also to our integrity and innocence in the world.

Such testimony is especially necessary given the cross under which Christians must suffer. The cross appears not only in the lowly status of the Christian life but also in the false accusations and slander brought against those who confess Christ. The Christian must be able to oppose such slander with the testimony of a good conscience. "Let them cry 'heretic, seditionist, apostate, deceiver,' and the like, as long as it is not true, as long as your conscience does not agree."[72]

The testimony of a good conscience not only allows us to defend ourselves against the slander of enemies, but it also gives us confidence that we shall be heard in our affliction by God, who has promised to deliver those innocent ones who are persecuted for God's sake. "A good conscience is like the firmest rock, on which the godly rely in their affliction, and with great and high courage they despise the threats of all adversaries."[73] A good conscience prevents us from seeking to vindicate on our own the wrong being done us, for its testimony to our innocence leads us to look first to God for help.[74]

Our obedience and godly life thus give us two defenses against the persecution of the world: the testimony of our own conscience, and the promise of God's deliverance. "For [the Word] alone produces true obedience and worship that is pleasing to God; and if we render this, we are able not only to defend ourselves with the witness of our conscience but also to look for help from God, whose voice we follow even in real danger."[75]

Because of the cross, the glory of the saints is not to be sought in their reputation among people but in the testimony of their own conscience. "Let every preacher learn, therefore, to have his boast based, not on what others say but within himself. . . . He regards the testimony of his own conscience as the substance of his glory."[76] When one has such testimony, then one has the kind of glory that cannot be taken away by the slander of the world: "outwardly disgraced but honored in conscience, despised among men but glorified before God."[77] The testimony of the good conscience once again manifests the *theologia crucis*: the innocence of the saints is hidden under the slander of the world; the deliverance of the saints is hidden beneath the persecution of the world.

Thus far Luther acknowledges the necessity of the testimony of a good conscience, but he seems to limit it to our lives *coram hominibus*, especially

72. *Der 112. Psalm Davids gepredigt*, 1526. W.A. 19.330.23–24, 26–27, 31–34; L.W. 13:415.
73. W.A. 44.298.12–19; L.W. 6:398–99.
74. *Operationes in Psalmos*, 1519–1521. *Psalms*, p. 370.
75. W.A. 42.24–27; L.W. 2:273.
76. W.A. 40(II).515.21–31; L.W. 27:118.
77. *Roemerbriefvorlesung*, 1515–1516. W.A. 56.527; L.W. 25:523.

with regard to the persecution that Christians suffer in the world. Christians are to have their glory in their conscience and not in the opinion of the world. However, Luther goes beyond this and relates the testimony of the conscience to our standing before God: on the day of judgment God will judge each of us as to whether we sought our glory in the world or in our conscience. " 'On that day, when God judges the secrets of men' (Rom. 2:16), the testimony of your conscience will stand either for you or against you: against you if you have your boast in others; for you if your conscience bears testimony to you . . . that you have done your duty rightly, in accordance with your calling."[78] To seek our glory within ourselves is to perform our calling for the glory of God and the salvation and good of mankind, and not for our own glory and good. On the day of judgment our conscience will testify as to whether we performed our office with integrity and sincerity. Thus it is clear that Luther not only allows for the testimony of conscience with respect to the Word of God, but also with respect to the way in which we obey that Word. "Nobody bears in mind that on Judgment Day God will demand from everyone an account of how he carried on his office or calling."[79]

In other words, Luther insists that we must have the testimony of our conscience not only that we lived in a calling commanded by God, but also that we performed that calling sincerely. Even though such testimony does not contribute to our justification before God, it is necessary. Such testimony will be demanded of our conscience on judgment day, and if it is lacking we will be condemned. "We have need of this testimony of our conscience that we have carried out our ministry well and have also lived a good life."[80] The testimony of a good conscience does not have to do with the forgiveness of sins, but with the discrimination between true and hypocritical works. Although such testimony does not justify, Luther insists that it is essential and will stand either for or against us on the day of judgment.

Thus, although the testimony of the conscience to its integrity does not justify us, it nevertheless helps to confirm and strengthen our faith in the mercy of God. The foundation of faith is always the forgiveness of sins; the testimony of the good conscience gives us further assurance that God is merciful toward us and that our faith is genuine.

> Although we must not rely on this, since we are justified, it puts my conscience at peace, that I do evil to no one, and thus I walk safely in God. . . . Now comes the confidence in the Lord that on the basis of this conduct we can be certain that God is well disposed toward us. . . . These are the testimonies of our conscience, if anyone has lived properly in his calling and did his duty. . . . Thus all who do good to their neighbor know that they are pleasing to God, since this is the testimony of our conscience, that we are conducting ourselves before the world in a holy manner.[81]

78. W.A. 40(II).154.17–22; L.W. 27:120.
79. *Auslegung des Johannis in Predigten*, 1537–1538. W.A. 46.618.25–33; L.W. 22:95–96.
80. W.A. 40(II).154.25–32, 155.15–23; L.W. 27:120–21.
81. W.A. 31(II).482.34–37, 483.1–16; L.W. 17:288–89.

The testimony of the good conscience tells us that our faith in the justifying mercy of God is manifesting itself in the world in love of neighbor and a life of holiness, and that such love and holiness are not the result of our own effort but of the goodness of God. On the basis of such testimony, we are assured of God's favor toward us, for we see that our faith is bearing fruit and is thus genuine.[82]

Luther clearly subordinates the confirming testimony of conscience to faith in the mercy of God in Jesus Christ.[83] Faith in God is founded only on the revelation of God's forgiveness as attested to the conscience by the Word of Christ and the Holy Spirit. The good conscience bears witness to the truth of our faith in Christ, because our faith is bearing fruit in obedience and love: "our obedience and holy works will be pleasing because of faith in Christ for their proper purpose, namely, that they are done not for the sake of righteousness but for the sake of testimony that we are pleasing to God and freely justified."[84] Our obedience and love bear witness to ourselves and to the world of our faith in the freely given mercy of God. Such testimony confirms our faith by showing that our faith is true, just as the lack of such testimony bears witness that our faith is not genuine. "The absence of love bears testimony against you that your faith is not true and that you have not received this friendship but have forfeited everything Christ has spent for you."[85]

Because works of love and the testimony of a good conscience bear witness to the truth of our faith, believers are to be exhorted to bring forth the fruits of faith in good works; "for unless these works follow faith, this is the surest possible sign that faith is not genuine."[86] The command of God takes the form of exhortation to believers to bring forth works that attest to the truth of their faith, and to confirm their faith by the testimony of a good conscience. It is therefore clear that Luther understands the command of God in a way quite similar to Calvin's third use of the law, although it does not have the same prominence in Luther that it does in Calvin. Indeed, Luther sums up the whole of the New Testament in terms of promises and exhortations.[87] Exhortation is especially necessary for those hypocritical Christians who think they can believe in Christ without being made clean. "Against those who have received the doctrine one must resort to exhortations, in order that they may walk in a manner worthy of their calling."[88]

Believers are to be exhorted to live lives of holiness, for such is the goal toward which we are called. "But we constantly strive to attain the goal, under his redemption or remission of sin, until we too shall one day become perfectly

---

82. W.A. 31(II).482.37, 483.1; L.W. 17:288.
83. W.A. 31(II).10.5–7; L.W. 16:15.
84. W.A. 40(II).456.1–9; L.W. 12:401.
85. *Auslegelt des Johannis in Predigten*, 1537. W.A. 45.694.17–19; L.W. 24:255.
86. W.A. 40(II).162.20–23; L.W. 27:127.
87. *De servo arbitrio*, 1525. W.A. 18.693.1–5; L.W. 33:150.
88. *Vorlesung ueber den 1. Brief des Johannes*, 1527. W.A. 20.699.26–36; L.W. 30:268–69.

holy and no longer stand in need of forgiveness. Everything is directed toward that goal."[89] The life of sanctification takes place under the forgiveness of sins and is made possible by the gift of the Holy Spirit. Therefore believers are not to become falsely secure in their faith, but are to strive more and more to conform to the goal of their calling, sanctification. The commandments of God are necessary both to set forth the goal and to exhort us to continual and progressive sanctification. "Thus we must constantly grow in sanctification and always become new creatures in Christ. This means 'grow' and 'do so more and more.' "[90] Our obedience to the commands of God not only witnesses to the truth of our faith, but also demonstrates that we are beginning to conform to the goal of our calling.

Because the testimony of a good conscience tells us that we have a genuine faith and are conforming to our call, it assures us that we are indeed children of God. "If this is my feeling, if I curse no one, hate no one, yes, sympathize with those who are troubled and afflicted, there we have the testimony of our conscience that we are children of God."[91] Given the danger of hypocrites wrongly arrogating the testimony of the gospel to themselves, the testimony of the conscience cannot only contradict faith in the gospel, as in the case of *Anfechtung*, but it must also confirm our faith in the gospel, by testifying that we are children of God on the basis of our sanctification. Such self-testimony strengthens our confidence in the mercy of God in Jesus Christ and also confirms our faith that we have been elected by God. Thus Luther endorses Peter's admonition "to confirm your call and election" (2 Pet. 1:10). "Therefore Peter wants us to confirm this election and call for ourselves with good works. . . . The fruit does not fail to strengthen faith and cause it constantly to do more and more good works."[92] A faith that bears fruit in good works bears witness that we have been elected, just as a faith that does not bring forth works testifies that we have not been elected.[93] Faith alone justifies, and not good works: yet good works and a good conscience testify that our faith is true. Only such testimony can make us certain that we are called by God.

Even the testimony of the Word and the sacrament to our conscience is not enough to make us certain that God has elected us. "Therefore, even if all the angels and the whole world were to testify that you had received the Lord's Supper profitably, it would be weaker testimony than that furnished by your conduct."[94] The testimonies of Word and sacrament to the conscience must find a corresponding testimony of the conscience to itself—that is, a good conscience growing out of sanctification and love—if we are to be certain

---

89. W.A. 50.642.36, 643.1–2; L.W. 41:166.

90. W.A. 50.643.19–26; L.W. 41:166.

91. W.A. 20.767.33–39; L.W. 30:308.

92. *Die ander Epistel S. Petri*, 1523–1524. W.A. 14.22.25–32; L.W. 30:158. Fredrik Brosche, "Luther on Predestination: The Antinomy and Unity Between Love and Wrath in Luther's Concept of God" (doctoral diss., Uppsala University, 1978), p. 193.

93. W.A. 42.669.27–38; L.W. 3:169–70.

94. *Fastenpostille*, 1525. St.L. XI.599; *Sermons* 2:211.

that Christ's testimony applies personally to us. Without such confirming testimony, the gospel and the sacrament do not profit us at all. If the absence of the testimony of a good conscience can completely falsify alleged faith in Jesus Christ, then its presence is an essential component in the assurance of faith in a sincere believer, even if Luther intends it only to confirm a faith otherwise founded on the testimony of Christ and the forgiveness of sins.

In spite of the theology of the cross, which emphasizes the contradiction between the testimony of Christ and the testimony of the conscience, Luther finds it necessary to incorporate into the assurance of faith the confirming testimony of a good conscience, since God's mercy only extends to those who sincerely believe in Christ. Our assurance of salvation cannot be based solely on the testimony of Christ to us; it must also be supported by the testimony of the conscience to itself.

It is clear, therefore, that according to Luther there is a testimony of the good conscience that does not contradict but actually confirms faith and trust in the mercy of God. Although the testimony of the good conscience also forms part of Luther's *theologia crucis* (that is, the witness of the conscience versus the slander and persecution of the world), another aspect of such testimony is a straightforward confirmation of faith (that is, that our faith is bearing fruit, and that we are assured thereby of our election and therefore of the mercy of God). The testimony of the good conscience has reference not only to our life *coram hominibus* but also to our faith *coram Deo*. "The consciousness of a life well spent is the assurance that we are keeping the faith, for it is through works that we learn that our faith is true."[95] Luther insists that the testimony of a good conscience is necessary in order that believers may have confidence that their faith in Christ is sincere. "Therefore man knows by the fruits of faith what kind of tree it is, and is proved by love and deed whether Christ is in him and he believes in Christ."[96] Believers should be exhorted to attain such testimony in order that they might confirm their calling and conform with the goal of their salvation—sanctification.

The testimony of the good conscience to the sincerity of our faith, however, must never be mistaken for the testimony concerning God's mercy in which faith trusts and believes. Although the testimony of the good conscience confirms our trust in God, it should never become the object of such trust: for the very conscience that assures us of the mercy of God because of its awareness of our good works can contradict the mercy of God toward us because of its awareness of our sin, especially in the midst of *Anfechtung*. The mercy of God toward sinners is revealed in Christ alone, and in Christ only should we trust, for his testimony to us will never change from mercy to wrath, as will that of the conscience. "To be sure, I can certainly feel whether I am merciful or angry; but when a trial presents itself, this confidence wavers.

95. W.A. 20.716.24–28; L.W. 30:279.
96. St.L. XI.24; *Sermons* 2:40.

Confidence in Christ, however, is the only thing that cannot be snatched away. He is a Rock, and he who stands on this rock will not be confounded."[97]

The testimony of the good conscience must never be confused with the testimony to the mercy and forgiveness of God; even those who have a good conscience remain sinners in need of forgiveness. When the conscience accuses us because of the sin that remains, or when the devil makes even our good works look like sins, we must turn away from the testimony of the conscience and listen to the Word of God alone. "Satan disturbs our conscience even when we do what is right. . . . But then one must close one's eyes and consider that God is wiser in His Word and that we are not saved by such vain works."[98]

On the one hand, Luther maintains that faith must be confirmed by the testimony of a good conscience, thereby assuring us that we have been truly called by God, for God is only merciful toward those who completely trust in Christ. On the other hand, Luther is aware that the testimony of the terrified conscience can also contradict our confidence in Christ, making it necessary to base our confidence solely on Christ, for the conscience can never testify to us that God is merciful toward those who are aware of their sins. Even though the good conscience confirms our faith and election, yet if we trusted in it before God as though it testified to sinners of God's mercy and grace, the same conscience could only stand against us. "Therefore I can put no trust whatsoever in my own holiness and purity. I have the Word all right and it says: This is the way you must live and love and have a good conscience, and this is pure and holy; but what is lacking is that I can never conclude that this is the way my heart is and never find within me a conscience which is as pure and good as the Word requires."[99]

In sum, the good conscience testifies to the truth of our faith, yet true faith trusts only in Christ and not in the testimony of conscience. "Therefore through him we can say before God: Although I am not pure and cannot have a good conscience, yet I cleave to him who possesses perfect purity and good conscience and offers them for me, indeed, gives them to me."[100] The command of God exhorts us to confirm our faith through the testimony of a good conscience to our obedience; yet the promise of God grounds our faith by revealing to us that God has mercy on those who feel and confess their sins.

> Wherefore God cares admirably for us by making us certain of two things: First, he teaches in Gal. 5:22 what good works are manifest. . . . [On the other hand], He has made us certain that they [the good works] are not sinless and faultless (so that our trust is not in them), with the result that we can acknowledge in a confession without doubt or falsity that we are sinners in all our works and are men whom mercy has found. Further, in order that we may have unfailing peace,

---

97. W.A. 20.768.22–28; L.W. 30:308–9.
98. W.A. 20.717.18–31; L.W. 30:280.
99. W.A. 36.365.28–33; L.W. 51:276.
100. W.A. 36.366.12–15; L.W. 51:277.

He has given us His Word in Christ, on which we rely with confidence, secure from all evil.[101]

Because of his experiences of *Anfechtung*, Luther was well aware that the consciences of all Christians, no matter how holy, have the capacity to contradict faith in the mercy of God; for once the conscience is made aware of sin, it cannot help but conclude that God is wrathful toward it. The foundation of faith, trust, assurance, and confidence must therefore be God's promise of mercy to sinners in Jesus Christ. Yet because of the danger of hypocrisy, Luther nonetheless claimed that the consciences of Christians must also confirm their faith by attesting to their conformity to their calling by works of love, thereby assuring them of the mercy of God and of their status as elect children of God: for God promises to have mercy only on those who sincerely believe in Jesus Christ. The theology of the cross leads Luther not to emphasize such conforming and strengthening testimony; but his axiom, "As you believe, so you have," makes it necessary for him to have such confirming testimony.

Luther exemplifies the dilemma in which both he and Calvin find themselves: The same conscience that testifies against the mercy of God in *Anfechtung*, turning us outside of ourselves to the testimony of Christ and the Holy Spirit, also testifies to the mercy of God toward us by confirming our faith in the mercy of God by a good conscience, making it possible for us to testify to ourselves that we are elect children of God on whom God has mercy. Given this dilemma, Luther's distinction between the foundation of assurance and its confirmation is understandable, yet it is also inherently unstable. In spite of Luther's impressive emphasis on the testimony of the Word of God to the conscience—as law, as gospel, and as command—he must also incorporate into the assurance of faith the testimony of the conscience to itself, for the Word of God only profits those who sincerely believe in it, and only the good conscience can attest to the sincerity of our faith, even if it is not meant to be the object of our faith. By confirming faith, and by testifying that we are elect children of God toward whom God has mercy, the good conscience constitutes a major exception to the theology of the cross, which in every other instance emphasizes the impossibility of moving from the perception of conscience to the true knowledge of God.

101. W.A. 8.82.3–14; L.W. 32:193.

PART TWO

CALVIN—THE FATHER HAS SENT THE SPIRIT OF THE SON INTO OUR HEARTS

5

THE LORD IS OUR
FATHER

This part of the book turns from the theology of Luther to the role that the testimony of the conscience plays in the assurance of faith in the theology of John Calvin. Although Calvin employs the theology of the cross within his interpretation, the question of the assurance of faith must be set within the context of his doctrine of God—that God is our Father in his Son through the Holy Spirit. Calvin understands God the Father as the fountain of every good (*fons omnium bonorum*). The Father is the source and origin of all divinity within the Trinity in relation to the Son and Holy Spirit. The Father is also the source and origin of every good thing of which we are aware as creatures of God, and the fountain from which we must seek all that we are aware we lack as fallen creatures of God.

God the Father, the fountain of every good, is therefore the object of the twofold knowledge of God as Creator and Redeemer, the counterpart to the knowledge of ourselves as created, fallen, and redeemed. "For, quite clearly, the mighty gifts with which we are endowed are hardly from ourselves; indeed, our very being is nothing but subsistence in the one God. Then, by these benefits shed like dew from heaven upon us, we are led as by rivulets to the spring itself. Indeed, our very poverty better discloses the infinitude of benefits reposing in God."[1] The knowledge of ourselves and the knowledge of God are inextricably related, because we cannot know ourselves as creatures without being led by the good things of creation to God, the source of all good things; and we cannot know ourselves as fallen without humbly and earnestly seeking from God all of the spiritual blessings that we lost in Adam. "Thus, from the feeling of our own ignorance, vanity, poverty, infirmity, and—what is more— depravity and corruption, we recognize that the true light of wisdom, sound virtue, full abundance of every good, and purity of righteousness rests in the Lord alone."[2]

1. *Inst.* I.i.1; O.S. III.31.10–21 (1:35–36).
2. *Inst.* I.i.1; O.S. III.31.26–29, 32.1 (1:36).

This relationship of what we are in ourselves making us aware of what we must seek from God is the analogy of faith (*analogia fidei*) or rule of faith (*regula fidei*) that should govern all interpretation of Scripture. "Now, if our interpretation be measured by this rule of faith, victory is in our hands. For what is more consonant with faith than to recognize that we are naked of all virtue, in order to be clothed by God? That we are empty of all good, to be filled by him?"[3] The truth attested by Scripture is that every good thing we lack must be sought from the Father alone, while every good thing that we receive we are to gratefully acknowledge as having flowed to us from God.

However, Calvin makes it clear that we cannot know God as our Father without also knowing God as our righteous and majestic Lord; for God originally gave us all good things in our creation so that we might respond in gratitude by mirroring God's holiness in our own holiness of life, thereby joining ourselves to God. The good things we receive from God are only properly used when we seek by means of them to bring our lives into correspondence with the life of God. After our fall into sin, and our subsequent pride and hypocrisy, we cannot acknowledge that we are destitute of all good things until we first look upon the nature of the Lord and compare our wisdom, strength, and righteousness to the Lord's. "Again, it is certain that man never achieves a clear knowledge of himself unless he has first looked upon God's face, and then descends from him to scrutinize himself."[4] We cannot know God as Father without knowing ourselves to be empty of every good; yet we cannot know ourselves to be empty of every good without first encountering the righteous judgment and majesty of God, to which our lives should correspond. "As a consequence, we must infer that man is never sufficiently touched and affected by the awareness of his lowly state until he has compared himself with God's majesty."[5] We cannot truly know ourselves unless we first look upon the majesty of the Lord and then compare ourselves with the Lord. When we do so, we will find that we are empty of every spiritual blessing, and the knowledge of our poverty will drive us outside ourselves to seek from the Father every good thing we lack.[6]

Thus, if Calvin's doctrine of God is to be fully understood, the true knowledge of God must be knowledge of God as Lord and Father. To know God as Father is to be assured that God is the fountain of every good, while to know God as Lord is to know that God gives us all good things in order that we might be conformed and united to God by holiness and righteousness of life. Although Calvin insists that we cannot know God as Father without simultaneously acknowledging God as Lord, we should not understand these as parallel or independent relationships; the Lordship of God must be seen within the context of the Fatherhood of God. To have true knowledge of God means to

---

3. *Praefatio ad regem Galliae*, O.S. III.12.26–34 (1:13).
4. *Inst.* I.i.2; O.S. III.32.10–18 (1.37).
5. *Inst.* I.i.3; O.S. III.33.18–20 (1:39).
6. *Inst.* I.i.1; O.S. III.32.1–4 (1:36–37).

be assured that the majestic and righteous Lord is our Father, the fountain of every good. Thus it is our Father who is the Lord; it is the majesty of the Father that makes us aware of our poverty; it is the goodness of the Father from which we seek all that we lack; it is the glory and holiness of the Father that we are to image by our grateful obedience. "This is life eternal, to know the one true God as Father and Jesus Christ whom he sent [John 17:3]. I say to know him, in order that we may offer to him the honor and worship that is due, so that He may be not only Lord to us, but also Father and Savior [Matt. 1:21], that we on our side be his children and servants, and accordingly dedicate our life to display his glory."[7]

Just as it was difficult for Calvin to sort out which knowledge precedes and brings forth the other—knowledge of God or of ourselves—so it was difficult for Calvin to set forth in final form which knowledge of God precedes and brings forth the other—knowledge of God as Lord or as Father. Although Calvin often says that we must first fear God as Lord and judge before we can call upon God as Father, he also insisted we can only fear God as Lord when we know with certainty that God wills to be our Father, in light of Ps. 130:4: "But there is forgiveness with you, so that you may be revered." The final shape of the *Institutes* indicates that Calvin was arguing for the priority of the knowledge of the mercy of God the Father; for there can be no genuine fear of God, no acknowledgment of sin, no repentance, no willing and sincere obedience to God, where God is not first known as the fountain of every good.

> Now, the first thing respecting God is, that we should acknowledge him to be beneficent and bountiful; for what would become of us without the mercy of God? Therefore, the true and right knowledge of God begins here, that is, when we know him to be merciful to us. For what would it avail us to know that God is just, unless we had a previous knowledge of his mercy and gratuitous goodness?[8]

This dynamic between the knowledge of God as Lord and Father will be examined more fully below, in order to clarify the prominence that Calvin gave to the knowledge of God as our Father.

The two kinds of self-knowledge that should lead to the knowledge of God as our Father—namely, the awareness of the gifts with which we are endowed, and the awareness of our poverty—mirror the twofold knowledge of God that Calvin uses as an organizing principle for the final edition of the *Institutes*. "First, as much in fashioning the universe as in the general teaching of Scripture the Lord shows himself to be simply the Creator. Then in the face of

---

7. *Catechismus Ecclesiae Genevensis*, C.O. 6:108; *Treatises* p. 129. See Benjamin B. Warfield, *Calvin and Augustine* (Philadelphia: Presbyterian and Reformed Publishing Co., 1956), pp. 173–76; Garret Wilterdink, *Tyrant or Father? A Study in Calvin's Doctrine of God*, 2 vols. (Bristol, Ind.: Wyndam Hall Press, 1985).

8. Comm. Jer. 9:24, C.O. 38:52; C.T.S. 17:52.

Christ [cf. 2 Cor. 4:6] he shows himself the Redeemer."[9] According to Calvin, it is one thing to know God as Father in the work of creation, and another thing to know God as Father in Jesus Christ: hence the twofold knowledge of God (duplex cognitio Dei). Yet if both the knowledge of God the Creator and the knowledge of God the Redeemer involve knowing God as our Father, why does Calvin distinguish between the two? Indeed, how can he distinguish between the two? And if it is true that in this "ruin of mankind no one now experiences God either as Father or as Author of salvation, or favorable in any way, until Christ the Mediator comes forward to reconcile us to him," then why does Calvin begin the *Institutes* with the knowledge of God the Creator?

Although the answer to these questions is complex, it is nonetheless possible to discern three reasons why Calvin distinguishes between the knowledge of God the Creator and the knowledge of God the Redeemer. The first has to do with Calvin's concern, in light of Rom. 1:18-32 and Acts 14 and 17, to render without excuse our inability to know God as our Father from the witness of the universe. The second reason has to do with the order of right teaching necessitated by this inexcusable ignorance of God. The third involves the confirmation of the assurance of believers that God is their Father. The first two reasons support the order of teaching in the *Institutes*, while the third argues for a reversal in the order of teaching that would reflect the order of assurance.

Calvin sets forth the first reason, rendering our ignorance of the Father without excuse, at the beginning of his discussion of the knowledge of God. "Here I do not yet touch upon the sort of knowledge with which men, in themselves lost and accursed, apprehend God the Redeemer in Christ the Mediator; but I speak only of the primal and simple knowledge to which the very order of nature would have led us if Adam had remained upright."[10] By beginning with the knowledge of God the Father as Creator, Calvin makes it clear that we would have been able to know God as our Father and Lord directly from the order of nature if Adam had remained upright. The fact that we can no longer know God as our Father from the testimony of the universe is not God's responsibility, but solely our own because of our fall from God in Adam. God the Father bestowed every good thing upon Adam, both for himself and for his posterity; yet Adam by his sin lost every good thing both for himself and for us, and thereby lost the ability to know God as his and our Father, the fountain of every good. Our ignorance of the Father is culpable, since it is caused by our fall from being children of God to become sinful creatures of God.

However, of God's own free mercy, God willed to be our Father again, even after we had destroyed ourselves as God's children and had subjected creation

---

9. *Inst.* I.ii.1; O.S. III.34.21–25 (1:40).
10. *Inst.* I.ii.1; O.S. III.34.10–14 (1:39–40).

to the curse. Thus the Father sent his only-begotten Son to become human in Jesus, and anointed him with the Holy Spirit to be the Christ, thereby bestowing on him every good thing that we lost in Adam, so that in him sinful humanity might again become children of the Father. By beginning with the knowledge of God the Creator, Calvin highlights both the enormity of our sin and the wonder of the mercy of God, not only in willing to be our Father by creating us as his children in Adam, but especially in willing to be the Father of rebellious, sinful humanity in Jesus Christ.

The second reason Calvin begins with the knowledge of God the Creator has to do with the order of right teaching made necessary by our fall in Adam and our subsequent inexcusable ignorance of the Father. According to Calvin, it is impossible to bring those who are ignorant of God directly to the knowledge of God the Redeemer in Jesus Christ the Mediator. Instead, the order of right teaching requires that we begin with something closer to the common understanding of all the ungodly. All people are imbued with an awareness that there is some god who is their maker, to whom worship and obedience are due. However, all people are completely ignorant of who that God is (*quis sit Deus*) and what God is like (*qualis sit Deus*). As a consequence, they worship false gods on the basis of human opinion alone. The order of right teaching therefore must begin with the true principle that is the basis of all idolatry—that there is one whom all are to worship and adore as their maker—in order to overthrow all of the false gods by clearly setting forth the true Creator, God the Father, who created through the Word by the Holy Spirit.

The knowledge of who the true God is, the Father and Lord, and what God is like, infinite and spiritual essence, leads directly to the knowledge of how God ought to be worshiped, in spirit and in truth. This is how Paul confronted the false worship of the people of Athens and Lystra, according to Calvin.

> If anyone wishes to discuss religion in general this will be the first point, that there is some deity to whom worship is due from men. But because there was no dispute about that, Paul passes on to the second point, that the true God ought to be distinguished from all fabrications. So he makes a beginning with the definition of God, so that he might prove from that how he ought to be worshipped, because the one thing depends on the other.[11]

The order of teaching of the *Institutes* follows Calvin's reading of the preaching of Paul to the ungodly. After the two introductory chapters that set forth the theme for the whole of the *Institutes*, Calvin establishes the first point in the order of right teaching, the universal human awareness that there is some god to whom worship is due (I.iii). Next, he shows how that awareness leads to idolatry and superstitious worship because of ignorance of who the true

---

11. Comm. Acts 17:24, C.O. 48:410; C.N.T.C. 7:112; cf. Comm. Acts 14:15, C.O. 48:326; C.N.T.C. 7:10–11.

God is and what God is like (I.iv–v). Finally, on the basis of Scripture, which is more certain than any human opinion, Calvin overthrows all idols and imaginary gods by clearly setting forth who the true God is and what God is like, so that we may know how God wills to be worshiped (I.vi–xiv, xvi–xvii). "All things will tend to this end, that God, the Artificer of the universe, is made manifest to us in Scripture, and that what we ought to think of him is set forth there, lest we seek some uncertain deity by devious paths."[12]

The knowledge of who God is, what God is like, and how God ought to be worshiped in turn leads to the knowledge of ourselves as fallen from our created nature, unable to fulfill our duty to worship God as we ought, and hence unable through our sin to know the Creator as our Father (II.i–v). This knowledge in turn leads us to know God as Father in the knowledge of Jesus Christ our Mediator (II.vi ff.). "Therefore although the preaching of the cross does not agree with our human inclination, if we desire to return to God our Author and Maker, from whom we have been estranged, in order that he may again begin to be our Father, we ought nevertheless to embrace it humbly."[13] In this way, the order of right teaching coincides with rendering inexcusable our ignorance of God as our Father, so that we might be led to know the Creator again as our Father in Jesus Christ through the Holy Spirit.

Once we are assured that God is our merciful Father in Jesus Christ, the knowledge of God as Father from the testimony of the universe confirms our assurance that the Creator is indeed our Father. It is necessary for believers to know the self-revelation of the Father in the universe, in order to confirm the assurance that God is our Father in Jesus Christ. "Nothing shall we find, I say, above or below, which can raise us up to God, until Christ shall have instructed us in his own school. Yet this does not prevent us from applying our senses to the consideration of heaven and earth, that we may thence seek confirmation of the true knowledge of God."[14]

Just as the knowledge of God the Creator shows us that it is because of our sin that we cannot know God as our Father, thereby driving us to Christ that God may again be our Father, so the knowledge of God the Redeemer leads us back to the knowledge of God the Creator, where our assurance that God is our Father is confirmed in a distinctive way. Before God fully reveals himself as our Father in our inheritance of the kingdom of God, God reveals himself as our Father in this life by restoring to us the inheritance of the good things of heaven and earth forfeited in Adam. "Since, therefore, this life serves us in understanding God's goodness, should we despise it as if it had no grain of good in itself?"[15] Our assurance that God is our Father must be founded in Jesus Christ alone, but it is incomplete unless we confirm it by knowing God as our Father in the creation and governance of the world.

---

12. *Inst.* I.vi.1; O.S. III.61.31–34 (1:71).
13. *Inst.* II.vi.1; O.S. III.320.33–36 (1:341).
14. *Argumentum in Genesin*, C.O. 23:9–12; C.T.S. 1:63–64.
15. *Inst.* III.ix.3; O.S. IV.173.3–10 (1:714–15).

We might summarize Calvin's use of the distinction between the knowledge of God the Creator and the knowledge of God the Redeemer in the following way. First, it takes away all excuse for our ignorance of God as our Father, since it is because of our loss of every good thing in Adam that we can no longer know God as the fountain of every good but rather encounter God as the wrathful judge of our sin. Second, in light of our ignorance of God, the order of right teaching demands that the true God whom all are to worship be set forth in distinction from all idols invented by human opinion, in order that we might know how our Creator wishes to be worshiped. Both of these concepts establish our sin as being the sole reason for the Father's sending forth his Son in Jesus Christ. Third, once we know God as our Father in Jesus Christ, our assurance is confirmed by the knowledge of the Father in the creation and governance of the universe, which has special regard for the community of believers.[16] The first two ideas clarify why Calvin began the *Institutes* with the knowledge of God the Creator, while the third would argue for a reversal of that order, since only those who have been adopted in Jesus Christ through the Holy Spirit can know the Creator as their Father.

All three concepts lying behind the distinction between the twofold knowledge of God directly involve the testimony of the conscience. It is our conscience that testifies to us that our sin is the reason we cannot infer from the order of nature that God is our Father; and yet it is also the conscience that makes us aware there is some divinity whom all ought to worship and adore, which is the first step in the order of right teaching. We can only enjoy the benefits that the Father freely bestows on us in creation when our conscience is certain that those good things are rightfully ours, through our adoption as children of God in the Son Jesus Christ. The next chapter will examine the knowledge of God and self that arises from the testimony of the conscience in the ungodly.

16. *Argumentum in Genesin*, C.O. 23:11; C.T.S. 1:64.

6

TO RENDER THE UNGODLY WITHOUT EXCUSE

Calvin, unlike Luther, wrote an orderly presentation of the Christian religion, a *summa religionis*, in order to instruct his readers in the teaching of true piety and religion. Thus, before the discussion here could turn to Calvin's understanding of the testimony of the conscience, the previous chapter established the way in which Calvin sets forth and orders his teaching, both with regard to the knowledge of God and of ourselves and with regard to the twofold knowledge of God. The order of Calvin's teaching in the *Institutes* sheds light on the issues under consideration. It is constantly necessary when dealing with Calvin to check his commentaries, lectures, sermons, and treatises against the *Institutes*, in order to make sure of setting forth a fair and accurate interpretation. Thus in the reading of Calvin one has a touchstone to guide interpretation that is lacking in Luther.

However, this advantage in Calvin's theology does not extend to his understanding of the conscience.[1] Like Luther, Calvin refers to the conscience virtually every doctrine he discusses, and yet (also like Luther) he has no sustained discussion of the conscience per se. He does define the conscience in the *Institutes*, and interestingly enough, both occasions of the definition occur in the middle of a discussion of Christian freedom, just as Luther's definition of the conscience occurs in the discussion of evangelical freedom in his *Judgment on Monastic Vows*. Calvin significantly expands upon his understanding of the conscience in other places, particularly when he discusses the natural law, so that a fairly consistent definition of the conscience emerges. The discussion of the conscience here will begin with the definition from

---

1. *Natural Theology*, trans. Peter Fraenkel (London: Geoffrey Bles: Centenary Press, 1946); Peter Brunner, "Das Problem der natuerlichen Theologie bei Calvin," *Theologische Existenz Heute* 18 (1935); Guenter Gloede, *Theologia naturalis bei Calvin* (Stuttgart: Kohlhammer, 1935); Edward A. Dowey, Jr., *The Knowledge of God in Calvin's Theology* (London and New York: Columbia University Press, 1952); T. H. L. Parker, *The Doctrine of the Knowledge of God: A Study in the Theology of John Calvin* (Edinburgh: Oliver & Boyd, 1952); T. F. Torrance, *Calvin's Doctrine of Man* (Grand Rapids, Mich.: Wm. B. Eerdmans, 1957); David Lee Foxgrover, "John Calvin's Understanding of Conscience" (Ph.D. diss., Claremont School of Theology, 1978).

Calvin's chapter on Christian freedom, but the overall discussion will be framed in light of the brief description Calvin gives of the functions of the conscience in his discussion of the law of God.

Christian freedom, for Calvin as for Luther, is freedom of the conscience, not freedom from political obedience; and so, in order to understand the nature of Christian freedom, Calvin must define the conscience.

> For just as when through the mind and understanding [*mente intelligentiaque*] men grasp a knowledge [*notitiam*] of things, and from this are said "to know" [*scire*], this is the source of the word "knowledge" [*scientia*]: so also, when they have a sense of divine judgment [*sensum divini iudicii*], as a witness joined to them, which does not allow them to hide their sins from being accused before the Judge's tribunal, this sense is called conscience.[2]

First of all, Calvin relates and distinguishes knowledge (*scientia*) and conscience (*conscientia*). Both are based upon a knowledge of reality that is outside the knower. Knowledge is based on the action of the mind or understanding grasping information about things, while conscience is based upon the awareness of God's judgment. The crucial difference between *scientia* and *conscientia* lies in the fact that knowledge per se (*simplex notitia*), once it has been gained through information about things, can remain closed up within the understanding or mind of the knowing subject. By this, Calvin seems to mean that no one, not even the known object (which presumably could be another person) necessarily needs to know what I know: I can hide what I know from other people.

The sense of divine judgment, which is the basis of the conscience, is also the knowledge of an external reality—namely, the judgment seat of God. However, unlike knowledge (*scientia/notitia*), the awareness of divine judgment cannot remain closed up within us, but rather continually places us before the judgment seat of God. To put it another way, the *sensus divini iudicii* is like a witness joined to us that does not allow us to hide what we know but testifies to us until it convicts us before the judge's tribunal. Unlike *scientia*, which begins with a knowledge of things but ends with knowledge within the mind, *conscientia* begins with an awareness of divine judgment, which then leads to a knowledge of ourselves in light of that judgment, only to bring us back in condemnation before that judgment. "A simple knowledge [*notitia*] could reside, so to speak, closed up in man. Therefore this awareness [*sensus*] which hales man before God's judgment is a sort of guardian appointed to man to note and spy out all his secrets that nothing may remain buried in darkness."[3]

---

2. *Inst.* III.xix.15; O.S. IV.295.8–25 (1:848).

3. *Inst.* III.xix.15; O.S. IV.295.20–24 (1:848). See David Bosco, "Conscience as Court and Worm: Calvin and the Three Elements of Conscience," *The Journal of Religious Ethics* 14 (1986): 333–55.

The awareness of judgment particularly spies out and accuses us of our sins, and once these sins are discovered our conscience bears witness against us before the judgment seat of God. The conscience therefore both arises from the awareness of divine judgment and also leads us back to the judgment seat of God, where we are convicted of our sins before God. "For it is a certain mean between God and man, because it does not allow man to suppress within himself what he knows, but pursues him to the point of convicting him."[4]

The fundamental difference between *scientia* and *conscientia*, therefore, is that while both are founded on a knowledge or awareness of a reality outside of us, *scientia* represents our knowledge of another thing, whereas *conscientia* represents our awareness of God's judgment of us. The knowing subject of *scientia* is the human being; the knowing subject of *conscientia* is God the judge, although we also share in the awareness of God's judgment of us. In fact, the proper function of conscience is to bring us to the same judgment of ourselves that God has. By definition, therefore, the judgment of conscience, because it is based on the awareness of divine judgment, should represent that same judgment. "As often, then, as the secret compunctions of conscience invite us to reflect upon our sins, let us remember that God himself is speaking with us. For that interior sense by which we are convicted of sin is the peculiar judgment seat of God, where he exercises his jurisdiction."[5] The testimony of conscience convicting us of sin should therefore be regarded as the judgment of God accusing us of sin. This is why conscience is a kind of mean (*quiddam medium*) between God and humanity.

If the *sensus divini iudicii* makes known to us our sins in order to hale us before the judgment seat of God, there must be some sort of standard or law by which the conscience arrives at its discernment of sin. What must be added to Calvin's definition of the conscience is the standard of self-judgment that arises out of the awareness of divine judgment. We find the needed piece in Calvin's discussion of the soul as an immortal, created essence. "Surely the conscience, which, distinguishing between good and evil, responds to God's judgment, is an undoubted sign of the immortal spirit. For how could a motion without essence penetrate to God's judgment seat, and inflict itself with terror at its own guilt?"[6]

The distinction between good and evil, arising in the conscience as it responds to God's judgment, gives the conscience the necessary standard or law by which sins should be discerned and accused, and this law should correspond to the law by which God judges us. This is precisely what we find in Calvin's definition of natural law: "This would not be a bad definition: natural law is that apprehension of conscience which distinguishes sufficiently between just and unjust, and which deprives men of the excuse of ignorance, while it proves

4. *Inst.* III.xix.15; O.S. IV.295.15–20 (1:848).
5. Comm. Gen. 4:9, C.O. 23:91–92; C.T.S. 1:205.
6. *Inst.* I.xv.2; O.S. III.175.13–17 (1:184).

them guilty by their own testimony."[7] The apprehension or recognition (*agnitio*) of conscience, which distinguishes sufficiently between good and evil, is the natural law; and the natural law should hold before us the sum total of our duties before God, thereby corresponding to the law of God, the Ten Commandments. "Now that inward law which we have above described as written, even engraved, upon the hearts of all, in a sense [*quodammodo*] asserts the very same things that are to be learned from the Two Tables."[8] The discussion below will explore to what degree the natural law corresponds to the two tables of the Decalogue.

Calvin not only distinguishes the conscience from the mind and understanding, but he also distinguishes the conscience from the will (*voluntas*). To say that the natural law is inscribed in the heart does not mean that the law is engraved on the will, so that we obey the law; rather, the conscience holds before the will the natural law by which its actions should be guided— that is, to pursue the good and abhor the evil—and then judges the actions of the will in light of its duty.[9] If, in light of the natural law, the conscience judges that the will does in fact demonstrate a lively and sincere pursuit of the good and shunning of the evil, that judgment gives rise to what Calvin calls the testimony of the good conscience.[10] If, however, the conscience judges that there is a lack of correspondence between the inclination and actions of the will and the natural law, then the conscience's testimony accuses the person of sin, thereby rendering the person condemned before the judgment seat of God. The condemning testimony of the conscience should therefore be considered to be the condemning judgment of God.[11]

To sum up Calvin's definition of the conscience, we might say that the conscience is the awareness of divine judgment that responds to that judgment by distinguishing between good and evil. The distinction between good and evil apprehended by the conscience generally corresponds with the law of God, and thus in some sense asserts the same things taught by the Ten Commandments—namely, that we are to worship God and to treat our neighbors justly and equitably. The conscience both holds this duty before the will in an *antecedent* way, as what ought to be done or avoided, and also judges the actions of the will in a *consequent* way as to whether they correspond to the natural law. If they do, then the conscience renders an approving testimony; if not, it renders a condemning testimony.[12] Since the conscience arises from the awareness of divine judgment, the testimony of the conscience should be regarded as the judgment we receive from God before God's tribunal.[13]

---

7. *Inst.* II.ii.22; O.S. III.265.7–11 (1:282).
8. *Inst.* II.viii.1; O.S. III.344.11–17 (1:368).
9. Comm. Rom. 2:15, *Iohannis Calvini Commentarius in Epistolam Pauli ad Romanos*, ed. T. H. L. Parker (Leiden: E. J. Brill, 1981), pp. 45–46 (henceforth *Commentarius*); C.N.T.C. 8:48.
10. *Inst.* III.xix.16; O.S. IV.295.32–34, 296.1–5 (1:849).
11. *Inst.* III.xix.15; O.S. IV.295.12–14 (1:848).
12. Comm. Rom. 2:15, *Commentarius* p. 45; C.N.T.C. 8:49.
13. *Inst.* III.xix.15; O.S. IV.295.12–20 (1:848).

Calvin clearly grounds the conscience in awareness of God's judgment, unlike Luther, who grounds the conscience in the syllogistic logic of the practical reason. Both theologians agree that the conclusions of the conscience render the whole person either acquitted or condemned before the judgment seat of God; but Calvin also grounds the beginning of the operation of the conscience in our awareness of divine judgment, whereas Luther grounds it on the major premises the mind gives to the conscience. In sum, Calvin associates conscience (*conscientia*) with consciousness (*conscius*) or awareness (*sensus*), whereas Luther associates conscience with the syllogism of practical reason, possibly indicating the Platonic versus Aristotelian influences in their anthropologies.

In light of this definition of conscience, what kind of knowledge of God and of God's law does the conscience yield, and what knowledge of ourselves arises in light of this?[14] The following discussion will consider (1) the conscience in its role in the awareness of divinity (*sensus divinitatis*), which brings with it the indelible knowledge that there is some god who ought to be worshiped; (2) the knowledge of God that arises from this awareness of divinity and the subsequent worship rendered to God; and (3) the natural law of conscience compared with the law of God, and the knowledge of self derived from the testimony of conscience.

The Awareness of Divinity

Since the conscience responds to the judgment of God by being an inner witness and monitor of what we owe God, the conscience must provide us with some sort of knowledge of God. According to the law of God, to which the natural law in some sense corresponds, our obligation toward God is grounded in God's relation to us as our Creator. Because God is our Creator, we owe God obedience and must submit to God's judgment. "Now what is to be learned from the law can be readily understood: that God, as he is our Creator, has toward us by right the place of Father and Lord; for this reason we owe to him glory, reverence, love and fear."[15] If the conscience corresponds to the first table of the law, then it must also set forth the basis of our obligation, namely, that God is our Maker, even if it does not necessarily know that Maker as Father and Lord. Were the conscience not to know God as Maker, our obligation to God would have no basis in anything other than brute fact. Calvin insists that all consciences are aware there is some god who created heaven and earth and who therefore must be obeyed: "for it has remained engraven on the conscience that the world was not formed by itself; that there was some heavenly majesty to which we must be subject."[16]

---

14. *Inst.* II.viii.1; O.S. III.344.14–17 (1:368).
15. *Inst.* II.viii.2; O.S. III.344.28–31 (1:369).
16. Sermon Job 32:1-3, C.O. 35:5–6; *Sermons from Job*, trans. Leroy Nixon (Grand Rapids, Mich.: Baker Book House, 1979), pp. 219–20. See Dowey, *The Knowledge of God in Calvin's Theology*, pp. 55–56.

The awareness that there is some god who created us, whose majesty we must worship and adore, is what Calvin means by *sensus divinitatis*. "There is within the human mind, and indeed by natural instinct, an awareness of divinity [*divinitatis sensum*]. . . . Since, then, men one and all perceive that there is a god and that he is their Maker, they are condemned by their own testimony because they have failed to honor him and to consecrate their lives to his will."[17] The awareness of divinity makes atheism impossible, according to Calvin. This does not mean that there will not be those who deny in word and deed that there is a God; but in spite of their denial, their consciences will feel what they desire not to believe. "Whence does this arise but from the vengeance of divine majesty, which strikes their consciences all the more violently the more they try to flee from it."[18] The same also holds true for those who laughingly deride the universally known obligation to worship God. Even though they attempt to free themselves from the fear of God by denying the judgment of God, the conscience testifies against them and gnaws away within them.[19] The conscience contains the awareness of divinity and seed of religion that make atheism and the rejection of religion impossible to maintain. Although the rejection of God and religion are possible in theory, such rejection can never be made without the conscience making us aware of what we desire to deny. "In like manner, when Dionysius the tyrant ridiculed his gods, he fought with God and defied him to a contest; for he attacked, in opposition to his conscience, such a deity as his mind could comprehend."[20]

The conscience makes us aware that there is some god (*esse aliquem Deum*) who ought to be worshiped and obeyed, making impossible the denial of God or religion; but this is not the same thing as knowing who the true God is (*quis sit Deus*) or what God is like (*qualis sit*). We cannot, according to Calvin, render to God due worship unless we first know who and of what nature God is. "For the true rule of godliness is precisely this, to have a clear grasp of who the God is, whom we worship."[21] The awareness that there is a God is not knowledge of the true God, and the awareness of our duty to render worship to God is not the same as true religion.[22] We cannot render to God the worship that is God's due until we know with certainty the God who created us. "We have to note that it is not enough for men to confess that there is some kind of divinity, and to endeavor to discharge themselves of their duty by serving god; but they must also have a certain firm belief, that they may not wander to and fro."[23]

17. *Inst.* I.iii.1; O.S. III.37.16–24 (1:43–44).
18. *Inst.* I.iii.2; O.S. III.38.32–33, 39.1–10 (1:45).
19. *Inst.* I.iii.3; O.S. III.39.23–28, 40.1–2 (1:46).
20. Comm. Isa. 36:18, C.O. 36:611; C.T.S. 15:97.
21. Comm. Acts 17:24, C.O. 49:410; C.N.T.C. 7:112.
22. *Inst.* I.ii.1; O.S. III.34.6–10 (1:39).
23. Sermon Eph. 2:11-13, C.O. 51:394–95; John Calvin's *Sermons on Ephesians*, trans. Arthur Golding, Leslie Rawlinson, and S. M. Houghton (Edinburgh: Banner of Truth Trust, 1973), pp. 179–80.

The conscience therefore holds before us as the law of our creation the duty to know with certainty the God who created us, so that we might know both whom we are to worship and how to worship properly.[24] The conscience, however, cannot by its own testimony provide itself with the certain and stable knowledge of God. The testimony of the conscience can only tell us that there is some god who created us, to whom we owe worship and obedience. In order to know who that God is, we must look to the revelation of God in the created world. It is there that God our Creator reveals to us that God is our Father.

The Awareness of the Powers of God

The testimony of the conscience can only tell us that there is some God whom all ought to worship and adore, but it cannot tell us who or of what sort that God is. The conscience must be instructed about these things from elsewhere, where the true God has revealed himself. According to Calvin, that self-revelation of God occurs in the whole workmanship of the world. "Lest anyone, then, be excluded from access to happiness, he not only sowed in men's minds that seed of religion of which we have spoken but revealed himself and daily discloses himself in the whole workmanship of the universe."[25] God's essence cannot be known, but God reveals himself in, and therefore can be known by, God's works. In particular, the works of the Creator reveal powers (*virtutes*) such as wisdom, righteousness, power, rectitude, and truth. "We must therefore admit in God's individual works—but especially in them as a whole—that God's powers [*Dei virtutes*] are actually represented as in a painting."[26]

The initial way by which we become aware of the powers of God is in the sustaining and governing of the universe by God. The eternity of God is revealed by the subsistence of all things in God; God's wisdom, in the perfect order of creation; God's goodness, in that there can be no other reason for creation; God's justice, because God defends the innocent and punishes the guilty; God's mercy, because God endures the wickedness of humanity with patience; and God's truth, because God is unchangeable.[27] Our awareness of these powers in the universe should then lead us to acknowledge God to be the source and fountain of them; "no drop will be found either of wisdom and light, or of righteousness or power or rectitude, or of genuine truth, which does not flow from him, and of which he is not the cause."[28] The works of creation reveal that the God who governs and sustains the universe is the fountain of every good (*fons omnium bonorum*).

Our awareness of God's powers should lead us to acknowledge that the Creator and Ruler of the universe is our Father. This is especially clear when

---

24. *Inst.* I.iii.3; O.S. III.40.13–18 (1:46). See Dowey, *The Knowledge of God in Calvin's Theology*, pp. 50–56.
25. *Inst.* I.v.1; O.S. III.44.30–31, 45.1–8 (1:51–52).
26. *Inst.* I.v.10; O.S. III.54.19–24 (1:63).
27. Comm. Rom. 1:21, *Commentarius*, p. 30; C.N.T.C. 8:32.
28. *Inst.* I.ii.1; O.S. III.34.25–37, 35.1–2 (1:40–41).

we contemplate the powers of God that are found within us as human beings. "For each one undoubtedly feels within the heavenly grace that quickens him . . . by adorning us with such great excellence he testifies that he is our Father."[29] Indeed, Calvin insists that the powers of God are only properly contemplated when we discern them within ourselves. "Now these powers appear most clearly in his works. Yet we comprehend their chief purpose, their value, and the reason why we should ponder them, only when we descend into ourselves and contemplate by what means the Lord shows in us his life, wisdom, and power, and exercises on our behalf his righteousness, goodness, and mercy."[30]

Our awareness of the powers of God within us should bear testimony that God is our Father, in that God has bestowed these gifts on us; whereas the powers of God revealed in God's governance of us reveal that we are to live as God's children, for we see in the governance of the world that God protects the innocent and punishes the guilty. However, since the innocent also suffer in this life, while the guilty often escape punishment, we should be awakened to the awareness of a future life where God's mercy and justice will be more clearly revealed.[31]

In sum, by the powers portrayed within us God reveals to us that God is our Father; by the powers portrayed in the governance of the world, God reveals that there is a future life where all God's children will inherit all good things and clearly know God as Father, while all the ungodly will be eternally punished.

The duty that the conscience holds before us—that is, to know who the God is who created us so that we might worship God in truth—can only be fulfilled by the knowledge that God is our Father, the fountain of every good. "It will not suffice simply to hold that there is one whom all ought to honor and adore, unless we are also persuaded that he is the fountain of every good, and that we must seek nothing elsewhere than in him."[32] Such knowledge should arise from our awareness of the powers of God manifested in the works of God. "For the Lord manifests himself by his powers, the force of which we feel within ourselves and the benefits of which we enjoy."[33] The awareness of the powers of God should therefore teach us piety, which is the knowledge that the Lord is our Father. "For this sense of the powers of God [*Virtutum Dei sensus*] is for us a fit teacher of piety, from which religion is born. I call 'piety' that reverence joined with love of God which the knowledge of his benefits induces."[34]

The knowledge of the true God in piety in turn should give birth to religion, which is the true worship of the true God. If we owe our very existence to

29. *Inst.* I.v.3; O.S. III.47.3–6, 19–22 (1:54–55).
30. *Inst.* I.v.10; O.S. III.54.24–29 (1:63).
31. *Inst.* I.v.10; O.S. III.54.3–7 (1:62).
32. *Inst.* I.ii.1; O.S. III.34.25–30 (1:40).
33. *Inst.* II.vi.4; O.S. III.325.35–38 (1:347).
34. *Inst.* I.ii.1; O.S. III.35.2–10 (1:41).

the fountain of every good, and God governs our lives with justice and righteousness, then we in turn should seek to obey the will of our Creator in all
things; and yet we are to render our service not out of fear of judgment, but
out of the knowledge that our Creator and Lord is our Father. "Here indeed
is pure and real religion: faith so joined with an earnest fear of God that this
fear also embraces willing reverence, and carries with it such legitimate worship as is prescribed in the law."[35] Because we know God as the fountain of
every good, we ought to trust in God, pray to God for every good thing that
we need, and thank God for all the good things that we receive. Thus, just
as piety arises out of the sense of the powers of God, true religion arises out
of piety, for from piety we learn that God the Father wishes to be worshiped
by trust, prayer, thanksgiving, and willing obedience.

However, the revelation of God through God's powers leads to true piety
and religion only if our minds *obey* the self-revelation of God in the universe;
we come to a true and certain knowledge of God if we contemplate and seek
God solely in God's works and follow the powers of God depicted in those
works back to their source.[36] The revelation of God through God's powers
would have led to true piety and religion *only if Adam had remained upright*.
Because of Adam's fall, our minds are unable to obey the self-revelation of
God in the universe in order to learn who God is (*quis sit Deus*) and of what
nature God is (*qualis sit Deus*), and consequently how God wishes to be
worshiped. "Our judgment, however, fails here before it discovers the nature
or character of God [*aut quis aut qualis sit Deus*]."[37] The objective manifestation
of God is sufficient in itself to lead to the true knowledge of God, and thus
removes any excuse for our ignorance of God. However, because of our dullness
and ingratitude resulting from the fall, we are led instead to idolatry and
superstition.

According to Calvin, we are all sufficiently aware of the powers of God in
the world to form some conception of divinity. However, this conception does
not hold to the manifestation of God in God's works; because of our blindness,
it is corrupted by the false imagination of the flesh. "Yet after we rashly grasp
a conception of some sort of divinity, straightaway we fall back into the ravings
or vain imaginings of our flesh, and corrupt by our vanity the pure truth of
God."[38] This is not to say that we all corrupt the truth of God in the same
way. Indeed, the imagination of the flesh gives rise to myriad false conceptions
of God; and yet all have in common the fact that they do not adhere or
correspond to the self-representation of God in God's works but corrupt the
truth of God by the vanity of the human mind.[39] Even the wisest of the
philosophers demonstrate that they also are subject to this vanity and ignorance.

---

35. *Inst.* I.ii.2; O.S. III.37.7–10 (1:43).
36. *Inst.* I.ii.2; O.S. III.36.5–12 (1:42).
37. Comm. Rom. 1:20, *Commentarius*, p. 30; C.N.T.C. 8:31–32.
38. *Inst.* I.v.11; O.S. III.55.3–6, 15–-20 (1:63–64).
39. *Inst.* II.v.11; O.S. III.55.20–23 (1:64).

At the heart of human dullness, according to Calvin, is the attempt to understand God according to the capacity of the human mind. Rather than subject our minds to the truth of God set forth in creation, we judge God and God's works according to our limited human standards of judgment. Thus we cannot help but develop carnal conceptions of God. The ignorance under which we labor is therefore a mixture of pride and boldness on the one hand, and fleshly weakness and darkness of mind on the other.[40] Our pride and boldness, or rashness and superficiality, are revealed by the fact that when we attempt to know God, we do not seek God where God has revealed himself—that is, in the powers set forth in God's works—but rather attempt to know God's essence. When this happens, we cannot help but give rise to idols, for we are attempting to understand the spiritual majesty of God's essence according to the limits of carnal human understanding. "Man's mind, full as it is of pride and boldness, dares to imagine a god according to its own capacity; as it sluggishly plods, indeed is overwhelmed by the crassest ignorance, it conceives an unreality and an empty appearance as God."[41] By attempting to penetrate to God's spiritual essence, we neglect where God has in fact revealed himself, and thus whatever god we conceive of must be an invention. "They do not therefore apprehend God as he offers himself, but imagine him as they have fashioned him in their own presumption."[42]

Another aspect of human dullness is the darkness and weakness of the human mind even when it attempts to know God in God's works. The powers of God set forth in creation do strike our minds with a taste of divinity (divinitatis gustus), which leads us to form some conception of divinity. However, our minds cannot rightly judge the works of God, and therefore fade away in ignorance before they come to a proper understanding of the powers of God. This darkness of mind is especially apparent when the human mind judges the governance and providence of God in the world; in its ignorance the mind thinks that all things are tumbled about fortuitously, and believes in fortune or chance instead of providence. The mind's limitations are also apparent in our contemplation of the works of God in general, for in contemplating creation we look only at the works and do not consider their author.[43]

This makes it clear that the darkness of the human mind is fundamentally based on ingratitude. Both the providence of God and the works of God reveal that our Creator and Lord is our Father, the fountain of every good. This is especially clear when we contemplate our own nature, which is a microcosm of the works of God in the universe. "For nothing is more preposterous than to enjoy the very remarkable gifts that attest the divine nature within us, yet to overlook the Author who gives them to us at our asking."[44] Our awareness

40. *Inst*. I.v.12; O.S. III.56.10–12 (1:65).
41. *Inst*. I.x.8; O.S. III.97.6–9 (1:108).
42. *Inst*. I.iv.1; O.S. III.41.9–15 (1:47).
43. *Inst*. I.v.11; O.S. III.55.6–15 (1:63–64).
44. *Inst*. I.v.6; O.S. III.50.29–31, 51.1–3 (1:58–59).

of the good things we perceive within ourselves and in the world should lead us back to God, the author and fountain of every good. By divorcing the gifts of God from their author, we claim for ourselves that which we have been given and demonstrate our fundamental ingratitude toward God. It does not matter if we acknowledge that the good things we have received come from nature or from other false gods, so long as we do not acknowledge God the Father to be our governor and the fountain of every good.

In sum, our pride and ingratitude make it impossible for us to know God as Father from the testimony of creation. On the one hand, we seek to know God apart from God's works, by investigating God's essence, and we wind up inventing an empty idol in place of God. On the other hand, we seek to know God's works apart from their author, and thus seek to enjoy the good things that God gives us without trusting in, praying to, or giving thanks to God the Father.[45] The fault for our ignorance of God is our own and is therefore without excuse. Even though we cannot overcome our ignorance of God on our own, we cannot pretend that we are thereby excused; the very conscience that holds before us the duty to know God also accuses us for failing in that duty. "And, indeed, we are not allowed thus to pretend ignorance without our conscience itself always convicting us of both baseness and ingratitude."[46]

The Worship of an Unknown God

The failure to come to a true knowledge of God the Father from the testimony of creation means that the conscience cannot be instructed in the certain truth of who God is and what God's nature is, and therefore cannot know with certainty how God is to be worshiped. In the place of the true knowledge of God stands human opinion about God; even if that opinion does not necessarily develop into the crassest form of idolatry, it is insufficient to lead us to the true knowledge of God. "And though nothing more harmful may result, yet to worship an unknown god by chance is no light fault."[47] The lack of certainty alone is enough to convince the ungodly that they do not worship the true God, for the true knowledge of God the Father brings with it certainty of conscience. "No, indeed, and however much they boast, yet because they continue to be perplexed in their consciences, they are bound to be held convicted by their own judgment of themselves."[48]

So serious is the error of worshiping an unknown god that Paul calls those who do so atheists, not because they deny that God exists but because they worship an idol in the place of God.[49] No matter how much we might exert ourselves, if we lack the certain knowledge of the true God, our consciences will always bear witness against us; it is the conscience that holds before us

---

45. *Inst.* I.v.15; O.S. III.60.2–8 (1:69).
46. *Inst.* I.v.15; O.S. III.59.24–29 (1:68–69).
47. *Inst.* I.v.13; O.S. III.58.15–20 (1:67).
48. Comm. Acts 17:22, C.O. 48:408–9; C.N.T.C. 7:110.
49. Comm. Eph. 2:12, C.O. 51:169; C.N.T.C. 11:148–49.

the duty to know with certainty the God we ought to worship. The inability of the mind to know the true God from the works of creation necessarily corrupts our worship.

The conscience as the seed of religion or sense of divinity does not lead to true religion, but rather to idolatrous superstition on the one hand or to the malicious denial of God on the other.[50] Superstition is a carnal form of worship arising from a carnal conception of God. "Indeed, whatever they afterward attempt by way of worship or service of God, they cannot bring as tribute to him, for they are worshipping not God but a figment and a dream of their own heart."[51] The superstitious first form an idol in their heart and mind, then pattern their worship of God on that idol.[52]

For Calvin, the two ways in which superstition consistently manifests itself are in images and ceremonies. Since the mind's conception of God is in carnal or earthly form, it follows that the worshiper would seek to give outward expression to that conception in an image of God. "Therefore the mind begets an idol: the hand gives it birth."[53] Even if God is not confined in the earthly image, the power or presence of God is confined to the image so that God is adored in the idol.[54] Ceremonies and other external forms of worship also correspond to the carnal knowledge of the divine, for they are earthly actions that set forth an empty appearance of worship. "Men have always, accordingly, been found addicted to ceremonies until they have been brought to the knowledge of that which constitutes true and acceptable religion."[55] It does not matter how zealously these ceremonies are observed, for the self-invented worship of self-invented gods is an open rejection of what God enjoins.[56] Indeed, Calvin seems to be of the opinion that the more religious the superstitious try to be, the more they depart from the true worship of God, so that the most religious among them may be said to be without God.[57] Because superstition is without God, it lacks stability and certainty and therefore is always adding new practices or ceremonies, for it never knows when it has discharged its duty. Superstition is therefore the uncertain and carnal worship of an unknown god.

The failure to know God as the fountain of every good also leads to hypocrisy, from which the superstitious are never free. The consciences of the superstitious remind them that the God they seek to worship is their judge; and yet they do not reverence God's majesty as they would in piety, out of love born of knowledge of God's benefits, but rather fear God out of hatred of God's judgment. Since they cannot escape God's judgment directly, they seek to

50. *Inst.* I.iv.1; O.S. III.40.31–32, 41.1–5 (1:47).
51. *Inst.* I.iv.1; O.S. III.41.13–20 (1:47–48).
52. *Inst.* I.iv.3; O.S. III.42.35–38 (1:49).
53. *Inst.* I.xi.8; O.S. III.97.9–11 (1:108).
54. *Inst.* I.xi.9; O.S. III.98.6–8 (1:109).
55. Comm. Ps. 50:14; C.O. 31:501; C.T.S. 9:269.
56. *Inst.* I.iv.3; O.S. III.42.31–35 (1:49).
57. Comm. Eph. 2:12, C.O. 31:501; C.N.T.C. 11:149.

escape it in their religious observances, by appearing to approach the God from whom they are fleeing.[58] Because hypocrites have a carnal understanding of God, they think that God's judgment, like a human's, stops with the outward appearance and does not extend to the heart. As a consequence, they give the appearance of worshiping the God whom they inwardly hate, all the while withholding the obedience of their consciences.

This hypocrisy, according to Calvin, is inevitable; for they alone worship God from the heart who are certain that God is their Father, the fountain of every good. "Indeed, no one gives himself freely and willingly to God's service unless, having tasted his fatherly love, he is drawn to love and worship him in return."[59] Only the knowledge of God arising from piety leads us to reverence God's majesty, for piety knows that the one whom we are to reverence and worship is the fountain of every good.[60] Because of the failure to know God as Father, the ungodly cannot reverence and love God as their Lord and Father, but can only fear him as their judge.[61] Both the carnal conception of God and the extorted fear of God's judgment corrupt the way in which the impious worship God; they do not worship in spirit, but with external ceremonies, nor do they worship in truth, but by withholding the obedience of their heart and conscience.[62] Hypocrisy in particular reveals the impossibility of rightly worshiping God on the basis of the testimony of the conscience alone, for when we know God only as our judge, we cannot willingly reverence and obey God, but must rather fear and flee God, disobeying under the external pretext of obeying.[63]

Unlike Luther, who roots all idolatry in the conscience's portrayal of God to itself (that is, that God is gracious to those who do good works and are aware of no sin in themselves), Calvin roots all idolatry in the carnal conceptions that we form of God on the basis of the taste of divinity we acquire from God's powers depicted in the works of creation. Idolatry for Calvin not only involves a false confidence in our own works—seen both in superstition and in hypocrisy—as it does for Luther, but also involves the carnality of our worship in images and ceremonies, thereby confusing the Creator with creation. Calvin therefore counters idolatry not only by properly depicting the grace of God in Jesus Christ, but also first by properly depicting God as Creator, thereby overcoming the confusion between Creator and creature. Calvin is also much more concerned with externals such as images and ceremonies than was Luther, categorically rejecting them, even apart from false trust of conscience in them, because they directly contradict God's nature as Spirit.

Both superstition and hypocrisy are based on the awareness that there is some god, governor and ruler of the world, who ought to be worshiped. As

58. *Inst.* I.iv.4; O.S. III.44.4–10 (1:50–51).
59. *Inst.* I.v.3; O.S. III.47.24–26 (1:55).
60. *Inst.* I.ii.1; O.S. III.35.5–8 (1:41).
61. *Inst.* I.iv.4; O.S. III.43.13–15 (1:50).
62. *Inst.* I.iv.4; O.S. III.44.4–10 (1:50–51).
63. *Inst.* I.iv.4; O.S. III.44.16–19 (1:51).

bad as these forms of impiety are, the summit of impiety is reached when both of these principles are denied—when God is deprived of judgment both in the governance of the world and in the testimony of the conscience. Calvin calls this state malice (*malitia*), for it represents a deliberate attempt to deprive God of the office of judge in order that the malicious might sin with impunity. "Accordingly, whoever heedlessly indulges himself, his fear of heavenly judgment extinguished, denies that there is a God."[64]

Calvin considers the denial of God's judgment to be atheism; this makes it clear that he is less concerned with theoretical atheism than with practical atheism. Those whose impiety has reached the level of malice may acknowledge the existence of some god or gods—as did the Epicureans—but by depriving God of judgment, they essentially deny God.[65] This is why, according to Calvin, David tells us that the fool says in his heart there is no God: "not that they deprive him of his being, but because, in despoiling him of his judgment and providence, they shut him up idle in heaven."[66] Calvin associates this form of impiety in particular with Epicurus.[67] This kind of impiety goes beyond superstition and hypocrisy in that it not only is unaware of those powers of God that teach us God is the fountain of every good, but it also strips from God those powers that teach us God is our Lord and governor. "Since, then, the glory of God consists in his justice, wisdom, judgment, power, and other attributes, all who deny God to be the governor of the world entirely extinguish, as much as they can, his glory."[68]

The ultimate goal in denying God as governor of the world is to extinguish the awareness of the judgment of God that is the basis of conscience. To deny that God is the judge of good and evil in the governance of the world is concomitantly to deny the distinction between good and evil that our conscience holds before us based on its awareness of God's judgment.[69] Those who make this denial do so in order to indulge in their sin with impunity, with no restraint from the voice of conscience (which even hypocrites feel), and with no remembrance of the fact that we will all have to give an account of our lives before the judgment seat of God.[70] The denial of the powers of God in governing the world has as its inevitable consequence the denial of the judgment of God in the conscience, so that we might sin without restraint.

This means that Calvin sees an affinity between the awareness of God's judgment in the conscience and the awareness of God's providential judgments in the world. Indeed, so close is the relationship that Calvin often seems to state that the knowledge of God's providence is inscribed upon the hearts of all in the same way as the sense of divinity, in order to render the ungodly

---

64. *Inst*. I.iv.2; O.S. III.42.3–6 (1:48).
65. Comm. Ps. 14:1, C.O. 31:136; C.T.S. 8:191.
66. *Inst*. I.iv.2; O.S. III.41.35–36, 42.1–3 (1:48).
67. Comm. Zeph. 1:12, C.O. 44:22; C.T.S. 29:217.
68. Ibid.
69. Ibid.
70. Ibid.

without excuse.[71] "All agree to this truth, that there is some God, and also that no dead idol can do anything, but that the world is governed by the providence and power of God, and further, that safety is to be sought from him."[72]

Calvin goes so far as to call this principle concerning the providence of God a preconception (*prolepsis*), clearly echoing Cicero's use of the term in *De natura deorum*.[73] Thus the knowledge of God's providential governance of the world seems to be given with the awareness that there is some god (*esse aliquem Deum*), which arises out of the conscience as *sensus divinitatis*. The awareness of judgment in the conscience tells us that there is one who judges the world, and the distinction between good and evil in the conscience tells us that there is one who distinguishes between good and evil in the world. To deny one, the way the malicious do, necessarily entails the denial of the other.

God does not allow the malicious denial of his judgment to succeed so entirely that the impious are never made aware of God's judgment and providence. God hales the impious deniers of God unwillingly before the judgment seat, not in order to heal them but to render them without excuse, so that they might feel what they strive so furiously to deny.[74] God does this not so that the malicious might begin to be restrained in their sinning out of fear of the judgment of God (as is the case with hypocrites, at least in their external behavior), but rather so that their denial of the providence of God might be condemned by their own lips. For when God hales the maliciously impious before God's tribunal and presses their consciences by adversity, they are led by the very feeling of nature to cry out to God and to acknowledge the governor whom they seek to deny.[75] Their invocation of God proves that they are not ignorant of the very thing they strive so hard to deny, the providence of God. "For nature in a manner teaches this, that we ought to flee to God when oppressed by evils; and even those who have no fear of God exclaim in their extreme miseries, 'God be merciful to us.' God has thus from the beginning rendered all mortals inexcusable."[76]

Thus God in the governance of the world awakens by adversity the conscience as *sensus divinitatis* and its indelible knowledge of the providence of God. "From this, my present contention is brought out with greater certainty, that a sense of divinity is by nature engraven on human hearts. For necessity forces from the reprobate themselves a confession of it."[77] Fear is not the cause of religion, but the seed of religion is stirred up and awakened by fear.[78]

71. Comm. Jonah 1:5, C.O. 43:213; C.T.S. 28:37.
72. Comm. Jonah 1:6, C.O. 43:215; C.T.S. 28:40.
73. Comm. Jonah 1:6; C.O. 43:217; C.T.S. 28:43.
74. *Inst.* I.iv.2; O.S. III.42.17–24 (1:49).
75. Comm. Ps. 107:6, C.O. 32:137; C.T.S. 11:249.
76. Comm. Lam. 2:18, C.O. 39:566; C.T.S. 21:379.
77. *Inst.* I.iv.4; O.S. III.44.19–27 (1:51); cf. Comm. Jonah 1:5, C.O. 43:212; C.T.S. 28:35–36.
78. Comm. Jonah 1:5, C.O. 43:212; C.T.S. 28:36; cf. Comm. Ps. 14:1, C.O. 31:136; C.T.S. 8:190.

The conscience, which holds before all people the duty to know the God of whose judgment it is aware, has a particularly strong and direct relationship to those powers of God that reveal God's judgment of the world, and it should move from the awareness of these powers to a knowledge of God as the source of those powers.

> This I take to mean that not only does he sustain the universe (as he once founded it) by his boundless might, regulate it by his wisdom, preserve it by his goodness, and especially rule mankind by his righteousness and judgment, bear with it in his mercy, watch over it by his protection; but also that no drop will be found either of wisdom and light, or of righteousness or power or rectitude, or of genuine truth, which does not flow from him, and of which he is not the cause.[79]

The two kinds of impiety Calvin describes, superstition and malice, are based on the failure to know either or both of these levels of the powers of God revealed in creation. Superstition and hypocrisy acknowledge both the awareness of divinity in the conscience and the awareness of the powers of God's governance and judgment of the world; yet because of their dullness and ingratitude, the superstitious fail to know God as the fountain of every good and thus fall into the carnal and hypocritical worship of self-invented idols. The malicious go so far as to deny even those powers of governance that reveal God as the judge of the world, and by so doing seek to extinguish the awareness of God's judgment.

Although both groups are impious, Calvin makes a consistent distinction between the two, suggesting that superstition and hypocrisy are lesser evils than the malicious denial of the providence and judgment of God. "If, however, we were to choose one of two evils, superstition is more tolerable than the gross impiety which obliterates every thought of a God."[80] It would be better, therefore, to leave superstitions in place than to remove them out of contempt for all religion. The superstitious at least acknowledge the command of conscience as the *sensus divinitatis* and are aware of the powers of God that reveal the glory and majesty of God's judgment of the world, while the malicious deny both God's judgment and their own conscience.

The clear suggestion of this distinction is that the superstitious, by retaining some true principles in their worship, can be instructed by the truth about God, whereas the malicious are beyond hope of recovery.[81] The awareness of divinity in the conscience is thus the irreducible foundation of both true and false religion. Only those consciences that have not extinguished the awareness that there is some god whom we ought to worship and adore can be instructed in the true knowledge of God. This is why the sense of divinity is the irreducible first step in the order of right teaching. "If anyone wishes to discuss religion

---

79. *Inst.* I.ii.1; O.S. III.34.30–37 (1:40–41).
80. Comm. Hab. 2:20, C.O. 43:561–62; C.T.S. 29:129.
81. Comm. Zeph. 1:12, C.O. 44:22; C.T.S. 29:218.

in general this will be the first point, that there is some deity to whom worship is due from men."[82]

And yet those who do acknowledge that there is some divinity whom all ought to worship are unable to come to the firm and certain knowledge of God from the testimony of creation, but are left instead with the uncertain and carnal worship of an unknown god.[83] Such ignorance of God is inexcusable, for our conscience itself convicts us of our dullness and ingratitude; and yet it is also incurable, since our taste of the powers of God in nature inevitably leads us to formulate human opinions about God, and opinion humanly conceived is the mother of all errors concerning the knowledge of God. "Human reason, therefore, neither approaches, nor strives toward, nor even takes straight aim at, this truth: to understand who the true God is or what sort of God he wishes to be toward us."[84] Not even communal agreement or ancient tradition can overcome this fundamental deficiency of human opinion regarding the knowledge of God. Idolatry cannot be overcome by human effort, but only by the self-witness of God in the Word and Holy Spirit. "Therefore, since either the custom of the city or the agreement of tradition is too weak and frail a bond of piety to follow in worshipping God, it remains for God to give witness of himself from heaven."[85]

The Cold and Faint Awareness of Sin

The conscience as the awareness of divine judgment gives rise both to the sense of divinity, which should lead us to knowledge of God, and to the distinction between good and evil, which should lead us to knowledge of ourselves. "There are two main parts in that light which yet remains in corrupt nature. Some seed of religion is sown in all: and also, the distinction between good and evil is engraven in their consciences."[86] The distinction between good and evil arises in the conscience in response to the awareness of God's judgment, and this distinction forms the standard by which we are rendered either accused or excused before God's judgment seat. This means that the distinction between good and evil that the conscience makes in response to God's judgment should in some way correspond to the distinction between good and evil that God makes in the law, which is the standard by which God judges us.

---

82. Comm. Acts 17:24, C.O. 48:410; C.N.T.C. 7:112. It is this point that Emil Brunner detected in the theology of Calvin and refused to surrender in light of Barth's criticism. See *The Christian Doctrine of the Church, Faith, and the Consummation*, trans. David Cairns (Philadelphia: Westminster, 1960), pp. 256–58.

83. *Inst.* I.v.12; O.S. III.57.21–24. It is this point that Karl Barth detected in Calvin and refused to surrender in light of Brunner's attempt to develop a "natural theology" out of Calvin. Brunner eventually clarified his position on natural theology, bringing it much closer to Calvin and Barth. See *The Christian Doctrine of God*, trans. Olive Wyon (Philadelphia: Westminster, 1949).

84. *Inst.* II.ii.18; O.S. III.261.10–15 (1:277–78).

85. *Inst.* I.v.13; O.S. III.58.32–34 (1:68).

86. Comm. John 1:5, C.O. 47:6; C.N.T.C. 4:12.

The distinction the conscience makes between good and evil is the basis of what Calvin means by natural law. "This would not be a bad definition: natural law is that apprehension of conscience which distinguishes sufficiently between just and unjust, and which deprives men of the excuse of ignorance, while it proves them guilty by their own testimony."[87] Calvin bases his understanding of conscience as natural law on Rom. 2:14-15, which he interprets as meaning that the Gentiles who are without the revealed law of God are condemned by the testimony of their own conscience, which stands in the place of the revealed law of God in rendering them without excusing ignorance. "The purpose of the natural law, therefore, is to render man inexcusable."[88]

If the natural law is to render the ungodly without excuse, then it must in some sense assert the same things as the revealed law of God.[89] Yet it is not necessary for the natural law to correspond to the law of God in all respects. "It is more than enough if their understanding extends so far that evasion becomes impossible for them, and they, convicted by the witness of their own conscience, begin even now to tremble before God's judgment seat."[90]

The deficiencies of the natural law are especially evident when it comes to the first table of the Decalogue, which has to do with the lawful worship of God. Even though the conscience bears witness to us that there is some god who ought to be worshiped, it utterly fails to be instructed either as to who God is or how God wants to be worshiped. "But man is so shrouded in the darkness of errors that he hardly begins to grasp through this natural law what worship is acceptable to God."[91] If we try to measure the natural law of conscience by the first table of the Ten Commandments, we find a complete lack of correspondence. "What soul, relying upon natural perception, ever had an inkling that the lawful worship of God consisted in these and like matters?"[92] Moreover, the impious are already convinced that they know who the deity is and how that deity wishes to be worshiped, so that they are not only ignorant of the first table of the law, but actively deny its truth when they hear it; "for they could never be persuaded that what the law prescribes concerning worship is the truth."[93] There is a complete contradiction between the worship of God based on the natural law and the worship of God presented in the law of God. Such a contradiction is attested by Calvin in his own life when he speaks of his tenacious resistance to the gospel based on his adherence to the superstition in which he had been raised.[94]

The natural law corresponds much more closely to the second table of the law, which applies more directly to the governance of human society.[95] Thus,

87. *Inst.* II.ii.22; O.S. III.265.7–11 (1:282).
88. *Inst.* II.ii.22; O.S. III.265.1–7 (1:281–82).
89. *Inst.* II.viii.1; O.S. III.344.11–17 (1:367–68).
90. *Inst.* II.ii.24; O.S. III.266.10–16 (1:283).
91. *Inst.* II.viii.1; O.S. III.344.17–20 (1:368).
92. *Inst.* II.ii.24; O.S. III.266.17–24 (1:283).
93. *Inst.* II.ii.24; O.S. III.266.24–30 (1:283–84).
94. Comm. Ps. Preface, C.O. 31:21; C.T.S. 8:xl.
95. *Inst.* II.ii.24; O.S. III.267.1–3 (1:284).

in the laws of all nations the same things are prohibited on the basis of natural law as are prohibited in the second table. "For together with one voice, they pronounced punishment against those crimes which God's eternal law has condemned, namely, murder, theft, adultery, and false witness."[96] Given this correspondence, Calvin can use this aspect of the natural law not only in a negative way, to remove the pretext of excusing ignorance and to condemn the ungodly by the witness of their conscience, but also in a positive way, by appealing to the natural law of conscience as both the source and the norm of all laws in the human community. "Hence, this equity alone must be the goal and rule and limit of all laws."[97]

Unlike Luther, however, Calvin does not primarily relate either the knowledge of the natural law, or the judgment of all human laws by the natural law, to the learned, who then are to teach and govern others. Rather, all people are given a knowledge of the natural law, and all people are given both the ability and the responsibility to test the correspondence between human laws and natural law. "Hence no man is to be found who does not understand that every sort of human organization must be regulated by laws, and who does not comprehend the principles of those laws."[98] The universality of the principles of equity is not compromised by the fact that disputes arise between people concerning individual laws, for such disputes could neither occur nor be arbitrated were the principles of equity not engraved in the minds and consciences of all.

Thus, unlike Luther, who thought that the natural law was only discerned by those whom God raised up as rulers and teachers, Calvin has a universal conception of both the understanding of the natural law and the ability of people to test all human law by this criterion. If Luther's view of the natural law might be conceived of as a lecture by a few to the many, Calvin's might be conceived of as an ongoing discussion and conversation among all. Not all are called to rule, but all are called to test the laws of rulers and are given the criterion by which to do so. It might well be that Calvin's famous statement concerning "nefarious perfidy" has its roots in this more universal distribution of the natural law in its positive political use.

The positive political use of the natural law of conscience should not, however, blind us to the fact that Calvin sees a "failure to endure" even in this arena. Calvin consistently singles out two areas in which the natural law is deficient. First, according to the perception of natural law, it is shameful to bear domination or oppression with patience, but is instead the mark of a moral and free person to cast off oppression and to avenge wrongdoing.[99] The natural law is not only ignorant of, but actually contradicts, the law of God

---

96. *Inst.* IV.xx.16; O.S. V.488.22–26 (2:1504–5).
97. *Inst.* IV.xx.16; O.S. V.488.3–12 (2:1504).
98. *Inst.* II.ii.13; O.S. III.256.34–39, 257.1–2 (1:272). See Josef Bohatec, *Calvin und das Recht* (Feudingen in Westfalen: Buchdruckerei G.m.b.H., 1934), esp. pp. 99–131.
99. *Inst.* II.ii.24; O.S. III.267.4–10 (1:284).

with regard to the patient suffering of evil. Second, the natural law is utterly blind to the sin of concupiscence. "But in all our keeping of the law we quite fail to take our concupiscence into account."[100] The philosophers only called "vices" those enticements to gross and outward sins, and took no account of desires that gently tickle the mind without our consent and with no external manifestation.

As will be seen, the failure of the natural law in both of these areas, especially the second, has profound effects with regard to our ability to know ourselves on the basis of the natural law. However, even this blindness is not excusable, "since it will not be right for them to covet what they know it is wrong for them to do."[101]

The conscience distinguishes between good and evil so that it might hold before us the good we ought to do and the evil we ought to avoid.[102] This means that the conscience functions in both an antecedent and a consequent way: it sets forth what we ought to do and also judges what we have done. "Notice Paul's scholarly definition of conscience—there are, he says, some arguments [rationes] which we adopt to defend a right course of action which we have taken, while on the other hand there are others which accuse and convict us of our evil deeds."[103] Calvin, like Luther, emphasizes the consequent judgment of conscience, yet neither he nor Luther ignores the antecedent judgment. One might relate the antecedent to the consequent in this way: precisely because our conscience will develop arguments to defend good actions and accuse and convict evil ones, and because these arguments will render us acquitted or convicted before God, we should follow the good the conscience sets before us, and shun evil.

According to Calvin, the antecedent judgment of the conscience should function in all people either as a fountain of modesty or at least as a check on sinning. We cannot decide to undertake an evil or sinful action without feeling the restraining interrogation of conscience. "When any man is tempted to do what is sinful, his conscience secretly asks him, what are you doing?"[104] Even the most obstinate and tenacious of sinners cannot avoid this interrogation.[105] Since the natural law of conscience tells us that murder, extortion, robbery, whoredom, deceit, and perjury are vices to be avoided, whenever we are tempted to commit one of these actions, our conscience will demand an account of how the action squares with its distinction between good and evil.

However, the antecedent judgment or interrogation of conscience is not sufficient to restrain the sinner's action: "for whenever men are prompted to sin by the lust of the flesh, they at first pause, and feel that something within

100. *Inst.* II.ii.24; O.S. III.267.11–16 (1:284).
101. Comm. Rom. 1:15, *Commentarius*, p. 46; C.N.T.C. 8:48–49.
102. Comm. Rom. 1:15, *Commentarius*, p. 46; C.N.T.C. 8:49.
103. Ibid.
104. Comm. Isa. 5:18, C.O. 36:117; C.T.S. 13:183.
105. Comm. Isa. 44:11, C.O. 37:113; C.T.S. 15:371.

restrains them, which would certainly keep them back, if they did not rush forward with opposing violence, and break through all opposition."[106] The most common way in which this happens, according to Calvin, is that sinners impose on their conscience, through the enticement of Satan, a false image of evil; they refuse to acknowledge sin as sin. " 'This is a trivial fault,' they say. 'Fornication is a mere game to God. Under the law of Grace God is not so cruel.' "[107] Sinners may even seek to excuse their sins by appeal to the providence of God.[108] The latter tactic was adopted by Calvin's opponents in Geneva, the Libertines, who used the doctrine of providence as a way of avoiding the distinction between good and evil in the conscience. "We have said that if one attributes everything to God . . . and says that man does nothing, then it will no longer be a matter of making conscience of anything."[109]

We may also overcome the antecedent judgment of conscience by imposing on the conscience a false image of the good, so that we can commit what is in fact a sinful action with the intention of pursuing the good. According to Calvin, this false image is imposed when we move from a general law to a particular course of action.[110] The illusory application of the general to the particular pertains to the conscience's apprehension of both tables of the law. Before his conversion, the apostle Paul knew of the general principle that God is to be worshiped, but he erred when it came to applying that principle to a particular action. Thus, out of thoughtless zeal for the law, he persecuted the church of Christ. "This is the position of those who deceive themselves with a good intention, as they call it, but with what is in fact a foolish fancy."[111]

The same false intention can arise for actions opposed to the general precepts of the second table. "In reply to the general question, every man will affirm that murder is evil. But he who is plotting the death of an enemy contemplates murder as something good. . . . Herein is man's ignorance: when he comes to a particular case, he forgets the general principle that he has just laid down."[112] This form of ignorance is closely related to hypocrisy for Calvin, for sinners allow themselves to do something in particular that they would generally condemn (especially in others). The ability of the conscience to be deceived by a good intention is one reason why Calvin places so much importance on the third use of the law and the necessity of the Holy Spirit in guiding the lives of the godly. "For we know all too well by experience how often we fall despite our good intention."[113]

The most drastic and dangerous way in which the antecedent judgment of conscience is overridden takes place when the sinner knowingly consents to

---

106. Comm. Isa. 5:18, C.O. 36:117; C.T.S. 13:183.
107. Comm. Eph. 5:6, C.O. 51:216; C.N.T.C. 11:198.
108. Comm. 1 Cor. 6:10, C.O. 49:393; C.N.T.C. 9:125.
109. C.O. 7:192; *Treatises Against the Anabaptists and Against the Libertines*, trans. Benjamin W. Farley (Grand Rapids, Mich.: Baker Book House, 1982), p. 250.
110. *Inst.* II.ii.23; O.S. III.265.21–24 (1:282).
111. Comm. 1 Cor. 2:8, C.O. 49:338–39; C.N.T.C. 9:55.
112. *Inst.* II.ii.23, O.S. III.265.24–30 (1:282).
113. *Inst.* II.ii.25; O.S. III.267.23–27 (1:284).

the urging of sin despite the protests of conscience, without imposing on the conscience any false conception of good and evil. "Out of such a disposition of mind come statements like this: 'I see what is better and approve of it, but I follow the worse.' "[114] Calvin calls this state of mind malice (*malitia*) and claims that it is more like madness than mere ignorance.[115] "Sometimes malice gets the upper hand so that, despite the protests of conscience, a man rushes into such wickedness with something like fury."[116]

Malice manifests a dangerous advance of sin beyond hypocrisy, and Calvin often associates it with reprobation. The danger of such malicious violation of the protests of conscience is that it will extinguish both the antecedent and the consequent judgment of conscience. Such a depraved state of mind existed in the people of Sodom and the scribes and Pharisees who crucified Christ, according to Calvin, and a similar danger lay in the teachings of the Libertines.[117] Calvin did not think that either malice or the extinguishing of the sense of good and evil was at all common, but they represent the furthest extreme of the overriding of the restraint of conscience.

Even though hypocrisy and malice prevent the interrogation of conscience from restraining sin, such ignorance does not excuse sin, as Plato thought; such ignorance of the good is itself the consequence of sin. "Wickedness and ignorance are therefore closely connected, but the connection is of such a nature that ignorance proceeds from the sinful disposition of mind."[118] The ignorance that is the condition for sinful actions is itself the result of sinful desires. "It is just this, that after God has given us a good rule, we are moved by ambition, hatred, pride, avarice. This is how everything is perverted."[119] Calvin singles out the desires of pride and ambition as the most common ways in which the antecedent judgment of conscience is perverted. "Ambition, like a violent wind, always carries men along so that they cannot stop themselves; hence it is that neither the testimony of conscience nor the judgment of God has much weight in them."[120]

Because the ignorance that makes sinful actions possible is itself the result of sinful desires, the conscience that is overridden by ignorance in its antecedent judgment will nonetheless render such ignorance culpable in its consequent judgment. "Besides, everyone is sufficiently, and more than sufficiently convinced by his own conscience, that his ignorance is closely connected with pride and indolence, and therefore voluntary."[121] The natural law of the conscience is not sufficient to guide our lives aright, given the

114. *Inst.* II.ii.23; O.S. III.265.31–35, 266.1 (1:282–83).
115. Comm. 1 Cor. 2:8, C.O. 49:338–39; C.N.T.C. 9:55.
116. Ibid.; cf. Comm. 1 Tim. 1:13, C.O. 52:258–59; C.N.T.C. 10:197.
117. Comm. Gen. 8:21, C.O. 23:260; C.T.S. 1:484.
118. Comm. Isa. 27:11, C.O. 27:11, C.O. 36:458; C.T.S. 14:263.
119. Sermon Job 16:1–9, C.O. 34:8–9; *Sermons from Job*, p. 98.
120. Comm. Jer. 20:12, C.O. 38:350; C.T.S. 19:41; cf. Comm. Dan. 6:14, C.O. 41:15–16; C.T.S. 24:368.
121. Comm. Deut. 29:4, C.O. 24:243; C.T.S. 3:289–90.

ignorance under which we labor, but it is sufficient to take away excusing ignorance, to make us aware of our sin, and to condemn us by our own testimony when we sin.[122]

The sufficiency of the consequent judgment of conscience is the purpose of the natural law, "that apprehension of the conscience which distinguishes sufficiently between just and unjust, and which deprives men of the excuse of ignorance, while it proves them guilty by their own testimony."[123] Although the ungodly wish to evade their ability to distinguish between good and evil, not even the most hardened sinner can evade being condemned by the testimony of conscience before the judgment seat of God. The pagans themselves give testimony to this phenomenon in the proverb that "Conscience is like a thousand witnesses."[124] "The eloquence, therefore, of the whole world will avail nothing to deliver those from condemnation, whose own conscience has become the judge to compel them to confess their fault."[125] Thus, Calvin appeals directly to the consciences of the ungodly, either to warrant their own voluntary complicity in the fall of Adam, their inability to blame the providence of God for their sin, or their inability to call God's decree of reprobation unjust.[126]

The awareness of sin that inevitably arises from the consequent judgment of conscience should lead us to descend within ourselves, in light of our awareness of divine judgment and the law of God, in order to humble ourselves and confess our sinfulness to God. However, this does not in fact happen, even though the consciences of the ungodly hold them guilty before God. Instead, they are either blinded by hypocrisy and pride, which keep them from coming to a serious awareness of their sin, or are filled with carnal security and contempt for God so that they are kept from a serious awareness of God's judgment.[127] The first error leads them to think that besides being sinners they also have the ability to merit the grace of God, while the second error leads them to think that God can be rendered merciful by self-invented expiations for sin.[128]

Even though we are aware of our sins by the accusing testimony of conscience, we are not aware of our inability to do anything but sin, because of our ignorance of the sin of concupiscence, which gives birth to all actual sins; thus we think that the solution lies not in the grace of repentance given by Christ, but in our own efforts to do good and shun evil.[129] Although we are aware that the wrath of God lies upon sinners before God's judgment seat,

---

122. Comm. 1 Pet. 1:14, C.O. 53:221–22; C.N.T.C. 12:244–45; Comm. Gen. 26:10, C.O. 23:261; C.T.S. 2:63; Comm. Ezek. 11:19–20, C.O. 40:246; C.T.S. 22:376.
123. *Inst.* II.ii.22; O.S. III.265.8–11 (1:282); cf. *Inst.* II.ii.24, O.S. III.266.11–16 (1:283).
124. Comm. Gen. 4:11, C.O. 23:89–90; C.T.S. 1:201–2.
125. Comm. Gen. 3:7, C.O. 23:63; C.T.S. 1:157.
126. Comm. Jer. 27:10, C.O. 38:550; C.T.S. 19:366.
127. Comm. Ps. 32:1, C.O. 31:314–15; C.T.S. 8:522–23.
128. Ibid.
129. *Inst.* II.i.3; O.S. III.230.20–23 (1:243).

we are not aware that the wrath of God can only be appeased by the death of the Son on the cross. Instead we think we can propitiate God with our imaginary satisfactions.[130] "The first error to lead them away from the right way was, that they tried to win the pardon which is freely offered, and received by faith alone. Thereafter countless kinds of propitiations were invented, from which satisfaction was made to God."[131]

This twofold error leads neither to genuine repentance nor to true forgiveness, but rather to the conviction that we can shield ourselves from the wrath of God by our self-chosen expiations so that we might wallow in our sins with impunity. In this way, the false repentance and expiation for sin based on the accusing testimony of the conscience lead back to and reinforce the false worship of God based on the awareness of divinity from the testimony of the conscience and the taste of divinity from the testimony of creation.[132]

In response to the awareness of sin and the judgment of God disclosed by the testimony of the conscience, sinners seek to offer imaginary expiations to God so that they may continue to sin with impunity. This is not to say that Calvin thinks that the offering of sacrifices before the coming of Christ was inherently ungodly and illusory. On the contrary, God set forth the sacrifice of Christ under the shadow of the type of sacrifice Israel was commanded to perform in the law of Moses, so that the faithful might be made aware of the judgment of death that lay on their sins and have faith in the future once-for-all sacrifice of Christ. The Gentiles, according to Calvin, imitated the outward form of Israelite sacrifices but did not at all understand their meaning.[133]

If sacrifices are offered in contrast to the sacrifice of Christ, they are offered unreasonably; but there is nothing unreasonable per se about sacrifices. "There is, therefore, nothing absurd in submitting to the eyes of sinners the judgment of death which they deserve, in order that, descending into themselves, they may begin seriously to abominate the sin in which they fondly indulged themselves."[134] Sacrifices were not meant to allow us to indulge in sins safe from the judgment of God, but were meant to cause us to descend into ourselves (*in se descendere*) to abhor our sin that deserves death, and thereby to seek the grace of forgiveness offered in the once-for-all sacrifice of Christ. Yet even if the Gentiles were ignorant of this aspect of the meaning of their sacrifices, they were still aware that one could not offer sacrifice for sin without a sincere heart. Even the heathen knew that they could not offer sacrifice with the intention of remaining in sin, although their hypocrisy led them to do just that.[135]

130. Comm. John 1:29, C.O. 47:26; C.N.T.C. 4:32–33.
131. Comm. Acts 10:43, C.O. 48:249; C.N.T.C. 6:315.
132. *Inst.* I.iv.4; O.S. III.43.33, 44.1–14 (1:50–51). Calvin is thinking especially of the sacrifice of the Roman mass: cf. Comm. Jonah 1:7, C.O. 43:218–19; C.T.S. 28:46; *Inst.* IV.xviii.15; O.S. V.430.17–22 (2:1443).
133. Comm. Exod. 29:38, C.O. 24:489; C.T.S. 4:293–94.
134. Comm. Exod. 29:38, C.O. 24:489; C.T.S. 4:294.
135. Comm. Ps. 50:16, C.O. 24:114; C.T.S. 9:274.

Thus the condemning testimony of conscience does not cause us to descend into ourselves to confess our sin, nor does it cause us to flee to the twofold grace set forth in Christ. Instead, it is perverted by hypocrisy, which has neither a serious awareness of sin nor of the judgment and wrath of God, and which therefore offers expiations in the hopes of indulging in sin with impunity.

At this point several things become clearer: the similarities and differences between Calvin and Luther on the relationship between the false worship of God that arises out of the testimony of the conscience, as well as one of the fundamental reasons Calvin begins his discussion of the twofold grace of Christ with repentance before moving to justification.

Both Luther and Calvin claim that the knowledge of self that arises from the testimony of the conscience renders the ungodly guilty of their sins before the judgment seat of God. Yet both also insist that the testimony of the conscience is unable to humble pride and break through hypocrisy so that the ungodly might know not only that they sin, but that they are *sinners*. Instead, both Luther and Calvin claim that convicted sinners still think they have enough strength of free will to counter their sin with good works in order to merit the grace and favor of God. For Luther, this is the sum and substance of all idolatry: the conviction that God is a judge who must be made gracious to us by our doing good works of the law, works that alone can remove the condemning testimony of the conscience. This understanding of idolatry accounts for Luther's primary emphasis on justification over sanctification; for even the conscience of believers will always tempt them, especially in the midst of tribulation (*Anfechtung*), into believing that God is a judge who can only be placated by good works.

While Calvin agrees that one of the fundamental errors arising out of the false knowledge of self is the belief that we have the ability to do what we ought to do and thereby merit the favor of God, he adds another dimension not as prominent in Luther—namely, that we seek to placate God's judgment not so much by doing good works as by offering self-invented ceremonies and sacrifices of expiation so that we might indulge in our sins with a peaceful conscience.

Just as Luther saw the exhortation to attain the favor of God by good works to be constitutive of the papacy, Calvin saw the desire to escape the judgment of God by ceremonies and sacrifices to be constitutive of the papacy. "For that vast chaos of ceremonies is indeed 'a den of robbers' . . . because hypocrites, hiding behind their cover, are confident that they are at liberty to do anything they like with impunity."[136] And just as Luther's version of the religion of conscience emerged in his autobiographical account of his experience under the papacy before his conversion, so also Calvin's version of the false and hypocritical knowledge of self is present in his account (whether or not it can

---

136. *De Scandalis*, O.S. II.199; *Concerning Scandals*, trans. John W. Fraser (Grand Rapids, Mich.: Wm. B. Eerdmans, 1978), p. 58.

be taken as genuinely autobiographical; I think it can) of the person trapped in the papacy before being freed by the gospel. "When, however, I had performed all these things, though I had some intervals of quiet, I was still far off from true peace of conscience; for, whenever I descended into myself, or raised my mind to thee, extreme terror seized me—terror which no expiations nor satisfactions could cure."[137]

For Luther, the sinner made aware by the conscience of sin and the judgment of God seeks to overcome both by doing works of the law; for Calvin, the same awareness of conscience leads the sinner to offer false expiations to God in order to sin with impunity. This accounts for the fundamental agreement between Luther and Calvin concerning faith in the priestly work of Christ as being the only basis of our justification and of our freedom from the wrath of God, as well as for Calvin's consistent emphasis on repentance and for his putting repentance before justification in discussing the twofold grace of Christ in the 1559 *Institutes*. Hypocrisy for Luther leads us to seek to justify ourselves before God on the basis of good works; hypocrisy for Calvin leads us to placate God with expiations and sacrifices so that we might continue to indulge in sin.

It is clear, therefore, that even though the conscience's distinction between good and evil is sufficient to condemn all people of their sin and make them aware of the judgment of God, the testimony of the conscience is not able to crush the self-love and pride of sinners so that they truly descend into themselves to attain a serious awareness of the judgment of God.[138] Both the malicious and the hypocritical fail to examine themselves before the judgment of God: the malicious, by scoffing at the judgment of God itself; the hypocritical, by relying on expiations to ward off God's judgment. "The wicked are, indeed, conscious to themselves of their guilt, but still they delight in their wickedness, harden themselves in their impudence, and laugh at threatenings. . . . As for hypocrites, if their conscience at any time stings them, they soothe their pain with ineffectual remedies."[139]

The malicious represent the worst form of escape from judgment, since they seek to pacify their consciences by directly scoffing at the judgment of God, thereby denying as much as in their power the existence of God.[140] The nethermost limit of the denial of God's judgment happens when the wicked succeed in extinguishing all sense of sin and divine judgment in their consciences.[141] Calvin thought that such depravity was (fortunately) quite rare. By far the most common and pervasive avoidance of sin and judgment is hypocrisy, which does not explicitly deny either its sin or the judgment of

137. *Responsio ad Sadoleti Epistolam*, C.O. 5:412; *A Reformation Debate*, ed. John C. Olin (Grand Rapids, Mich.: Baker Book House, 1976), p. 88.
138. Comm. Ps. 32:2, C.O. 31:317; C.T.S. 8:527.
139. Comm. Ps. 32:2, C.O. 31:317; C.T.S. 8:526–27.
140. Comm. Isa. 57:21, C.O. 37:321–22; C.T.S. 16:221.
141. Comm. Eph. 4:19, C.O. 51:206; C.N.T.C. 11:188.

God, but avoids a true awareness of either by placing false coverings over itself so as to attain peace of conscience.[142]

Although the testimony of conscience can give us no more than a "cold and faint knowledge of sin,"[143] the awareness of sin and judgment that remains in the conscience keeps us from attaining our goal of pacifying the conscience by avoiding the judgment of God. "That is why God awakens the sleeping consciences, . . . so that in spite of themselves they must recognize their poverty and feel their vices, although they wish to sleep in them."[144] All seek to attain peace, either by stupefying their consciences and denying the judgment of God, or by putting the judgment of God at bay with propitiatory sacrifices; and yet the conscience can at any time be awakened by God, so that these efforts to attain peace can never succeed. We cannot have peace with God by avoiding our sinfulness and the judgment of God. We cannot have God as our Father if we will not allow God to be our Lord and judge.

The conscience of the ungodly therefore cannot be successfully pacified, nor can it lead to genuine repentance. The sinner should understand all compunctions of conscience as a summons to the judgment seat of God. "For that interior sense by which we are convicted of sin is the peculiar judgment-seat of God, whereby he exercises his jurisdiction."[145] Such compunctions are nothing other than incentives to repentance; and yet, instead of submitting to the judgment of God in acknowledgment of our sin, we boldly rebel against that judgment. "Hence it appears how great is the depravity of the human mind; since, when convicted and condemned by our own conscience, we still do not cease either to mock, or to rage against our Judge."[146]

Even though we suffer pangs of conscience, we do not as a consequence turn away in abhorrence from our sin to love and desire justice instead, which constitutes true repentance; we wish to keep on sinning, and thus resist the compunctions of conscience and judgment of God.[147] The stings of conscience in the ungodly do not represent signs of repentance, but rather the pain that God makes them bear for loving sin and hating righteousness.[148] Hypocrites may feign repentance during such awakenings of conscience to the judgment and wrath of God, but when the awareness passes, they think they have escaped the judgment of God and thus turn back to their pride and rebellion against God.[149] They never attain to a genuine awareness of the judgment of God, nor do they descend into themselves in light of that judgment to acknowledge their sin and humble their pride.[150]

---

142. Comm. Gen. 3:7, C.O. 23:64; C.T.S. 1:159.
143. Ibid.
144. Sermon Matt. 27:11–26, C.O. 46:887–901; *Sermons on the Saving Work of Christ*, trans. Leroy Nixon (Grand Rapids, Mich.: Baker Book House, 1980), pp. 128–29.
145. Comm. Gen. 4:9, C.O. 23:91–92; C.T.S. 1:205–6.
146. Ibid.
147. Comm. Matt. 27:3, C.O. 45:754; C.N.T.C. 3:175.
148. Comm. Rom. 7:15, *Commentarius*, p. 148; C.N.T.C. 8:148.
149. Comm. Exod. 8:8, C.O. 24:98–99; C.T.S. 3:161.
150. Comm. Ezek. 18:30, C.O. 40:454; C.T.S. 23:259.

God therefore awakens the consciences of the ungodly, not in order to lead them to repentance, but to render them without excuse by arousing the condemning testimony of the conscience. This is not only true when God in his providence afflicts the ungodly, it is even true when God encounters them with the Word. Even though the ungodly secretly despise the Word of God, when they hear it they cannot help but be made aware of its power, and their rage against the Word is forced into the open. This is necessary so that hypocrisy may be exposed. Hypocrites pretend to worship the God from whom they flee, but when they hear the Word of God they cannot help but openly blaspheme God. In this way the Word of God discloses the thoughts of many hearts (Luke 2:35). "But the truth is that, when men's minds are in Satan's grip, if they are being pressed by the Word, impiety is bound to break out."[151]

Even though this is an accidental property of the Word of God and not its proper function, it is necessary in order to bring hypocrisy into the open. The Word of God strikes the consciences of the reprobate and enrages them, because "they feel that they are being pressed by their Judge."[152] Thus not all who hear the Word of God are improved by it; indeed, the reprobate are in fact made more obstinate and rebellious. According to Calvin, this reaction is inevitable when the Word is proclaimed outwardly without the inward testimony of the Holy Spirit.[153] Without the Holy Spirit, the Word of God only removes all excusing ignorance of God by awakening the condemning judgment of conscience.[154] It does not, however, lead us to repentance and faith, but causes our impiety and hatred of God to erupt all the more. "The Word of God is a seal to our hearts, and is a hot iron that wounds the conscience of bad men, so that their impiety burns more strongly."[155] This suggests that Calvin will be much more explicit about the relationship of the Holy Spirit to the revelation of the law than was Luther; for without the Holy Spirit, the Word of God leads the ungodly further and further away from God.

There is yet another reason why the preaching of the Word cannot of itself lead to repentance or faith: if the Word of God makes the consciences of the ungodly feel that they are being pressed by their judge, how can they help but flee from God when all they are aware of is wrath? The conscience, even when awakened by God, can by definition only make us aware of the judgment of God, and sinners have no choice but to flee from that judgment. "Indeed, the more grievously their conscience pricks them, the more they rage against God and show their anger to Him. They want access to be given to them by God, but because they find nothing but His wrath they flee from His sight."[156] It has already been seen how the ungodly want God to be favorable to them

---

151. Comm. Acts 7:54, C.O. 48:166; C.N.T.C. 6:216.
152. Comm. Acts 5:33, C.O. 48:112; C.N.T.C. 6:151.
153. Comm. Matt. 13:14, C.O. 45:360; C.N.T.C. 2:67.
154. Comm Ezek. 2:3, C.O. 40:65; C.T.S. 22:113.
155. Comm. Matt. 21:45, C.O. 45:598; C.N.T.C. 3:23.
156. Comm. Heb. 12:17, C.O. 55:181; C.N.T.C. 12:198.

without their acknowledging God as their judge; Calvin is also aware that we cannot allow ourselves to submit to the judgment of God unless we know that God is favorable to us.

Just as we cannot have God as our Father without knowing God as our Lord and judge, so also we cannot have God as our Lord and judge without also knowing God as our Father. For "no obstacle can be greater or more destructive than when we think that God is irreconcilable."[157] The awakening of the conscience therefore cannot lead to repentance and conversion to God, for the conscience can only know God as a judge. The failure to know God as Father from the testimony of the world and from a sense of God's powers leaves the conscience no choice but to know God as judge, and the awakening of such a conscience can only lead to the false repentance of a Cain or Judas.[158] We are only converted to God, and only truly acknowledge our sin, when we are aware of the mercy of God.[159] Without the simultaneous awareness of God's mercy, the awareness of sin and judgment in the conscience leads only to rebellion against God. "Almost all have their consciences burdened with guilt, and having never experienced the power of divine grace which might lead them to betake themselves to it, either proudly gnaw at the bit or fill the air with unavailing complaints, or, giving way to desperation, faint under their afflictions."[160]

This point suggests that Calvin will explicitly deal with the problematic relationships of law and gospel that we saw in Luther. Indeed, such statements by Calvin may give a strong indication of why his discussion of repentance *follows* his discussion of faith in the 1559 *Institutes*. "This voluntary confession is always conjoined with faith; for otherwise the sinner will continuously seek lurking places where he may hide himself from God."[161] The failure to know God as Father and Lord through the awareness of the powers of God in creation ultimately means that the knowledge of ourselves as sinners under judgment will not lead to repentance. Instead, the false knowledge of self leads back into and reinforces the false knowledge of God. A true knowledge either of God or of ourselves cannot come from the testimony of creation or the testimony of conscience; it must come from God's testimony in the Word of Scripture through the Holy Spirit.

157. Comm. Isa. 55:9, C.O. 37:290; C.T.S. 16:169.
158. Comm. Ps. 32:5, C.O. 31:319–20; C.T.S. 8:530–31.
159. Comm. Isa. 55:9, C.O. 37:290; C.T.S. 16:170.
160. Comm. Ps. 28:1, C.O. 31:280; C.T.S. 8:465.
161. Comm. Ps. 32:5, C.O. 31:319–20; C.T.S. 8:530–31.

7

CREATED TO BE CHILDREN
OF THE FATHER

As the previous chapter explained, the false knowledge of self that arises out of the condemning testimony of the conscience directly reinforces the false knowledge of God derived from the taste of divinity provided by the universe. The attempt of hypocrites to propitiate the wrath of God by sacrifices reinforces the superstitious worship that arises out of the carnal conception of God, while the attempt to merit the favor of God by works reinforces the worship of hypocrites, who flee the God whom they outwardly profess to approach. The attempt of the wicked to deny the condemning testimony of conscience directly reinforces the malicious denial that there is some god who ought to be worshiped.

In light of this mutual reinforcement of the false knowledge of God and self, the inability to know God as Lord and Father based on awareness of the powers of God manifested in creation makes it impossible for those made aware of their sins and the condemning judgment of God to repent. Sinners flee from God when they know God as judge and not also as Father. Thus, it is necessary for God to bear witness to himself in Scripture, so that we might know the Creator as Father and Lord, in distinction from all false gods. And yet our inability to know God as Father from the testimony of creation is rooted in our inability to know ourselves as children of God. It is our sin, of which we are made at least dimly aware by the condemning judgment of conscience, that is the basis of our inability to know God as Father in creation, and that therefore leads to idolatry. In creation itself not only is God's favor toward us set forth, but also God's curse against sin.[1] One of the reasons Calvin begins the *Institutes* with the knowledge of God the Creator is to show that it is solely because of our sin that we cannot know God as Father from creation, making it necessary for God to send Jesus Christ the Mediator. Thus, even the testimony of Scripture to God the Father as Creator would not make it possible for sinners to know God, unless God revealed himself as Father not only to creatures but also to *sinful* creatures.[2]

---

1. *Inst.* II.vi.1; O.S. III.320.19–26 (1:341).
2. *Inst.* II.vi.1; O.S. III.320.10–13 (1:341).

Both of these aspects of the knowledge of God the Creator will be explored in this section—the setting forth of God the Father as Creator by Scripture, in order to distinguish God from idols; and the setting forth of our sin (in Adam) as being the sole cause of our inability to know God as Father even in light of the scriptural witness to the Creator. The immediate transition, however, will be from the false knowledge of God arising out of the conscience as awareness of divinity (*sensus divinitatis*) to the true knowledge of God the Creator based on the witness God bears in Scripture through the Holy Spirit.

The conscience's sense of divinity makes us aware that there is some deity who is to be worshiped, and therefore holds before us our duty to know with certainty who God is and what sort of God we are to worship. In order to make this knowledge of God possible, God manifests himself in creation so that we might come to the knowledge of God from our awareness of God's powers. Yet we do not come thereby to a knowledge of the true God, but rather dream up idols rooted in human opinions about divinity arising from the task of divinity that we derive from the universe.

This failure to know who God is (that is, the Lord as Father, the fountain of all good [*fons omnium bonorum*]) leads to a concomitant failure to know what the nature of God is (that is, Spirit), for human opinion cannot help but form a carnal conception of God, thereby confusing the Creator with creation. At best, such false knowledge of God leads to superstitious and hypocritical worship; at worst, it leads to the malicious denial of God's providential governance of the earth and judgment of humans. Although Calvin views superstition as a lesser evil than atheism, because it does not deny the testimony of conscience that there is some deity whom all ought to worship and adore, superstition leads further away from God. "Human reason, therefore, neither approaches, nor strives toward, nor even takes a straight aim at, this truth: to understand who the true God is or what sort of God he wishes to be toward us."[3]

It is impossible to come to a true knowledge of God on the basis of human opinion alone, even if that opinion is buttressed by the common consent of a whole community and strengthened by a long tradition. Opinion humanly conceived is the source of all idolatry, which at best leads us to worship an unknown god, and at worst leads us to deny that there is a god who ought to be worshiped. "Therefore, since the custom of the city or the agreement of tradition is too weak and frail a bond of piety to follow in worshipping God, it remains for God himself to give witness of himself from heaven."[4]

The witness that God gives to himself from heaven is found in Scripture. Scripture fulfills the duty the conscience holds before us to know who and of what sort the God is whom we must worship. "Not only does he teach the elect to look upon a god, but also shows himself as the God upon whom they

---

3. *Inst.* II.ii.18; O.S. III.261.13–15 (1:278).
4. *Inst.* I.v.13; O.S. III.58.32–34 (1:68).

are to look."[5] In order to do this effectively, Scripture must meet the following conditions: first, it must give a basis or foundation for the knowledge of God that transcends human opinion, in order to instruct the conscience with certainty; second, it must set forth what sort of God the Creator is—that is, Spirit—in order to annihilate all carnal deities and carnal worship founded on human opinion; and third, it must clearly depict who the true God is, our Father and Lord, in order to distinguish God from the false throng of idols.

The Self-Witness of the Creator

Calvin insists that Scripture must be understood as having proceeded directly from God, as the "living words of God," so that the witness of God to himself might be received with a certainty not possible on the basis of human opinion. "For by his Word, God rendered faith unambiguous forever, a faith that should be superior to all opinion."[6] For this reason, Calvin emphatically rejects the Roman position that the authority—and therefore the truth—of Scripture rests upon the decision of the Christian community in making it canonical, for that would place Scripture under the authority of human opinion, thereby destroying its certainty. "Yet, if this is so, what will happen to miserable consciences seeking firm assurance of eternal life if all promises of it consist in and depend solely upon the judgment of men?"[7]

The validity of Scripture cannot be established in human opinion, since that would place Scripture in the same realm of uncertainty that gives rise to idolatry. Nor can the truth of Scripture be validated by the testimony of conscience, because it is precisely the conscience that needs to be instructed by certain truth outside itself and needs to know that such truth comes directly from God. "Thus, the highest proof of Scripture derives in general from the fact that God in person speaks in it."[8] If such proof cannot come from the opinion of the community or from the testimony of the conscience, then it must come directly from God, by the inner testimony of the Holy Spirit. "If we desire to provide in the best way for our consciences . . . we ought to seek our conviction in a higher place than human reasons, judgments, or conjectures, that is, in the secret testimony of the Spirit."[9] Therefore, in order that consciences might be established in the truth with certainty, it is necessary to say that God bears witness to himself from heaven by the external witness of the Word of Scripture and the internal witness of the Holy Spirit. "For as God alone is a fit witness of himself in his Word, so also the Word will not find acceptance in men's hearts before it is sealed by the inward testimony of the Spirit."[10]

5. *Inst.* I.vi.1; O.S. III.61.1–4 (1:70).
6. *Inst.* I.vi.2; O.S. III.62.6–7 (1:71).
7. *Inst.* I.vii.1; O.S. III.66.8–12 (1:75).
8. *Inst.* I.vii.4; O.S. III.68.30, 69.1 (1:78).
9. *Inst.* I.vii.4; O.S. III.69.7–11 (1:78).
10. *Inst.* I.vii.4; O.S. III.70.1–5 (1:79).

The conscience needs to be instructed with certainty by the Word and Spirit of God, and is in this sense a point of contact for the self-witness of God. Those, like the malicious, who deny the voice of conscience cannot even hope to be instructed by the Word. Yet the conscience cannot be understood as a sufficient condition for the reception of the Word of God with certainty, for that certainy requires the internal testimony of the Spirit, sealing the truth of the Word of God on our minds, hearts, and consciences. Without the inner testimony of the Spirit, the Word of God does not meet with receptiveness from the conscience, but rather presses the conscience with the judgment of God, making its hypocrisy and impiety manifest and leading to the violent rejection of the Word of God. "Therefore . . . those whom God does not enlighten by the Spirit of adoption are . . . only the more blinded by the Word of God."[11] The conscience only attains certainty of the truth it seeks when it rests not in its own testimony about God, but when it hears the witness that God bears to himself by the inner testimony of the Holy Spirit.[12]

Calvin states that the Word of God is an image whereby God manifests himself in order to be made known to us. Yet the way in which God the Creator bears witness to himself in his Word cannot be different from the way in which God manifests himself in his works: otherwise, our failure to know God from the testimony of creation would be excusable. We do, according to Calvin, acquire a taste of divinity from our experience of the powers of God in creation, but we judge these powers inaccurately and carnally, and do not acknowledge God to be the fountain of every good.[13] Because we do acquire a taste of divinity, it is not true to say that we have no awareness of God, even if that awareness leads to idolatry. For this reason, Calvin uses the metaphor of spectacles to describe the scriptural witness to God the Creator; the Scriptures also set forth God by manifesting God's powers in creation, but they do so far more clearly and powerfully than we do on the basis of our taste of divinity, which gets perverted by our ingratitude and blindness.[14] The Scriptures clearly set forth the powers of God depicted in God's works in a way superior to the way in which these powers are known in creation, so that our clear awareness of them will lead us to a true knowledge of our Creator as our Father and Lord. "We must come, I say, to the Word, *where God is truly and vividly described to us from his works*, while these very works are appraised not by our depraved judgment but by the rule of eternal truth."[15]

Calvin's doctrine of Scripture as God's witness to himself from heaven does not therefore change his fundamental epistemology: namely, that God's essence cannot be known, for there God is hidden in majesty; God must rather be known through our awareness of God's powers as set forth in creation. "For

---

11. Comm. Matt. 13:14, C.O. 45:361; C.N.T.C. 2:67.
12. *Inst.* I.vii.5; O.S. III.71.15–17 (1:80).
13. *Inst.* I.v.15; O.S. III.60.2–6 (1:69).
14. *Inst.* I.vi.1; O.S. III.60.25–30 (1:70).
15. *Inst.* I.vi.3; O.S. III.63.25–28 (1:73), my emphasis.

the Lord manifests himself by his powers, the force of which we feel within ourselves and the benefits of which we enjoy."[16] Scripture clearly depicts these powers by giving the divine interpretation of God's works, and by clearly setting forth the God who is the fountain of every good, so that we might come to know God through the awareness of these powers. Calvin thinks that such a depiction of the powers of God is given in Exod. 34:6-7 (Vulg.). Commenting on these verses, Calvin says: "Now we hear the same powers enumerated there that we have noted in the shining of heaven and earth: kindness, goodness, mercy, justice, judgment, and truth."[17] The witness of God in Scripture to the powers set forth in God's works, and our knowledge of God by our living awareness of those powers, is destined for the same goal as were the powers of God manifested in creation—namely, the piety that gives birth to religion.[18]

God Is Spirit

Scripture can fulfill its second necessary function, that of rejecting all idols and superstitious worship, on the basis of what God is like (*qualis sit*). "Therefore, that exclusive definition, encountered everywhere, annihilates all the divinity that men fashion for themselves out of their own opinion: for God himself is the sole and proper witness of himself."[19] The witness of God to himself in Scripture not only transcends all human opinion about God, but it also entails the rejection of all deities invented by human opinion. In particular, Scripture rejects all of the carnal conceptions people have formed of divinity, which form the basis of superstitious worship, by explicitly and categorically rejecting all images and likenesses of God (cf. Exod. 20:4).

Again, it must be noted that Calvin's categorical rejection of the use of images in worship constitutes a genuine disagreement with Luther. Luther did not hear in the Second Commandment a clear and certain command of God. Calvin did, on the basis of the nature of God: "without exception he repudiates all likenesses, pictures, and other signs by which the superstitious have thought he will be near them."[20] The full ramifications of this disagreement will be seen in Chapter 13's discussion of Calvin on Christian freedom.

According to Calvin, the human mind has a strong inclination toward forming carnal conceptions and images of God. It makes no difference whether those conceptions are given external expression by the physical construction of idols; all that we conceive of God on our own, apart from God's witness to himself in Scripture, is idolatry. "For whence came the beginning of idols but the opinion of men?"[21] We are always in danger of straying from the truth of God's

16. *Inst*. I.v.9; O.S. III.53.14–16 (1:62).
17. *Inst*. I.x.2; O.S. III.86.14–22 (1:97–98).
18. *Inst*. I.x.2; O.S. III.87.16–19 (1:98).
19. *Inst*. I.xi.1; O.S. III.88.17–25 (1:99–100).
20. *Inst*. I.xi.1; O.S. III.89.3–6 (1:100).
21. *Inst*. I.xi.4; O.S. III.92.14–15 (1:104).

self-witness by believing our own thoughts and by falling into superstition. The only way we can avoid falling back into idolatry is to strictly follow and adhere to the witness God bears to himself in Scripture. "Hence, there emerges the beginning of true understanding when we reverently embrace what it pleases God there to witness of himself."[22] This is what Calvin means by saying that all right knowledge of God is born of obedience.

In particular, Scripture sets forth God's essence as infinite and spiritual, not so much to give us direct knowledge of God's essence, but to banish from our minds any thoughts or opinions that might confuse the Creator with creation. "Surely, his infinity ought to make us afraid to try to measure him by our own senses. Indeed, his spiritual nature forbids our imagining anything earthly or carnal about him."[23] The prohibition of images and of all human opinion about God is based upon God's infinite and spiritual essence. Since God is Spirit, God can neither be conceived of nor worshiped carnally, for that would be to worship the creature instead of the Creator. On this basis, Scripture annihilates all deities and worship that arise from human opinion, which are inevitably finite and carnal.

The Fount of Every Good Thing

The scriptural teaching about God's infinite and spiritual essence reveals what God is like, but not who God is. In order to more vividly depict who God the Creator is, Scripture sets God forth as being three persons or subsistences in one essence. "For he so proclaims himself the sole God as to offer himself to be contemplated clearly in three persons."[24] More concretely, God attests himself in Scripture as Father, Son, and Holy Spirit, in such a way that all three are one God and yet are distinct persons or subsistences within the single infinite and spiritual essence of God.

Calvin was convinced that the technical language developed by the church to defend this scriptural self-proclamation of God—Trinity, consubstantial (*homoousios*), and person (*persona*) or subsistence (*subsistentia*)—was itself warranted by Scripture, in accordance with his maxim that all right knowledge of God is born of obedience.[25] These terms were used by the church out of necessity to defend the truth of Scripture from attack by heretics such as Arius, Sabellius, and Servetus. Yet Calvin thought that the truth of Scripture could be set forth to teachable and pious people without using these terms. "Indeed, I could wish they were buried, if only among all men this faith were agreed on; that Father and Son and Spirit are one God, yet the Son is not the Father, nor the Spirit the Son, but that they are differentiated by a peculiar quality."[26]

22. *Inst.* I.vi.2; O.S. III.63.9–12 (1:72).
23. *Inst.* I.xiii.1; O.S. III.108.23–33, 109.1 (1:120–21).
24. *Inst.* I.xiii.2; O.S. III.109.19–23 (1:122).
25. *Inst.* I.xiii.3; O.S. III.112.11–15 (1:124).
26. *Inst.* I.xiii.5; O.S. III.113.29–31, 114.1–2 (1:126).

Although Calvin realized the danger of setting forth the distinctions between Father, Son, and Holy Spirit by means of human analogies, he still thought it necessary to make those distinctions as they are expressed in Scripture: "to the Father is attributed the beginning of activity, and the fountain and wellspring of all things; to the Son, wisdom, counsel, and the ordered disposition of all things; but to the Spirit is assigned the power and efficacy of that activity."[27] These distinctions do not apply to the essence of the godhead, for Father, Son, and Holy Spirit are all one God with regard to that essence, but rather to the mutual relations among the subsistences within the godhead. Nonetheless, Calvin insists that within the one essence of God, apart from any reference to the created world, God is Father to the Son and Holy Spirit. In the triune relationship itself, even though the Son and Holy Spirit are one essence with the Father, it is still appropriate to say, in accordance with Scripture, that the Father is the beginning and fountainhead of deity (*fons ac principium deitatis*).[28]

By setting forth one God as Father, Son, and Holy Spirit, Scripture distinguishes the true God from all other idols by depicting God the Father as the fountain of all good things not only in relation to the world, but also in relation to the Son and Holy Spirit, so that it is proper to call the Father the fountain of all divinity. The term "Father" therefore names God in relation to the Son and Holy Spirit before it describes God in relation to the world or humanity. The fountain of every good is only known by participation in the triune life of God itself: for the Son and Holy Spirit bring about our participation in the powers of God that can only come from the Father. No creature will be able to know or call on God as Father without being engrafted into the Son by the Holy Spirit.

Scripture goes on to depict God more clearly by bearing witness to the six days of creation and the Sabbath; again, the focus is on the self-attestation of God as Father in this work. God created heaven and earth in order to show himself as a Father to humanity, whom he created to be God's children. "But we ought in the very order of things to contemplate God's fatherly love toward mankind, in that he did not create Adam until he had lavished upon the universe all manner of good things."[29] The whole purpose of creation was to bring human beings into the life of the Trinity, so that we might live as children of the Father in unity with the Son through the Holy Spirit. God the Father therefore created all things through the Son as God's wisdom by the Holy Spirit as God's power. By contemplating the order of creation we are to admire the wisdom of the Creator (through the Son), and by becoming aware of the powers of God bestowed within us (by the Holy Spirit) we are to know ourselves as children of the Father.

27. *Inst.* I.xiii.18; O.S. III.132.7–11 (1:142–43).
28. *Inst.* I.xiii.25; O.S. III.145.12–17 (1:153).
29. *Inst.* I.xiv.2; O.S. III.154.11–20 (1:161–62).

The testimony of Scripture to the work of creation further assures us of this by revealing that God willed to be our Father even before we were created, by lavishing every good thing on us before we were created. "How great ingratitude would it be now to doubt whether this most gracious Father has us in his care, who we see was concerned for us even before we were born!"[30] The work of God in the six days of creation reveals to us that the Creator is none other than our Father, who is not only the fountain of all divinity within the godhead, but also the fountain of every good thing in relation to humanity. "We are therefore to await the fullness of all good things from him alone and to trust completely that he will never leave us destitute of what we need for salvation, and to hang our hopes on none but him!"[31]

The knowledge of God as our Father from the testimony of Moses to the six days of creation tells us who God is and what God's nature is, thereby laying the foundation for piety and religion—the true and spiritual worship of God. "We are therefore, also, to petition him for whatever we desire; and we are to recognize as a blessing from him, and thankfully to acknowledge, every benefit that falls to our share. So, invited by the great sweetness of his beneficence and goodness, let us study to love and serve him with all our heart."[32]

We should not, however, limit the fatherly love and care of God to the beginning of creation, as though after that point the world could go on its way without the Father's care and nourishment. The knowledge of God the Creator is only complete when we come to the scriptural witness to God's providential care. Thus even though in general "philosophers teach and human minds conceive that all parts of the universe are quickened by God's secret inspiration,"[33] we must move beyond that general conception to see God's special care in everything, for in all of the happenings of the world God continues to reveal fatherly care for us.[34] Even so apparently natural an act as the rising of the sun is in reality a special act of God whereby we are to be reminded of God's fatherly favor toward us.

However, it should be noted that even though the providential action of God has as its focus and purpose the revelation of God as Father in the work of caring for and nourishing creation and humanity, it also reveals that God is Lord and judge of creation. As was seen in the preceding chapter, the conscience's sense of divinity is aware of those powers of God in the world by which God reveals his government and judgment of the world, even though the malicious attempt to deny God's judgment exists both in the world and in their consciences. However, even the hypocrites who do not deny the providential judgment of God are seriously aware neither of the wrath of God

30. *Inst.* I.xiv.22; O.S. III.172.32–34, 173.1–6 (1:182).
31. *Inst.* I.xiv.22; O.S. III.173.15–18 (1:182).
32. *Inst.* I.xiv.22; O.S. III.173.18–24 (1:182).
33. *Inst.* I.xvi.1; O.S. III.188.17–19 (1:198).
34. *Inst.* I.xvi.1; O.S. III.188.26–30 (1:198).

against sin, nor especially of the fatherly favor of God in the continual governance of the world. The witness of Scripture to God's providential care for the world attests both to God's fatherly favor and to God's lordly judgments; yet the heart of the knowledge of God's providence is the assurance of the godly that the Lord and Ruler of heaven and earth is none other than the Father, the fountain of every good. "His solace, I say, is to know that his Heavenly Father so holds all things in his power, so rules by his authority and will, so governs by his wisdom, that nothing can befall except he determine it."[35]

Because it is the pious who know the Ruler of the world as Father, the church is the special focus of God's fatherly care for the world. "I speak not only concerning mankind; but, because God has chosen the church to be his dwelling place, there is no doubt that he shows by singular proofs his fatherly care in ruling it."[36] The knowledge of God as Father in the governance of the world is consequently something peculiar to the godly in the church. Unbelievers, on the other hand, will find it difficult if not impossible to know God as Father from the governance of the world, given the revelation of God's judgments and curses, which awaken the condemning testimony of their conscience. Indeed, apart from faith in Christ it is impossible to know God the Creator as our Father.

The scriptural self-attestation of God the Creator depicts God as Father not only in relationship to the Son and Holy Spirit but also in relationship to humanity, by portraying the work of creation through the Son and Holy Spirit. The whole purpose of the creation and governance of heaven and earth is that humanity might know God as its Father in the Son by the Holy Spirit. This means that the related knowledge of ourselves as created has at its heart the knowledge of ourselves as children of God. "To conclude once for all, whenever we call God the Creator of heaven and earth, let us at the same time bear in mind that . . . we are indeed his children, whom he has received into his faithful protection to nourish and educate."[37]

Humanity was created in order to know and live under God as the fountain of every good, so that it might petition God for every good thing, acknowledge all things as God's benefits, and thank the Father for them; allured by the sweetness of God's benefits, humanity was to love and serve God with sincere obedience from the heart. To put this another way, humanity was created in the image of God by having bestowed on its immortal yet created soul the powers that come from God, especially wisdom and righteousness. In grateful response for these things freely given by the Father, humanity was to strive by obedience and holiness of life to become united with God, thereby attaining the goal of its creation.

---

35. *Inst.* I.xvii.11; O.S. III.215.8–15 (1:224).
36. *Inst.* I.xvii.6; O.S. III.210.10–13 (1:219).
37. *Inst.* I.xiv.22; O.S. III.173.11–15 (1:182).

Calvin calls the image of God, oriented toward the knowledge of and obedience to God as Father, the integrity (*integritas*) of the soul. "Accordingly, the integrity with which Adam was endowed is expressed by this word [image], when he had full possession of right understanding, when he had his affections kept within the bounds of reason, all his senses tempered in right order, and he truly referred his excellence to exceptional gifts bestowed upon him by his Maker."[38] By acknowledging God as the fountain of every good, humanity in Adam was to be drawn toward the love and service of God by holiness of life, in order thereby to become united to the Father in the Son by the Holy Spirit and attain eternal life.[39]

On the one hand, Calvin insists that the knowledge of God as the fountain of every good would in itself spontaneously lead to willing obedience to God and the mirroring of God's glory by our holiness of life.[40] On the other hand, Calvin states that God not only created humanity in the image of God, but also gave it God's Word of command in order to hold humanity in reverence and in obedience to the Word; for it is by obedience alone that we can keep and use safely the good things given us by God.[41] We only truly know God as Father, the fountain of every good, when we reverence and obey God as Lord; for this reason, over and above the distinction between good and evil that Adam knew on the basis of conscience, God gave his Word of command and prohibition to Adam. "And this, truly, is the only rule of living well and rationally, that men should exercise themselves in obeying God."[42] God cannot be known as Father without being reverenced as Lord; and God cannot be feared as Lord if we are not assured that God is our Father. The image of God in Adam and Eve involved both knowing God as Father and mirroring God's holiness as Lord by keeping themselves subject to his Word. In this way, they were to be led to eternal life by being joined to God, the highest good (*summum bonum*).

This basis makes possible a better understanding of Calvin's use of the scriptural witness to the knowledge of God the Creator. From all eternity, God in essence is Father, Son, and Holy Spirit. Out of his own boundless goodness, God wished to be Father to humanity, and so created the heavens and the earth through the Son by the Holy Spirit, and lavished upon them every good thing before they were created. The works of God in the six days of creation and in the providential care for and governance of creation reveal the Creator to be our Father. Even though God's actions in the world reveal both fatherly favor and severe judgments, the goal of the witness of providence is that we might know the Governor and Ruler of the world to be our Father, the fountain of every good. Humanity was created in the image of God in

---

38. *Inst.* I.xv.3; O.S. III.178.26–30 (1:188).
39. *Inst.* I.xv.8; O.S. III.186.1–2 (1:195).
40. Comm. Gen. 2:9, C.O. 23:39; C.T.S. 1:118.
41. Comm. Gen. 2:16, C.O. 23:44, C.T.S. 1:127.
42. Comm. Gen. 2:16, C.O. 23:44; C.T.S. 1:126.

order to trust in and thank God as Father and to reverence God as Lord. The image of God made it possible for us truly to know and sincerely to obey and worship God as Father and Lord, to be led thereby from the good things the Father gives us back to the fountain itself, the *summum bonum*, so that in union with God we might attain eternal life.

All of this makes it abundantly clear that if we can no longer know God as Father or reverence and obey God as Lord, the fault lies neither with God nor with our created nature, but solely with us. Calvin's use of the knowledge of God the Creator not only distinguishes the true God from all idols formed by human opinion, but also removes every excuse from our inability to know our Creator as Father or to obey our Maker as Lord.

The Loss of Every Good in Adam

Scripture goes on to show the cause of our ills by bearing witness to the fall of Adam and Eve from God. It is this fall, and not any deficiency in God or in creation, that prevents us from knowing God as Father and ourselves as God's children. According to Scripture, Adam and Eve did not remain united to the fountain of every good by willing and grateful obedience to God's Word. Instead, through the temptations of Satan in the mouth of the serpent, they turned away from reverencing God by disbelieving God's Word of command. "For Adam would never have dared oppose God's authority unless he had disbelieved in God's Word."[43] Their disbelief was therefore the root of the fall, and it opened the floodgates to all of the other sins—ambition, pride, ingratitude, blindness, and lust—that presently afflict us and prevent us from truly knowing either God or ourselves.[44] Finally, unbelief led inexorably to disobedience, not only in discreet acts, but even in the desires of our hearts, so that our deepest affections are nothing but rebellion against the will of God.[45]

By falling away from God, the fountain of every good, Adam lost all of the spiritual powers that God had bestowed upon him in order that he might be led to union with God in eternal life, and thus lost the integrity of soul that constituted the image of God within him: "in place of wisdom, virtue, holiness, truth, and justice, with which adornments he had been clad, there came forth the most filthy plagues, blindness, impotence, impurity, vanity, and injustice."[46] The fall of Adam not only entailed the loss of every good thing that constituted the life of the soul, but it also meant the spewing forth from the soul of every evil thing. The absence of good inevitably means the production of evil. "For our nature is not only destitute and empty of good, but so fertile and fruitful in every evil that it cannot be idle."[47]

---

43. *Inst.* II.i.4; O.S. III.232.22–23 (1:245).
44. *Inst.* II.i.4; O.S. III.232.6–9 (1:245).
45. *Inst.* II.i.4; O.S. III.232.17–19 (1:246).
46. *Inst.* II.i.7; O.S. III.236.14–17 (1:250).
47. *Inst.* II.i.8; O.S. III.238.7–9 (1:252).

The loss of the good and the production of evil in Adam also entailed the corruption of nature and subjected nature to the curse of God. As a consequence, the whole of creation not only bears witness to the fatherly favor of God, but also to the righteous wrath and curse of God upon our sin. "Before the fall, the state of the world was a most fair and delightful mirror of the divine favour and paternal indulgence toward man. Now, in all the elements we perceive that we are cursed."[48] Nor did Adam by his fall lose every good thing for himself alone, or subject only himself to the curse; for God had decreed that in Adam all of humanity would both have and lose all of the good things bestowed by God. This is both the root and the meaning of original sin for Calvin. Thus Calvin's definition of original sin includes both the loss of the good things of the soul that makes us liable to the wrath of God, and the production of evil things brought about by the lack of goodness, wisdom, righteousness, and power.[49]

Calvin clearly builds his entire understanding of the nature, scope, and effects of original sin on the Adam and Christ typology in Rom. 5:19: "For just as by one man's disobedience the many were made sinners, so by the one man's obedience the many will be made righteous." He uses this text, as did Augustine before him, to show that original sin affects the descendants of Adam not by imitation of Adam, as the Pelagians claimed, but by communication from Adam, in the same manner in which we receive righteousness from Christ.[50] Adam, by losing all the good things given by God for the life of his soul, is therefore the fountain of every evil and corruption afflicting human nature and creation. "But we will not find the beginning of this pollution unless we go back to the first parent of all, as its source [fontem]."[51] By contrast, Christ must be the fountain of every good thing set forth by the Father, in whom we recover all that we lost in Adam. "Adam and Christ are therefore, as it were, the two origins, or roots, of the human race."[52]

What is more, if Christ is the fountain from which we recover all that we lost in Adam, then Christ reveals with certainty what good things were lost in Adam. If God the Father offers us wisdom, righteousness, power, and life in Christ, then we know that we lack those things and that they must have been lost in Adam. Calvin follows the Augustinian model of saying that the supernatural gifts were totally lost in Adam, while the natural gifts were corrupted. "Among these are faith, love of God, charity toward neighbor, zeal for holiness and for righteousness. All these, since Christ restores them in us, are considered adventitious, and beyond nature: and for this reason we infer that they were taken away. On the other hand, soundness of mind and uprightness of heart were withdrawn at the same time."[53]

48. Comm. Gen. 3:17, C.O. 23:73; C.T.S. 1:173.
49. *Inst.* II.i.8; O.S. III.236.33–35, 237.1 (1:251).
50. *Inst.* II.i.6; O.S. III.234.32–35, 235.1 (1:248).
51. *Inst.* II.i.6; O.S. III.234.18–20 (1:248).
52. Comm. 1 Cor. 15:45, C.O. 49:558–59; C.N.T.C. 9:339.
53. *Inst.* II.ii.12; O.S. III.254.37, 255.1–7 (1:270).

The loss of the supernatural gifts, and the corruption of the natural, mean that even if some good remains, it does not suffice in directing our lives aright so that we might attain the kingdom of God; rather it renders us without excuse. Calvin in particular focuses on the conscience as the primary light remaining in the darkness, both as the seed of religion and as the distinction between good and evil. "There are two main parts in that light which yet remains in corrupt nature. Some seed of religion is sown in all: and also, the distinction between good and evil is engraven in their consciences."[54] And yet, as was seen in the preceding chapter, the conscience does not lead to the true knowledge of God, nor does its distinction between good and evil lead to the doing of good and shunning of evil. "But what is the fruition at last, save that religion comes to monstrous birth in a thousand superstitions, and conscience corrupts all judgment, confounding vice with virtue?"[55]

The conscience does, however, accuse us for failing in our duty both to know God and to obey God's will, and holds before us our sin as the reason we can neither know God as Father nor ourselves as God's children from our contemplation of the universe. The curse of God, which has come upon us in the person of Adam, is manifested throughout creation and awakens the accusing testimony of the conscience within us. Thus it is our sin and guilt that have brought upon us the curse of God manifested in creation, and it is therefore our sin alone that prevents us from knowing God as Father from the testimony of creation.

> The natural order was that the frame of the universe should be the school in which we were to learn piety, and from it pass over to eternal life and perfect felicity. But after man's rebellion, our eyes—wherever they turn—encounter God's curse. This curse, while it seizes and envelops innocent creatures through our fault, must overwhelm our souls with despair. For even if God wills to manifest his fatherly favor to us in many ways, yet we cannot by contemplating the universe infer that he is Father. Rather, conscience presses us within and shows in our sin just cause for his disowning us and not regarding or recognizing us as his sons. Dullness and ingratitude follow, for our minds, as they have been blinded, do not perceive what is true. And as all our senses have become perverted, we wickedly defraud God of his glory.[56]

The accusing testimony of the conscience keeps us from coming to a true knowledge of God as Father and Lord from observation of creation, and makes us instead unavoidably aware of the judgment of God, which we try to avert by superstitious and hypocritical worship or to deny by malicious sinning. The self-witness of God the Father almighty, Creator of heaven and earth, is necessary in order to annihilate all self-invented divinity and worship based

---

54. Comm. John 1:5, C.O. 47:6; C.N.T.C. 4:12.
55. Ibid.
56. *Inst.* II.vi.1, O.S. III.320.13–26 (1:341).

on human opinion by setting forth the true Creator as our Father. But given our fall in Adam and the resulting curse of God, even the testimony of Scripture to the Creator as Father would not be enough to lead us to a true knowledge of God. "Therefore, since we have fallen from life into death, the whole knowledge of God the Creator that we have discussed would be useless unless faith also followed, setting forth for us God our Father in Christ."[57]

God the Creator cannot be known as Father by creatures who have by their sin destroyed themselves as children of God, unless God sets himself forth as the Father of sinners in the person of the only-begotten Son. Those who profess to worship the Creator, even on the basis of the scriptural witness, without embracing Jesus Christ, do not worship the true God, because they cannot know God as Father apart from Jesus Christ. "For even if many men once boasted that they worshiped the Supreme Majesty, the Maker of heaven and earth, yet because they had no Mediator it was not possible for them truly to taste God's mercy, and thus be persuaded that he was their Father."[58]

In Adam, we lost every good thing that God the Father had bestowed upon us for the life of our souls; in Christ, God manifests himself as Father to us by freely bestowing upon empty sinners every good thing. In order to know God as Father, therefore, we must know ourselves as sinners who are empty of every good, so that we might seek in Christ both the removal of every evil thing with which we are afflicted and the bestowal of every good thing that we lack. The testimony of the conscience makes us aware of our sin, but it does not humble us by the knowledge that we are empty in ourselves; while the testimony to the Creator, both in nature and in Scripture, does not set forth God as Father to sinners. Hence Scripture must contain within itself, beyond its witness to the Creator, testimony to our own lack of every good, and must set forth Jesus Christ as the one whom the Father has made the fountain of every good for sinners.

---

57. *Inst.* II.vi.1; O.S. III.320.5–13 (1:340–41).
58. *Inst.* II.vi.4; O.S. III.326.9–15 (1:347–48).

8

THE LAW AS THE TRUE
PREPARATION FOR
CHRIST

Because we have forfeited the good things the Father gave us in Adam—the things that would have made it possible for us to attain eternal life by being joined with God—and have instead become subject to sin, guilt, death, and the curse of God, we cannot know God as Father from the work of creation. As sinners, we can only know God as Father in the person of the Redeemer and Mediator, Jesus Christ. "Surely, after the fall of the first man no knowledge of God apart from the Mediator has had power unto salvation."[1]

Thus, in order once again to know our Creator as Father, the fountain of every good, we must embrace the preaching of Christ crucified, for it is Christ who has been made the wisdom of God by the Father. "Therefore, although the preaching of the cross does not agree with our human inclination, if we desire to return to God our Author and Maker, from whom we have been estranged, in order that he may again begin to be our Father, we ought nevertheless to embrace it humbly."[2] The first use of the law has as its purpose the overcoming of the opposition of human inclination to the preaching of the cross, so that we may be led to embrace it humbly.

Calvin's reference to Christ crucified as being the only one in whom we can know God as Father is not meant to exclude the people of Israel who lived before the coming of Christ. Instead, Calvin makes it explicit that whereas the pagan religions are condemned as having no reference to Christ, the same cannot be said of the Jews; for in the law, Christ was set before the people of Israel as the one in whom they were to know God as Father.[3] The people of Israel not only had Christ set before them in the law, but were also adopted as children of God by being engrafted into the only-begotten Son.[4]

Calvin does not mean that Christ was clearly and explicitly set before the people of Israel, for that is the office of the gospel; but he does mean that

---

1. *Inst.* II.vi.1; O.S. III.320.37, 321.1 (1:341).
2. *Inst.* II.vi.1; O.S. III.320.33–36 (1:341).
3. *Inst.* II.vi.1; O.S. III.321.12–18 (1:342).
4. *Inst.* II.vi.1; O.S. III.321.25–26 (1:342).

Christ was truly and efficaciously promised to the people of Israel by being set before them in shadows and types, beginning with Adam and Eve, who received the promise that the head of the serpent would be crushed (Gen. 3:15), and including the promise to Abraham that in his seed all the nations will be blessed. In particular, Calvin sees in the Davidic kingship a type of the one who was to come: "And there is no doubt that our Heavenly Father willed that we perceive in David and his descendants the living image of Christ."[5] On the basis of the promise made to David, the people of Israel were led to trust and hope in the fulfillment of the promise in Christ, even when they were led away into captivity and exile.[6] Israel was adopted as God's children in the covenant founded on Jesus Christ, and only hoped that God would be Father to them as the basis of the messiah promised and set before them in the image of David.

Calvin therefore does not understand the law given to Moses by God as mutually exclusive with Christ, but rather as the whole form of religion and worship by which God set Christ before Israel in types, images, and shadows.[7] Calvin focuses on the whole cultus of Israel set forth by Moses, in particular the Levitical priesthood and the sacrifices for sin, as being types and images of the priestly office of Jesus Christ, for they pointed the people of Israel to the once-for-all sacrifice that Christ was to offer on the cross, thereby making it possible for sinners to know God as their Father. "Hence he was then surely known in the same image in which he with full splendor now appears to us."[8] The law of Moses also includes the Davidic kingship, which is an image of the kingly office of Christ. "From this it follows that both among the whole tribe of Levi and among the posterity of David, Christ was set before the eyes of the ancient folk as in a double mirror."[9] God attested to Israel that God was their Father in Jesus Christ, by setting forth Christ as priest and king in the images of the Davidic kingship and the Levitical priesthood.

The law of Moses, taken in this broad sense, and the gospel of Jesus Christ cannot be understood as though they were setting forth two different covenants or two different ways of salvation, as though Israel knew God only as the righteous judge of works while the church knows God as gracious Father in Christ. Instead, both Israel and the church are to know God as their Father in Jesus Christ and are to be adopted as children by God's gracious mercy alone. "The covenant made with all the patriarchs is so much like ours in substance and reality that the two are actually one and the same."[10] The gospel does not then do away with the law of Moses, but clearly and directly sets forth the same Jesus Christ who was set before Israel under the types and

---

5. *Inst.* II.vi.2; O.S. III.322.21–22 (1:343).
6. *Inst.* II.vi.4; O.S. III.325.4–9 (1:346).
7. *Inst.* II.vii.1; O.S. III.326.27–34 (1:348).
8. *Inst.* II.ix.1; O.S. III.398.11–14 (1:423).
9. *Inst.* II.vii.2; O.S. III.328.3–5 (1:350).
10. *Inst.* II.x.2; O.S. III.404.5–7 (1:429).

images of its kings and priests.[11] The gospel of Christ differs from the law of Moses only in the clarity of its manifestation of God as our Father in Jesus Christ. "From this we infer that, where the whole law is concerned, the gospel differs from it only in clarity of manifestation."[12] Christ as prophet clearly attests God as Father by pointing to himself as the fountain of every good set forth by the Father, whereas the previous prophets of Israel pointed to the same fountain in shadows, images, and types.

Thus, to refer to one of Calvin's favorite images, the revelation of the gospel differs from the testimony of the prophets in the same way that early dawn differs from the sunrise. The same things are seen in both; but what the prophets of Israel set forth in shadows, Christ brings fully to light.[13] Indeed, in keeping with this metaphor, Calvin claims that there was a progressive increase in the clarity of revelation from Adam and Abraham to Moses and the rest of the prophets, up to and including Malachi and John the Baptist, until Christ, "the Sun of Righteousness," dawned in his gospel.[14] This progressive revelation of God as Father in Jesus Christ represents the way in which God instructed the chosen people in God's truth. Since the people of Israel were not able to bear the full revelation of God in Christ, God tutored them like children under the shadows, images, and types of the law of Moses, gradually increasing the light of revelation until Christ appeared as the prophet who fulfilled and brought to clarity all that had been set forth by the prophets of Israel.[15]

In sum, the people of Israel are not to be excluded from the revelation of God as Father in the only-begotten Son, for God attested himself as their Father in the Davidic kingship and the Levitical priesthood, which are images and types of Christ as king and priest. The only difference between the law of Moses in this broad sense and the gospel of Jesus Christ is the clarity of the revelation of God as Father in Jesus Christ, for "the gospel points out with the finger what the law foreshadowed under types."[16] Christ as prophet fulfills all the prophecy of Israel by clearly attesting God as Father through himself as priest and king, thereby confirming the promises given to Adam, Abraham, and David, and giving substance and reality to the sacrifices of the Levitical priesthood.[17]

Within the otherwise remarkable consistency of Calvin's theology from the 1536 *Institutes* to the edition of 1559, one development that can be traced in his theology is his increasing understanding of the law of Moses in this broad sense. It first emerges in the 1539 *Institutes* in Calvin's polemic against the Anabaptists; but by the 1559 edition, Calvin clearly and explicitly places his

11. *Inst.* II.ix.4; O.S. III.401.32–35 (1:427).
12. *Inst.* II.ix.4; O.S. III.402.9–11 (1:427).
13. *Inst.* II.ix.1; O.S. III.399.20–22 (1:424).
14. *Inst.* II.x.20; O.S. III.420.3–13 (1:446).
15. *Inst.* II.vii.2; O.S. III.328.10–13 (1:350).
16. *Inst.* II.ix.3; O.S. III.401.20–21 (1:426).
17. *Inst.* II.ix.1; O.S. III.399.4–10 (1:424).

discussion of the law in the narrow sense—that is, the Ten Commandments as interpreted by Jesus—within the context of the law in the broad sense, as the testimony of God as our Father in the images and types of Christ set forth in the whole law of Moses. Calvin is clearly moving away from his earlier law-gospel theology of the 1536 *Institutes*, worked out in dependence on Luther's Small Catechism, where the law is primarily understood as the commandments of God revealing our sin and God's wrath, toward an understanding of law-gospel as the different ways in which God reveals himself as our Father in Jesus Christ.

In the 1559 *Institutes*, Calvin brackets his discussion of the law in the narrow sense by new material. He precedes his discussion of the Ten Commandments by a discussion of God attesting himself as Father to Israel under the Davidic kingship (II.vi) and the Levitical priesthood (II.vii.1–2). He follows his discussion of the Ten Commandments with a comparison of the law and the gospel in terms of the clarity of the manifestations of Christ in the prophets compared with Christ as prophet (II.ix). That is followed by a discussion that sets forth the unity of the covenants made in the Old and New Testaments with Israel and in Christ by noting the difference of their mode of dispensation (II.x–xi).

Although the primary opponents against whom Calvin is arguing in these sections are Servetus and the Anabaptists (cf. II.x.1), especially in the chapters added in 1539 (II.x–xi), it is also clear that the material added in 1559 (II.vi–vii.1–2; ix), which immediately surrounds the discussion of the Ten Commandments, is arguing against an exaggeration of the understanding of law and gospel set forth by Luther. "Hence, also, we refute those who always erroneously compare the law with the gospel by contrasting the merit of works with the free imputation of righteousness."[18] It is neither necessary nor accurate to see Luther as the one against whom Calvin is arguing in these sections; but it is necessary to point to this development in Calvin's thought about the law, for it represents an increasingly different emphasis than that found in the theology of Luther. Although both Luther and Calvin agree that the Old Testament contains attestations of God's mercy as well as commandments and threats, it is nonetheless true that when Luther thinks of the law of Moses he thinks of the Ten Commandments in their theological use, whereas when Calvin thinks of the law of Moses he thinks of "the form of religion handed down by God through Moses" that sets forth God as Father to Israel in Christ under the double image of the tribe of Levi and the posterity of David.

This means that Calvin, in contrast to Luther, forces us to understand the Ten Commandments not as prior to, but as already contained within, the self-revelation of God the Father in Jesus Christ. This point will have direct implications on how Calvin understands the impact of the law in the narrow sense upon the conscience. On the one hand, it will mean that we cannot

18. *Inst.* II.ix.4; O.S. III.401.22–24 (1:426).

acknowledge that we are sinners who lack every good thing unless we at the same time know God as Father; on the other hand, it will mean that the principal use and proper purpose of the law will be in the lives of those who have already been adopted as children by the Father, and that this third use of the law will itself be given a christological meaning and shape just like the rest of the law of Moses.

The Revelation of Our Poverty

The law in the narrow sense—that is, the Ten Commandments as interpreted by Jesus Christ—must be understood in the context of the law in the broad sense, as both rooted in and bearing witness to the covenant of adoption fulfilled in Jesus Christ. Paul, according to Calvin, will oppose the law in the narrow sense to the covenant of grace only to argue against justification by works of the law, and not to oppose the law itself to the grace of adoption.[19] The Ten Commandments were given within the covenant of free adoption in Christ and cannot be understood apart from that context. However, within that context, the law in its narrow sense serves a necessary and important function by revealing our sin and emptiness so that we might seek in Christ both forgiveness of sin and every good thing that we lack.[20]

Even though God revealed himself as Father to sinners in Jesus Christ both to Israel and to the Church, this revelation does not profit those who do not acknowledge they are sinners who lack every spiritual good, for "we know what Christ is only when we understand what the Father has given us in him and what blessings he brings to us. But that knowledge begins with a sense of our poverty. For to desire a remedy one must first be conscious of one's ills."[21] The awareness of our poverty and sin is the necessary preparation for seeking the good things the Father has set forth in Christ. This is clearly stated in Jesus' invitation to sinners in Matt. 11:28: "Come to me, all you that are weary and are carrying heavy burdens, and I will give you rest." According to Calvin, "Christ means by 'ye that labour and are heavy-laden' those whose consciences are afflicted by the guiltiness of eternal death and are inwardly so moved by their wretchedness that they faint. For this failure makes us fit to receive His grace."[22]

The one who invites us to himself, in order that our burdens might be lifted and our emptiness filled, is none other than the crucified. To those not aware of their own poverty, the claim that the fountain of every good set forth by the Father is found in Christ crucified is inherently ridiculous and self-contradictory. To seek eternal life from a dead man, to ask for forgiveness from a man who was condemned and cursed, and to flee to an execution site as a refuge offering eternal salvation—all this seems as illogical as seeking ice-cold

19. *Inst.* II.vii.2; O.S. III.329.2–6 (1:351).
20. *Inst.* II.vii.8; O.S. III.334.21–25 (1:357).
21. Comm. John 4:10, C.O. 47:81; C.N.T.C. 4:91.
22. Comm. Matt. 11:28, C.O. 45:320–21; C.N.T.C. 2:25.

water in a fiery furnace or light from utter darkness. "And, of course, when they laugh at our simplicity they seem to be exceedingly clever in their own eyes. But I maintain that what they lack is the principal thing in true wisdom, a sense of conscience."[23] It is only those whose consciences are aware of their own sin and poverty who embrace the preaching of Christ crucified with eagerness and humility, for only they despair of their own wisdom so that they might seek the wisdom of God in the cross.

No one, according to Calvin, can escape the condemning testimony of the conscience. The whole purpose of the conscience in the impious is to remove the excuse of ignorance from their sinning, and to pronounce them guilty and condemned by their own testimony before the judgment seat of God.[24] The condemning testimony of the conscience would not be possible if the natural law of conscience did not in some way correspond with the law of God in the Ten Commandments.[25] However, given our voluntary blindness and ingratitude, we know that there is a God whom we are to worship, but not who that God is or how God wishes to be worshiped.[26] Because we do not know the true God, we form carnal conceptions about God, rooted in human opinion, and therefore worship false gods with carnal ceremonies, in superstition and hypocrisy; or we deny the judgment of God altogether in order that we might sin with impunity.

The conscience does hold before us the distinction between good and evil, and more closely corresponds to the second table of the Law; but this distinction does not succeed in guiding our lives aright. It only condemns us by our own testimony when we sin. However, because of our pride and self-love, this condemning testimony of the conscience does not lead us to descend within ourselves before the judgment of God so that we might humble ourselves before God and acknowledge our impotence and unrighteousness.[27] Instead, our cold awareness of sin and the judgment of God either leads us to the twofold error of hypocrisy—thinking that we have the ability to counter our sins by good works and that we can propitiate God's wrath by performing self-invented sacrifices—or to the denial of the voice of conscience in malice and carnal security. Both hypocrisy and carnal security keep us from a true knowledge of ourselves and hence prevent us from seeking the grace of Christ.[28]

The problem with the knowledge of God and the knowledge of ourselves arising from the testimony of the conscience would seem to lie in the fact that the natural law of the conscience asserts the same thing as the two tables of the Ten Commandments only in a sense. Such an imperfect knowledge of the

---

23. *De Scandalis*, O.S. II.173; *Concerning Scandals*, trans. John W. Fraser (Grand Rapids, Mich.: Wm. B. Eerdmans, 1978), pp. 19–20.
24. *Inst.* II.ii.22; O.S. III.265.7–11 (1:282).
25. *Inst.* II.viii.1; O.S. III.344.11–17 (1:368).
26. *Inst.* II.viii.1; O.S. III.344.17–20 (1:368).
27. *Inst.* II.viii.1; O.S. III.344.20–23 (1:368).
28. Comm. Matt. 11:28, C.O. 45:320; C.N.T.C. 2:25.

law is sufficient to condemn us before God by our own testimony, but it is not sufficient to overcome our pride and self-love so that we might truly descend within ourselves and confess our poverty and iniquity. It would seem, therefore, that the solution to this impasse would lie in the revelation of the Ten Commandments to the conscience, setting forth the true knowledge of God in the law and bringing us to a knowledge of ourselves before the righteous judgment of God. In other words, the imperfect and dull testimony of the conscience must be awakened and strengthened by the perfect and clear testimony of the law, in order to bring us to a true knowledge of ourselves. "Accordingly (because it is necessary both for our dullness and for our arrogance), the Lord has provided us with a written law to give us a clearer witness of what was too obscure in the natural law, shake off our listlessness, and strike more vigorously our mind and memory."[29]

To begin with, the testimony of the law sets forth the knowledge of God the Creator that we should have been able to learn from our awareness of God's powers depicted in the works of creation. "Now what is to be learned from the law can be readily understood: that God, as he is our Creator, has toward us by right the place of Father and Lord; for this reason we owe him glory, reverence, love, and fear."[30] The true knowledge of who God is and of what sort God is in turn makes it clear what the proper worship of God is—namely, grateful and sincere obedience to God's will.[31] In particular, the law sets forth the character of God's holiness, which we are to mirror in our own holiness of life. "Now it will not be difficult to decide the purpose of the whole law: the fulfillment of righteousness to form human life to the archetype [*exemplar*] of divine purity."[32] The law sets forth the holiness of our Father to which we are to conform our lives, so that we might both express the image of God and be joined and cleave to God.

Because God is our Creator who made us in God's image, if we cannot conform our lives to God's holiness, the fault cannot be God's but must be ours.[33] The holiness of God set forth in the law as the archetype to which we are to conform especially reveals the sinfulness of our lust, about which the natural law of conscience had been completely ignorant. "For the natural man refuses to be led to recognize the diseases of his lusts."[34] The conformity of our lives to the holiness of God is not to be external, as hypocrites think, but is to spring from a pure heart and conscience. Any desire or motion of the heart or conscience not in accord with the holiness of God is a mortal sin.[35] The lust and concupiscence we find in our hearts cannot be attributed to God

29. *Inst.* II.viii.1; O.S. III.344.24–27 (1:368).
30. *Inst.* II.viii.2; O.S. III.344.28–31 (1:369).
31. *Inst.* II.viii.2; O.S. III.344.35–37, 345.1–3 (1:369).
32. *Inst.* II.viii.51; O.S. III.390.15–20 (1:415).
33. *Inst.* II.viii.2; O.S. III.345.8–14 (1:369).
34. *Inst.* II.ii.24; O.S. III.397.5–7 (1:422).
35. *Inst.* II.viii.58; O.S. III.397.5–7 (1:422).

our Creator, but are instead the ultimate result of the fall of Adam rooted in his faithlessness.[36]

In sum, the law, by setting forth the holiness of God, sets forth the pattern of life that we could have attained as we were originally created by God, and therefore reveals to us how empty we now are of any ability to express the image of God in our lives and how utterly sinful and unrighteous we are before God. The revelation of our emptiness, our inability to conform our lives to God's law, is directed against our self-confidence and ambition, by which we think we can merit God's favor by virtuous works. The revelation of our sinfulness, especially the disclosure of the sin of concupiscence, is directed against our pride, in which we imagine that our external works constitute our righteousness before God.

The law reveals that the Creator is our Father and Lord whom we are to reverence, and sets forth the way in which we are to express reverence, namely by obeying God's commands with sincerity of heart. Once we have been taught by the law who the true God is and how God wills to be worshiped, we are then to descend into ourselves and judge ourselves by the standard of divine judgment and righteousness. When we do so, we come to realize that our sin makes us unworthy to be considered God's children, while our impotence makes it impossible for us to recover our status as children on our own.[37] Calvin in particular focuses on the way in which the teaching of the law reveals the twofold error made by hypocrisy in response to the accusing testimony of the conscience apart from the law—that is, the illusion of free will and the illusion of righteousness protecting us from God's wrath—in such a way as to make us seek in the twofold grace of Christ (*duplex gratia Christi*) what we mistakenly sought in ourselves—the righteousness whereby we might be considered God's children, and the power by which we might begin to live before God as his children.[38]

The realization of our own emptiness is not possible, however, until the teaching of the law awakens the conscience to its inability to fulfill the law, the resulting sin and guilt, and the wrath of God and sentence of death that inexorably lie upon us as guilty and impotent sinners. "For the conscience cannot bear the weight of iniquity without soon coming before God's judgment. Truly, God's judgment cannot be felt without evoking the dread of death. So also, constrained by the proofs of its impotence, conscience cannot but fall straightway into deep despair of its own powers."[39] The awareness of divine judgment on sin leads to the dread of death, while the proofs of its impotence lead to deep despair of its own powers; it is these emotions of the conscience that generate genuine humility and self-abasement.

---

36. *Inst.* II.i.4; O.S. III.232.17–19 (1:246).
37. *Inst.* II.viii.3; O.S. III.345.15–22 (1:369).
38. Comm. Lev. 19:18, C.O. 24:726; C.T.S. 5:198–99.
39. *Inst.* II.viii.3; O.S. III.345.22–32 (1:369–70).

The conscience of the impious has an awareness of sin, but it is a cold and half-dead awareness; it has an awareness of judgment, but one not serious enough to bring about the horror of death. The essential functioning of the conscience is short-circuited by pride and self-love, so that its accusing testimony results not in humility but in hypocrisy. It is therefore necessary for the conscience to be awakened by the teaching of the law so that it might come to a genuine knowledge of its sin and a serious awareness of the judgment of God. "While the law convicts and reproves us, it arouses us to return to a consideration of the judgment of God."[40]

It is the nature of the Word of God to cite consciences in accusation before the judgment seat of God.[41] The proper function of the Word of God, therefore, is to dispel the darkness of unbelief and to remove the blindness of hypocrisy.[42] For this reason, Paul places prophecy above speaking in tongues. "The unbeliever is reproved . . . because, when he listens, his conscience accepts its own judgment through what it is taught."[43] This power of the Word of the law was indicated by God when the law was promulgated to Moses and the people of Israel at Mount Sinai with thunder and lightning and other portents of wrath, "because the Law was given to cite slumbering consciences to the judgment-seat, that, through fear of death, they might flee for refuge to God's mercy."[44]

The fact that the natural law of the conscience only in a sense teaches the same thing as the Ten Commandments makes the teaching of the law by God necessary if we are to be humbled by the awareness of eternal death and our utter impotence; however, the same fact makes it possible for the conscience to appropriate the teaching of the law, to descend within itself, and to come to a serious awareness of its own impotence, sin, and the wrath of God. In this sense, there is no doubt that the conscience is a necessary and indelible point of contact (*Anknuepfungspunkt*) for the Word of God, awakening the knowledge of sin and the awareness of judgment in even the most hardened sinners.[45]

It is clear, therefore, that Calvin, like Luther, operates on one level with an order of teaching that involves first the law, then the gospel. The law reveals both our unrighteousness, which keeps God from regarding us as God's children, and our impotence, which keeps us from living as God's children. By citing our consciences before the judgment seat of God, the law causes us to descend into ourselves, to despair of our own powers, and to feel the wrath of God, so that we might seek in Christ all that our conscience tells us we

40. Comm. Rom. 5:12, *Commentarius*, p. 111; C.N.T.C. 8:112.
41. Comm. Heb. 4:12, C.O. 55:50; C.N.T.C. 12:51.
42. Comm. Heb. 4:12, C.O. 55:52; C.N.T.C. 12:53.
43. Comm. 1 Cor. 14:24, C.O. 49:527; C.N.T.C. 9:299.
44. Comm. Exod. 19:16, C.O. 24:201; C.T.S. 3:327.
45. Comm. Heb. 4:12, C.O. 55:52; C.N.T.C. 12:53.

lack.[46] The question of the order of teaching will be addressed further at the end of this chapter.

The Beginning of Repentance

The judgment of the conscience is specifically related to repentance. The accusing testimony of conscience must be considered as a summons to repentance. The awakening of the conscience by the law is the beginning of repentance, the necessary condition both for repentance itself and for the reception of God's pardon. In order to understand what Calvin means by the beginning of repentance, the discussion of repentance proper must be anticipated by Calvin's definition of repentance: "On this account, in my judgment, repentance can thus be well defined: it is a true turning of our life to God, *a turning that arises from a pure and earnest fear of him*; and it consists in the mortification of our flesh and of the old man, and in the vivification of the Spirit."[47] The pure and earnest fear of God, which is the beginning of repentance, arises when the conscience is summoned before the judgment seat of God to give an account of its actions.[48]

The summoning of the conscience before the tribunal of God not only leads us to despair so that we seek in Christ all that we lack; it is also the beginning of repentance, which is the necessary condition for our acceptance of God's pardon. "Hence we infer that the doctrine of repentance ought always to accompany the promise of salvation; for in no other way can men taste the goodness of God than by abhorring themselves on account of their sins, and renouncing themselves and the world."[49] God makes the offer of reconciliation, forgiveness, and pardon contingent upon repentance; for the serious abhorrence of sin, which is the beginning of repentance, opens the door for God's pardoning mercy.[50] The pardon of God in Jesus Christ is not to be understood as yet another way in which hypocrites can escape a serious acknowledgment of their own sin and of God's judgment. Only those who anticipate the eschatological judgment of God by judging and condemning themselves by the testimony of their conscience shall be spared that judgment and receive pardon.[51]

Thus Calvin agrees with Luther that God pardons only those who acknowledge they are sinners subject to the wrath of God; but his reason for doing so is different. For Luther, the acknowledgment of our sin and God's wrath is necessary so that we despair of our own works and acknowledge that works cannot justify us before God. For Calvin, the anticipation of the condemnation of God by the self-condemnation of conscience is the necessary condition for

---

46. *Responsio ad Sadoleti Epistolam*, C.O. 5:397; *A Reformation Debate*, ed. John C. Olin (Grand Rapids, Mich., Baker Book House, 1976), p. 66.
47. *Inst.* III.iii.5; O.S. IV.60.1–5 (1:597), my emphasis.
48. *Inst.* III.iii.7; O.S. IV.61.10–18 (1:599).
49. Comm. Isa. 55:7, C.O. 37:288; C.T.S. 16:166.
50. Comm. Lev. 22:27, C.O. 24:593; C.T.S. 4:460.
51. Comm. Jer. 5:9, C.O. 37:618–19; C.T.S. 17:273–74.

pardon because God does not want us to abuse forgiveness by using it as a way of indulging in our sins with impunity.

Calvin states that it is the *beginning* of repentance—the anticipation of God's judgment by the conscience—that is the necessary condition for pardon, in order to make it clear that God does not pardon us because of our newness of life. Here he fundamentally agrees with Luther against the Roman Catholic and even Augustinian conception of the relationship between justification and repentance. But in distinction from Luther, who is primarily concerned with the hypocrite who trusts in his own works even while claiming to believe in Christ, Calvin is primarily concerned with the hypocrite who uses the forgiveness of sins in Christ as a way of avoiding the judgment of God in order to indulge in sinning with impunity. "Whence it also appears that He so pardons sinners as still to hate their sins, since He only absolves those who voluntarily condemn themselves, nor admits any into His favour except those who forsake their sins."[52]

Calvin understands repentance as the necessary condition of forgiveness not because our newness of life contributes anything to our pardon before God—for that pardon springs solely from God's grace and free mercy—but because God does not want hypocrites to use pardon as a pretext for sinning with impunity. "But as he would not have men to abuse his indulgence and forbearance, he lays down this condition—that they must repent of their former life and change for the better."[53] It is the beginning of repentance, the condemning testimony of the conscience against its own sin, that is the necessary condition of forgiveness—not the fruit of repentance, the testimony of the good conscience that we are beginning to live like children of God. The beginning of repentance is the anticipation of God's judgment by our own conscience, and this keeps us from using forgiveness to indulge in sin with impunity.

This concern to prevent the abuse of forgiveness by hypocrites governed Calvin's decision to place his discussion of repentance before his discussion of justification and forgiveness in the 1559 *Institutes*, even though both flow from Christ and neither is given to us as a reward for merit.[54] Calvin's discussion of repentance before justification must not be understood as a disagreement with Luther, for Luther consistently maintained that faith in Christ brings newness of life, and this insistence necessitated his bitter break with the antinomians, against whom he wrote, "There is no Christ who died for sinners who afterwards do not desist from their sin and lead a new life."[55] However, the theology of the cross, especially manifested in tribulation (*Anfechtung*), reinforced Luther's concern with the hypocrisy of legalism and led him to place justification before sanctification in the order of right teaching.[56] Calvin's

52. Comm. Lev. 22:27, C.O. 24:593; C.T.S. 4:460–61.
53. Comm. Jonah 3:10, C.O. 43:260–61; C.T.S. 28:115.
54. *Inst.* III.iii.1; O.S. IV.55.8–15 (1:592–93).
55. *Von den Konziliis und Kirchen*, 1539. W.A. 50:599.21–23; L.W. 41:114.
56. W.A. 18.65.9–31, 66.1–20; L.W. 40:82–83; W.A. 10 (III).2–7; L.W. 51:70–72.

understanding of God as Father in Jesus Christ means that the awakened conscience must seek both justification and repentance in Christ alone, so that neither grace theologically precedes or is contingent upon the other, as both flow simultaneously from Christ. However, given his concern with antinomian hypocrisy, Calvin discusses repentance first to make it clear that God only pardons those who condemn themselves on account of their sins.

In sum, repentance is not the cause of pardon, as though it merits or calls forth God's forgiveness; but the beginning of repentance is the necessary condition (*conditio sine qua non*) of pardon, because God pardons only those who condemn themselves.

The conscience awakened by the law testifies that we are impotent sinners under sentence of eternal death before the judgment seat of God. This condemning testimony on the one hand humbles us so that we seek in Christ all that we lack in ourselves, especially forgiveness and repentance, while on the other hand it is the beginning of repentance itself, which is the necessary condition (but not the cause) of pardon. The condemning testimony of the conscience is only possible under the teaching of the law of God, and yet this condemning testimony is possible because of the general correspondence between the natural law of conscience and the Ten Commandments.

This point, however, raises a serious question: Is the work of the Holy Spirit necessary even for the beginning of repentance, or is this beginning within the capacity of the conscience? Beyond this question, a further one arises, for repentance involves not only hatred of sin but also voluntary turning toward God. The law may indeed—and Calvin says it always does—awaken the conscience to a serious awareness of its sin and the judgment of God; but how can we voluntarily turn to God when we are aware of God only as a condemning judge? Thus the question arises for Calvin just as it did for Luther: Can we genuinely descend within ourselves and acknowledge our own sin and emptiness when we do not already know that God wills to be our gracious Father?

With regard to the first question, Calvin claims that the ability of the consciences of the impious to appropriate the testimony of the law does not lead to an abhorrence of sin, but rather to an increase in sin. "There is no doubt that the more closely the conscience is struck with awareness of its sin, the more its iniquity grows. For stubborn disobedience is then added to transgression."[57] The law does in fact inexorably and unavoidably make the consciences of the impious aware of their sin and of the judgment and curse of God against sin; but this does not lead them to condemn themselves and seek the grace of God in Christ, but rather increases the gravity and severity of their sin by taking away every pretext and excuse they had devised to avoid both a serious knowledge of their sin and a direct awareness of the judgment of God. "It follows from this that sin is increased by the law, because the authority of the Lawgiver is then despised and His majesty degraded."[58] Not

57. *Inst.* II.vii.7; O.S. III.333.3–14 (1:355–56).
58. Comm. Rom. 5:20, *Commentarius*, p. 118; C.N.T.C. 8:119.

even the awareness of eternal death in the conscience is enough to humble sinners, but rather makes them more high-handed.[59] "For the reprobate always freely desire to evade God's judgment. Now, although that judgment is not yet revealed, so routed are they by the testimony of the law and of conscience, that they betray in themselves what they have deserved."[60]

Of itself the awakened conscience of the ungodly does not humble their pride, destroy their self-love, lead them to seek what they lack in Christ, or bring about even the beginning of repentance. The pride of the ungodly is only increased by the condemning testimony of the conscience, even when that testimony is awakened and reinforced by the testimony of the law. This is a serious qualification of many of the claims Calvin apparently makes about the emotions engendered in the conscience by the law per se bringing about humility and self-abasement. Calvin repeatedly insists that the law itself increases sin and pride, so that only the Holy Spirit can humble the pride of the impious. "For where God's Spirit does not reign, there is no humility, and men ever swell with inward pride, until God thoroughly cleanse them. It is necessary that God should empty us by his special grace."[61] Only the work of the Holy Spirit can bring about a genuine acknowledgment by the conscience of its own sin and emptiness. "It is true that for a sinner to beg forgiveness demands a sorrow of conscience and displeasure at himself. *But it is wrong to infer from this that repentance, which is the gift of God, is contributed by men as the movement of their own heart.*"[62]

While it is true, therefore, that Christ invites to himself only those "whose consciences are afflicted by the guiltiness of eternal death and are inwardly so moved by their wretchedness that they faint," we should not be led to think that Christ finds such people in the world who are thus prepared and fit to come unto him. "Now although this preparation for receiving the grace of Christ takes all the heart out of men, yet we must note that it is the gift of the Holy Spirit, *for it is the beginning of repentance, to which none can attain by his own efforts.* For Christ did not mean to teach what a man can do on his own, but only how they must be affected who come to Him."[63] Thus the self-condemnation of the conscience, which alone prepares us to receive the grace of God, is itself dependent not only on the external testimony of the law, but also on the inward regeneration of the Holy Spirit. "It then follows that the beginning of the fear of God is the regeneration of the Spirit."[64] God may make reconciliation contingent upon the beginning of repentance, but it is also God whose Spirit works repentance in us to remove the impediments that keep God's pardon from us. "We hence see that God is not only inclined

59. Comm. 1 Cor. 15:56, C.O. 49:564; C.N.T.C. 9:346.
60. *Inst.* II.vii.9; O.S. III.335.21–29 (1:358).
61. Comm. Heb. 1:16, C.O. 43:516; C.T.S. 29:52.
62. Comm. Luke 15:20, C.O. 45:509; C.N.T.C. 2:223, my emphasis.
63. Comm. Matt. 11:28, C.O. 45:320–21; C.N.T.C. 2:25, my emphasis.
64. Comm. Jer. 32:39, C.O. 39:40; C.T.S. 20:212.

to pardon when men repent, but that it is his peculiar office to remove the obstacles."[65] The awareness in the conscience of our impotence and eternal death, which makes us long for grace, is itself the work of God's grace within us.[66]

Without this inward working of the Holy Spirit, we cannot ever hope to be prepared to receive God's grace, for the very longing for the grace of God is itself awakened in our hearts by the Holy Spirit.[67] The testimony of the law, which awakens and reinforces the condemning testimony of the conscience, is necessary but not sufficient to bring about the awareness of our poverty. It is the proper work of the Holy Spirit to awaken this sense of our inner poverty, thereby preparing us to receive the grace of Christ: "there are even very many who are not affected by their emptiness until the Spirit of God with His own fire kindles hunger and thirst in our hearts. It is the office of the Spirit, therefore, to give us an appetite for His grace."[68]

Although Calvin, like Luther, describes the relationship of the law to the conscience in a way that makes the conscience the point of contact for the teaching of the law, Calvin is much more explicit than Luther (in the commentaries and not, oddly enough, in the *Institutes*) that this point of contact only serves to increase sin where the Spirit of God is not also at work. The gift of the Spirit alone awakens the conscience to a genuine awareness of its own sin and poverty under the testimony of the law, thereby initiating repentance and preparing us to receive the grace of Christ.

All this only accentuates the second problem noted above; for even if it is true that it is the office of the Holy Spirit to give us an appetite for grace by creating within us a true awareness of our poverty and sinfulness before the judgment seat of God, the question still remains as to how the self-condemned sinner will seek the grace of God when all he or she is aware of is the wrath and judgment of God. As has been seen, it is impossible for the awakened conscience to seek God, for the conscience can only testify that God is an angry judge. This is why the impious rage, blaspheme, and flee from God when the condemning testimony of their conscience is awakened. Thus the beginning of repentance must not only depend on the work of the Holy Spirit making us aware of God's judgment and our calamity, but it must also depend on an awareness of God's mercy offered to sinners.[69] There can be no true acknowledgment of our sin and emptiness where there is only the awareness of divine judgment; and yet both the testimony of the conscience and the testimony of the law can only bring us before the judgment seat of God.

The purpose of making us aware of divine judgment is not to close us up in our sin under wrath, but rather to lead us to seek the grace of God offered

65. Comm. Mic. 5:13, C.O. 43:382–83; C.T.S. 28:324.
66. Comm. Jer. 24:7, C.O. 38:465; C.T.S. 19:232.
67. Comm. Zech. 12:10, C.O. 44:334; C.T.S. 30:361.
68. Comm. John 7:37, C.O. 47:180; C.N.T.C. 4:197.
69. *Inst.* II.vii.8; O.S. III.334.15–25 (1:356–57).

in Christ. "For we ought to be so affected by the judgment of God that we shall not look for hiding places to flee from the presence of the judge, but shall go straight to Him to ask His forgiveness."[70] Yet we cannot go straight to God to ask forgiveness if we do not in any sense know of that forgiveness even as we are aware of God's judgment.[71] The awareness of sin and divine judgment, therefore, is not sufficient to lead us either to begin to repent or to seek the grace of God in Jesus Christ, unless that sense of divine judgment is joined with a promise of divine favor. "In short, the sense of God's judgment, unless conjoined with the hope of forgiveness, strikes men with terror, which must necessarily engender hatred."[72] Where God is only known as a severe judge, the sinner will either seek to flee God or will be led in despair to wage war against God. "For this reason all threats are vain without a taste of the mercy of God."[73]

Just as the beginning of repentance is the necessary condition for the acceptance of God's mercy, so the sense of God's mercy is the necessary condition for the beginning of repentance. "We must then remember that the beginning of repentance is a sense of God's mercy."[74] Calvin bases this claim on Ps. 130:4: "But there is forgiveness with you, so that you may be revered." Without knowing of God's forgiveness, it is impossible for the sinner not to flee from God. It is the mercy of God alone that truly gives birth to the fear of the Lord, which is the beginning of repentance. "For except men know God to be ready to be at peace with them, and feel assured that he will be propitious to them, no one will seek him, no one will fear him."[75]

Calvin uses this insight to critique the teaching of the "papist doctors" about repentance; for even though they, like Calvin, insist on a serious awareness of our sin and God's judgment, they teach nothing about freely offered pardon and therefore make true repentance impossible.[76] This reinforces the claim made above that Calvin's placement of repentance before forgiveness does not compromise his teaching concerning the free grace of forgiveness. Just as faith is not found where there is no repentance (against antinomian hypocrites), so also repentance is not found where there is not faith in God's pardon (against legalistic hypocrites). "When a man is awakened with a lively sense of the judgment of God, he cannot fail to be humbled with shame and fear. Such self-dissatisfaction wouldn't however suffice, unless at the same time there were added faith, whose office is to raise up the hearts which were cast down in fear, and to encourage them to pray for forgiveness."[77] Just as we cannot have genuine faith in the forgiveness of our sins where we do not anticipate

70. Comm. John 8:9, C.O. 47:190; C.N.T.C. 4:208.
71. Comm. Acts 3:18, C.O. 48:71; C.N.T.C. 6:101.
72. Comm. Ps. 130:4, C.O. 32:335–36; C.T.S. 12:132.
73. Comm. Ezek. 1:1, C.O. 40:24; C.T.S. 22:55.
74. Comm. Hos. 6:1, C.O. 42:319; C.T.S. 26:215.
75. Comm. Hos. 3:5, C.O. 42:264–65; C.T.S. 26:135.
76. Comm. Isa. 55:7, C.O. 37:289; C.T.S. 16:167.
77. Comm. Ps. 130:4, C.O. 32:335; C.T.S. 12:130.

the judgment of God by condemning ourselves and repenting of our sins, so also we never genuinely condemn ourselves and repent of our sins where we are not assured that God will in fact forgive our sins.[78] The knowledge of God's mercy must be present at the same time as we feel the condemning testimony of our conscience. Otherwise, we will either use the promise of mercy to indulge in our sins, or we will despair under the judgment of God and either flee from or rage against God.[79] "These two things then ought not to be separated, and cannot be,—the acknowledgment of our sins, which will humble us before God,—and the knowledge of his goodness, and a firm assurance as to our salvation."[80]

One way in which Calvin understands the simultaneity of the acknowledgment of our sins and the knowledge of God's mercy is by speaking of the inseparability of the whole of God's truth revealed to humanity, that is, the law and the gospel, or the threats and the promises of God. According to Calvin, faith apprehends both the threats and the promises, and separates neither the promise of forgiveness nor the knowledge of God's mercy from the acknowledgment of sin. "God embraces each quality in his word, as he cites all who have sinned to his tribunal, and gives them a hope of reconciliation."[81] This clearly accounts for the placement in the 1559 *Institutes* of the discussion of the law in the narrow sense within the context of the law in the broad sense: for the law only profits those who genuinely acknowledge their impotence and unrighteousness, and that can only happen when they at the same time apprehend God's mercy.[82]

In sum, not only is the testimony of the conscience, awakened by the testimony of the law, insufficient to lead us to a sincere awareness of our sin and poverty without the inner working of the Spirit; but even that inner working of the Spirit would not be enough if we were unable to know with certainty that our judge is none other than our Father. Thus Calvin prays that God may "so influence us by thy Spirit within, that we, being really humbled, may acknowledge thee as our judge and Father—our judge, in order that we may be displeased with ourselves, and being touched by thy judgment, we may condemn ourselves,—and our Father, in order that we may, not withstanding, flee to that mercy which is daily offered to us in the Gospel, through Christ Jesus our Lord."[83]

However, Calvin also claims that the awareness of God's mercy occurs prior to our awareness of sin and judgment. We can only acknowledge God as judge, and can only condemn ourselves as sinners, when we are already assured that God is our Father in Jesus Christ. "Now, the first thing respecting God is,

---

78. Comm. Jer. 26:3, C.O. 38:515–16; C.T.S. 19:311.
79. Comm. Hab. 3:2, C.O. 43:567–68; C.T.S. 29:139.
80. Comm. Mic. 7:9, C.O. 43:414; C.T.S. 28:377.
81. Comm. Dan. 9:13, C.O. 41:149–50; C.T.S. 25:170; cf. *Inst.* III.ii.7.
82. Comm. Jer. 10:24, C.O. 38:92; C.T.S. 18:61.
83. Comm. Jer. 31:21, C.O. 38:678; C.T.S. 20:111.

that we should acknowledge him to be beneficent and bountiful; for what would become of us without the mercy of God? Therefore the true and right knowledge of God begins here, that is, when we know him to be merciful towards us. For what would it avail us to know that God is just, except we had a previous knowledge of his mercy and gratuitous goodness?"[84] The knowledge that God is our judge—a knowledge given by the conscience as the sense of divine judgment (sensus divini iudicii) and reinforced by the testimony of the law—is of no profit unless it follows the knowledge that God is our beneficent and merciful Father.

This precedence of the knowledge of God as gracious Father over the knowledge of the Father as Lord and judge emerges consistently in the arrangement of the Institutes of 1559: the knowledge of God as the fountain of every good is discussed before the knowledge of the righteous judgment of God in the opening chapter (I.i); piety, arising from knowledge of God as Father, is discussed before religion, which reverences the Father as Lord (I.ii); the knowledge of the Creator as Father (I.xiii–xiv) precedes the knowledge of the Father as Lord and ruler of the world (I.xvi–xviii); the knowledge of God as Father of sinful creatures in Jesus Christ precedes the knowledge of God as judge in the law (II.vi–viii); and the knowledge of Christ as the source of every blessing for sinners precedes the discussion of both repentance and justification (III.ii–xi).

This consistent pattern becomes especially clear in the context of Calvin's discussion of the knowledge of ourselves as impoverished sinners, knowledge that prepares us to receive the grace of Christ. Not only is the condemning testimony of conscience unable to humble us without the inner working of the Holy Spirit, but it is also unable to lead us to seek the grace of Christ unless it follows upon our knowledge that God wills to be our Father in Jesus Christ. Indeed, Calvin can even say that it is the awareness of God's grace itself that leads us to condemn and humble ourselves before God. "And surely the more anyone has tasted of the grace of God, the more ready he is to condemn himself, and as unbelief is proud, so the more anyone proceeds in the faith of God's grace, he is thus humbled more and more before him."[85]

The order of right teaching and preaching by 1559 is not "first law, then gospel," as seen in Luther and detected earlier in Calvin, but first the distinguishing of the Father and Lord as Creator from all idols, and then the revelation of God as Father to fallen sinners in Jesus Christ, which is the basis, along with the testimony of the law and the work of the Spirit, of our acknowledgment of our sin and poverty so that we take refuge in Christ. "So, also, Christ entered upon his preaching: 'The Kingdom of God has come near; repent, and believe in the Gospel' [Mark 1:15]. First he declares that the treasures of God's mercy have been opened in himself; then he requires

84. Comm. Jer. 9:24, C.O. 38:52; C.T.S. 17:500.
85. Comm. Ezek. 16:63, C.O. 40:400–1; C.T.S. 23:184, my emphasis.

repentance; finally, trust in God's promises."[86] The beginning of repentance is indeed the necessary condition for faith and trust in God's mercy; but the knowledge of the offer of God's mercy to sinners in Jesus Christ is the basis for the beginning of repentance. First, God offers to again be the Father of sinners in Jesus Christ (the law in the broad sense and the gospel); then he requires repentance (the law in the narrow sense), which leads to the acceptance of the offer of God's mercy in faith.

This concept represents a significant theological development beyond Luther, making it impossible to understand the mature Calvin of the 1559 *Institutes* within Luther's law-gospel framework, in spite of all the similarities Calvin shares with Luther. Even though both agree that the law must awaken the conscience so that it despairs of its powers and condemns its righteousness, Calvin is clearer than Luther about the role played by the Holy Spirit in bringing about the awareness of our poverty in the conscience, and Calvin moves beyond Luther by seeing the Ten Commandments within the context of the knowledge of God as the Father of sinners in Jesus Christ.

---

86. *Inst.* III.iii.19; O.S. IV.76.32–34, 77.1–2; (1:613).

9

THE IMAGE OF
THE INVISIBLE FATHER
IN JESUS CHRIST

The testimony of the law, which brings about the humbling of our self-love and pride through the awakening of conscience to our calamity, poverty, nakedness, and disgrace, is given by God within the context of God's testimony to himself as the Father of sinful creatures in Jesus Christ. Calvin claims that the knowledge of ourselves as empty of every good and as condemned to eternal death before the judgment seat of God is the necessary preparation for knowing God as Father in Jesus Christ, and is also based on a prior knowledge of the offer of God's mercy in Jesus Christ. According to Calvin's position as it took shape by 1559, we must have a certain knowledge of God's offer to be our Father in Jesus Christ before we can begin to repent; but we must begin to repent, under the testimony of the law that reveals our unrighteousness and impotence, before we can accept God's offer.

Both the beginning of repentance as our submission to the testimony of the law, and our acceptance of God as our Father in Jesus Christ, are brought about by the working of the Holy Spirit within us and not by the inherent powers of the conscience per se (as a point of contact [*Anknuepfungspunkt*]). Without the inner testimony of the Holy Spirit, the testimony of the law does not bring about genuine self-knowledge, but rather increases our sin by inflaming our pride or by making us rage at God in despair.

This chapter turns from the knowledge of ourselves as condemned sinners to the knowledge of God as the merciful Father of sinners in Jesus Christ. Just as the offer of God to be our Father formed the context of Calvin's discussion of the knowledge of ourselves as impoverished sinners, so also the knowledge of ourselves as impoverished sinners, brought about by the awakening of the conscience, forms the context for Calvin's discussion of God as the Father of sinners in Jesus Christ, both in terms of his understanding of the person and work of Jesus Christ as Mediator and in terms of his understanding of our participation in Jesus Christ by faith through the Holy Spirit.

At the heart of Calvin's understanding of Jesus Christ is the description of Christ found in the confession of faith in 1 Tim. 3:6, "He [God] was revealed in flesh." This confession lies behind Calvin's understanding of Jesus Christ both as the self-revelation of God the Father (that is, Christ as the image of the invisible God) and as the Mediator between God and humanity (that is, Jesus as the Christ anointed by the Holy Spirit to be prophet, king, and priest). Thus Calvin begins his discussion in the *Institutes* of the person and work of Christ with a statement that is in accord with the Definition of Chalcedon, but interpreted in light of 1 Tim. 3:16: "Now it was of the greatest importance for us that he who was to be our Mediator be both true God and true [hu]man [*verum esse et deum et hominem*]."[1]

Calvin does not, like Anselm, argue for the necessity of Christ as true God and true human on the basis of what must obtain if there is to be reconciliation between God and sinful humanity, but rather on the basis of the free decision of God the Father.[2] In light of Eph. 1:3-8, Calvin claims that the decree of the Father upon which the incarnation depends has as its purpose God's adoption of sinners by their election into Jesus Christ.[3] God the Father willed to adopt sinners as God's children, and thus sent his only-begotten Son to be the Mediator between God and humanity by the Son's becoming true God and true human.[4] "We will know why Christ was promised from the beginning: to restore the fallen world and to restore lost men."[5] For this reason, even before Christ, the promise of the coming of the Mediator was always held before the people of Israel in the image of sacrifices, to indicate that the purpose for his coming lay in the free decision of God the Father to reconcile sinners to God by the blood of Christ.[6]

Even though it is impossible to establish an external necessity for the fact that the Mediator must be both true God and true human, or God manifested in the flesh, apart from the decree of God the Father, it is possible to understand why God willed that our Mediator be the incarnate Son of God. One such reason is related to the way human beings as creatures of God come to know God, even apart from their sinfulness. As was seen in the discussion of the knowledge of God the Creator, we cannot know the Creator's essence, but must come to know God by the manifestation of God's powers. "For the Lord manifests himself by his powers, the force of which we feel within ourselves and the benefits of which we enjoy."[7] These powers—wisdom, righteousness, life, goodness, mercy, and so on—are depicted in the works of creation. "We must therefore admit in God's individual works—but especially in them as a

---

1. *Inst.* II.xii.1; O.S. III.437.3–4 (1:464). See E. David Willis, *Calvin's Catholic Christology* (Leiden: E. J. Brill, 1966), pp. 60–100; Wilhelm Niesel, *The Theology of Calvin*, trans. Harold Knight (Grand Rapids, Mich.: Baker Book House, 1980), pp. 110–19; Edward A. Dowey, Jr., *The Knowledge of God in Calvin's Theology* (New York and London: Columbia University Press, 1952), Chapter IV; and T. H. L. Parker, *Calvin's Doctrine of the Knowledge of God* (Edinburgh: Oliver & Boyd, 1969), chap. 5.
2. *Inst.* II.xii.1; O.S. III.437.4–8 (1:464).
3. *Inst.* II.xii.5; O.S. III.442.33–36 (1:469).
4. *Inst.* II.xii.5; O.S. III.442.37–39 (1:469).
5. *Inst.* II.xii.4; O.S. III.440.28–31 (1:467).
6. *Inst.* II.xii.4; O.S. III.440–42 (1:467–68).
7. *Inst.* I.v.9; O.S. III.53.14–16 (1:62).

whole—that God's powers are actually represented as in a painting."[8] This is true not only in the works of creation as a whole, but also in terms of humanity as a microcosm of creation and as the highest of God's works.

The testimony of Scripture and the Holy Spirit to God the Creator does not circumvent this way of knowing God, but instead corrects our corrupted judgment of God's works so that we might become properly aware of the powers of God already depicted in creation, just as spectacles help those with poor eyesight to see more clearly. Thus if the Father is to make himself known to the children of Adam, he must do so by setting forth and depicting his powers in his works in the creaturely sphere—that is, in the humanity of Jesus Christ. This is especially necessary after the fall, because our minds are even more bound by carnality than they were at creation. "Otherwise, God's majesty is too lofty to be attained by mortal men, who are like grubs crawling upon the earth."[9]

It is precisely because we are children of Adam that God must reveal himself as our Father not only in the creaturely sphere in general, but in the life of a child of Adam in particular. Humanity, the greatest work depicting the powers of God in creation, both received and lost in Adam all the good things the Father had freely bestowed upon us, so that we might out of gratitude seek to unite ourselves to God by holiness of life and thereby attain the kingdom of God.[10] Because we human creatures have lost every good spiritual thing God had bestowed upon us in Adam, and have subjected creation itself to the curse of God because of our sin, the powers of God by which we might come to know God as Father again cannot be set forth in the works of creation in general, but must be set forth in the life of a human being in particular. "The name 'heir' is attributed to Christ as manifested in the flesh; for in being made man and putting on the same nature as us, He took on Himself this heirship, in order to restore to us what we had lost in Adam."[11]

Jesus Christ as "God manifested in the flesh" means Jesus Christ as the fountain of every good who reveals the invisible Father in his humanity. It is in this sense that Calvin calls Jesus Christ "the image of the invisible God" (cf. Heb. 1:3; Col. 1:15). "For God would have remained hidden afar off if Christ's splendor had not beamed upon us. For this purpose the Father laid up with his only-begotten Son all that he had to reveal himself in Christ so that Christ, by communicating his Father's benefits, might express the true image of his glory."[12] God the Father reveals himself to sinners in Jesus Christ by granting Christ every good thing that we lack, so that Christ might reveal the Father by revealing the fountain of every good in himself. "Moreover, if

8. *Inst.* I.v.10; O.S. III.54.19–21 (1:63).
9. *Inst.* II.vi.4; O.S. III.325.20–22 (1:346).
10. *Inst.* II.i.5; O.S. III.232.39, 233.1–5 (1:246).
11. Comm. Heb. 1:2, C.O. 55:10–11; C.N.T.C. 12:7.
12. *Inst.* III.ii.1; O.S. IV.8.11–15 (1:544).

apart from *God* there is no salvation, no righteousness, no life, yet *Christ* contains all these in himself, God is certainly revealed."[13]

To put it another way, by not only setting forth the good things we lack, but by being for us the source of every good thing, Jesus Christ sets forth the powers of God and also sets forth God himself in his humanity, thereby truly being God manifested in the flesh. "The sum is, that God in Himself, that is, in His naked majesty, is invisible . . . to the human understanding; and that He is revealed to us in Christ alone, where we may behold Him as in a mirror. *For in Christ He shows us His righteousness, goodness, wisdom, power, in short, His entire self.*"[14] God reveals himself as the Father of the children of Adam and Eve by sending his only-begotten Son to become human, thereby revealing the fountain of every good in the humanity of Jesus Christ. In this way, Jesus Christ, as God manifested in the flesh, is the image of the invisible God, apart from whom it is impossible to know God as Father.

The Wonderful Exchange

Calvin depicts Christ as the fountain of every good in three distinct but inseparable ways: in the event of the incarnation (the Son of God becoming the Son of humanity); in the event of the anointing by the Spirit (the threefold office of Christ); and in the event of his death and resurrection. All three moments depict Christ as the fountain of every good to sinners by means of the wonderful exchange: Christ takes away all evil that our conscience tells us we have, and gives us every good thing that our conscience tells us we lack.

> This is the wonderful exchange [*mirifica commutatio*] which, out of his measureless benevolence, he has made with us; that, becoming Son of man with us, he has made us sons of God with him; that, by his descent to earth, he has prepared an ascent to heaven for us; that, by taking on our mortality, he has conferred his immortality upon us; that, accepting our weakness, he has strengthened us by his power; that, receiving our poverty upon himself, he has transferred his wealth to us; that, taking the weight of our iniquity upon himself (which oppressed us), he has clothed us with his righteousness.[15]

Following the dynamic of the wonderful exchange in each of the three moments of the person and work of Jesus Christ will establish a more complete understanding of Christ as the fountain of every good offered to sinners by the Father. It is Jesus Christ himself who forms the primary foundation of the assurance of faith.

The Incarnation of the Son

With regard to the incarnation, the only-begotten Son of God becomes a child of Adam in order to remedy the two major problems of which the awakened

---

13. *Inst.* I.xiii.13; O.S. III.125.34–37 (1:137).
14. Comm. Col. 1:15, C.O. 52:85–86; C.N.T.C. 11:308, my emphasis.
15. *Inst.* IV.xvii.2; O.S. V.343.29–32, 344.1–6 (2:1362).

conscience under the law makes us aware—namely, our impotence to become children of God, and our sin that makes us subject to God's curse and condemns us to eternal death before the judgment seat of God. With regard to the first problem—our inability to live as children of God, by which means alone we inherit the kingdom of God—the Son of God, who alone is the head of the kingdom of God by right, takes upon himself our mortal humanity in order to make the children of Adam into children of God, thereby bestowing on us every good thing. "Ungrudgingly he took our nature upon himself to impart to us what was his, and to become both Son of God and Son of man in common with us. In this way we are assured of the inheritance of the Heavenly Kingdom; for the only Son of God, to whom it wholly belongs, has adopted us as his brothers."[16] By taking what is ours—our human nature—upon himself, the only-begotten Son freely bestows on us by grace what is his alone by nature, namely to be a child of God, so that we might become children of God by our adoption into Christ.

Jesus Christ must therefore be the only Son of God not only according to his divinity, but also according to his humanity. He could not make us, who are only human, into children of God by adoption if he himself were not the Son of God by nature even according to his humanity. "We therefore hold that Christ, as he is God and man, consisting of two natures united but not mingled, is our Lord and the true Son of God even according to, but not by reason of, his humanity."[17] Were Christ not the Son of God by nature even according to his humanity (*secundum humanitatem*), then neither we nor the patriarchs of old could have been adopted as children of God, nor could we know God as Father; for God can be our Father only as we are engrafted into God's only-begotten Son, Jesus Christ.[18]

Yet Jesus Christ cannot be the only-begotten Son of God by reason of his humanity (*ratione humanitatis*), for that would be to deny the sheer grace of the incarnation. By assuming our human nature in a hypostatic union, the Son bestows upon humanity something it could never achieve on its own: to *be* the only-begotten Son of God. For this reason Calvin agrees with Augustine that the assumption of the humanity of Jesus Christ into union with the Son of God is the mirror of God's free grace. "And the man Christ [*homo Christus*] would not be the mirror of God's inestimable grace unless this dignity had been conferred upon him, that he should both be the only-begotten Son of God and be so called."[19] The bestowal of such dignity and excellence on the humanity of Jesus thus comes from the same grace by which we are adopted as children of God by being made one with him, even while that same humanity is the means of our adoption. Only the one who is the Son of God by nature even according to his humanity can give the power to the children of Adam

---

16. *Inst.* II.xii.2; O.S. III.439.1–9 (1:465–66).
17. *Inst.* II.xiv.4; O.S. III.463.14–18 (1:486); cf. *Inst.* II.xiv.6; O.S. III.466.15–21 (1:489).
18. *Inst.* II.xiv.5; O.S. III.465.24–28 (1:488).
19. *Inst.* II.xiv.5; O.S. III.464.18–19, 465.1–2 (1:487–88).

to become children of God by adoption.[20] For this reason, the eternal Son of God obeyed the decree of the Father to become incarnate in Jesus Christ, that we might be adopted as God's children and made heirs of the kingdom in him.

With regard to the second problem the law reveals to our conscience—our sin and unrighteousness—the only-begotten Son of God became a human being to take the place of disobedient and condemned Adam, in order both to render the obedience to God that Adam did not render, and to take away our sin and guilt by taking them upon himself and dying for them, thereby satisfying the wrath of God against sin.[21] It was necessary for Jesus Christ to be true human, for otherwise he could not have taken the place of Adam both in obeying the Father and in subjecting our flesh to death in order to satisfy God's judgment; and yet it was also necessary for Jesus Christ to be true God, for only in that way could he triumph over the sin and death that he took upon himself. "In short, since neither as God alone could he feel death, nor as man alone could he overcome it, he coupled human nature with divine that to atone for sin he might submit the weakness of the one to death; and that, wrestling with death by the power of the other nature, he might win victory for us."[22] The Son of God in the humanity of Jesus Christ subjects himself to the curse and wrath of God by taking our place as a guilty sinner before the judgment seat of God, and overcomes the power of sin, guilt, and the curse of death by rising from the dead by the power of his divinity.

At the heart of Calvin's understanding of the incarnation lies the wonderful exchange: the Son of God becomes human in order to remove every evil thing from us and to bestow on us every good thing we lack. The Son of God becoming the Son of humanity makes it possible for impotent sinners to become adopted children of God and heirs of the kingdom of God, forming the basis of our regeneration; while the Son of God in the place of Adam makes it possible for the Father to regard humanity as his children even though God might justly regard us as enemies, because Christ takes our iniquity upon himself and gives us his righteousness, forming the basis of our justification.[23] In these two ways, we can see how Jesus Christ, in the event of the incarnation, is the fountain of every good and therefore the image of the invisible God, for in him we find both freedom from our iniquity and power to become children of God and heirs of eternal life.

The Anointing of Jesus as the Christ

Calvin further shows Jesus to be the fountain of every good thing given to us by the Father, and therefore the foundation of our faith in God, by his being anointed as Christ by the Holy Spirit. "Therefore, in order that faith may find

20. *Inst.* II.xiv.7; O.S. III.468.12–20 (1:491).
21. *Inst.* II.xii.3; O.S. III.439.21–28 (1:466).
22. *Inst.* II.xii.3; O.S. III.439.28–29, 440.1–3 (1:466).
23. *Inst.* II.xii.3; O.S. III.440.13–18 (1:466–67).

a firm basis for salvation in Christ, and thus rest in him, this principle must be laid down: the office enjoined upon Christ consists of three parts. For he was given to be prophet, king, and priest."[24] By "office" (*munus*) Calvin means the office of being the Christ, the anointed one of God the Father. The anointing of Christ is not done with oil but with the Holy Spirit. The bestowal of the Spirit on Christ, and the enjoining of this threefold office on him, gives a solid basis for faith because it clearly reveals that in Jesus Christ is to be found every good thing the Father wishes to bestow upon us. "Christ was filled with the Holy Spirit and loaded with a perfect abundance of gifts, that he might impart them to us, according to the measure, of course, which the Father knows to be appropriate (Eph. 4:7). So from him as the only source we draw whatever spiritual blessings we possess."[25] To call Jesus the Christ is the same as to call him the fountain from which we must draw every good thing. In this way, Jesus' office of being the Christ corresponds to and further fills out Jesus Christ as the image of the invisible God.

Calvin claims that the term "Messiah" especially refers to the office of Christ as king (which, interestingly enough, is the office in which Christ actually bestows on us every good spiritual thing we lack), but it also refers to Christ as prophet and priest. As the one anointed by the Holy Spirit to be prophet, Jesus Christ is the last of the prophets to bear witness to the Father, and is also the consummation of all prophecy. "We see that he was anointed by the Spirit to be herald and witness of the Father's grace."[26] The prophetic office of Christ refers not only to the actual preaching and witness of Jesus Christ himself, but also to Christ's witness to God the Father through the Holy Spirit in the continual preaching of the gospel from Pentecost to the last day. Yet Christ bears witness to the Father's grace not by pointing us directly to the Father—for the Father is hidden in majesty and cannot be directly known—but rather by proclaiming himself to be the one in whom the Father has revealed himself by depositing every good thing in Jesus.

The gospel that Christ declared, which the church continues to declare empowered by his prophetic office, clearly sets forth Jesus Christ as the fountain of every good sent to us by the Father, and in that way bears witness to the Father. "That is, outside Christ there is nothing worth knowing, and all who by faith perceive what he is like have grasped the whole immensity of heavenly benefits."[27] Christ as prophet in the gospel sets himself forth as the image of the invisible God, the fountain of every good, in order that we might believe in the gospel and thus be engrafted into Jesus Christ by faith. Without Christ as prophet offering himself to us in the gospel, the wonderful exchange in Christ would profit no one.

---

24. *Inst.* II.xv.1; O.S. III.472.3–7 (1:494).
25. *Catechismus Ecclesiae Genevensis*, C.O. 2:22; *Treatises*, p. 95.
26. *Inst.* II.xv.2; O.S. III.473.17–19 (1:496).
27. *Inst.* II.xv.2; O.S. III.474.7–15 (1:496). See J. F. Jansen, *Calvin's Doctrine of the Work of Christ* (London: J. Clarke, 1956).

The central part of Christ's threefold office, and the one most directly related to his being anointed by the Father, is Christ as king. Calvin takes great pains to insist that Christ's kingdom is a spiritual one, both to reassure those rulers who might think that Christ challenges their earthly domain, and more importantly to caution Christians against conceiving of Christ's rule in temporal ways. For Christ is not a king who rules us by giving us temporal blessings and peace; instead, he gives us eternal blessing and spiritual peace while we labor under temporal hardship and the cross, just as Christ himself did not ascend to the right hand of the Father before he had been crucified. Christ gives us power to endure the cross in this life so that we might inherit the kingdom of God, by sharing with us the Holy Spirit the Father has bestowed on him as king. "Such is the nature of his rule, that he shares with us all that he has received from the Father."[28] Christ the king is therefore the fountain from which comes to us the Holy Spirit, which was so abundantly bestowed upon him.[29] "For the Spirit has chosen Christ as his seat, that from him might abundantly flow the heavenly riches of which we are in such need."[30] Christ as king bestows upon Christians the same Spirit with which he was anointed by the Father, and leads them safely through the warfare of the cross to the eternal kingdom that he rules at the right hand of the Father.

To say that Jesus Christ is king is therefore the same as to confess that Jesus Christ is Lord. It is through Jesus Christ that God the Father exercises dominion over the earth, especially over the godly, whom God governs by the Spirit.[31] We should not conceive of Jesus Christ as Lord and king according to his divinity as the eternal Son of God, but rather primarily according to his humanity. In other words, humanity in Jesus Christ has been exalted to a dignity it could never claim on its own, namely to be Lord in the place of the Father, at the right hand of the Father. "Such great majesty would not be appropriate for a mere man, but nevertheless the Father exalted Him in the self-same nature in which He was humbled. . . . Of course we acknowledge that God is the Ruler, but His rule is actualized in the man Christ [*sed in facie hominis Christi*]."[32] The exaltation of Jesus Christ to the right hand of the Father means not only that Christ is the king who bestows on us the Holy Spirit, but also that he is the one who exercises Lordship in the place of God the Father. His will must therefore be obeyed, and he will punish every disobedience not only now but in the last judgment, which will be the final act of his rule.[33]

The anointing of Christ as king corresponds with the same movement of the bestowal of good we saw in Jesus Christ as the Son of God even according

28. *Inst.* II.xv.4; O.S. III.476.23–29 (1:499).
29. *Inst.* II.xv.5; O.S. III.477.11–16 (1:500).
30. *Inst.* II.xv.5; O.S. III.478.4–8 (1:500).
31. *Inst.* II.xv.5; O.S. III.479.12–14 (1:501).
32. Comm. 1 Cor. 15:27, C.O. 49:549; C.N.T.C. 9:327.
33. *Inst.* II.xv.5; O.S. III.479.25–34 (1:501).

to, if not by reason of, his humanity. Christ as king is the one who rules at the right hand of the Father even according to his humanity, and who bestows on us the Holy Spirit so that we might become heirs with him of the kingdom of God. Christ as king thus forms the basis of our sanctification, according to Calvin; for Christ not only gives us the Spirit that enables us to live as children of God and makes us heirs of the kingdom, but he is also the Lord and judge before whose judgment seat we all must stand, who therefore requires the obedience he makes possible by the bestowal of the Holy Spirit.[34] Christ as king also provides the pattern for holiness of life; for just as Christ did not ascend to the Father before he was crucified and raised, so our newness of life arises from our participation in his death and resurrection, and the same pattern of crucifixion and resurrection should be expressed in our lives.

The third office Christ received from the Father by his anointing is that of priest. This office has to do with the expiation of our sins and the satisfaction of God's wrath, which are necessary if God is to regard sinners as God's children, and if sinners are to regard God as their Father. "Hence, an expiation must intervene in order that Christ as priest may obtain God's favor for us and appease his wrath."[35] Calvin bases his understanding of Christ as priest almost entirely upon Hebrews 7–10, where Christ is set forth as having made the once-for-all expiatory sacrifice for our sins by his death on the cross. "To sum up his argument: the priestly office belongs to Christ alone because by the sacrifice of his death he blotted out our guilt and made satisfaction for our sins."[36]

Even though Calvin discusses this office of Christ third, this is not meant to diminish its importance, for it is the "principal point on which our whole salvation turns," for without Christ as priest washing away our sins with his sacrifice, we would not be able to know the grace of, nor be able to call upon, God the Father. "Hence arises not only trust in prayer, but also peace for godly consciences, while they safely lean upon God's fatherly mercy and are surely persuaded that whatever has been consecrated through the Mediator is pleasing to God."[37] Christ as priest, by his once-for-all sacrifice of himself for our sins, both renders the Father propitious and favorable toward us, and makes it possible for us to call upon God as our Father with confidence and assurance.

Christ in his office as priest therefore represents the further removal of every evil from sinners that is discerned in Calvin's description of Christ as the one in whom the Son of God became human in order to take the place of Adam, to render obedience to the Father, and to satisfy the wrath of God by taking our sins upon himself and dying for them. Christ as priest forms the basis for Calvin's discussion of justification, which consists of the forgiveness

---

34. C. O. 6:22; *Treatises*, p. 96.
35. *Inst.* II.xv.6; O.S. III.480.1–6 (1:501).
36. *Inst.* II.xv.6; O.S. III.480.12–15 (1:502).
37. *Inst.* II.xv.6; O.S. III.480.26–30 (1:502).

of sins and the imputation of righteousness. Christ as priest therefore represents the other half of the wonderful exchange, for as priest Christ takes upon himself every evil thing we have (sin, guilt, the curse of God, and eternal death) in order as king to bestow on us every good thing we lack (sanctification, justification, the grace of God, and eternal life).

The Obedience of Jesus Christ

Calvin's discussions of the incarnation and the anointing of Jesus in the threefold office of Christ have as their object the setting forth of Jesus Christ as the fountain of every good given to sinners by God the Father in the wonderful exchange. "What we have said so far concerning Christ must be referred to this one objective: condemned, dead, and lost in ourselves, we should seek righteousness, liberation, life, and salvation in him."[38] However, thus far Calvin has only discussed the *person* of the Mediator. In order to make it clear that the totality of what we as sinners lack in ourselves is found in Jesus Christ, and to found the assurance of faith in him alone, it is necessary to discuss the saving work of Jesus Christ, especially his death, resurrection, ascension, and coming in judgment. "This we must do not only to be persuaded that he is its author, but to gain a sufficient and stable support for our faith, rejecting whatever could draw us away in one direction or another."[39]

It is at this point, when he is going to discuss how Christ reconciles us to God, that Calvin explicitly introduces the context of the knowledge of ourselves as sinners condemned under the curse and wrath of God. This knowledge in turn has the effect of making our reconciliation with God hinge upon the assurance that our sins have been expiated by a sacrifice, and that God's curse and wrath have been taken from us once for all. "No common assurance is required, for God's wrath and curse always lie upon sinners until they are absolved of guilt."[40] Such self-knowledge also has the effect of removing the scandal or offense of the cross; for only sinners aware of the wrath of God can embrace the death of Christ as the satisfaction for their sins, and hence as the basis of their reconciliation with God.[41] Only awakened consciences know that God cannot be known as Father with assurance unless a sacrifice for sins intervenes to reconcile them to God.

However, the awareness of the wrath of God in the conscience raises a major theological problem for Calvin: How can we say that God only begins to be our Father when the death of Christ reconciles us to the Father, when the whole basis of our reconciliation lies in the Father's free, gracious love for sinners, on the basis of which he sent Christ to be our Redeemer? How can the love of the Father be both the cause and the effect of the death of Christ?

---

38. *Inst.* II.xvi.1; O.S. III.481.23–24, 482.1–4 (1:502).
39. *Inst.* II.xvi.1; O.S. III.483.1–5 (1:504).
40. *Inst.* II.xvi.1; O.S. III.483.5–12 (1:504).
41. Sermon Isa. 53, C.O. 35:619; *Sermons on Isaiah's Prophecy of the Death and Passion of Christ*, trans. and ed. T. H. L. Parker (London: James Clarke and Co., 1956), p. 60.

According to Calvin, although it is true that God reconciles us to himself because God first loves us, it is nonetheless the case that our sin and unrighteousness keep God from completely accepting us. In order to remove all barriers to God's love for us, God the Father sent Jesus Christ to take upon himself all that makes impossible our full fellowship with God, especially our unrighteousness, so that we might be completely joined to the Father. "Therefore, by his love the Father goes before and anticipates our reconciliation in Christ. . . . But until Christ succors us by his death, the unrighteousness that deserves God's indignation remains in us, and is accursed and condemned before him."[42] God wills to be the Father of sinners, and yet God cannot embrace them as children because of their unrighteousness, which summons forth God's wrath against them. Therefore, he sends Christ to take upon himself their unrighteousness, guilt, curse, death, and damnation, in order that they might be fully joined to God in Jesus Christ. In this way, the death of Christ is the effect of God's love for us; because God first loves us, God reconciles us to himself in the death of Jesus Christ.

Yet the love of God must also be understood as the effect of the death of Christ, not because it changes God from being a wrathful judge to being a merciful Father, but because God's love for sinners can only be known with assurance in the death of Jesus Christ. Apart from that we can only be aware of God as a wrathful and damning judge. "If then we would be assured that God is pleased with and kindly disposed toward us, we must fix our eyes and minds on Christ alone."[43] Thus when Calvin says that the death of Christ reconciles God to us so that God might become our loving Father instead of our wrathful judge, this must be understood as referring to the awareness of God in our conscience. According to the testimony of conscience, God is a wrathful judge of sinners until the death of Christ intervenes, in light of which we come to regard God no longer as a judge but as a loving Father. In this way the love of God is the *cause* of the death of Christ with regard to the prevenient love of the Father in sending Jesus Christ for us; it can also be said to be the *effect* of the death of Christ with regard to the awareness of the conscience of the believer. "God interposed His Son to reconcile Himself to us because He loved us. . . . As to the feeling of faith, God began to love us in Christ."[44]

God wills that we first be aware of God's wrath against our sin, not because God first begins to love us when Christ dies for us, but because we will not otherwise embrace the love that God has for us in Jesus Christ. Although Calvin often states that this knowledge of our sin and God's wrath comes from the testimony of the law, in another sense it comes from the death of Christ itself. If the Father wills to remove all that separates us from the Father by

42. *Inst.* II.xvi.3; O.S. III.484.37–40, 485.1–4 (1:506).
43. *Inst.* II.xvi.3; O.S. III.485.4–7 (1:506).
44. Comm. 1 John 4:10, C.O. 55:353–54; C.N.T.C. 5:291–92.

sending Jesus Christ to take our place as sinners condemned by God, then it necessarily follows that in the death of Jesus Christ we are not only made aware of the love of God for us, but also of who we are and of what we deserve before the judgment seat of God. "For we gather how frightful our faults are and how God hates them from the greatness of the sufferings of the Son of God. By His grievous afflictions He has testified to us on the one hand His infinite goodness and the love He bears us; but on the other we must contemplate what our iniquities deserve in the sight of God."[45]

It is the suffering and death of Jesus Christ that ultimately causes us to descend into ourselves in order that we might know our sin and guilt and God's curse and sentence of eternal death; and it is also the death of Jesus Christ that is the sole basis of our assurance of the love of God for us as sinners. In the cross and death of Jesus Christ we become aware of what we would have deserved apart from him, so that we might fully embrace the mercy of the Father in Jesus Christ.

Calvin's explicit treatment of the way in which Jesus Christ attained salvation for us is grounded in the wonderful exchange. God sends Jesus Christ to take upon himself every evil thing that separates us from God, in order to bestow upon us every good thing that unites us with God. Although both aspects of this exchange are essential, the banishing of all that separates us from God is the basis for the bestowal of every good thing, just as the bestowal of every good thing is the goal and purpose of the taking away of sin and wrath.

The way in which Christ has both taken away our sin and has acquired righteousness for us is "by the whole course of his obedience."[46] Although the whole of Christ's life was one of willing obedience to the will of the Father, Calvin nonetheless sees the heart of that obedience in Christ's free sacrifice of himself for our sins on the cross.[47] By obeying the will of the Father to take the place of guilty sinners accursed by God, Christ not only takes away all our unrighteousness, but also renders the obedience by which we might be reckoned as righteous before God.[48] The obedience of Christ unto death on the cross is the basis of our justification, which consists of the forgiveness of our sins and the imputation of his righteousness.

However, it is the forgiveness of sins based on the sacrifice of Christ that Calvin emphasizes. "But because trembling consciences find repose only in sacrifice and cleansing by which sins are expiated, we are duly directed thither; and for us the substance of life is set in the death of Christ."[49] The sacrifice that expiates our sins is not one that pays God back what we owe but cannot pay, as in the satisfaction scheme of Anselm, but is rather one in which God transfers our sin, guilt, curse, death, and damnation to the incarnate Son of

---

45. Sermon Isa. 53, C.O. 35:648–49; *Sermons on Isaiah's Prophecy*, p. 104.
46. *Inst.* II.xvi.5; O.S. III.486.1–2 (1:507).
47. *Inst.* II.xvi.5; O.S. III.487.7–9 (1:508).
48. *Inst.* II.xvii.5; O.S. III.512.17–38, 513.1–2 (1:532).
49. *Inst.* II.xvi.5; O.S. III.487.13–16 (1:508).

God. The transfer onto Christ is graphically depicted by the New Testament accounts of Christ's trial and condemnation before Pilate. Jesus' arraignment and condemnation testify that he stood in the place of sinners condemned by God; and yet Pilate's testimony to his innocence attests that he was being condemned not for his own sin and guilt but for ours.[50] The condemnation before the judgment seat of Pilate reveals that in Jesus Christ the Son of God has taken our place as sinners condemned before the judgment seat of God and has forgiven our sins by taking our guilt upon himself. "This is our acquittal: the guilt that held us liable for punishment has been transferred to the head of the Son of God [Isa. 53:12]."[51]

The transfer of our curse onto the Son of God is openly attested by his death on the cross, for the cross was accursed not only by human but primarily by divine judgment (cf. Deut. 21:23). "Hence, when Christ is hanged upon the cross, he makes himself subject to the curse. It had to happen in this way in order that the whole curse—which on account of our sins awaited us, or rather lay upon us—might be lifted from us, while it was transferred to him."[52] By taking upon himself the curse of God on the cross, Christ fulfilled the expiatory sacrifices set forth in the law of Moses. The whole purpose of sacrifices of expiation was to transfer the curse of God from the sinner to the sacrificial object. In the death of Jesus Christ on the cross, the curse lying upon our sin is taken from us and laid upon the only-begotten Son of God, making Jesus Christ the once-for-all sacrifice for sin.[53]

In light of this transfer, even when our consciences accuse us of sin before God, we can be confident that we will not be rejected by God, because the curse has been transferred from us to Jesus Christ. "We cannot fail to be assured that he will pardon our sins and accept us as his well-beloved children, righteous and blameless, since our curse was abolished on this tree that our Lord Jesus Christ was hanged upon."[54] The condemnation of Jesus Christ is our acquittal before God, and the curse of God on Jesus Christ brings the blessing and favor of God upon us.

If Jesus Christ was subject to the curse of God when he took our place as guilty sinners, then he must also have been subject to the death to which our sins made us captives. "Death held us captive under its yoke; Christ, in our stead, gave himself over to its power to deliver us from it."[55] Yet it is not primarily physical death that oppresses us, but the eternal death that results from our rejection and damnation by God. If Christ genuinely took our place, he must have subjected himself to our eternal rejection and damnation by God. This is indicated by the Apostles' Creed, when it speaks of Christ's

50. *Inst.* II.xvi.5; O.S. III.489.10–13 (1:509).
51. *Inst.* II.xvi.5; O.S. III.489.16–20 (1:509–10).
52. *Inst.* II.xvi.6; O.S. III.489.23–27 (1:510).
53. *Inst.* II.xvi.6; O.S. III.490.10–14 (1:510).
54. Sermon Isa. 53, C.O. 35:624; *Sermons on Isaiah's Prophecy*, pp. 70–71.
55. *Inst.* II.xvi.7; O.S. III.491.11–15 (1:511).

descent into hell: "he paid a greater and more excellent price in suffering in his soul the terrible torments of a condemned and forsaken man."[56] The cry of dereliction on the cross is the public testimony to this suffering of Christ's soul under the eternal rejection and damnation of God, even to the point of feeling God's condemning wrath in his conscience.[57] Christ held back nothing when he obeyed the will of the Father in taking our place; he not only took upon himself our sin and guilt, and not only accepted God's curse and death, but also took our place as a sinner utterly forsaken, condemned, and damned by God. We cannot take our place in heaven unless the Son of God first takes our place in hell.

The obedience of Jesus Christ even unto death on the cross represents the fulfillment of that part of the wonderful exchange whereby all the evils that separate us from God are transferred from us to the incarnate Son of God. However, since Jesus Christ is true God as well as true human, it follows that he did not take all of our evils upon himself to be overcome by them, but rather in order to overcome them for us. Thus, even though our reconciliation with God is complete on the cross, the victory of the Son of God over all the evils that he took upon himself is accomplished in his resurrection.[58] If the death of Jesus Christ represents the fulfillment of the transfer of every evil to him, the resurrection represents the beginning of the bestowal upon us of all his blessings. Just as Christ by his death takes our unrighteousness upon himself, so by his rising he bestows his righteousness upon us; as his death means the putting to death of the old person of sin within us, so his resurrection means the bestowal of newness of life upon us; and as his death means that we no longer need to fear death, so his resurrection is the pledge of our resurrection from the dead.

However, it is Jesus Christ's ascension that truly begins the bestowal of all good things upon us in Jesus Christ, for it is in his ascension to the right hand of the Father that Jesus Christ inaugurates God's kingdom.[59] In particular, it is only in his ascension into heaven that Jesus Christ exercises his office as king, not only by governing heaven and earth as the vice-regent of the Father, but primarily by bestowing the Holy Spirit, which he himself received from the Father, upon the elect.[60] This does not mean that Jesus Christ no longer remains our priest after his death—for one of the benefits of the ascension is Christ's intercession for sinners before the throne of the Father—but it does mean that Jesus Christ only begins to reign as king when he ascends to the right hand of the Father.

As the obedience of Jesus Christ unto death on the cross is the basis of our justification and forgiveness, so the ascension of Jesus to the right hand of the

56. *Inst.* II.xvi.10; O.S. III.495.21–27 (1:516).
57. *Inst.* II.xvi.11; O.S. III.496.21–23 (1:517).
58. *Inst.* II.xvi.13; O.S. III.500.12–16 (1:521).
59. *Inst.* II.xvi.14; O.S. III.501.22–25 (1:522).
60. Comm. John 7:38, C.O. 47:182; C.N.T.C. 4:199.

Father is the basis of our repentance and sanctification.[61] The exalted humanity of Jesus Christ is the pledge that we also will inherit the kingdom of God, of which Christ is the king, and is also the fountain from which we receive the Holy Spirit, which both protects us from our enemies—sin, the world, and Satan—and brings us to the inheritance of the kingdom by means of newness of life.[62]

Just as Jesus began to take our place by his obedience from the time of his incarnation onward but only fulfilled his obedience upon the cross, so also Jesus Christ began to rule as king after his ascension into heaven but will only fulfill his office as king at the last judgment.[63] Even though no one, including the faithful, will escape the judgment of the king on that day, the coming judgment is a terror only to the ungodly. To the faithful, it is part of the mercy of the Father, seen in light of the awakened conscience, that the one who has been ordained by God to be our judge is the one who died for our sins and who now rules on our behalf. "No mean assurance, this—that we shall be brought before no other judgment seat than that of our Redeemer, to whom we must look for our salvation!"[64]

Thus both the beginning and the end of Calvin's discussion of how Jesus Christ won salvation for us have special reference to the problem of divine judgment that arises in awakened consciences. Not only the death of Jesus Christ, but also his coming in judgment, take away the fear of God's judgment from our consciences, making it possible for us to know God as Father in Christ, so that we might be empowered by the Spirit of Christ to live as God's children and to inherit God's kingdom.

The whole of Calvin's Christology has as its purpose and goal the depiction of Christ as the fountain of every good, offered to sinners by the Father, in whom we find salvation from all that oppresses us, reconciliation with God, and the bestowal of every good thing we need in order to inherit the kingdom of God. All of this is meant by Calvin to underscore the fact that Jesus Christ is the sole foundation of our knowledge and assurance that God is our merciful Father. "In short, since rich store of every good abounds in him, let us drink our fill from this fountain, and from no other."[65] However, even though the fountain of every good is found in Jesus Christ alone, that fountain benefits no one to whom it is not offered, or who does not accept it by faith. It is precisely in his office as prophet that Christ offers himself to all in the preaching of the gospel, and engrafts us into himself by faith through the illumination of the Holy Spirit.

61. Sermon Eph. 4:7–10, C.O. 51:552; *Sermons on the Epistle to the Ephesians*, trans. Arthur Golding, Leslie Rawlinson, and S. M. Houghton (Edinburgh: Banner of Truth Trust, 1973), p. 359.

62. *Inst.* II.xvi.16; O.S. III.503–4 (1:524–25).

63. *Inst.* II.xvi.17; O.S. III.504.27–31 (1:525).

64. *Inst.* II.xvi.18; O.S. III.506.2–9 (1:526).

65. *Inst.* II.xvi.19; O.S. III.508.15–17 (1:528).

10

THE TRUE WITNESS OF
THE FATHER

Every good thing that we need for our salvation has been given to us by the Father in Jesus Christ alone. "Therefore, we shall find angels and men dry, heaven empty, the earth barren, and all things worthless if we want to partake of God's gifts otherwise than through Christ."[1] This, combined with the knowledge of God the Creator, is the basis of Calvin's rejection of all idolatry, which both confuses the Creator with creation and seeks to partake of the good things of God apart from the incarnate Son of God. "For whatever titles they may give the god they worship, yet because they reject Him without whom they cannot come to God, and in whom God has concretely manifested Himself to us, what have they but some creature or creation of their own?"[2]

The knowledge of God the Father from creation makes it clear that God is an infinite, spiritual essence invisible and unknowable to creatures; whereas the knowledge of God the Son makes it clear that Jesus Christ is the image of the invisible God, apart from whom there is no true representation of God.[3] Jesus Christ is the self-revelation of God the Father to humanity, for he alone is God manifested in the flesh, and he alone is the image of the invisible Father who communicates the Father's benefits to us.

Even though our faith can only be in the one true God, we cannot have faith in God the Father apart from faith in Jesus Christ, his only-begotten Son.[4] There are two reasons for this. The first has to do with the greatness of God's glory, and the creaturely limitations and sinful carnality of the human mind. "Our acuteness is very far from being capable of ascending so high as to comprehend God. Hence all thinking about God without Christ is a vast abyss which immediately swallows up our thoughts."[5] Even before the fall, we creatures could not know God's essence, but only know God through

---

1. Comm. John 1:16, C.O. 47:16–17; C.N.T.C. 4:23.
2. Comm. 1 John 2:22, C.O. 55:325; C.N.T.C. 5:260–61.
3. Comm. Col. 1:15, C.O. 52:84–85; C.N.T.C. 11:308.
4. *Inst.* III.ii.1; O.S. IV.8.9–15 (1:544).
5. Comm. 1 Pet. 1:20, C.O. 55:226; C.N.T.C. 12:250.

awareness of the powers depicted in the works in the universe. After the fall, our dullness and ingratitude prevent us even from knowing God in that way; therefore, in order that carnal human beings might come to know him, the Father manifested himself in a creature, the incarnate Son of God. "In this sense Irenaeus writes that the Father, himself infinite, becomes finite in the Son, for he has accommodated himself to our little measure lest our minds be overwhelmed by the immensity of his glory."[6]

Jesus Christ, who is God manifested in the flesh, is the only object of faith that leads to faith in God the Father, for since he is the incarnate *Son of God*, he is the only creature in whom we can have faith without committing idolatry, and since he is the *incarnate* Son of God, he is the only self-revelation of the invisible God suited to our fallen, creaturely capacity.[7] "God is revealed to us in no other way than in Christ. . . . While God is incomprehensible to us in Himself, yet His form appears to us in the Son."[8]

The other reason why faith in God the Father is impossible without faith in Jesus Christ has to do with our consciences' awareness of divine judgment and wrath. Apart from Jesus Christ, who alone reveals the mercy and love of God the Father, we flee from God even when we make the pretense of approaching God. "Hence, as soon as mention is made of God, we must necessarily be filled with dread, and if we approach Him, His justice is like fire, which will utterly consume us."[9] God manifests himself to us in Jesus Christ not only to accommodate our cognitive capacity, but also to reconcile us to God. The Father makes himself finite in Jesus Christ in order to reveal himself to sinful *creatures*, and God reveals mercy in Jesus Christ in order to reveal himself as Father to *sinful* creatures. "It is evident from this that we cannot believe in God except through Christ, in whom God in a manner makes Himself little, in order to accommodate Himself to our comprehension, and it is Christ alone who can make our consciences at peace, so that we may dare come in confidence to God."[10] God *reveals* his mercy to us in Jesus Christ, for apart from God manifested in the flesh the Father would remain hidden from us in glory; and God reveals his *mercy* to us in Jesus Christ, for apart from the Mediator the conscience prevents us from approaching God, whom it dreads as a wrathful judge of sinners.

In sum, faith in God is only possible by faith in Jesus Christ, for in Jesus Christ God has revealed himself as the fountain of every good for sinful creatures. But because we are empty in ourselves, we must be joined to Christ by faith in order to receive the good things the Father wishes to give us. "In God, indeed, is the fountain of life, righteousness, power, and wisdom; but this fountain is hidden and inaccessible to us. Yet in Christ the wealth of all

6. *Inst.* II.vi.4; O.S. III.325.41, 326.1–3 (1:347).
7. *Inst.* II.vi.4; O.S. III.325.20–22 (1:346).
8. Comm. Heb. 1:3, C.O. 55:12; C.N.T.C. 12:8.
9. Comm. 1 Pet. 1:20, C.O. 55:226–27; C.N.T.C. 12:250.
10. Comm. 1 Pet. 1:20, C.O. 55:227; C.N.T.C. 12:250.

these things is laid before us that we may seek them in him. Of His own will He is ready to flow to us, if only we make room for Him by faith."[11] Even though the Father has bestowed upon Christ every good thing that we lack, the riches of Christ benefit no one who is not joined to Christ by faith in order to participate in Jesus Christ and all his blessings. "Therefore, to share with us what he has received from the Father, he had to become ours and to dwell within us. We also, in turn, are said to be 'engrafted unto him' (Rom. 11:17), and to 'put on Christ' (Gal. 3:27); for . . . all that he possesses is nothing to us until we grow into one body with him."[12]

Just as faith has as its object not God in himself, but Jesus Christ the image of the invisible Father, who was sent to be our wisdom, righteousness, sanctification, and life, so also faith has as its purpose our being made one with Jesus Christ so that we might receive the wisdom, sanctification, righteousness, and life that he alone can bestow upon us. Over and above the good things that faith receives from Christ—especially the twofold grace of justification and repentance—Calvin is concerned that faith should unite us with Jesus Christ himself. This is why his discussion of faith in the *Institutes* precedes his discussion of both repentance and justification: unless faith engrafts us into Christ himself, we can become partakers neither of justification nor of sanctification.

Calvin's definition of faith, corresponding to his emphasis on God the Father, is therefore significantly different from Luther's understanding of faith, which is especially if not exclusively associated with forgiveness and justification, in light of his theology of the cross and his experience of trial (*Anfechtung*). It would have been unimaginable for Luther to discuss repentance and sanctification before justification. However, for Calvin the primary object and basis of faith is neither justification nor sanctification, but Jesus Christ, the image of the invisible Father; therefore Calvin can discuss repentance and justification in either order, depending on the needs of the church he is instructing. Both graces flow from Christ, and faith receives both simultaneously and inseparably when it engrafts us into Jesus Christ himself.

Just as the forgiveness and justification found in Christ was for Luther directed at the conscience terrified by the law in its awareness of sin and wrath, for Calvin Christ as the fountain of every good is directed to the conscience that has been made aware of its poverty and emptiness. For Calvin, the assurance of faith is primarily founded on the assurance of the conscience that Jesus Christ dwells in us and we in Christ, so that he might take away all of the evils of which the conscience makes us aware (ignorance, impotence, sin, guilt, death, and wrath) and freely bestow on us all the good things the conscience testifies we lack (wisdom, sanctification, justification, life, and blessing). Only in this way do the faithful have the confidence and boldness to call upon God as "Abba, Father!"

11. Comm. John 1:16, C.O. 47:16–17; C.N.T.C. 4:23.
12. *Inst.* III.i.1; O.S. IV.1.8–19 (1:537).

Christ is the image of the invisible Father, in whom the Father is revealed to us in a way suited to our limited capacity. Yet no one can know Christ as the fountain of every good, and hence be joined to him by faith, apart from the illumination of the Holy Spirit. The Father cannot be known apart from Jesus Christ, the Father's image, and Jesus Christ cannot be known except by the illumination of the Spirit given by the Father. "It all comes back to this: It is the Father's gift that the Son is known, for by His Spirit He opens the eyes of our minds and we perceive the glory of Christ which otherwise would be hidden from us. But the Father, who dwells in light inaccessible and is Himself incomprehensible, is revealed to us by the Son, His lively image, and in vain do we seek Him elsewhere."[13]

Even though the Father makes himself finite in the Son, and offers himself in a way that can be known by sinful creatures, such is the blindness of our mind and the fear of our conscience and heart that we cannot even know that image apart from the Spirit of the Father.[14] Hence it is by the illumination of the Holy Spirit alone that we know God the Father in the image of the Son, and it is therefore by the power of the Spirit that we become engrafted into Jesus Christ so that we might partake of him and all his blessings. "For when we conceive the benefits of Christ with the mind, this happens by the illumination of the Holy Spirit, it is by his persuasion that they are sealed in our hearts. Hence whatever gifts are offered us in Christ, we receive them by virtue of the Spirit."[15] Calvin therefore often describes the Holy Spirit as the "Spirit of adoption" (Rom. 8:5; Gal. 4:6) because it bears witness to us that God is our Father in Jesus Christ, and is the power by which we are engrafted into Christ.[16]

Faith in Christ is the knowledge of Jesus Christ as the image of the glory of God the Father, by the illumination of the Holy Spirit; and faith engrafts us into Jesus Christ and makes us one with him and all his benefits, by the power of the Holy Spirit. Faith is therefore based on the triune life of God: "to the Father is attributed the beginning of activity, and the fountain and wellspring of all things; to the Son, wisdom, counsel, and the ordered disposition of all things; but to the Spirit is assigned the power and efficacy of that activity."[17] God the Father, the fountain of all things, reveals himself in the incarnate Son, who as the wisdom of God is the image of the invisible Father, by the power of the Holy Spirit, which reveals the Father in the Son and engrafts us into him. "For these two things must be joined: there can be no knowledge of Christ until the Father enlightens by His Spirit those who are blind by nature; and yet it is useless to seek God unless Christ leads the

13. Comm. Matt. 11:27, C.O. 45:319–20; C.N.T.C. 2:24; cf. Comm. John 6:46, C.O. 46:150; C.N.T.C. 4:165.
14. Comm. Matt. 16:17, C.O. 45:473; C.N.T.C. 2:185.
15. C.O. 6:38; *Treatises*, p. 102.
16. *Inst.* III.i.1; O.S. IV.1.20–24 (1:537).
17. *Inst.* I.xiii.18; O.S. III.132.8–11 (1:152–53).

way, for the majesty of God is higher than man's senses can reach."[18] The assurance of faith is ultimately grounded in the trinitarian self-revelation of God.

Christ Offered to Us in the Gospel

The discussion so far has not settled all of the issues that are related to faith according to Calvin. For even if Christ is the fountain of every good, which we can only know and be engrafted into by the Holy Spirit, the question remains: How do we know that the Father offers Jesus Christ *to us* to be accepted by faith? The answer is that God the Father offers Jesus Christ to us in the preaching of the gospel, which includes the testimony of Scripture and the sacraments. "This, then, is the true knowledge of Christ, if we receive him as he is offered by the Father: namely, clothed with his gospel. . . . And there, surely, the treasures of grace are opened to us; for if they had been closed, Christ would have benefited us little."[19]

Jesus Christ as the fountain of every good thing must be offered to us by the gospel; and Jesus Christ was anointed by the Holy Spirit in order to be the true and final witness to the Father in the preaching of the gospel. In other words, Jesus Christ is both the image of the Father, and offers himself as such to the world through his office as prophet by the preaching of the gospel: "Jesus Christ being raised from the dead and having performed the charge that was laid on him by God the Father, was our redeemer and also the bringer of the same message to us, not for once only, but by the continued preaching of it, so much so that he will have his mouth open even to the end, to witness to us that in him we shall surely find all that we can wish for to bring us to the heavenly life."[20] Without Christ as prophet proclaiming himself to us in the gospel and thus bearing witness to the Father, all that he had done for our salvation would have been to no effect. The once-for-all reconciliation effected on the cross in the wonderful exchange must be offered to us in the gospel, to be accepted by faith, if we are in fact to be reconciled to God.[21]

Because Jesus Christ is the image of the invisible Father, Christ's testimony in the preaching of the gospel is really the testimony of the Father to the Father's grace and mercy toward us in Christ.[22] This point is of fundamental importance for establishing the conscience in assurance and certainty.[23] Unless God takes the initiative by bearing witness to God's mercy in the Word, we

18. Comm. John 6:46, C.O. 47:150; C.N.T.C. 4:165.
19. *Inst.* III.ii.6; O.S. IV.13.15–20 (1:548).
20. Sermon Eph. 2:16-19, C.O. 51:413–14; *Sermons on the Epistle to the Ephesians*, trans. Arthur Golding, Leslie Rawlinson, and S. M. Houghton (Edinburgh: Banner of Truth Trust, 1973), pp. 200–201.
21. Sermon Isa. 53, C.O. 35:670–71; *Sermons on Isaiah's Prophecy of the Death and Passion of Christ*, trans. and ed. T. H. L. Parker (London: James Clarke and Co., 1956), p. 130.
22. *Inst.* II.xv.2; O.S. III.473.17–18 (1:496).
23. *Inst.* III.ii.7; O.S. IV.16.18–22 (1:550–51).

can never have confidence that God is in fact merciful toward us: "for we cannot be fully convinced respecting God's favour, except he anticipates us by his word, and testifies that he will be propitious to us whenever we flee to him."[24] Because it is axiomatic that God is true and cannot lie, God's witness in the gospel of Jesus Christ establishes our minds, hearts, and consciences in certainty, which all human opinion taken together is unable to do.[25] The assurance of faith is based on the fact that in the gospel God's mercy is joined with God's truth; God bears witness to us that he wills to be our Father in Jesus Christ: "for it would not help us at all to know that God is true unless he mercifully attracted us to himself. Nor would it have been in our power to embrace his mercy if he had not offered it with his word."[26]

Given the fact that the preaching of the gospel comes to us through the ministry of human beings, it is important for the conscience to be certain that God himself is bearing witness to us of God's mercy; for the conscience makes us aware of God's judgment and wrath against sinners.[27] We only attain such certainty when God not only testifies that God is our Father in Jesus Christ through the gospel, but when God confirms that testimony in our consciences by the witness of the Holy Spirit. "But just as Jesus Christ is the faithful witness of the Father, so He confirms us by the Holy Spirit, and we pray that He will do it more and more."[28]

The preaching of the gospel should not be divorced from the testimony of the sacraments of baptism and the Lord's Supper, for they also offer Christ to us so that we might be engrafted into him by faith, although they derive their power from the gospel.[29] According to Calvin, the sacraments have as their primary purpose the assurance of the consciences of believers in the salvation found in Christ. "This will be of great value for understanding the nature of sacraments, for, if they are covenants, then they contain promises, which may awaken men's consciences to an assurance of salvation."[30] Unlike Zwingli, who claimed that sacraments bear witness of our faith to others, Calvin, like Luther, taught that sacraments are primarily testimonies of God's grace to our consciences.[31] The sacraments, as physical signs employed in the testimony of the gospel, are part of the accommodation of God to the carnal capacity of our minds, for in them "he condescends to lead us to himself even by these earthly elements, and to set before us in the flesh a mirror of spiritual blessings."[32]

---

24. Comm. Mic. 7:18, C.O. 43:429; C.T.S. 28:401–2.
25. Comm. John 3:33, C.O. 47:73; C.N.T.C. 4:83.
26. *Inst.* III.ii.7; O.S. IV.16.4–9 (1:550).
27. Comm. John 20:23, C.O. 47:441; C.N.T.C. 5:207.
28. Sermon Acts 1:4–5, C.O. 48:597; *Sermons on the Saving Work of Christ*, trans. Leroy Nixon (Grand Rapids, Mich.: Baker Book House, 1980), p. 211.
29. Comm. 2 Cor. 5:19, C.O. 50:72; C.N.T.C. 10:79.
30. Comm. 1 Cor. 11:25, C.O. 49:490; C.N.T.C. 9:249.
31. *Inst.* IV.xiv.1; O.S. V.259.2–8 (2:1277).
32. *Inst.* IV.xiv.3; O.S. V.260.27–29 (2:1278).

The sacrament of baptism sets forth the spiritual blessings of the twofold grace of Christ, repentance and justification, while the sacrament of the Lord's Supper offers us the gift of eternal life that is ours in Christ. However, at the heart of both sacraments is the testimony that Jesus Christ is ours and that we are engrafted into Christ. Thus, with regard to baptism, Calvin states, "Lastly, our faith receives from baptism the advantage of its sure testimony to us that we are not only engrafted into the death and life of Christ, but so united to Christ himself that we become sharers in all his blessings."[33] This union with Christ is even more directly attested in the Lord's Supper, which Calvin wanted celebrated at least once a week. "Godly souls can gather a great assurance and delight from this Sacrament; in it they have a witness of our growth into one body with Christ such that whatever is his may be called ours."[34]

Thus the sacraments, like the gospel, set forth Christ into whom we are to be engrafted by faith and in whom we are to participate; and yet neither form of the prophetic testimony of Christ would bear any fruit without the inner illumination of the Holy Spirit.[35] Only the Holy Spirit can establish certainty in the conscience that God is bearing witness to himself through the human ministry of the gospel and the sacraments. Nonetheless it is essential that both the preaching of the gospel and the administration of the sacraments be undertaken by the church under the authority of and in faithful obedience to Christ the prophet.[36] All preaching of the gospel and all administering of the sacraments must be tested by the witness that God bears to Christ in the testimony of Scripture. "Moreover, as we are commended to seek Christ in the Scriptures, so He declares that our work will not be fruitless, for there the Father bears witness to the Son in such a way that He will manifest Him to us beyond all doubt."[37] Just as there is no good from the Father that we should seek outside of Christ, so there is no testimony from the Father that we should hear apart from Christ in the gospel.[38]

Faith has as its object Jesus Christ himself, as he offers himself to us in the preaching of the gospel and the administration of the sacraments, illumined by the testimony of the Holy Spirit. The human ministers of the gospel are to preach nothing other than Jesus Christ as he is attested in Holy Scripture, so that those who hear them may be certain in their consciences that they are hearing Jesus Christ himself. However, we only become certain that the gospel is the testimony of Christ himself when the Holy Spirit reveals Christ to us through the gospel and sacraments and confirms their truth to our consciences. The Holy Spirit that anointed Christ as prophet must accompany

33. *Inst.* IV.xv.6; O.S. V.289.6–9 (2:1307).
34. *Inst.* IV.xvii.2; O.S. V.343.21–24 (2:1361–62).
35. *Inst.* IV.xiv.8; O.S. V.266.5–10 (2:1284).
36. Comm. John 3:11, C.O. 47:60; C.N.T.C. 4:69–70.
37. Comm. John 5:39, C.O. 47:125; C.N.T.C. 4:139.
38. *Inst.* IV.viii.7; O.S. V.139.22–28 (2:1155).

the preaching of the gospel now, for "he received anointing, not only for himself that he might carry out the office of teaching, but for his whole body that the power of the Spirit might be present in the continuing preaching of the gospel."[39]

Faith is therefore the sure and certain knowledge that God is our Father in Jesus Christ, based on the testimony of the gospel and the illumination of the Holy Spirit. "Now we possess a right definition of faith if we call it a firm and certain knowledge of God's benevolence toward us, founded upon the truth of the freely given promise in Christ, both revealed to our minds and sealed upon our hearts through the Holy Spirit."[40] The knowledge of God's benevolence toward us is equivalent with knowing God as our Father in Jesus Christ. "[Faith] may be defined thus: a sure and steadfast knowledge of the fatherly goodness of God towards us, as through the gospel he declares that he will be, for the sake of Christ, our Father and Savior."[41] Because the treasure of goodness set forth in Jesus Christ benefits no one who does not have faith in Christ, faith distinguishes the elect or godly from the reprobate.[42]

However, if Calvin is seeking a definition of faith that distinguishes the children of God from the reprobate, then he immediately confronts a problem that arises both in the testimony of Scripture (especially Luke 8:4-15 and parallels, and Heb. 6:4-8) and in the everyday experience of the church: there are many who appear, not only to others but to themselves, to be believers and to possess the faith that seals their adoption as children of God. "For though only those predestined to salvation receive the light of faith, and truly feel the power of the gospel, yet experience shows that the reprobate are sometimes affected by almost the same feeling, so that even in their own judgment they do not in any way differ from the elect (cf. Acts 13:48)."[43] According to Calvin, such people, as Heb. 6:4 states, have "tasted the heavenly gifts" by the Holy Spirit, so that they may seem to believe in Christ, but such a taste is not in itself the seal of adoption brought by the Spirit; instead it only renders them even more without excuse.

Yet Calvin is also aware of the problem this description of temporary faith creates for the assurance of believers; how are we to know that our faith is the seal of adoption by the Holy Spirit and not simply a taste of the heavenly gifts found in Christ? As this question itself indicates, if Christ benefits only those who truly believe in him, then in order to assure ourselves of salvation, we must not only believe in Jesus Christ, but we must also be certain that our faith in Christ is genuine. The way in which Calvin answers the problem posed by temporary faith will therefore establish the criteria for the rest of his treatment of genuine faith and assurance.

39. *Inst.* II.xv.2; O.S. III.473.19–22 (1:496).
40. *Inst.* III.ii.7; O.S. IV.16.31–35 (1:551).
41. *Catechismus Ecclesiae Genevensis*, C.O. 6:44; *Treatises*, p. 105.
42. *Inst.* III.ii.30; O.S. IV.40.8–9 (1:576).
43. *Inst.* III.ii.11; O.S. IV.20.28–32 (1:555).

Calvin's solution to the problem of temporary faith is twofold. On the one hand, he establishes the foundation of our assurance by stating that the seal of our adoption by the Holy Spirit gives us a confidence in God as our Father that far transcends the taste of the heavenly gifts given to the reprobate: for "only in the elect does that confidence flourish which Paul extols, that they loudly proclaim Abba, Father."[44] The faithful rely on God's mercy and truth in the gospel of Christ, and hence are certain that God is their Father, whereas the reprobate only have a "confused awareness of grace" and a "fleeting awareness" of God's truth. Such a confused and fleeting awareness of God's grace and truth in the gospel is quite different, according to Calvin, from the "firm and certain knowledge of God's benevolence toward us" that is given to God's children.

On the other hand, Calvin suggests that the apparent confidence in God that arises from a confused awareness of God's grace is corrupted by a carnal security far removed from faith. Thus he bids the godly to examine their hearts to see if confidence in the flesh might be perverting their faith.[45] By this self-examination Calvin does not mean the discernment of the testimony of a good conscience, for such testimony is directed against a lower and grosser kind of hypocrisy than temporary faith. Rather he means that the godly are to be simultaneously aware of God's mercy and of God's wrath. The awareness of God's wrath upon their sins does not lead them to despair of God's mercy, but rather leads them both to repent and to flee to God's mercy. "Therefore, at the same time they conceive him to be at once angry and merciful toward them, or toward their sins. For they unfeignedly pray that his wrath be averted, while with tranquil confidence they nevertheless flee to him for refuge."[46]

The godly not only have a firm and certain knowledge that God is their Father, sealed on their consciences by the Holy Spirit, but at the same time they have an awareness of God as their Lord and judge, and consequently an awareness of the gravity of their sin and poverty. Only the godly simultaneously have confidence in God as their Father while they fear God as their Lord and judge. Just as the assurance of conscience that God is Father does not abolish the awareness of conscience that God is Lord, so also the fear of conscience caused by God's wrath on sin does not undermine, but rather strengthens, faith in God as Father. The knowledge of God as Lord keeps us from ever trusting in ourselves, while the knowledge of God as Father keeps us from ever despairing of God's love and mercy. "The Lord at one and the same time encourages our faith and subdues our flesh."[47] The consciences of the children of God are simultaneously aware of God as the fountain of every good in Jesus Christ and of themselves as empty of every good, and in this way they can be assured that their faith is genuine and not temporary.

44. *Inst.* III.ii.11; O.S. IV.21.4–9 (1:555).
45. *Inst.* III.ii.11; O.S. IV.21.14–16 (1:555).
46. *Inst.* III.ii.12; O.S. IV.22.36–38, 23.1–4 (1:557).
47. Comm. Heb. 6:5, C.O. 55:72; C.N.T.C. 12:76.

Only by inwardly embracing the promise of the gospel can we gain the kind of assurance that will give genuine peace to the conscience. The godly whose conscience is aware of God's judgment and wrath, in light of their own poverty and sin, can only know God as Father when they know Christ as the fountain of every good for themselves. "Now it is an assurance that renders the conscience calm and peaceful before God's judgment. . . . Briefly, he alone is a believer who, convinced by a firm conviction that God is a kindly and well-disposed Father toward him, promises himself all things on the basis of his generosity."[48] The gospel sets forth God as the fountain of every good for all sinners in Jesus Christ. The foundation of the assurance of faith is established when the believer embraces the promise of the gospel as being true not only for all sinners, but as being true for himself or herself, so that the believer can confidently pray for and await every good thing from God the Father through Jesus Christ. "To trust in Christ as Mediator, and to rest with assurance in God's fatherly love, to dare boldly to promise ourselves eternal life, and not to tremble at death and hell, this, as they say, is a holy presumption."[49]

In other words, faith brings assurance to the conscience that God is Father when it embraces Jesus Christ as the fountain of every good in the gospel, and thus knows that it is engrafted into Jesus Christ himself so that all that Christ has can be considered its own.

Assurance Amid Trials of Conscience

Consonant with the simultaneity of faith and fear, Calvin does not want us to think that faith gives an assurance of conscience that is untouched by anxiety or doubt. The anxiety and doubt of conscience in the faithful do not mutually exclude, but rather reinforce, assurance and certainty in God's mercy. "Far, indeed, are we from putting their consciences in any peaceful repose, undisturbed by any tumult at all. Yet, once again, we deny that, in whatever way they are afflicted, they fall away and depart from the certain assurance received from God's mercy."[50]

The trials the faithful undergo in their hearts have to do with the opposition between what God promises them in the gospel and what they are aware of in themselves. This opposition is especially strong in the conscience itself, because of its awareness of its poverty and sin on the one hand, and the judgment and wrath of God on the other. "And so, whether adversities reveal God's wrath, or the conscience finds in itself the proof and ground thereof, thence unbelief obtains weapons and devices to overthrow faith."[51] Temptation therefore arises when the conscience makes us aware of the opposition between the promises of God in the gospel and the knowledge of who we are in ourselves, and it seeks to overthrow faith by having us base our knowledge

48. *Inst.* III.ii.16; O.S. IV.26.29–32 (1:561–62).
49. Comm. Eph. 3:12, C.O. 51:184; C.N.T.C. 11:164.
50. *Inst.* III.ii.17; O.S. IV.27.30–34 (1:562).
51. *Inst.* III.ii.20; O.S. IV.30.27–35 (1:566).

of God on our knowledge of ourselves. Since even the godly are weak sinners, then God must be a wrathful judge and cannot be their Father. This is similar to Luther's description of *Anfechtung* as it arises in the conscience; only in Luther the awareness of conscience contradicts the forgiveness of sins, whereas in Calvin the awareness of conscience contradicts the knowledge of God as Father, the fountain of every good.

Calvin, like Luther, can ascribe the onset of temptation either to Satan or to God. Thus, on the one hand Calvin will say, "Now I call it spiritual temptation when . . . the devil so works in our imaginations that God is a deadly enemy to us, and we can no longer have recourse to Him; and we know that he never has to be merciful toward us."[52] Yet on the other hand, Calvin can ascribe temptation directly to God, which would then be the principal temptation believers can endure, "that is to say, when God has summoned them in their consciences, that He has made them to feel His fury, that He has persecuted them in such a way that they did not know where they stood with Him."[53] The conscience that knows God as Father in the testimony of the gospel can also know God as wrathful judge in its testimony to itself. Thus the conscience contains within itself the seeds by which temptation can arise, either by the work of Satan or by the work of God.

In sum, temptation arises because the testimony of Jesus Christ in the gospel is contradicted by the testimony of the conscience to itself. The truth of the gospel is therefore hidden from the believer under the appearance of its opposite. Our present experience does not confirm, but rather denies, that all of the good things God the Father wishes to give us in Jesus Christ are in fact ours.

> Our circumstances are all in opposition to the promises of God. He promises us immortality: yet we are surrounded by mortality and corruption. He declares that He accounts us just: yet we are covered with sins. He testifies that He is propitious and benevolent toward us: yet outward signs threaten His wrath. What then are we to do? We must close our eyes, disregard ourselves and all things connected with us, so that nothing may hinder or prevent us from believing that God is true.[54]

Given the inherent and unresolvable contradiction between the promises of the gospel and the present state of ourselves and the world, the temptation that arises out of this contradiction can only be overcome when we cling to the truth of the Word of God in the gospel and ignore all that contradicts it, especially the testimony of the conscience; for faith is grounded neither in our present experience nor in the testimony of the conscience, but in the

---

52. Sermon Job 1:1, C.O. 33:22–23; *Sermons from Job*, trans. Leroy Nixon (Grand Rapids, Mich.: Baker Book House, 1979), p. 4.
53. Sermon Job 16:1–9, C.O. 34:12; *Sermons from Job*, p. 103.
54. Comm. Rom. 4:20, *Commentarius*, p. 97; C.N.T.C. 8:99; cf. Comm. Phil. 4:7, C.O. 53:62; C.N.T.C. 11:290.

Word of God alone.[55] For this reason Calvin distinguishes between the knowledge of faith (*cognitio fidei*) and the knowledge of experience (*cognitio experimentalis*).[56] We are promised every good thing in Jesus Christ by the gospel, but we only possess those things by faith and hope, not by present experience. "Although, therefore, Christ offers us in the gospel a present fullness of spiritual benefits, the enjoyment thereof ever has hidden under the guardianship of hope, until, having put off corruptible flesh, we be transfigured in the glory of him who goes before us."[57] This does not mean that God may not at times confirm the truth of God's promises by what we experience in the world; but such confirmation by experience is always secondary to faith in the Word, for experience will yet again contradict the Word, but God can never lie.

When the faithful do cling to the Word of God in the midst of temptation, the awareness of sin and wrath in their consciences actually has the effect of strengthening faith; for anxiety of conscience before the wrath of God leads us to trust even more firmly in the mercy of God offered in the gospel. "For nothing so moves us to repose our assurance and certainty of mind in the Lord as distrust of ourselves, and the anxiety occasioned by the awareness of our ruin."[58] We cannot have faith in God's mercy without becoming simultaneously aware of our calamity in our consciences, for we cannot trust in God as our merciful Father without simultaneously reverencing and fearing God as our majestic Lord.[59] The awareness of God's majesty is directed toward the knowledge of ourselves as impoverished sinners, whereas the testimony of the gospel is directed toward the knowledge of God as the merciful Father of sinners in Jesus Christ. "Accordingly, nothing prevents believers from being afraid and at the same time possessing the surest consolation; according as they turn their eyes now upon their vanity, and then bring the thought of their minds to bear upon the truth of God."[60] In ourselves we are empty of every good, and hence we must fear God; but in the gospel God offers us every good, and hence we must simultaneously trust in God.

Yet the simultaneity of faith and fear must be more precisely defined in relationship to our being engrafted into Jesus Christ by faith. Otherwise one could claim, as did "certain half-papists," that faith and fear alternate in the consciences of the godly, as they behold what they are in themselves apart from Christ, and then what God offers them in Jesus Christ. "If, they say, you contemplate Christ, there is sure salvation: if you turn back to yourself, there is sure damnation."[61] Such a position would totally negate faith, for at the heart of faith is the assurance that we are engrafted into Christ so that we

---

55. Comm. Acts 2:25, C.O. 48:44; C.N.T.C. 6:70.
56. Comm. Joel 3:17, C.O. 42:596; C.T.S. 27:136.
57. *Inst.* II.ix.3; O.S. III.400.36, 401.1–3 (1:426).
58. *Inst.* III.ii.23; O.S. IV.33.14–17 (1:569).
59. *Inst.* III.ii.23; O.S. IV.33.19–23 (1:569).
60. *Inst.* III.ii.23; O.S. IV.33.29–32 (1:569).
61. *Inst.* III.ii.24; O.S. IV.34.24–25 (1:570).

dwell in him and he in us, whereas the position of the "half-papists" severs that unity. The simultaneity of assurance and fear must ultimately be set in the context of the unity of the believer with Christ.

> For we await salvation from him not because he appears to us afar off, but because he makes us, engrafted into his body, participants not only in all his benefits but also in himself. . . . Since Christ has been imparted to you with all his benefits that all his things are made yours, that you are a member of him, indeed one with him, his righteousness overwhelms your sins; his salvation wipes out your condemnation; with his worthiness he intercedes that your unworthiness may not come before God's sight. Surely this is so: We ought not to separate Christ from ourselves or ourselves from him.[62]

The temptation with which the anxiety of conscience confronts us is precisely to see ourselves as cut off from Christ, and to judge our relationship to God on that basis. Faith overcomes this temptation, and benefits from the humbling of pride and self-confidence it brings, when it not only ignores the testimony of the conscience that contradicts the Word of God in the gospel, but when it also clings firmly to the unity we have with Jesus Christ. On the basis of our participation in Christ, especially in light of the wonderful exchange, we can better appreciate how assurance and fear can be simultaneously present in the faithful: for the sins and wrath of which our conscience makes us aware have been taken from us by Jesus Christ, whereas Christ himself and every good thing of his have been granted to us.

The opposition of the testimony of the conscience to the testimony of Christ in the gospel, combined with the temptation of the conscience to judge the believer apart from the believer's union with Christ, makes it clear why Calvin insists on the illumination and power of the Spirit in creating faith and engrafting us into Christ. For if the gospel transcends all that we can know by our experience of the world, then our minds cannot know Jesus Christ as the fountain of every good apart from the illumination of the Spirit.[63] By illumining to our minds the testimony of the gospel to Christ, the Spirit at the same time engrafts us into Christ himself. "To sum up: Christ, when he illumines us into faith by the power of the Holy Spirit, at the same time so engrafts us into his body that we become partakers of every good."[64]

Yet the illumination of the mind itself would not be sufficient to establish faith in Jesus Christ, for the temptations of the heart and conscience offer even stronger resistance to the gospel than does the dullness of the human mind. "For the Word of God is not received by faith if it flits about in the top of the brain, but when it takes root in the depth of the heart that it may be an invincible defense to withstand and drive off all the stratagems of

---

62. *Inst.* III.ii.24; O.S. IV.34.26–38 (1:570).
63. *Inst.* III.ii.33; O.S. IV.44.6–10 (1:580).
64. *Inst.* III.ii.35; O.S. IV.46.30–32 (1:583).

temptation."[65] Consequently, just as the mind cannot be certain of the truth of the gospel apart from the illumination of the Spirit, so also the heart cannot be assured of the truth of the gospel apart from its being sealed on the heart, and especially on the conscience, by the Holy Spirit.[66] "There is nothing of Christ, then, in him who does not hold the elementary principle, that it is God alone who enlightens our minds to perceive His truth, and who by His Spirit seals it on our hearts, *and by His sure attestation to it confirms our conscience.*"[67]

Even though the gospel itself bears witness to the conscience that God wills to be our Father in Christ, it is only the testimony of the Holy Spirit that gives confidence and assurance to the conscience so that it dares to call upon God as Father. "Therefore we may know that this is the nature of faith, that conscience has, by the Holy Spirit, a sure witness of God's good will toward itself, and relying on this, it confidently calls on God as Father."[68] Only the testimony of the Holy Spirit can seal the truth of our adoption on the conscience, so that we boldly and confidently cry Abba, Father, and confidently await every good thing from God, including the inheritance of the kingdom of God and eternal life. "Faith, therefore, having grasped the love of God, has promises of the present life and of that to come [1 Tim. 4:8], and firm assurance of all good things, but of such sort as can be perceived from the word."[69] The Holy Spirit bears witness to the conscience that we have been engrafted into Jesus Christ by faith, and hence made participants not only in every good thing of his, but also in Christ himself.

---

65. *Inst.* III.ii.36; O.S. IV.46.34–37 (1:583).
66. *Inst.* III.ii.36; O.S. IV.47.1–6 (1:584).
67. *Responsio ad Sadoleti Epistolam*, C.O. 5:405; *A Reformation Debate*, ed. John C. Olin (Grand Rapids, Mich.: Baker Book House, 1976), pp. 78–79, my emphasis.
68. Comm. 1 Cor. 2:12, C.O. 49:342; C.N.T.C. 9:59.
69. *Inst.* III.ii.28, O.S. IV.38.9–11 (1:574).

11

THE CONFIRMATION OF ADOPTION IN UPRIGHTNESS OF LIFE

The object of faith, according to Calvin, is neither justification nor regeneration, but Jesus Christ himself, the image of the invisible Father, in whom the Father has taken away all the evil that afflicts us and has given us every good thing that we lack. The primary object of faith, therefore, is neither forgiveness of sins nor newness of life, but union with Christ. Jesus Christ offers himself to us in the gospel as the fountain of every good sent to sinners by the Father. The Holy Spirit illumines our minds and seals on our hearts the knowledge of Christ, thereby engrafting us into Christ so that we not only participate in all of his benefits but also in himself.[1] Unlike Luther, who associates faith almost exclusively with the forgiveness of sins and the justification of the ungodly in Jesus Christ, Calvin consistently associates faith with the knowledge of God the Father in Jesus Christ, who has been made by the Father into the fountain of every good that we as sinners lack. Regeneration and justification are two of these good things; however, Calvin's explicit discussion of sanctification and justification must be seen within the larger context of Jesus Christ himself as the fountain of every good.

Just as it is impossible to do justice to Calvin's understanding of the twofold grace of Christ (*duplex gratia Christi*) without setting it in the context of Christ as the image of the invisible God, so also it is impossible to do justice to Christ as the fountain of every good without explicitly taking up in particular the twofold grace of Christ. "With good reason, the sum of the gospel is held to consist in repentance and forgiveness of sins [Luke 24:47; Acts 5:31]. Any discussion of faith, therefore, that omitted these two topics would be barren and mutilated and well-nigh useless."[2] Although Jesus Christ bestows upon us every good thing we lack—among them wisdom, righteousness, power, sanctification, life—it is nonetheless true that the twofold grace of Christ is at the heart of these benefits. This corresponds to the testimony of the awakened conscience under the law; for although the conscience is aware that it

1. *Inst.* III.ii.24; O.S. IV.34.28–31 (1:570).
2. *Inst.* III.iii.1; O.S. IV.55.2–8 (1:592).

lacks every good thing that it needs for its spiritual life, it is in particular aware of its impotence and unrighteousness. Thus, while we find in Christ every good thing, it is important to Calvin that in particular we find the twofold grace of repentance and forgiveness of sins.

Since faith unites us to Christ, both graces of repentance and justification flow simultaneously and inseparably from Jesus Christ to the believer. Were it possible, both would be discussed at the same time.[3] Neither grace, in other words, has either a temporal or a theological priority over the other, since Jesus Christ is the source of both. "Since, therefore, it is solely by expending himself that the Lord gives us these benefits to enjoy, he bestows them both at the same time, the one never without the other."[4] Although justification and sanctification must be distinguished, they cannot be separated, and for this reason both logic and the order of teaching demand that Calvin discuss both at the same time. However, given the nature of human language and the linear nature of human thought, it is impossible to do so. Calvin begins with repentance.

Repentance Before Justification

More than any other single element of Calvin's theology, including the doctrine of election, the transition from faith to repentance raises the question whether Calvin has subverted Luther's reformation theology by subsuming justification under sanctification. There is no doubt that Luther placed justification before sanctification in the order of teaching, especially given his continual battles over justification not only with Rome but also with Karlstadt, the radical reformers, Erasmus, and others. Calvin, however, begins with repentance, and by doing so—even in light of the simultaneity of the twofold grace of Christ—he gives repentance a distinctive emphasis in the Calvinist tradition that endures to this day. Even though this emphasis does not set Calvin at odds with Luther, it does distinguish him from Luther. The question must therefore be asked: Why did Calvin make his transition in the order of right teaching from faith to repentance?

There are two basic reasons why Calvin moves from faith to repentance. On the one hand, against the Roman Catholic and even Augustinian definition of justification, Calvin wants to make it clear that repentance and regeneration do not make justification by faith alone unnecessary, for the godly continually need to be justified even as they are being renewed. On the other hand, against the Libertine and antinomian perversion of justification by faith, Calvin wants to make it clear that one cannot be justified by participation in Christ's righteousness without also being renewed by participation in Christ's sanctification.[5]

---

3. *Inst.* III.iii.1; O.S. IV.55.8–11 (1:592).
4. *Inst.* III.xvi.1; O.S. IV.249.11–19 (1:798).
5. *Inst.* III.iii.1; O.S. IV.55.11–15 (1:593).

Although Calvin shares Luther's concern that justification by faith not be collapsed into sanctification, Calvin became increasingly concerned in his life as a reformer with the antinomian abuse of the gospel. If Luther was concerned that the light of the gospel would be extinguished by theologians and preachers once more turning the gospel into the law, Calvin was equally concerned that the light of the gospel would be put out by the depravity of life of those who confessed Jesus Christ with their lips while denying their confession of faith with their lives.[6] For Calvin the gospel can be lost as much by the dissolute lives of those who profess faith as by the legalism of those who call themselves Christians. If Luther was particularly sensitive to the problem of nomian hypocrisy, Calvin was equally sensitive to antinomian hypocrisy. By placing his discussion of repentance after faith, Calvin makes it clear that a true understanding of the gospel directly entails newness of life.

Yet another reason for this transition has to do with Luther's way of presenting repentance and faith, especially as that is echoed in the Augsburg Confession drafted by Melanchthon. As noted earlier, Calvin was beginning to move away from his acceptance of Luther's understanding of "first law, then gospel"—which is explicitly set forth in the order of the 1536 *Institutes*—to an understanding of repentance that is born of the knowledge of the mercy of the Father, on the basis of Ps. 130:4, "But there is forgiveness with you, so that you may be revered." In the 1559 *Institutes* Calvin frames his treatment of the first use of the law within the context of the self-revelation of God as Father to sinners in Jesus Christ, especially in the Old Testament law of Moses. The continuation of that development is seen here, for by placing repentance after faith in Jesus Christ, Calvin takes issue with Luther on two points: first, that repentance does not precede faith but is rather born of faith; second, that repentance is not primarily directed toward the forgiveness of sins but toward newness of life.

With regard to the first point, Calvin unequivocally states: "Now it ought to be a fact beyond controversy that repentance not only constantly follows faith, but is also born of faith."[7] According to Luther and Melanchthon, repentance is born of the preaching of the law that precedes the gospel and that terrifies the conscience by the revelation of its sin and God's wrath. "Properly speaking, repentance consists of two parts: one is contrition, that is, terror smiting the conscience with a knowledge of sin, and the other is faith, which is born of the gospel."[8] According to Calvin, repentance is not born out of the terror of the conscience prior to faith in the gospel, but is rather born of faith in the gospel. We only begin to apply ourselves seriously to repentance when we know God as our merciful Father in Jesus Christ. "For while Christ the Lord and John preach in this manner: 'Repent, for the

---

6. Comm. 1 Tim. 1:19, C.O. 52:263–64; C.N.T.C. 10:202.
7. *Inst.* III.iii.1; O.S. IV.55.16–17 (1:593).
8. "The Augsburg Confession," *The Book of Concord*, ed. Theodore Tappert (Philadelphia: Fortress Press, 1959), pp. 34–35.

kingdom of Heaven is at hand' [Matt. 3:2], do they not derive the reason for repenting from grace itself and the promise of salvation?"[9] Even though Calvin agrees with Luther and Melanchthon that the fear of God is the beginning of repentance, he insists that such genuine fear of God does not arise unless God is known as our Father by faith; "no one will ever reverence God but him who trusts that God is propitious to him."[10] By placing his discussion of repentance immediately after faith in Jesus Christ, Calvin emphasizes his shift away from Luther by insisting that repentance is born of faith. It is the gospel itself that calls us to, and is the basis of, repentance.

Calvin also disagrees with Luther about the goal of repentance. According to Luther, the first part of repentance is contrition arising from a conscience terrified by the knowledge of its sins, while the second part is the consolation of the conscience by faith in forgiveness offered in the gospel.[11] "There are two elements in true repentance: recognition of sin and recognition of grace; or, to use the more familiar term, the fear of God and trust in mercy."[12] Although Calvin, as we have seen, claims that the beginning of repentance is the preparation for and a necessary condition of faith in forgiveness, he does not include faith in forgiveness in his definition of repentance, for that would be to collapse repentance into justification. This is not to say that Luther in fact collapses justification into sanctification, but rather that Luther equates repentance with the reaction of the conscience to the revelation of the law and the gospel. "Can true repentance stand apart from faith? Not at all. But even though they cannot be separated, they ought to be distinguished."[13]

The other half of repentance is not the consolation of conscience brought about by faith in forgiveness, but is rather the newness of life wrought in us by the Spirit of Christ, our Lord and king. "When they understand vivification as the happiness that the mind receives after its perturbation and fear have been quieted, I do not agree. It means, rather, the desire to live in a holy and devoted manner, a desire arising from rebirth; as if it were said that man dies to himself that he may begin to live to God."[14] By placing his discussion of repentance after faith in Christ but before faith in forgiveness, Calvin distinguishes his position on repentance from that of Luther. Repentance does not precede the preaching of the gospel but is rather born of faith in the gospel; and repentance does not have its goal in the forgiveness of sins but in newness of life.

The Definition of Repentance

Repentance is inseparably connected to the forgiveness of sins, but it must be distinguished from forgiveness. The true meaning of repentance is not the

---

9. *Inst.* III.iii.2; O.S. IV.56.11–14 (1:593).
10. *Inst.* III.iii.2; O.S. IV.56.35–37 (1:594).
11. *In Epistolam S. Pauli ad Galatas Commentarius*, 1535. W.A. 40(I).224; L.W. 26:126–27.
12. *Ennaratio Psalmi LI*, 1532. W.A. 40(II).317.35–37; L.W. 12:305.
13. *Inst.* III.iii.5; O.S. IV.59.20–22 (1:597).
14. *Inst.* III.iii.3; O.S. IV.58.2–6 (1:595).

consolation of a conscience terrified by its sins, but rather the turning of the mind, heart, and conscience away from sin toward obedience to God. Repentance does in fact begin with the fear of conscience before the judgment seat of God, but it leads to the desire to attain the testimony of a good conscience by putting off sin and devoting one's life to the will of God. "On this account, in my judgment, repentance can thus be well defined: it is the true turning of our life to God, a turning that arises from a pure and earnest fear of him; and it consists in the mortification of our flesh and of the old man, and in the vivification of the Spirit."[15]

Although repentance arises from a pure and earnest fear of God, it cannot arise from a sense of divine judgment alone; for when God is only known as judge, the sinner cannot truly turn to God, but rather placates God with external observances and hypocritical worship while inwardly fleeing from God's judgment. Calvin explicitly defines repentance in contrast to this hypocritical obedience to God.[16] The heart of repentance is the sincere devotion and self-surrender of our life to the will of God, and that can only arise when we know that God is our merciful Father, for "no one will ever reverence God but him who trusts that God is propitious to him."[17]

However, repentance is also born of the awareness that God is our Lord and judge in Jesus Christ. Sincere repentance arises from a pure and earnest fear of God in the conscience, when the conscience is haled before the judgment seat of God.[18] One of the central functions of the conscience is to render an account of all our words and deeds and to defend a right course of action. Before we can incline to repentance, our conscience must be awakened by the need to render an account to Christ, whom God has appointed to be our judge. Repentance is inevitably born of faith because we cannot know Jesus Christ without coming to know him as our Lord and judge.[19] "For to know *the fear of the Lord* is to share the knowledge that each of us will have to give account of all his actions before the judgment-seat of Christ, and if a man seriously considers that, he cannot but be moved by fear and shake off all his carelessness."[20] Repentance is therefore rooted in the knowledge that the same Jesus Christ who has been given to us by the Father as the fountain of every good has also been exalted to the right hand of the Father to be our king, Lord, and judge.

The fear of the Lord and the abhorrence of our sins that result from our standing before the judgment seat of Christ the king are the necessary conditions for the reception of the forgiveness of sins that comes from Christ as priest. "Now the hatred of sin, which is the beginning of repentance, first

15. *Inst.* III.iii.5; O.S. IV.60.1–5 (1:597).
16. *Inst.* III.iii.6; O.S. IV.60.23–27 (1:598).
17. *Inst.* III.iii.2; O.S. IV.56.36–37 (1:594).
18. *Inst.* III.iii.7; O.S. IV.61.10–18 (1:599).
19. Comm. 2 Cor. 5:10, C.O. 50:65; C.N.T.C. 10:71.
20. Comm. 2 Cor. 5:8, C.O. 50:66; C.N.T.C. 10:71.

gives us access to the knowledge of Christ, who reveals himself to none but poor and afflicted sinners."[21] This is the third reason why Calvin places his discussion of repentance before his discussion of justification and forgiveness; for God only forgives those who condemn themselves.[22] However, two qualifications need to be made.

First, in opposition to the Roman definition and practice of penance, to say that the beginning of repentance is the necessary condition (*conditio sine qua non*) of faith in forgiveness is not at all the same as making it the *cause* of forgiveness.[23] Repentance is not required in order that God's mercy might be extended to us, for repentance is born of faith in Jesus Christ, and the knowledge of mercy is the cause of repentance. "For this reason, when God offers forgiveness, he usually requires repentance of us in return, implying that his mercy ought to be a cause for men to repent."[24]

Second, to say that repentance is the necessary condition for forgiveness is not to say that the beginning of repentance is a preparation for the grace of God that we can perform on the basis of the conscience apart from the Spirit of God. "This fact stands firm: wherever the fear of God flourishes, the Spirit has worked toward the salvation of man."[25] The one before whose judgment seat we stand is the same one who gives us the Holy Spirit so that we may in fact fear him and repent, namely Jesus Christ in his office as king.

Although it proceeds from an earnest fear of the Lord, repentance itself consists of two parts: mortification and vivification. By mortification Calvin means the putting to death of the old person of sin with all of that person's sinful desires.[26] By vivification Calvin means the newness of life granted to us by the reign of the Spirit within us.[27] Calvin is continually at pains to emphasize that there can be no newness of life where the old person is not continually put to death, even though such a death is not an end in itself but the beginning of newness of life. The fear of conscience and the hatred of sin from which repentance proceeds are also fundamental to what Calvin means by mortification of the flesh; however, our mortification and vivification do not, like the fear of the Lord, arise when we stand before the judgment seat of Christ, but rather when we are engrafted into Jesus Christ. "Both things happen to us by participation in Christ. For if we truly partake in his death, 'our old man is crucified by his power, and the body of sin perishes' [Rom. 6:6], that the corruption of the original nature may no longer thrive. If we share in his resurrection, through it we are raised up into newness of life to correspond with the righteousness of God."[28]

---

21. *Inst.* III.iii.20; O.S. IV.77.19–23 (1:614).
22. See the discussion of this issue in chap. 8.
23. *Inst.* III.iv.3; O.S. IV.88.21–25 (1:626).
24. *Inst.* III.iii.20; O.S. IV.77.29–32 (1:614).
25. *Inst.* III.iii.21; O.S. IV.79.8–9 (1:616).
26. *Inst.* III.iii.8; O.S. IV.62.21–24 (1:600).
27. *Inst.* III.iii.8; O.S. IV.62.28–30 (1:600).
28. *Inst.* III.iii.8; O.S. IV.63.6–11 (1:600–601).

It may now be seen more clearly why repentance is born of faith. Faith engrafts us into Jesus Christ so that we participate not only in all of his benefits, but also in himself. Repentance is brought about by our participation in the power of Christ's death and resurrection in particular, by which we are brought into correspondence with the righteousness of God.

The Renewal of the Image of God

The image of God is meant to express our correspondence with the righteousness and holiness of God.[29] The goal of our participation in the death and resurrection of Christ is therefore the restoration of the image of God within us. "Therefore, in a word, I interpret repentance as regeneration, whose sole end is to restore in us the image of God that had been disfigured and all but obliterated through Adam's transgression."[30] Such restoration is not completed once and for all in this life, but is a lifelong process in the godly. Our participation in the death of Christ does not utterly obliterate our sin, but keeps sin from reigning within us. Our participation in the resurrection of Christ, the vivification of the Holy Spirit, means that our lives are brought into correspondence with the righteousness of God, not that we actually fulfill the righteousness of God in our lives. "But sin ceases only to reign; it does not cease to dwell in them."[31]

Even though repentance breaks the dominion of sin within the godly, it does not at all remove from them the need for the forgiveness of sins. The full restoration of the image of God is therefore the ever-future goal toward which the godly are to strive, and not a present attainment in which they can safely rest. However, the beginning of the restoration of the image of God, and its continual progress, is a reality in the lives of the godly. "Now this is not to deny a place for growth; rather I say, the closer any man comes to the likeness of God, the more the image of God shines in him. In order that believers may reach this goal, God assigns to them a race of repentance, which they are to run throughout their lives."[32] By the restoration of the image through our participation in the death and resurrection of Christ, our lives begin to correspond to the righteousness of God.

The principal use and proper purpose of the law of God—that is, the third use—has its locus in this restoration of the image of God by our participation in Christ.[33] The law sets forth the archetype of the holiness of God to which our lives must conform if we are to express the image of God. "For God has so depicted his character in the law that if any man carries out in deeds whatever is enjoined there, he will express the image of God, as it were, in his own life."[34] Since the goal of regeneration and repentance is to restore the

---

29. See chap. 7.
30. *Inst.* III.iii.9; O.S. IV.63.11–14 (1:601).
31. *Inst.* III.iii.11; O.S. IV.66.26–30 (1:603).
32. *Inst.* III.iii.9; O.S. IV.65.7–11 (1:601).
33. *Inst.* II.vii.12; O.S. III.337.23–25 (1:360).
34. *Inst.* II.viii.51; O.S. III.390.15–20 (1:415).

image of God within us, the law of God has a positive role to play in the Christian life by setting forth the pattern of holiness into which we are to be transformed. "The object of regeneration is to manifest in the life of believers a harmony and agreement between God's righteousness and their obedience, and thus confirm the adoption that they have received as sons [Gal. 4:5; cf. 2 Pet. 1:10]. The law of God contains in itself that newness by which his image can be restored in us."[35] The godly can measure their progress in repentance, and discern how far they have yet to go, by measuring their lives by the law of God. "Briefly, the more earnestly any man measures his life by the standard of God's law, the surer are the signs of repentance that he shows."[36] The law, therefore, sets before us the righteousness of God to which our lives are to conform in repentance, and teaches us the will of God that our lives are to image in obedience.

Such instruction by the law is essential for the godly, for the conscience on its own is utterly ignorant of how God wants to be worshiped. "For no man has attained to such wisdom as to be unable, from the daily instruction of the law, to make fresh progress toward a purer understanding of the divine will."[37] Our obedience must conform to the righteousness revealed in God's law, and not to some pattern we invent. "We must not construct for ourselves our favorite new pattern of righteousness apart from the Word of God, but must allow ourselves to be ruled by God's command."[38] The godly must continually be taught the will of God by the law, so that they may constantly have held before them the goal toward which they are to strive and the archetype of holiness to which their lives are to conform.

Over and above such instruction, the law is necessary to exhort the faithful to obedience. "Again, because we need not only teaching but also exhortation, the servant of God will also avail himself of this benefit of the law; by frequent meditation upon it to be aroused in obedience, be strengthened in it, and be drawn back from the slippery path of transgression."[39] Such exhortation is not given so that we may be encouraged by our own ability to fulfill the law, for then the law would only accuse us of our own impotence; rather "the Lord instructs by their reading of it those whom he inwardly instills with a readiness to obey."[40]

More importantly, such exhortation takes place without the curse of the law being unleashed on the conscience, either as a threat to coerce obedience or as a condemnation of our lack of perfect obedience. "Now, the law has power to exhort believers. This is not a power to bind their consciences with a curse, but one to shake off their sluggishness, by repeatedly urging them,

---

35. *Inst.* III.vi.1; O.S. IV.146.14–18 (1:684).
36. *Inst.* III.iii.16; O.S. IV.72.31–33 (1:609).
37. *Inst.* II.vii.12; O.S. III.337.35–37, 338.1 (1:360).
38. Comm. Luke 1:6, C.O. 45:19; C.N.T.C. 1:6.
39. *Inst.* II.vii.12; O.S. III.338.1–4 (1:360–61).
40. *Inst.* II.vii.12; O.S. III.338.21–22 (1:361).

and to pinch them awake to their imperfection."[41] The curse of the law has been abrogated for believers by Christ's becoming a curse for us on the cross. For Calvin, as for Luther, the abrogation of the law from the conscience has to do with the curse of the law, and not with the command of the law per se. "What Paul says of the curse unquestionably applies not to the ordinance itself but solely to its force to bind the conscience."[42]

In sum, for Calvin as for Luther, the exhortation of the law does not compel obedience by threatening the curse and promising justification, but rather stirs up the obedience of those who have already been granted the willingness to obey by the Holy Spirit, with the confidence that they do not obey as servants of a judge but as children of a gracious Father.[43] Because Christ as priest frees us from the curse of the law while Christ as king renews the image of God within us, the law has a positive role in the life of believers, not terrifying our consciences with the awareness of sin and wrath, but teaching us the pattern of holiness to which we are to conform our lives, and exhorting us to do so, so that we might express the image of God by our obedience.

God renews his image within us through repentance in order to join us to himself; because God is holy, only those who are holy can be brought into union with God. The fundamental reason for our obedience is therefore the nature of God: we must be made holy because God is holy (Lev. 19:2; 1 Pet. 1:15-16). "When we hear mention of our union with God, let us remember that holiness must be its bond."[44] Holiness of life is not the basis of our union with God, but it is the means by which God brings those whom he has freely adopted into fellowship with himself. By holiness Calvin in particular means a pure conscience: "for God is not deceived, as men are, by outward pretense, but looks to faith, that is, to the truth of the heart."[45] The purpose of repentance, therefore, is to join us to God by holiness of life, which arises from our participation in the death and life of Christ, which restores the image of God in us. Repentance thus brings about the testimony of a good conscience that our lives are in harmony and agreement with the righteousness of God as set forth in the law, the archetype of divine purity.

However, Calvin presses the goal of repentance beyond conformity to the archetype of the law; for the image of God that was all but obliterated in Adam is only restored when we participate in the death and resurrection of Jesus Christ, who is himself the image of the invisible God. Therefore, the pattern or archetype to which we ought to conform, and the image of God we ought to express, are found in none other than Jesus Christ. "And to wake us more effectively, Scripture shows that God the Father, as he has reconciled

41. *Inst.* II.vii.14; O.S. III.339.26–28 (1:362).
42. *Inst.* II.vii.15; O.S. III.340.14–16 (1:363).
43. Comm. Gal. 5:23, C.O. 50:526; C.N.T.C. 11:126.
44. *Inst.* III.vi.2; O.S. IV.147.29–37 (1:685–86).
45. Comm. Eph. 1:4, C.O. 51:148; C.N.T.C. 11:126.

us to himself in his Christ [cf. 2 Cor. 5:18], has in him stamped the likeness [cf. Heb. 1:3] to which he would have us conform."[46]

This christological focus of repentance distinguishes the life of the Christian from that enjoined by philosophers. They urge us to live a life of virtue in accordance with our nature, whereas God wills that our lives express the pattern set forth in Christ.[47] Therefore, it is not the holiness of God as set forth in the law of Moses per se that is the archetype to which we are to conform, but rather the image of God as set forth in Jesus Christ. Even though holiness of life is the bond of union by which God joins us to himself, Jesus Christ is the bond of adoption in whom we become children of God and through whom we can know God as our Father. "For we have been adopted as sons by the Lord with this one condition: that our life express Christ, the bond of our adoption."[48]

We are therefore under a double obligation to conform our lives to the righteousness of God. First, as creatures made in the image of God, our repentance has as its object the mirroring of the holiness of God by our holiness and obedience. Second, repentance has as its goal expressing Christ, the bond of our adoption, in our lives. There are therefore two patterns of righteousness: the third use of the law of Moses (the Ten Commandments), and the example of Jesus Christ himself. "Accordingly, unless we give and devote ourselves to righteousness, we not only revolt from our Creator with wicked perfidy but we also abjure our Savior himself."[49] Although Calvin insists that we are under obligation both to our Creator and to our Redeemer, he subsumes the former obligation under the latter, so that we truly express the image of God our Creator when we are conformed to the image of God our Redeemer, Jesus Christ.

Jesus Christ not only renews the image of God within us when we participate in his death and resurrection, but Christ's self-denial, cross, and resurrection are the pattern all Christians are to represent in their own lives.[50] Just as Jesus Christ did not ascend to the right hand of God the Father as our king before he had first obeyed the Father unto death on the cross, so also the Father conforms our lives to Christ's by leading us to the inheritance of the kingdom through the cross.[51] Because God has destined us to be conformed to Christ by having us share in his cross in this life, we must also set our minds on our life hidden with Christ in God, so that even as we partake in his suffering and death we can hope with confidence in the power and triumph of his resurrection.[52]

---

46. *Inst.* III.vi.3; O.S. IV.148.11–13 (1:686).
47. *Inst.* III.vi.3; O.S. IV.148.18–23 (1:686).
48. *Inst.* III.vi.3; O.S. IV.148.23–26 (1:686–87).
49. *Inst.* III.vi.3; O.S. IV.148.27–29 (1:687).
50. *Inst.* III.viii.1; O.S. IV.161.23–26 (1:702).
51. *Inst.* III.viii.1; O.S. IV.161.36–38, 162.1–4 (1:702).
52. *Inst.* III.ix.6; O.S. IV.177.3–6 (1:719).

In sum, the death and resurrection of Jesus Christ in which we participate not only renew the image of God within us, but also become the pattern we are to express in our lives. It should be noted that Luther also subsumes the Ten Commandments under the example of Christ that we are to imitate. For Luther, however, this example is primarily found in the happy exchange: just as Christ took our sins from us and gave himself to us on the cross, so we should share one another's burdens and give to those in need (see especially *The Freedom of a Christian*).

This means that even though the third use of the law finds its locus in the life of repentance, the real goal of repentance is not set forth in the law of Moses but in the gospel of Jesus Christ. Repentance is born of faith in the gospel because faith knows Jesus Christ as the image of the Father, which we cannot truly know unless we "put on Christ" and are transformed into his image. We initially receive the gospel as the right knowledge of God in Christ, but it must pass into our hearts and our daily living and transform us or else it is not true knowledge of the gospel.[53] Those who claim to know Jesus Christ from the gospel but who do not put on Christ by participating in his death and resurrection do not in fact have a true knowledge of Christ. "For it is a doctrine not of the tongue but of life."[54] We cannot know Jesus Christ as the image of God, the fountain of every good, without also knowing Jesus Christ as our Lord and king who transforms us into himself. Similarly, we cannot be illumined by the Holy Spirit into the right understanding of Jesus Christ in the gospel without having the affections of our hearts transformed by the same Spirit. Nor can we know God as our Father and Lord in Christ without showing ourselves to be God's children and servants.[55]

In sum, we cannot know Jesus Christ as the image of God through faith in the gospel without being transformed into that image by repentance. "In short, the teaching of the gospel is a living mirror in which we contemplate God's image and are transformed into it, as Paul teaches in 2 Cor. 3:18. Where the conscience is not clear, there can be only the empty ghost of knowledge."[56]

Obedience Confirms Assurance

The testimony of a good conscience that arises out of our conformity to Jesus Christ has as it primary purpose the confirmation that our knowledge of Christ is genuine and our confession of faith sincere. "What we say has little weight without a corresponding life, and he therefore joins to confession a good conscience."[57] The good conscience bears witness that our lives correspond to the gospel of Jesus Christ in which we believe and which we confess. For

---

53. *Inst.* III.vi.4; O.S. IV.149.28–32 (1:688). Note the direct echo of the *Paraclesis* of Erasmus in this formulation of Calvin's.

54. *Inst.* III.vi.4; O.S. IV.149.16–23 (1:687–88).

55. Comm. 1 John 2:3, C.O. 55:311; C.N.T.C. 5:245.

56. Ibid.

57. Comm. 1 Pet. 3:16, C.O. 55:263; C.N.T.C. 12:290.

this reason, Calvin says that a good conscience is the way we protect and hold fast to a true understanding of the gospel.[58] Those who do not protect their faith with a good conscience, and whose lives do not correspond to the gospel they profess, will inevitably fall away from the faith, even if they began with a proper understanding of the gospel.[59] Those who cast aside a good conscience make shipwreck of their faith (1 Tim. 1:19), because they think that faith in Christ can be combined with a disobedient and dissolute life. "The metaphor of shipwreck is very apt, for it suggests that if we wish to reach port with our faith intact, we should make a good conscience the pilot of our course, or otherwise there is danger of shipwreck: faith may be sunk by a bad conscience as by a whirlpool in a stormy sea."[60]

Those who wish to preserve the treasure of the true knowledge of Christ in the gospel should keep it in the vault of a good conscience, which keeps our faith from being taken from us.[61] Indeed, just as Adam lost the good things freely bestowed upon him in creation through his disobedience, so we only keep the good things that the Father bestows on us in Jesus Christ by our obedience and good conscience. "Let others know, that what God has given may at any time be taken away, except good conscience be as it were the guard to preserve God's gifts and benefits, so that they may not at any time fall away or be lost."[62]

The testimony of a good conscience is necessary to prove that our faith in Christ is sincere. It is relatively easy to boast of faith in the gospel before others, much as Calvin thought that many in his day boasted of their faith in the gospel simply because of the popularity of the Reformation. The truth of our faith is confirmed by a good conscience, which, according to Calvin, it is impossible to feign. "There is nothing commoner or easier than to boast of faith and a good conscience, but there are very few who prove by their deeds that they are free from every trace of hypocrisy. . . . Every profession of faith which does not prove itself by a good conscience and manifest itself in love is insincere."[63] The testimony of a good conscience is therefore the only way to confirm and preserve true faith in the gospel, while a bad conscience will shipwreck faith and is the mother of all heresies.

The testimony of a good conscience also allows believers to profess the gospel with boldness so that others hear it with power, whereas a bad conscience subjects both the person and the gospel to ridicule. "Besides, integrity of conscience alone is that which gives us confidence to speak as we ought. . . . The defense of the tongue will avail little unless the life corresponds

---

58. Comm. 1 Tim. 1:19, C.O. 52:263; C.N.T.C. 10:202.
59. Ibid.
60. Ibid.
61. *Advertissement Contre L'Astrologie Qu'on Appelle Iudiciaire*,C.O. 7:513; Mary Potter, trans., "A Warning Against Judiciary Astrology and Other Prevalent Curiosities," *Calvin Theological Journal* 18 (1983):160.
62. Comm. Jer. 22:24, C.O. 38:397; C.T.S. 19:120.
63. Comm. 1 Tim. 1:5, C.O. 52:254; C.N.T.C. 10:191–92.

with it."[64] All of the godly, and especially those called to the public ministry of the gospel, should take care to examine themselves for the testimony of a good conscience, which testifies that their lives conform to their profession of faith. Without such testimony, they stand in danger both of losing their own faith and of subjecting the gospel to the ridicule of the ungodly.

If the goal of our adoption by God is conformity to Jesus Christ, and the testimony of a good conscience tells us that our lives do in fact express Christ, the bond of our adoption, then the testimony of a good conscience not only confirms to us that our faith is sincere, but it also confirms our adoption and election as children of God. "One argument whereby we may prove that we are truly elected by God and not called in vain is that our profession of faith should find its response in a good conscience and an upright life."[65] Indeed, the conformity of our lives to the gospel, of which the testimony of a good conscience informs us, is the most certain mark by which the children of God can distinguish themselves from the impious.[66]

Such confirmation of our adoption and election is not, according to Calvin, to be taken as the foundation of our knowledge and assurance of our adoption, as though it were the basis of our confidence in God as our Father in Jesus Christ; instead, since the purpose and goal (not the foundation and basis) of our adoption by God is conformity to Christ as the image of God, the testimony of a good conscience confirms that we have not been adopted in vain. "But because He chooses and calls us for the purpose of being pure and spotless in His sight, purity of life is rightly regarded as the illustration and evidence of election, whereby the faithful not only show to others that they are the sons of God, but also confirm themselves in this faith, but in such a way that they place their foundations elsewhere."[67] Even if the good conscience does not constitute the foundation of faith, it is nonetheless true that its absence invalidates the profession of faith: "every profession of faith which does not prove itself by a good conscience and manifest itself in love is insincere."[68]

Calvin was as concerned that faith in the gospel would be lost because of the absence of the testimony of a good conscience in believers as Luther was concerned that faith in the gospel would be lost by the legal knowledge of God based in the testimony of the conscience of believers. As we have seen, Luther did allow for a significant and necessary role for the testimony of a good conscience in confirming faith and election. Nevertheless, he preferred to delegate the testimony of a good conscience to the sphere before the world, whereas the terrified conscience was more the norm before God, within the context of the theology of the cross. The testimony of a good conscience is hidden in the Christian under the slander and accusations of the world, while

---

64. Comm 1 Pet. 3:16, C.O. 55:263; C.N.T.C. 12:290.
65. Comm. 2 Pet. 1:10, C.O. 55:449; C.N.T.C. 12:333.
66. Comm. Rom. 8:9, *Commentarius*, p. 164; C.N.T.C. 8:164.
67. Comm. 2 Pet. 1:10, C.O. 55:450; C.N.T.C. 12:333–34.
68. Comm. 1 Tim. 1:5, C.O. 52:259; C.N.T.C. 10:191–92.

faith in forgiveness is hidden under the awareness of sin and wrath in the conscience. Calvin, on the other hand, emphasizes the importance of the testimony of a good conscience before God more than he does its role before the world, because of its necessary function in confirming the goal and purpose of our adoption, repentance, and regeneration, without undermining or replacing the foundation and basis of our adoption, the forgiveness of sins. "Therefore, as works have regard to men, so conscience refers to God. A good conscience, then, is nothing but inward integrity of heart."[69]

A good conscience therefore has as its proper forum the life of the Christian in God's sight (*coram Deo*), and it signifies a sincere and heartfelt desire to obey God and to correspond with God's righteousness. This means that one does one's duty with regard for God alone, regardless of what other people may think or do. " 'Conscience toward God' means this, that one performs his duty, not from a regard for men, but for God."[70] In this sense, the good conscience seeks to please God alone; those who act out of a desire to gain the approval of other humans can be said to lack a good conscience.[71]

Thus, even if we are subjected to human disgrace because of our obedience to God, we should value the testimony of a good conscience more than the praise of the whole world. "For no one will prove that he heartily loves virtue, but he who, being content with God as his only witness, does not hesitate to submit to any disgrace, rather than decline from the path of duty."[72] This does not mean that we should not also seek to have a good reputation among people; but the desire for a good reputation must always be secondary to the desire to maintain a good conscience before God, lest we come to fear other people more than God. "The first concern is certainly to be a good man, and this is secured not only by outward deeds but by an upright conscience; but the second concern is that the people among whom you live should acknowledge you to be the good man whom you are."[73] The first consideration is foundational, for the godly must act out of a good conscience before God even when the whole world accuses them of sin and evil. A good conscience seeks approval from God alone.

The testimony of a good conscience is therefore necessary not only in confirming the faith and adoption of the godly, but also in sustaining the godly in the face of the rejection of the world and the assaults of Satan.[74] The testimony of a good conscience tells us that we are undertaking our task through the call and commandment of God, and thus not only sustains us against the false accusations of the wicked, but also leads us to hope in God as the defender and vindicator of God's own cause.[75] It is in this sense that the godly can

---

69. *Inst.* III.xix.16; O.S. IV.295.31–34 (1:849).
70. Comm. 1 Pet. 1:19, C.O. 55:248–49; C.N.T.C. 12:274–75.
71. Comm. 1 Thess. 2:4, C.O. 52:147; C.N.T.C. 8:342.
72. Comm. Gen. 39:11, C.O. 23:506; C.T.S. 2:298–99.
73. Comm. 2 Cor. 8:21, C.O. 50:104; C.N.T.C. 10:117.
74. Comm. Ps. 41:8, C.O. 31:422; C.T.S. 9:121.
75. Comm. Ps. 4:1, C.O. 31:58–59; C.T.S. 8:39.

appeal to their integrity before God in their prayers; not that their integrity is sufficient to justify them before God, but it testifies that their cause is God's cause while their enemy's is not.[76] However, such confidence would not be sufficient in and of itself if it did not lead the godly to commit their cause and its vindication to God in prayer.[77] Because the testimony of conscience tells us that the cause is not ours but God's, it leads us to call upon God to vindicate the cause and to defend God's honor. If instead "any man, trusting to the testimony of a good conscience which he enjoys, neglects the exercise of prayer, he defrauds God of the honor which belongs to him, in not referring his cause to him, and in not leaving him to judge and determine it."[78]

The relationship of the testimony of the good conscience to prayer begins to indicate some of the limitations and qualifications Calvin places upon the conscience. The first limitation arises from God as Father, the fountain of every good; the second arises from God as Lord and judge, whose judgment is far keener and more penetrating than that of even the godly conscience. The first qualification arises when Calvin comments on 2 Cor. 1:12, "For our boast is this, the testimony of our conscience that we have behaved in the world, and still more toward you, with holiness and godly sincerity, not by earthly wisdom but by the grace of God." Calvin asks how such boasting in the testimony of conscience squares with Paul's statement that the one who glories should glory in the Lord (2 Cor. 10:17). Taking his cue from the phrase "by the grace of God" in 2 Cor. 1:12, Calvin says: "Firstly, Paul is not setting himself over against God as if he had anything of his own or that came from himself. Secondly, he does not make his salvation depend on the integrity he claims or put any confidence in it. Lastly, it is God's gifts of which he is boasting so that he is glorifying God as their sole author to whom they are all to be ascribed."[79]

In this way, glorying in the testimony of a good conscience not only leads us to entrust our lives and cause to God in prayer, but more importantly it leads us to acknowledge God as the fountain of every good, from whose grace alone comes the testimony of a good conscience. "First, we must acknowledge that everything good in us has been received from God, claiming nothing for ourselves; next, we must hold fast this foundation, that our assurance of salvation depends solely on God's mercy; finally, we must rest in God as the sole author of all good things."[80] To glory in the testimony of a good conscience means to acknowledge God as the fountain of every good, from whose mercy salvation freely flows to us in Jesus Christ through the Holy Spirit. Such glorying does not lead us to think that we are sufficient unto ourselves, or that we have merited the blessings of God by our holiness of life, but rather

76. Comm. Ps. 7:8, C.O. 31:83; C.T.S. 8:84.
77. Comm. Ps. 17:1, C.O. 31:159; C.T.S. 8:235.
78. Comm. Ps. 17:1, C.O. 31:159; C.T.S. 8:236.
79. Comm. 2 Cor. 1:12, C.O. 50:17; C.N.T.C. 10:15–16.
80. Ibid.

glorifies the grace of God.[81] The testimony of a good conscience that confirms our adoption does not lead us to trust in our own gifts, but leads us to glorify God the Father, the fountain of every good, and to trust in God's mercy alone, which is the primary foundation of the assurance of faith.

The second limitation on the testimony of a good conscience, namely that God's judgment transcends that of the conscience, arises when Calvin writes an exegesis on 2 Cor. 10:17, "Let the one who boasts, boast in the Lord." Here Calvin states that Paul is not speaking of the glorying mentioned above, which acknowledges God alone as the author of all good things, but of the glorying that results from the acknowledgment of the judgment of God, before which we stand or fall. Although the testimony of a good conscience confirms our faith by attesting that our life corresponds with the gospel we profess, Calvin does not want the believer to equate the self-judgment of conscience with the judgment of the Lord, before which even the good conscience must be judged. The believer knows better than anyone else how easily seduced we are by a good opinion of ourselves, and how self-love can blind us to our own sins. Thus the testimony of a good conscience can never replace the judgment of God, nor can it be directly equated with it. "For since nearly everybody is blinded by an excess of self-love, we ought not to rest secure in our own estimate of ourselves. . . . For we should remember that the right of pronouncing judgment upon us is reserved to God alone for we are not competent judges in our own cause."[82]

Calvin is confident that the judgment of conscience is sufficient to disclose the sincerity or hypocrisy of our faith, by whether we long from our heart to be conformed to Christ; but he is also sure that the judgment of conscience can never be equated with the judgment of God. Even when our conscience does not accuse us, we cannot assume we are innocent; for the judgment of God so transcends the human judgment of conscience that it can overthrow it in a moment. "For our perception is poor, but God is penetrating beyond measure. We are far too lenient in what we think about ourselves, but God is a very strict Judge."[83]

The testimony of a good conscience may rightly and necessarily declare the sincerity of our faith based on the genuineness of our repentance, but the testimony of conscience is never adequate to declare us justified before God. We can only be certain that we are justified before God when God declares that we are justified in Jesus Christ. The testimony of a good conscience must always accompany, but can never replace, the faith in Jesus Christ that alone justifies us and assures our consciences before the judgment seat of God.

81. Comm. Gal. 6:4, C.O. 50:260; C.N.T.C. 11:110–11.
82. Comm. 2 Cor. 10:17, C.O. 50:122; C.N.T.C. 10:137–38.
83. Comm. 1 Cor. 4:4, C.O. 49:365; C.N.T.C. 9:88.

12

THE FOUNDATION OF ADOPTION
IN THE FORGIVENESS
OF SINS

Faith has as its object neither justification nor repentance per se, but Jesus Christ. Faith unites us with Jesus Christ and engrafts us into him so that we become participants not only in all of his blessings but also in himself. Yet of all the good things that faith receives out of participation in Christ, it is the twofold grace of Christ—repentance and justification—that is the most important for us to know, according to Calvin.[1] This twofold grace is given simultaneously and inseparably. Nonetheless, Calvin begins his discussion with repentance, primarily to counter the kind of antinomian hypocrisy that sees the gospel as something to talk about but not as something to which to conform one's life; such hypocrites use the gospel as a cover to enable themselves to indulge in sin with impunity.[2] Repentance has as its goal the transformation of our lives into conformity with Christ, the image of God, by our participation in his death and resurrection and expression of his death and resurrection in our lives.

The testimony of a good conscience is necessary to attest to us that our faith in Jesus Christ is sincere inasmuch as our lives have begun to express Christ. Those who boast of faith in the gospel, but lack the testimony of a good conscience arising out of repentance, will lose both their faith and the gospel. The testimony of a good conscience is essential, not to justify us before God, but to confirm the sincerity of our faith in Jesus Christ through the testimony that our lives are more and more conformed to his archetype.

The priority of repentance over justification in the order of Calvin's teaching should not, therefore, be read as a prioritizing of repentance before justification in our relationship to God. Beginning with repentance enables Calvin to demonstrate more clearly not only the necessity of repentance in the life of faith, but also the continual and lifelong necessity of justification by faith. If

---

1. *Inst.* III.xi.1; O.S. IV.182.3–8 (1:725).
2. *Advertissement Contre L'Astrologie Qu'on Appelle Iudiciaire*, C.O. 7:514; Mary Potter, trans., "A Warning Against Judiciary Astrology and Other Prevalent Curiosities," *Calvin Theological Journal* 18 (1983).

the greatest danger with regard to repentance is the libertine abuse of the gospel, the greatest danger with regard to justification by faith is the collapsing of justification into repentance and regeneration. Both Osiander and the Roman sophists and schoolmen, who themselves follow the lead not only of Lombard but also of Augustine, limit forgiveness of sins and justification by faith to the beginning of the Christian life, after which the sanctifying grace of the Holy Spirit renders us righteous before God. "Indeed they so describe the righteousness of the regenerated man that a man once for all reconciled to God through faith in Christ may be reckoned righteous before God by good works and be accepted by the merit of them."[3]

By discussing justification after repentance and renewal, Calvin shows not only that faith in Christ cannot be divorced from the conformity of our lives to Christ, but also clearly distinguishes justification from repentance. He shows that faith in Christ is essential for the whole of the Christian life even in light of our renewal into obedience and good works. By placing repentance before justification, Calvin opposes the libertine collapse of repentance into justification; by placing justification after repentance, Calvin opposes the scholastic and Augustinian collapse of justification into repentance. Far from undermining the doctrine of justification by faith, such a procedure can more emphatically demonstrate that justification by faith is the foundational grace given by Christ, for it alone makes it possible for us to know God as a Father instead of as a judge, and for God to know us as God's children rather than as sinful enemies. "For unless you first of all grasp what your relationship to God is, and the nature of his judgment concerning you, you have neither a foundation on which to establish your salvation nor one on which to build piety toward God."[4]

Repentance arises out of a pure and earnest fear of the judgment of God and strives for an integrity of heart and testimony of a good conscience in light of God's judgment seat; but repentance itself cannot acquire a verdict or judgment from God attesting our righteousness before God. In order that we might be justified before God and know God as our Father, we must receive the righteousness of Jesus Christ by faith.

Reckoned as Children of the Father

Calvin's definition of justification places it squarely within the context of our judgment before the divine tribunal, making clear the juridical meaning that justification has for him. "He is said to be justified in God's sight who is both reckoned righteous in God's judgment and has been accepted on account of his righteousness."[5] Before the judgment seat of God, the sinner qua sinner cannot be reckoned righteous or accepted by God, but rather receives the condemnation and rejection of God. "Now he is justified who is reckoned in

---

3. *Inst.* III.xiv.11; O.S. IV.230.1–9 (1:778).
4. *Inst.* III.xi.1; O.S. IV.182.14–20 (1:726).
5. *Inst.* III.xi.2; O.S. IV.182.25–27 (1:726).

the condition not of a sinner, but of a righteous man; and for that reason, he stands firm before God's judgment seat while all sinners fall."[6] To be justified therefore means to stand before God's judgment seat and receive the testimony to one's righteousness, not from one's conscience, but from God. "Thus, justified before God is the man who, freed from the company of sinners, has God to witness and affirm his righteousness."[7]

According to Calvin, there are only two mutually exclusive ways in which we can receive this justifying testimony from God: on the basis of our obedience in fulfilling the law, or on the basis of our faith in the obedience of Christ, who fulfilled the law in our place. As already discussed, not even the regenerate can receive justification before God's judgment seat by their works; hence it follows that we can be justified only by faith in Jesus Christ. "Therefore, we explain justification simply as the acceptance with which God receives us into his favor as righteous men. And we say that it consists in the remission of sins and the imputation of Christ's righteousness."[8]

The definition of justification as the remission of sins and the imputation of righteousness means that justification is rooted in Christ's office of priest, just as repentance was rooted in his office as king. Our sins are forgiven when Christ takes them upon himself on the cross and dies for them once for all, and righteousness is imputed to us when we by faith embrace the obedience of Christ in our stead.[9] Our sin was once for all transferred to the head of the Son of God in the cross and death of Jesus Christ, whereas righteousness was once for all bestowed on sinners in his resurrection from the dead. When we are engrafted into Jesus Christ by faith, this once-for-all exchange becomes an event in our lives as well, so that our sins are forgiven, and the righteousness of Christ is given to us to be received by faith.

Calvin contrasts his understanding of justification with the position of Osiander on the one hand and that of the Roman schoolmen on the other. Both those positions neglect the eternal efficacy of Christ's office as priest, and consequently collapse justification into regeneration and sanctification. Osiander jeopardizes the priestly office of Christ by stating that we are justified by our union with Christ's divinity, which contains within itself the eternal righteousness of God, and by claiming that in our union with Christ's essential divinity we ourselves are made righteous.

With regard to the first issue, Calvin does not deny that the righteousness of God is the source of the righteousness we receive from Christ; however, that righteousness cannot be bestowed directly upon sinners by God, but must be bestowed on us in the righteousness of the divine and human Mediator, particularly in his death and resurrection as priest.[10]

---

6. *Inst.* III.xi.2; O.S. IV.182.30–32 (1:726).
7. *Inst.* III.xi.2; O.S. IV.182.35–36, 183.1 (1:726).
8. *Inst.* III.xi.2; O.S. IV.182.25–29 (1:727).
9. Comm. 2 Cor. 5:21, C.O. 50.74; C.N.T.C. 10:81–82.
10. *Inst.* III.xi.8; O.S. IV.190.12–16 (1:735).

With regard to the second issue, Osiander is correct in insisting that God justifies none whom God does not renew, but he fundamentally errs by identifying justification with that renewal.[11] Even though our regeneration brings about a correspondence between our lives and the image of God in Christ, it does not eradicate sin, but only breaks its dominion. Thus, even though the regenerate receive the testimony of a good conscience, they still must acknowledge that this does not acquit them before the judgment seat of God.[12] By collapsing justification into sanctification, Osiander removes the peace and assurance that the conscience should have in faith before the judgment seat of God. "No portion of righteousness sets our consciences at peace until it has been determined that we are pleasing to God, because we are entirely righteous before him."[13] For this reason, our righteousness must not be found in ourselves but in Christ, so that even though our consciences accuse us of the sin that remains in us, we can still stand with confidence before the judgment seat of God.[14]

The same problem of collapsing justification into sanctification arises in the scholastic theologians, for they define justification in such a way as to identify it with being made righteous by the Spirit of sanctification. Thus they attempt to found the assurance of conscience in the hope of reward for the merits of our regenerate works.[15] According to Calvin, the source of this misunderstanding is Peter the Lombard, who obscured and perverted Augustine even as he tried to follow him, and who therefore set scholasticism on a path that led toward a new kind of Pelagianism. However, even Augustine is criticized by Calvin for defining justification in such a way as to subsume it under sanctification.[16] The effect of Augustine's identification of justifying grace with sanctification is the same seen with Osiander, for peace of conscience cannot be established on the basis of what God is doing within us, but only on the basis of what God freely gives us, apart from our deserving, in Jesus Christ.[17]

Even though Calvin would not disagree with Augustine that those whom God justifies in Christ God also sanctifies, he nevertheless insists that when it comes to the assurance of conscience of its justification before God, we must ignore what God is doing within us, including the testimony of a good conscience, and look solely to the righteousness of Christ. "We conclude from this that the question is not what men are in themselves, but how God regards them, not because purity of conscience and integrity of life are distinguished from the free favour of God, but because, when the reason for God's love to us and His acknowledgement of us as just is questioned, it is necessary that

---

11. *Inst.* III.xi.11; O.S. IV.193.29–30 (1:739).
12. *Inst.* III.xi.11; O.S. IV.193.30–33 (1:739).
13. *Inst.* III.xi.11; O.S. IV.194.1–4 (1:739).
14. *Inst.* III.xi.11; O.S. IV.195.12–15 (1:740–41).
15. *Inst.* III.xi.15; O.S. IV.199.8–13 (1:745).
16. *Inst.* III.xi.15; O.S. IV.200.2–6 (1:746).
17. Comm. Rom. 3:21, *Commentarius*, pp. 68–69; C.N.T.C. 8:71.

Christ should be seen as the one who clothes us with His own righteousness."[18] The foundation of our faith in God as our Father in Jesus Christ is not the testimony of a good conscience within us, but the testimony of forgiveness and imputed righteousness in Jesus Christ.

Calvin was convinced that the reason other theologians could collapse justification into sanctification was that they had not seriously summoned their consciences before the judgment seat of God. So long as we do not summon our consciences before the eschatological judgment of God, we can delude ourselves into thinking that we are justified by what God is doing within us. To counter this presumption, we must apply our minds to the seriousness of God's judgment when we are called to account for ourselves.[19] "Let us behold him, I say, sitting in judgment to examine the deeds of men: who will stand confident before his throne?"[20] We should contemplate the way the judgment of God is depicted in the written law of God, along with the curse pronounced on those who do not abide by everything in the law (Deut. 27:26). "In short, this whole discussion will be foolish and weak unless every man admit his guilt before the Heavenly Judge, and concerned about his own acquittal, willingly cast himself down and confess his nothingness."[21]

The eschatological judgment of God will allow nothing to remain hidden; it will awaken the conscience to testify against us concerning all of the sins we had either forgotten or tried to bury.[22] The last judgment will disclose not only the hypocrisy of the ungodly, but also the unavoidable hypocrisy of the pious; for there are none who are not deceived by self-love into thinking better of themselves than they ought.[23] We only appreciate the judgment of God when we are aware that it transcends the judgment of ourselves arising from our conscience; all that appears to be righteous before us is an abomination before God.[24]

Once we have placed ourselves before the severity of God's eschatological judgment as depicted in Scripture, we should descend into our own consciences in order to examine ourselves rigorously, apart from the distortion of self-love.[25] When our consciences are placed before God's tribunal, they rightly judge their works by the standard of divine judgment and are thus stripped of all confidence in their worth before God.[26] Only in this way can arrogance and complacency be cast down. The arrogant imagine they possess a righteousness that allows them to stand acquitted before God's judgment; the complacent seek to evade God's judgment altogether so that they can

18. Comm. Rom. 4:3, *Commentarius*, p. 82; C.N.T.C. 8:84.
19. *Inst.* III.xii.1; O.S. IV.208.12–15 (1:755).
20. *Inst.* III.xii.1; O.S. IV.208.23–24 (1:755).
21. *Inst.* III.xii.1; O.S. IV.209.15–17 (1:756).
22. *Inst.* III.xii.4; O.S. IV.211.19–24 (1:758).
23. *Inst.* III.xii.4; O.S. IV.211.28–32 (1:758).
24. *Inst.* III.xii.4; O.S. IV.211.36–38, 212.1–2 (1:759).
25. *Inst.* III.xii.5; O.S. IV.212.5–7 (1:759).
26. *Inst.* III.xii.5; O.S. IV.212.5–7 (1:759).

indulge in their vices with impunity. "Such sloth is no less to be shaken off than any confidence in ourselves is to be cast away in order that we may without hindrance hasten to Christ, and empty and hungering, may be filled with his good things."[27]

The pure and earnest fear of God that is the beginning of repentance is also the necessary preparation for and context of justification by faith. Our response to being summoned by God to give an account of ourselves leads us both to seek to put the life of sin to death so that we might be conformed to the righteousness of God in our lives, and to despair of any confidence in our own righteousness before God, including the righteousness that God works within us by repentance. "For God so begins [repentance] . . . in his elect, and progresses in it gradually, and sometimes slowly, throughout life, that they are always liable to the judgment of death before his tribunal."[28] Consequently, when the consciences of the godly are summoned before the judgment seat of God, they renounce their sin and despair of their own righteousness, taking refuge in the righteousness of Christ.[29] "Now, if we ask in what way the conscience can be made quiet before God, we shall find the only way to be that unmerited righteousness he conferred upon us as a gift of God."[30]

The expiating sacrifice of Christ on the cross is the sole foundation for the peace and tranquility of the conscience before the judgment seat of God and is the foundation of the confidence and assurance of the godly that God is their Father. "In short, we must seek peace for ourselves solely in the anguish of Christ our Redeemer."[31] Such assurance can never arise on the basis of our renewal, but only by the forgiveness of sins and the imputation of righteousness that we receive by participation in Christ.

> For, as Paul attests, faith is not true unless it asserts and brings to mind that sweetest name of Father—nay, unless it opens our mouth freely to cry, "Abba, Father" [Gal. 4:6; Rom. 8:15]. He expresses this more clearly elsewhere: "In Christ we have boldness and access with confidence through faith in him" [Eph. 3:12]. This surely does not take place through the gift of regeneration, which, as it is always imperfect in this flesh, so contains in itself manifold grounds for doubt. Therefore, we must come to this remedy: that believers should be convinced that their only ground for hope for the inheritance of a Heavenly Kingdom lies in the fact that, being engrafted in the body of Christ, they are freely accounted righteous.[32]

---

27. *Inst.* III.xii.8; O.S. IV.214.35–38 (1:762).
28. *Inst.* III.xi.11; O.S. IV.193.33–36 (1:739).
29. *Inst.* III.xii.4; O.S. IV.211.14–16 (1:758).
30. *Inst.* III.xiii.3; O.S. IV.217.12–14 (1:765).
31. *Inst.* III.xiii.4; O.S. IV.219.35–36 (1:767).
32. *Inst.* III.xiii.5; O.S. IV.220.14–24 (1:768).

The foundation of our peace of conscience in Jesus Christ, and the basis of our assurance that God is our Father, lie in the forgiveness of sins and imputation of righteousness attained by our participation in Christ, and not in the grace of regeneration that is given inseparably with the grace of justification.

Calvin explicitly contrasts this foundation of assurance with the Roman teaching on moral conjecture, which maintains that we can only gain assurance that we are in a state of grace by finding within ourselves the testimony of a good conscience. On this basis, we can conjecture that we are leading sanctified lives, and thus that we are in a state of grace. Calvin claims that such a position shakes the assurance of faith to its foundations.

> For what sort of peace of mind shall we possess, if it were decided from our works whether we are acceptable to God? I hold, therefore, that from the main foundation of the Papists there springs nothing but constant disturbance of conscience. On that account, we teach that we must have recourse to the free promise of mercy which is offered to us in Christ, so that we may know with certainty that we are reckoned righteous by God.[33]

The foundation of our assurance lies not in what God is doing within us by the gift of regeneration, but rather in the promise of what God freely gives to us in Jesus Christ.[34] Doubt and uncertainty cannot help but arise when we bring our works into consideration to found our assurance. Therefore, even though Calvin is at pains to show that faith in justification is never found apart from repentance and newness of life, he is equally at pains to establish the foundation of the assurance of conscience in justification alone, for it is only by faith in the reconciling death of Christ that "we may have in heaven instead of a judge a gracious Father."[35]

Founding and Confirming Assurance

So far, however, the most important question is left unresolved. Calvin states that the presence of the testimony of a good conscience confirms faith and assurance, not only in light of persecution by our enemies, but also before God. "Without comparison with others, while they examine themselves before God, the purity of their own conscience brings them some comfort and confidence."[36] How is this comfort and confidence acquired before God by the testimony of a good conscience to be harmonized with Calvin's insistence that the sole foundation of our assurance lies in the mercy of God alone?

> The agreement lies in this: that the saints, when it is a question of the founding of their own salvation, without regard for works turn their eyes solely to God's

---

33. Comm. 1 Cor. 4:4, C.O. 49:365; C.N.T.C. 9:88–89.
34. *Inst.* III.xiii.4; O.S. IV.219.14–17 (1:767).
35. *Inst.* III.xi.1; O.S. IV.182.6–7 (1:725).
36. *Inst.* III.xiv.18; O.S. IV.236.25–27 (1:785).

goodness. Not only do they betake themselves to it before all things as the beginning of blessedness but they repose in it as the fulfillment of this. A conscience so founded, erected, and established is established also in the consideration of works, so far, that is, as these are testimonies of God dwelling and ruling in us.[37]

The beginning and end of the foundation (*fundamentum*) of our assurance of salvation lie in the goodness of God, especially in the free promise of righteousness, and not in the consideration of works. However, once the conscience is founded on the righteousness of Christ, it can also establish itself by a consideration of works, not as meriting the grace of God, but as testimonies of the fatherly goodness of God within us.[38] Because God is the fountain of every good, we can know God as such not only in the gift of righteousness in Jesus Christ, but also in the gift of sanctification through the Holy Spirit. Therefore, the consideration of works and testimony of a good conscience not only strengthen and confirm our faith in God's goodness, but they also confirm our adoption and election by God. "When, therefore, the saints by innocence of conscience strengthen their faith and take from it occasion to exult, from the fruits of their calling they merely regard themselves as having been chosen as sons by the Lord."[39] Once faith has been established in the goodness of God, apart from works, it may also be established in the goodness of God made known in our good works and in the innocence of our conscience.

Calvin does not intend, however, that there be two parallel foundations of faith and assurance, one in the promise of righteousness, the other in the evidence of sanctification (even though his language may at times suggest such a pattern). Instead, he wishes to give continual priority to the free mercy of God as the irreducible foundation of the assurance of faith, and relegates the testimony of a good conscience to the secondary, a posteriori confirmation of faith so founded.[40] The primary revelation of God as our Father is not the testimony of the conscience but the testimony of the gospel, in which Christ sets himself forth as the fountain of every good for sinners.

The gospel remains the irreducibly prior source and foundation of the knowledge of God as our Father in Jesus Christ; but the gospel has as its goal the transformation of our lives into Jesus Christ our Lord and king. Therefore, when our knowledge of God from the gospel brings about the transformation of our lives, such transformation does not constitute the foundation of our faith, but rather its a posteriori confirmation. "For although everyone has a witness to his faith from his works, it does not follow that it is founded on them, but they are a subsequent proof added as a sign. The certainty of faith dwells only in Christ's grace."[41] The testimony of a good conscience only

37. *Inst*. III.xiv.18; O.S. IV.236.31–38 (1:785).
38. *Inst*. III.xiv.18; O.S. IV.237.1–5 (1:785).
39. *Inst*. III.xiv.19; O.S. IV.237.11–14 (1:785).
40. *Inst*. III.xiv.19; O.S. IV.237.14–20 (1:785–86).
41. Comm. 1 John 2:3, C.O. 55:311; C.N.T.C. 5:246.

confirms faith a posteriori because the knowledge of God is founded in Jesus Christ, the fountain of every good given to us by the Father, as attested in the gospel.[42] When the knowledge of God in Jesus Christ transforms our lives into the image of Christ, such transformation cannot be the foundation of our knowledge of God the Father, but rather serves as its secondary confirmation.

The other reason that the testimony of a good conscience is only a secondary confirmation of faith has to do with the relationship between justification and sanctification. Although regeneration itself bears witness to God as Father within us, its testimony, if taken on its own, or even if taken together with justification but made foundational, would be ambiguous at best and would more than likely place us under the wrath of God. "For there is nowhere that fear which is able to establish full assurance. And the saints are conscious of possessing only such an integrity as intermingled with many vestiges of the flesh . . . for indeed, if works be judged by themselves, by their imperfection they will no less declare God's wrath than by their incomplete purity they testify to his benevolence."[43] The testimony of a good conscience, taken by itself, would not set us before God the propitious Father, but before God the condemning judge. Such testimony only confirms our knowledge of God as our Father in Jesus Christ when the assurance of conscience is founded on the certainty of the promise testifying to us of the Father's mercy.

In a paradoxical way, the consciences of the pious simultaneously accuse them of iniquity, thereby driving them toward confidence in the sacrifice of Christ, and testify to their integrity, thereby confirming the genuineness of their faith in Christ.

> For who can be found whose heart reproves him in nothing? I reply: the godly are accused like this so that they may at the same time be absolved. For they need to be seriously pierced inwardly by their sins, that terror may train them in humility and self-hatred; but presently they flee to Christ's sacrifice where they have sure peace. Yet from another angle the apostle says that they are not accused, because although they may acknowledge that they fail in many respects, they are still sustained by this testimony of conscience, that they truly and sincerely fear God and desire to submit to His righteousness.[44]

This conjunction of the accusing and sustaining testimony of conscience is paradoxical, if not contradictory, if it is taken as addressing the same issue; but the paradox is resolved when each issue is seen in its own light. If the question is: On what basis can I know God as my Father, and can God regard and accept me as his child? then the conscience testifies to us that it cannot be on the basis of who we are in ourselves but only by who we are in Jesus Christ—that is, those who are forgiven and justified by faith alone. But if the

---

42. Comm. 1 Cor. 3:11, C.O. 49:354; C.N.T.C. 9:74.
43. *Inst.* III.xiv.19; O.S. IV.237.20–32 (1:786).
44. Comm. 1 John 3:21, C.O. 55:243; C.N.T.C. 5:280.

question is: For what purpose has God adopted me as God's child in Jesus Christ? then the conscience testifies to us that we are living in accordance with the purpose and goal of our adoption by striving to show ourselves to be children of God.

The testimony of a good conscience cannot replace the necessity for the assurance of the conscience in the mercy and goodness of God, any more than the assurance of conscience in forgiveness can remove the necessity for the testimony of a good conscience confirming our adoption by demonstrating that our lives are beginning to be conformed to Christ. Justification is the irreducible basis, and sanctification is the irreducible goal, of our adoption as children of God in Jesus Christ.[45] God cannot be united with sinful humanity except on the basis of the forgiveness of sins and imputed righteousness.[46] However, the Lord does not unite sinners to himself to let them remain sinners, but rather to conform them to himself by holiness of life, by which they will be joined to God in eternal life. This conformity of the children of God with their Father has only begun in this life and will not be complete until the last day, when the children will be made perfect.[47]

The foundation and basis of the union of the pious with God lies in the free mercy and forgiveness of God, while the means by which God brings the pious into unity with him is by conforming them to God's holiness by the sanctification of the Holy Spirit. "Therefore if one seeks the first cause that opens for the saints the door to God's Kingdom, and hence gives them a permanent standing-ground in it, we at once answer: Because the Lord in his own mercy has adopted them once for all, and keeps them continually. But if the question is the manner, we must proceed to regeneration and its fruits."[48]

Calvin's greater emphasis on sanctification and the testimony of a good conscience is possible because of his theology of God as our Father in Jesus Christ, which allows him not only to subsume sanctification under justification as the foundation of our assurance that God is our Father, but also to subsume justification under sanctification as the goal and purpose of our adoption. In spite of his greater emphasis on repentance and regeneration, however, Calvin consistently agrees with Luther that our assurance lies in the forgiveness of sins alone. "I certainly admit that we are regenerated to newness of life by the grace of Christ, but when it is a question of the assurance of salvation, we ought to be thinking about free adoption alone, which is bound up with the expiation of sins."[49]

However, there is in Calvin's theology a distinctive foundation of assurance that is not found in Luther's theology. According to Calvin, faith in Christ is

---

45. *Responsio ad Sadoleti Epistolam*, C.O. 5:348–49; *A Reformation Debate*, ed. John C. Olin (Grand Rapids, Mich.: Baker Book House, 1976), p. 69.

46. *Inst.* III.xi.21; O.S. IV.205.7–10 (1:751).

47. *Inst.* III.xviii.1; O.S. IV.271.7–10 (1:822).

48. *Inst.* III.xvii.6; O.S. IV.259.22–26 (1:809).

49. Comm. Acts 15:11, C.O. 48:35; C.N.T.C. 7:42; cf. Comm. John 3:16, C.O. 47:65; C.N.T.C. 4:75.

not directed to the grace of justification or sanctification per se, but to Jesus Christ himself as the fountain of every good. The primary purpose and effect of faith is neither to justify us before God nor to sanctify us in conformity to God, but to engraft us into Jesus Christ himself, so that we may partake not only of all his blessings but also in himself. The bond of our union with Christ, and the power that creates faith within us, is the Holy Spirit, who illumines our minds and seals on our hearts the knowledge of Jesus Christ as the fountain of every good. "To sum up: Christ, when he illumines us into faith by the power of his Spirit, at the same time so engrafts us into his body that we become partakers of every good."[50]

Thus, even though the grace of justification is the ground of our assurance before God when compared to the grace of sanctification, it is only by our participation in Christ himself that we are even justified or sanctified.[51] The object of our faith is therefore Jesus Christ himself, "who became for us wisdom from God, and righteousness and sanctification and redemption" (1 Cor. 1:30), so that the ultimate foundation of our assurance of salvation, over and above the particular grace of justification, is our participation in Jesus Christ himself. "In brief, because all his things are ours and we have all things in him, in us there is nothing. Upon this foundation, I say, we must be built if we would grow into a holy temple to the Lord."[52]

Because Jesus Christ contains within himself all the good things that our consciences make us aware we lack, the assurance of faith that God is our merciful Father and we are God's well-beloved children lies in the knowledge that Christ is one with us and we are one with him. "For our assurance, our glory, and the sole anchor of our salvation are that Christ the Son of God is ours, and we in turn are in him sons of God and heirs of the Kingdom of Heaven, called to a hope of eternal blessedness by God's grace, not by our worth."[53] First in order of assurance comes the knowledge that we are united by faith to Jesus Christ, the image of the invisible Father, in whom we find every good thing we lack; next in order of assurance is the forgiveness of sins and imputation of righteousness that we receive by participation in Christ, through which we have in heaven a propitious Father instead of a wrathful judge; and finally, confirming the sincerity of our faith in Jesus Christ and in the forgiveness of sins, is repentance, through which we are conformed to God the Father by expressing God's image in Jesus Christ in our own lives, thereby showing ourselves to be adopted children of the Father in Jesus Christ.

This order of assurance is reflected in Calvin's discussions of prayer and the assurance of election. As was seen above, Calvin claims that the testimony of a good conscience gives confidence to the faithful in their prayers, and also

50. *Inst.* III.ii.35; O.S. IV.46.30–32 (1:583).
51. *Inst.* III.xvi.1; O.S. IV.249.14–19 (1:798).
52. *Inst.* III.xv.5; O.S. IV.244.19–30 (1:793).
53. *Inst.* III.xvii.1; O.S. IV.235.20–24 (1:803).

confirms their election or adoption by God the Father. However, in his discussions both of prayer and of election, Calvin grounds the assurance of our prayer and election primarily in the knowledge of Jesus Christ as the image of the Father, then in the forgiveness of sins in Jesus Christ, and only subsequently in the testimony of a good conscience.

Calvin states that prayer is the necessary and inevitable exercise of faith. Faith knows that all good things have been given to us by the Father in Jesus Christ, but such knowledge would not be fruitful if we did not ask for these things from the Father through Christ. "But after we have been instructed by faith to recognize that whatever we need and whatever we lack is in God, and in our Lord Jesus Christ, in whom the Father willed the fullness of his bounty to abide [cf. Col. 1:19; John 1:16] so that we may all draw from it as from an overflowing spring, it remains for us to seek in him, and in prayers to ask of him, what we have learned to be in him."[54] Jesus Christ as prophet offers himself to us in the gospel as the fountain of every good given to us by God the Father. The faith that so grasps Jesus Christ cannot help but call upon God the Father through Jesus Christ, to bestow upon us all of the good things of which we know ourselves to be destitute. The Holy Spirit that seals the testimony of the gospel on our hearts and minds thereby gives our hearts the assurance to cry out boldly, "Abba, Father!"[55] Thus the foundation of the assurance in God from which prayer spontaneously and confidently arises is the knowledge of God as Father, the fountain of every blessing, in Jesus Christ, through the witness of the gospel and the Holy Spirit.

Within the context of the knowledge of Christ as the fountain of every good, the proper foundation of and preparation for prayer is the confession of sin and the plea for forgiveness. "Nor should anyone, however holy he may be, hope that he will obtain anything from God until he is freely reconciled to him; nor can God chance to be propitious to any but those whom he has pardoned."[56] God cannot grant the prayers of sinful children, even of those who have begun to be made holy, without pardoning their sins. Nor will the consciences of believers, aware as they are of their own sin and of God's judgment, allow them to approach God with the assurance that God is their Father unless they rely on the mercy of God.[57]

With faith founded on Jesus Christ and on the grace of forgiveness, the prayers of the faithful are also strengthened by the testimony of a good conscience, which confirms their confidence that they are children to whom the Father has promised to be gracious.[58] This does not mean that God answers their prayers as a reward for their godliness. Rather, the godly strengthen their confidence in God by knowing themselves to be sincere believers in

---

54. *Inst.* III.xx.1; O.S. IV.297.9–19 (2:850).
55. *Inst.* III.xx.1; O.S. IV.297.23–26 (2:851).
56. *Inst.* III.xx.9; O.S. IV.306.23–27 (2:860).
57. *Inst.* III.xx.9; O.S. IV.307.8–11 (2:860).
58. *Inst.* III.xx.10; O.S. IV.308.1–8 (2:861).

Christ.[59] Such testimony of integrity is a necessary part of the believer's confidence in calling upon God. "For no heart can ever break into sincere calling upon God that does not at the same time aspire to godliness."[60] Consequently, the godly need to appeal directly to their integrity before God without regard to others. "The godly man enjoys a pure conscience before the Lord, thus confirming himself in the promise with which the Lord comforts and supports his true worshippers."[61]

However, the testimony of a good conscience only confirms our trust in God's promises, by attesting that we are the true believers to whom they apply; it does not constitute the foundation of our confidence that our prayers will be heard by God: "his assurance his prayers will be answered rests solely upon God's clemency, apart from all consideration of personal merit."[62] Even when David was aware of the rightness of his cause in the face of his enemies, he did not trust in his integrity, but rather in the mercy of God, to which he appealed not as a righteous person but as a sinner in need of pardon. "While those to whom David was opposed were wicked men, and he was perfectly conscious of the rectitude of his cause as regards them, he freely acknowledged his sin before God as a condemned suppliant. We are to hold this as a general rule in seeking to conciliate God, that we must pray for the pardon of our sins."[63] Although the faithful confirm their faith by the testimony of a good conscience, and thereby prove that they are children to whom God has promised to be gracious, they nonetheless can only know God as their Father, and have confidence that God will hear their prayers, on the basis of the forgiveness of sins.[64]

Calvin's discussion of prayer therefore confirms the order of confidence and assurance noted above. The foundation of our confidence that God is our Father is the knowledge of Jesus Christ as the fountain of every good through the witness of the gospel and the illumination of the Holy Spirit. With regard to the twofold grace that faith receives from this fountain, the grace of forgiveness and imputed righteousness assures our consciences that God is our Father and not our judge. The grace of regeneration confirms this faith a posteriori by attesting that we are living as children of God; but this testimony could never stand alone before the judgment seat of God as the basis of our assurance.

The same pattern appears in Calvin's theology when it comes to the question of our confidence of our election. Calvin builds his understanding of the assurance of election on Rom. 8:30: "And those whom he predestined he also called; and those whom he called he also justified; and those whom he justified

59. *Inst.* III.xx.10; O.S. IV.308.12–15 (2:862).
60. *Inst.* III.xx.10; O.S. IV.308.19–21 (2:862).
61. *Inst.* III.xx.10; O.S. IV.308.30–33 (2:862).
62. *Inst.* III.xx.10; O.S. IV.308.33–34 (2:862).
63. Comm. Ps. 143:2, C.O. 32:400; C.T.S. 12:249.
64. Ibid.

he also glorified." Calvin maintains that the primary testimony of our election comes from the call of God, with justification being the next sign of election.[65] The glorification of the saints, which begins in this life with their regeneration, is not taken by Calvin as a sign of election on a par with the call and justification, but is rather referred to the Day of Jesus Christ. This already indicates that Calvin will subsume the confirmation of election by the testimony of a good conscience under the assurance of election by justification and (especially) the call.

The primary, if not exclusive, focus of Calvin's discussion of assurance of election is the call of God. The call of God to faith in Jesus Christ through the gospel manifests the election of the children of God, which is otherwise hidden in the secret will of the Father: "accordingly, it may properly be termed his 'attestation'."[66] Although Calvin includes the preaching of the gospel in his understanding of the call, he terms preaching the universal call that is common to the elect and reprobate, which profits no one without the special call of the illumination of the Holy Spirit.[67] Because election has to do with who receives the illumination of the Holy Spirit, while reprobation has to do with who does not, then "the call" as a testimony of election means the bestowal of the Holy Spirit through the preaching of the gospel.[68] By creating faith in Jesus Christ as he offers himself to us in the preaching of the gospel, the Holy Spirit simultaneously bears testimony to us of our election and adoption by God the Father.[69] "For the testimony of the Spirit is nothing but the sealing of our adoption."[70] For this reason, the attestation of our election is given by the call of God, in which the Spirit of adoption bears witness to us that we are children of God, and gives us the confidence to cry, Abba, Father! "Adoption by God precedes the testimony of adoption given by the Holy Spirit. But the effect is the sign of the cause. And you dare to call God your Father only by the instigation and incitement of the Spirit of Christ. Therefore it is certain that you are the sons of God."[71]

This does not mean that the gospel becomes irrelevant as a testimony to election. Even though the gospel as the universal call of God is useless without the illumination of the Spirit as the special call of God, the saints are not to attain assurance of election by inwardly contemplating the Holy Spirit apart from the Word of God, but are rather to base their confidence in the truth of the Word that has been illumined for them by the Holy Spirit. "In the meantime, I do not deny that to be assured of our salvation we must begin with the Word, and that our confidence ought to be so intent as to call upon

65. *Inst.* III.xxi.7; O.S. IV.379.3–6 (2:931).
66. *Inst.* III.xxiv.1; O.S. IV.410.11–14 (2:964).
67. *Inst.* III.xxiv.8; O.S. IV.419.13–24 (2:974).
68. *Inst.* III.xxiv.2; O.S. IV.412.15–17 (2:967).
69. Comm. Rom. 8:30, *Commentarius*, p. 183; C.N.T.C. 8:182.
70. Comm. John 6:40, C.O. 47:147; C.N.T.C. 4:162.
71. Comm. Gal. 4:6, C.O. 50:227–28; C.N.T.C. 11:75.

God as our Father."[72] In particular, the consciences of the godly attain more confidence by the universal nature of the gospel, as embodied, for instance, in 1 Tim. 2:4, which says that God our Savior "desires all men to be saved and to come to the knowledge of the truth." "But why does he say 'all'? It is that the consciences of the godly may rest more secure, when they understand there is no difference among sinners provided faith be present."[73] The call of God is the testimony of our election because in it the Holy Spirit illumines our minds and seals on our hearts the truth of the gospel in which Jesus Christ offers himself to us.

The call of God as the testimony of our election therefore provides the foundation for Calvin's solution to the question, which he acknowledges to be profoundly disturbing, concerning the revelation of our election.[74] The danger with such a question is that it immediately disturbs the conscience of the believer by leading it to seek a testimony concerning its election beyond the testimony of the gospel and Holy Spirit, or to seek a revelation of God as Father apart from Jesus Christ as offered to us in the gospel. But God the Father is hidden in himself, and has only revealed himself in Jesus Christ, the image of the invisible God.[75] In Jesus Christ alone, the fountain of every good that would otherwise be hidden in God the Father is offered to us. "First, if we should seek God's fatherly mercy and kind heart, we should turn our eyes to Christ, on whom alone God's Spirit rests [cf. Matt. 3:17]."[76]

The purpose of our election has no other goal than to engraft us into Jesus Christ by faith through the power of the Holy Spirit, so that we might participate not only in every good thing that God wishes to bestow on us, but also in Christ himself. Since God the Father is revealed only in Jesus Christ, and since election has as its purpose our engrafting into Jesus Christ, we will find assurance of our election neither in ourselves nor in God, but in Christ.

> Accordingly, those whom God has adopted as his sons are said to have been chosen not in themselves but in his Christ [Eph. 1:4]. . . . But if we have been chosen in him, we shall not find assurance of our election in ourselves; and not even in God the Father, if we conceive him as severed from his Son. Christ, then, is the mirror wherein we must, and without self-deception may, contemplate our own election.[77]

The assurance of our election comes with our being engrafted into Jesus Christ by faith; just as Jesus Christ as the image of the invisible God is the foundation and object of faith, so also he is the mirror in which we might behold our election. Therefore, "we have a sufficiently clear and firm testimony

---

72. *Inst.* III.xxiv.3; O.S. IV.413.28–31 (2:968).
73. *Inst.* III.xxiv.17; O.S. IV.430.13–15 (2:985).
74. *Inst.* III.xxiv.4; O.S. IV.414.23–25 (2:969).
75. *Inst.* III.xxiv.4; O.S. IV.414.36–38, 415.1–4 (2:969).
76. *Inst.* III.xxiv.5; O.S. IV.415.27–32 (2:970).
77. *Inst.* III.xxiv.5; O.S. IV.415.36–39, 416.1–4 (2:970).

that we have been inscribed in the book of Life [cf. Rev. 21:27] if we are in communion with Christ."[78] This is why the call of God is the testimony of our election; for in the universal call of the gospel Jesus Christ offers himself to us, and in the special call of the Holy Spirit we are in fact engrafted into Jesus Christ by faith. "Now he gave us that sure communion with himself when he testified through the preaching of the gospel that he had been given to us by the Father to be ours with all his benefits."[79] The assurance of our election is further strengthened when we remember that Jesus Christ will never cast away any whom the Father gives to him.[80] Thus the assurance of our election comes in the call of God, in which Jesus Christ testifies to us that he is the fountain of every blessing given to us by the Father, and in which the Spirit of adoption illumines our minds to the truth of the gospel and unites us to Jesus by faith.

Yet if this is the case, what about Calvin's claim that the testimony of a good conscience confirms our election and calling by God? On the basis of 2 Pet. 1:10 Calvin states: "one argument whereby we may prove that we are truly elected by God and not called in vain is that our profession of faith should find its response in a good conscience and an upright life."[81] This does not mean that the response of a good conscience forms the fundamental testimony of our election; rather, the good conscience *confirms* our call, and, as we have seen, it is the call that is the foundational testimony of our election. However, the purpose and goal of our calling and election are that we be conformed to God by holiness of life. Therefore, a good conscience testifies that we are living in accordance with the purpose of our call; however, the call remains the fundamental testimony that assures our conscience of our election.[82]

> But because he chooses and calls us for the purpose of being pure and spotless in His sight, purity of life is rightly regarded as the illustration and evidence of election, whereby the faithful not only show to others that they are sons of God, but also confirm themselves in this faith, but in such a way that they place their foundations elsewhere.
>
> This assurance of which Peter speaks should not, in my opinion, be referred to conscience, as though the faithful acknowledged themselves before God to be elect and called. I take it simply of the fact itself that calling is shown to be confirmed by a holy life.[83]

The lack of the testimony of a good conscience falsifies the call of God of which the ungodly hypocrites boast, because the Spirit that attests our election is never given without bestowing newness of life on the children of God. For

---

78. *Inst.* III.xxiv.5; O.S. IV.416.7–9; (2:970).
79. *Inst.* III.xxiv.5; O.S. IV.416.7–9 (2:970–71).
80. *Inst.* III.xxiv.6; O.S. IV.417.2–3 (2:971).
81. Comm. 2 Pet. 1:10, C.O. 55:449; C.N.T.C. 12:333.
82. Comm. 2 Pet. 1:10, C.O. 55:450; C.N.T.C. 12:334.
83. Ibid.

this reason, the children of God can confirm themselves in their calling by the testimony of a good conscience; but the testimony of their election must first be given to their conscience by the gospel and the Holy Spirit.

In sum, not only is Calvin in fundamental agreement with Luther regarding the relationship between justification and sanctification and the assurance of faith—that is, that the conscience only has peace before God by the forgiveness of sins and the imputation of righteousness—but Calvin also sees an additional, and even more basic, foundation of the assurance of faith. According to Calvin, faith has as its object not Jesus Christ the justifier of sinners, as in Luther, but Jesus Christ the image of the invisible God, in whom is found the fountain of every good. Both the assurance of faith, and the knowledge and assurance of our election by God the Father, are founded on the self-revelation of God the Father in Jesus Christ his only-begotten Son through the illumination of the Holy Spirit. "It has been said that we must be drawn by the Spirit to be aroused to seek Christ; so, in turn, we must be warned that the invisible Father is to be sought solely in this image."[84]

By making Jesus Christ as the fountain of every good the primary object of faith, Calvin has two ways of guarding against the possibility of placing the testimony of a good conscience at the foundation of the assurance of faith: faith only knows God as Father in Jesus Christ his image, and faith can only regard God as the Father of sinners by the forgiveness of sins. However, one cannot know God as Father without striving to live as a child of God; therefore repentance and the testimony of a good conscience arise from and confirm the knowledge of God the Father in Jesus Christ.

Nonetheless, Calvin is in complete agreement with Luther that all that Jesus Christ did for the salvation of the world is of no account unless we have faith in Jesus Christ. God in Jesus Christ is not only merciful to sinners, who therefore believe this to be true; but God is merciful *only* toward those sinners who believe in Christ. In order to be fully assured of salvation, we must not only trust in Jesus Christ, but we must *know* we trust in Jesus Christ; we must not only have confidence in God's promise of mercy to sinners in Jesus Christ, we must also know ourselves to be believing sinners to whom God promises to be merciful. For both Luther and Calvin, this involves not only our knowing that we find assurance and peace of conscience in Jesus Christ alone—which is itself a form of reflexive self-knowledge, even if its object is outside ourselves—but we must also know that our faith is sincere and not hypocritical, by finding within ourselves both the fear of God and the testimony of a good conscience.

Luther and Calvin emphatically maintain that the testimony of a good conscience does not have to do with the foundation of assurance, but rather with its confirmation—indeed, Calvin seems to be more conscious of the necessity of this distinction than Luther. However, for both theologians the

84. *Inst.* III.ii.1; O.S. IV.9.1–3 (1:544).

lack of the testimony of a good conscience invalidates any alleged assurance in Jesus Christ. If the lack of the testimony of a good conscience can completely falsify an alleged assurance of faith in Jesus Christ, it follows that its presence contributes directly to the assurance of faith in Jesus Christ. Calvin makes clear this direct contribution of the testimony of the good conscience to the assurance of faith.

> The saints, when it is a question of founding and establishing their own salvation, without regard for works turn their eyes solely to God's goodness. . . . A conscience so founded, erected, and established is established also in the consideration of works, so far, that is, as these are testimonies of God dwelling and ruling in us. . . . Inasmuch, therefore, as this reliance upon works has no place unless you first cast the whole confidence of your mind upon God's mercy, it ought not to seem contrary to that upon which it depends.[85]

So long as we first place the whole of our confidence in the mercy of God, we may then place part of our confidence in the testimony of a good conscience. The same claim is made by Luther, in spite of Luther's attempts to found the assurance of faith in the justification of sinners.

> These are excellent and golden consolations for the conscience. These are testimonies that bring joy to our conscience, as Peter says (2 Pet. 1:10), "Be the more zealous to confirm your call," and Paul says (2 Cor. 1:12), "the testimony of our conscience." Although we must not rely on this, yet, since we are justified, it puts my conscience at peace, that I do evil to no one, and thus I walk safely in God. Now comes the confidence in the Lord that on the basis of this conduct we can be certain that God is well disposed toward us.[86]

Such a secondary source of assurance is even more important given the fact that both Luther and Calvin were convinced that one could hypocritically embrace the promise of forgiveness, but one could not feign the testimony of a good conscience, given by the Spirit of sanctification to the elect. They both insist that faith is founded on the testimony of Christ to the conscience in the gospel and the sacraments through the illumination of the Holy Spirit; but they also insist that such faith is useless without the self-testimony of a good conscience. Luther and Calvin consistently deny that such testimony could or should directly found the assurance of faith; they distinguish between the foundation (*fundamentum*) of faith and its a posteriori confirmation (*confirmatio*). But given their claim that only those who sincerely believe in Jesus Christ have a gracious God, reinforced by the doctrine of election, such a distinction remains inherently unstable. The possibility of the testimony of a good conscience founding the assurance of faith cannot in principle be avoided, even if neither theologian intended it.

---

85. *Inst.* III.xiv.18; O.S. IV.31–33, 35–40 (1:785).
86. *In Esaiam Prophetam D. Doc. Martini Lutheri Enarraciones*, 1527. W.A. 31(II).482.31–37, 483.1–3; L.W. 17:288.

Luther and Calvin ultimately sought to avoid founding the assurance of faith in the testimony of a good conscience by qualifying such testimony by the awareness of a terrified conscience before the judgment seat of God. The same conscience that confirms and strengthens our faith in God's mercy also drives us to ground our faith in the mercy of God. Both testimonies of the conscience—to our godliness, and to our sin—must be simultaneously present in believers, the former to confirm faith, the latter to ground faith in the gospel.

The inherent instability of their distinction between the foundation and confirmation of the assurance of faith is illumined by the two almost mutually exclusive testimonies that Luther and Calvin root in the same conscience. On the one hand, the conscience of the believer makes it essential that we testify to ourselves concerning the mercy of God toward us—that is, that we are the godly to whom God has promised to be merciful. On the other hand, the conscience of the believer makes it impossible for us to testify to ourselves concerning the mercy of God, for the fact that God is merciful toward sinners is something that God alone can attest to our conscience in the gospel of Jesus Christ through the witness of the Holy Spirit. The testimony of a terrified and awakened conscience makes it necessary to begin with the testimony of Jesus Christ to the conscience in order to pacify and assure the conscience of the mercy of God, but the danger of hypocrisy makes it necessary to include the testimony of a good conscience to itself to confirm and strengthen its assurance in the mercy of God in Jesus Christ.

It would remain for later generations to discover that the hypocrisy of an alleged testimony of a good conscience can be just as pernicious as that of an alleged consolation of conscience, especially when the former is made much more foundational for the assurance of believers, as in Article XVIII of the Westminster Confession. It is not accurate, however, to maintain, as many have done, either that such a reversal is not in principle possible in Luther's theology, or that such a reversal in fact took place in Calvin's theology. Indeed, it is Calvin who offers the most promising way out of this dilemma of a christological starting point and an anthropological conclusion (Barth) by his unique doctrine of Jesus Christ as the image of the invisible Father in the wonderful exchange.

Calvin does not succeed in escaping the dilemma, however, because the one good thing that is not found in the wonderful exchange is the grace of election; that remains hidden in the Father and is only revealed by the special call of the Holy Spirit through the universal call of the gospel. Without the illumination of the Holy Spirit, given only to the elect, Jesus Christ does not profit us at all, for without faith "all that he has suffered and done for the salvation of the human race remains useless and of no value to us."[87]

---

87. *Inst.* III.i.1; O.S. IV.1.11–13 (1:537).

Luther also seeks to ground the assurance of faith in the objective truth of the happy exchange once for all enacted between God and sinners in the death and resurrection of Christ.

> Therefore if sin makes you anxious, and if death terrifies you, just think that this is an empty specter and an illusion of the devil—which is what it surely is. For in fact there is no sin any longer, no curse, no death, and no devil, because Christ has conquered and abolished all these. Accordingly, the victory of Christ is utterly certain: the defects lie not in the fact itself, which is completely true, but in our incredulity. It is difficult for reason to believe such inestimable blessings.[88]

However, Luther qualifies the objective efficacy of this once-for-all event by his unyielding axiom: "To the extent that you believe this, to that extent you have it. If you believe that sin, death, and the curse have been abolished, they have been abolished, because Christ conquered and overcame them in Himself."[89]

There is not one event of reconciliation in Christ for Luther and Calvin, but two: the happy exchange in Christ, and our faith in Christ. So long as God is not simply merciful to sinners in Jesus Christ, but only to those sinners who believe in Jesus Christ, it is impossible for Luther and Calvin, in speaking of the assurance and certainty of faith, not to add some form of self-testimony of the conscience to the testimony of Jesus Christ. We may begin with the promise of mercy in Jesus Christ, but we must eventually come to know ourselves, by the testimony of a good conscience, as those to whom God has promised to be merciful.

88. *Galatas Commentarius*, 1535. W.A. 40(I).444.19–24; L.W. 26:284–85.
89. Ibid.

13

BUILDING UP THE ADOPTED CHILDREN OF GOD

This chapter will examine the freedom of the conscience in Calvin's theology. The discussion will both reinforce his fundamental agreement with Luther concerning the assurance of conscience in justification alone, and illuminate a significant area where Calvin disagrees with Luther: namely, in his understanding of the uses and limitations of Christian freedom.

According to Calvin, the freedom of the Christian conscience is of fundamental importance for the Christian faith, particularly with regard to the antecedent judgment of conscience. "For it is a thing of prime necessity, and apart from a knowledge of it, consciences dare undertake almost nothing without doubting; they hesitate and recoil from many things; they constantly waver and are afraid."[1] The freedom of the conscience has to do with the impact of justification by faith on the antecedent judgment of the conscience of the believer, so that the conscience of the believer might be certain that whatever it undertakes is commanded or permitted by God and will be pleasing to God when it is haled before the judgment seat of God.[2]

For Calvin, Christian freedom is an essential component of Christian salvation, in contrast to Calvin's opponents, who think that it is concerned with trivial externalities like eating and drinking, or the Roman theologians who think that it does away with all discipline (a charge to which Calvin will directly respond). "But, as we have said, unless this freedom be comprehended, neither Christ nor gospel truth, nor inner peace of soul, can rightly be known."[3] Justification by faith not only brings peace and assurance to the conscience in light of its *consequent* judgment before the tribunal of God—that is, that we who know ourselves to be sinners are forgiven and considered righteous in Jesus Christ—but also by its *antecedent* judgment before the judgment seat of the Lord—that is, that we can be certain that all we undertake to do is pleasing to God.

---

1. *Inst.* III.xix.1; O.S. IV.282.13–16 (1:833).
2. Comm. Gal. 5:1, C.O. 50:243; C.N.T.C. 11:92.
3. *Inst.* III.xix.1; O.S. IV.282.33–34, 283.1 (1:834).

The Threefold Freedom of Christians

Calvin, like Luther, speaks of Christian freedom as having three parts, the first and most important of which is the freedom of the conscience from the law with regard to its justification before God: "The consciences of believers, in seeking assurance of their justification before God, should rise above and advance beyond the law, forgetting all law righteousness."[4] When it is a matter of our righteousness before God, the conscience must set aside the law and its works, and embrace the mercy of God in Jesus Christ alone.[5] Only in this way can consciences attain certain assurance of being reckoned righteous before the judgment seat of God.[6] This first and basic freedom of the conscience reinforces the consistent tendency demonstrated in Calvin's theology to make justification by faith alone the foundation of the certainty and assurance of the conscience in the grace of God.

This freedom, however, does not mean that believers are freed from the law altogether. Even though the law contributes nothing to the grace of justification, it is functionally related to the grace of sanctification. Therefore, although the conscience is freed from the law with regard to its justification before God, it is not freed with regard to its sanctification, for the law still exhorts and teaches believers to be conformed to the goal of their calling.[7] In this regard the law retains a place, for it exhorts us to the holiness of life that is the purpose of our adoption. "The whole life of Christians ought to be a sort of practice of godliness, for we have been called to sanctification. Here it is the function of the law, by warning men of their duty, to arouse them to a zeal for holiness and innocence."[8]

However, when it is a question of the basis of our calling, then the law has no place in the conscience. We have been adopted by God solely on the basis of forgiveness of sins and imputation of righteousness, and on no other basis can we know God as our Father. "But where consciences are worried how to render God favorable, what they will reply and with what assurance they will stand should they be called to his judgment, there we are not to reckon what the law requires, but Christ alone, who surpasses all perfection of the law, must be set forth as righteousness."[9] The conscience is freed from the law with regard to its justification before God, but not with regard to its sanctification before God, for it continues to urge, teach, and exhort believers unto holiness of life.

However, not even the teaching and exhortation of the law are effective in the life of believers apart from justification by faith. Even though the law continues to urge believers to obedience, the law per se is not the basis of

4. *Inst.* III.xix.2; O.S. IV.283.5–7 (1:834).
5. *Inst.* III.xix.2; O.S. IV.283.13–17 (1:834).
6. *Inst.* III.xix.2; O.S. IV.283.18–20 (1:834).
7. *Inst.* III.xix.2; O.S. IV.283.20–23 (1:835).
8. *Inst.* III.xix.2; O.S. IV.283.25–29 (1:835).
9. *Inst.* III.xix.2; O.S. IV.283.29–33 (1:835).

the apostolic exhortations found in Scripture. "Rather, they derive their most powerful exhortations from the thought that our salvation stands upon no merit of ours but solely upon God's mercy."[10] We are not exhorted to obey God so that we might attain a gracious Father; for in that way we would always be subjected to the curse of the law on account of our imperfect obedience, which might compel us to obey out of fear but would not draw us to obey out of gratitude. Rather, we are exhorted to obey God so that we who already know God as Father might willingly show ourselves to be God's children, knowing that even our imperfect obedience will be accepted by our Father in Christ.

The second part of Christian freedom, therefore, consists of freedom of conscience from the compulsion of the law.[11] Those who do not know God as Father by justification can only obey God grudgingly, the way servants obey harsh masters, afraid to offer their defective works lest the curse of God be unleashed upon them. Only those who know God as their Father on the basis of justification alone can willingly and freely obey God, for they are confident that God will accept and be pleased by their defective obedience on the basis of God's free mercy. "Such children ought we to be, firmly trusting that our services will be approved by our most merciful Father, however small, rude, and imperfect these may be."[12] It is again clear why Calvin wanted our obedience as children to be an a posteriori confirmation of our faith in God the Father, for we only reverence God with the obedience of a good conscience when we are assured that God is our merciful Father who will be pleased by our obedience on the basis of our justification by faith alone.

The third form of freedom, and the part at the heart of the controversy with Rome, is the freedom of the conscience from external things that are in and of themselves neutral or indifferent.[13] If the first part of freedom has to do with the consequent judgment of conscience, while the second part has to do with the motivation of conscience, the third part has specifically to do with the antecedent judgment of conscience. "Here begins a weighty controversy, for what is in debate is whether God, whose will ought to precede all our plans and actions, wishes us to use these things or those."[14] The problem is a delicate one, for once the conscience becomes ensnared by viewing some external things as necessary before God, it becomes more and more entangled and bound by scruples until it dares to undertake nothing.[15] "For all those entangled in such doubts, wherever they turn, see offense of conscience everywhere present."[16]

The freedom of the conscience with regard to external things that are themselves indifferent has to do with our use of the goods of creation that

10. *Inst.* III.xvi.3; O.S. IV.251.14–16 (1:800).
11. *Inst.* III.xix.4; O.S. IV.284.28–30 (1:836).
12. *Inst.* III.xix.5; O.S. IV.285.35–37 (1:837).
13. *Inst.* III.xix.7; O.S. IV.286.27–29 (1:838).
14. *Inst.* III.xix.7; O.S. IV.287.14–16 (1:839).
15. *Inst.* III.xix.7; O.S. IV.286.35, 287.1–5 (1:839).
16. *Inst.* III.xix.7; O.S. IV.287.19–21 (1:839).

God has given to us, such as food, drink, clothing, and housing. In order to have such freedom in external matters, believers must be certain that God the Father has indeed given them the good things of creation for their use and enjoyment: "there is no legitimate possession of any good thing unless our conscience witnesses that it is rightly ours."[17] Even though every good created thing was given to humanity in Adam, humanity lost its rightful claim to those things when Adam fell from God.[18]

Therefore, although people commonly think that humans naturally have dominion over the created world, it is in truth only those who have been adopted as children of the Father in Jesus Christ who can legitimately claim the earth as their inheritance. "Commonsense does indeed hold that the riches of the earth are naturally intended for our use, but, since our dominion over the world was taken from us in Adam, every good gift of God that we touch is defiled by our stains and it on its side is unclean to us, til God graciously helps us and, by incorporating us into the Body of His Son, makes us anew lords of the earth, so that we may legitimately enjoy as our own all the wealth He supplies."[19] Only those who have been adopted as children of God in Jesus Christ can know God the Creator as their Father, and therefore be assured that the good things of creation are freely given by God for their use and enjoyment. "It is not lawful for us to seize for ourselves the food which He has intended for His own household. But Christ by whom we are adopted into the family also admits us into the fellowship of this right, so that we may enjoy the whole world with God's blessing."[20]

It can now be seen that the whole discussion in Book I of the *Institutes* of the knowledge of God the Creator as our Father has legitimacy and efficacy only for those who have been adopted by God in Jesus Christ. "For believers especially, this ought to be a testimony of divine benevolence, wholly destined, as it is, to promote their salvation. For before he shows us openly the inheritance of eternal glory, God wills by lesser proofs to show himself to be our Father. These are the benefits that are daily conferred on us by him."[21] Thus the testimony of the conscience that we may legitimately use and enjoy the good things of creation comes only from the testimony of the gospel, that God the Creator is our Father, and we are God's children, by our adoption in Jesus Christ.[22] Only believers, therefore, have freedom of conscience with regard to the good things of creation, so that they might be assured that nothing in creation is forbidden them or is in itself defiled.[23]

17. Comm. 1 Tim. 4:4, C.O. 52:297; C.N.T.C. 10:241.
18. Comm. Heb. 2:5, C.O. 55:24; C.N.T.C. 12:21.
19. Comm. 1 Tim. 4:5, C.O. 52:297; C.N.T.C. 10:241.
20. Comm. Heb. 2:5, C.O. 55:24; C.N.T.C. 12:21–22.
21. *Inst.* III.ix.3; O.S. IV.173.3–8 (1:714–15); cf. Comm. Rom. 4:13, C.O. 49:77; C.N.T.C. 8:91–92.
22. Comm. 1 Tim. 4:5, C.O. 52:297; C.N.T.C. 10:241.
23. *Inst.* III.xix.8; O.S. IV.288.6–9 (1:840).

However, even though believers may legitimately and freely use the good things of creation, it is necessary for the consciences of believers to be assured of this right. If our consciences are not assured of their freedom in Jesus Christ, but rather harbor the superstitious opinion that some external thing is prohibited, then we should not partake of that thing lest we violate our conscience before God. For this reason, the weak in faith, who still harbor superstitious opinions about externals, should not be compelled by the strong to act against their conscience, even if what they are compelled to do is in itself good and pure before God. "But they who are deeply moved in any fear of God, when they are compelled to commit many things against their conscience, are overwhelmed and fall down with fright."[24]

Not only does violation of the conscience lead the weak to fall from faith in the mercy of God, but it also (and more importantly) demonstrates contempt for God. By doing something that their conscience testifies to them is sinful before God, they do sin against God, even though the deed in itself is not sinful. "For anyone who boldly sets out on something that is against his conscience, is showing a certain contempt for God."[25] Calvin claims that we act against conscience, and therefore show contempt for God, not only when we commit an act that we are certain displeases God, but also when we undertake an act that we are not sure will please God. "Where such doubt exists, therefore, anyone who goes against the testimony of his conscience is rightly accused of prevarication."[26]

It does not matter, therefore, if the work we perform is pleasing to God in the Word if our conscience is not assured that the work is pleasing to God, "since our works are right only when they please God and have the testimony of conscience that they please him."[27] The weak in faith should not be encouraged to do something that lacks the testimony of their conscience as pleasing to God; God will approve their adherence to their conscience, even if they are led by a superstitious opinion.[28] The weak should not be compelled to act with an uncertain or hesitant conscience, but should be allowed their superstitious observances until they are strengthened in the assurance of their freedom of conscience in these external matters.[29]

The faithful can only be certain that what they are about to undertake is pleasing to God on the basis of the Word of God, which attests to them the dominion over creation they have regained in Jesus Christ, and which therefore offers them all good things from the liberality of God the Father. This necessarily entails the rejection of all human laws that have been invented either to command or to prohibit the use of those good things. "To condemn all that

---

24. *Inst.* III.xix.8; O.S. IV.287.33–35 (1:840).
25. Comm. 1 Cor. 8:7, C.O. 49:433; C.N.T.C. 9:176–77.
26. Comm. Rom. 14:23, *Commentarius*, p. 304; C.N.T.C. 8:301–2.
27. *Inst.* IV.xiii.20; O.S. V.257.18–20 (2:1275).
28. Comm. Rom. 14:6, *Commentarius*, p. 294; C.N.T.C. 292–93.
29. Ibid.

is not of faith is to reject all that is not supported and approved by the Word of God."[30] The ultimate purpose and objective of the freedom of the conscience with regard to indifferent externals is to free the conscience from subjugation to any and all human laws. A human law is said to bind the conscience when it states that something is in and of itself necessary to be observed before God, regardless of the consequences; that is, when it commands deontologically. "Here it comes about that a law is said to bind the conscience when it simply binds a man without regard to other men, or without taking them into account."[31] A law is binding in this sense before God alone, regardless of its consequences or effects in the human community, making it a sin to violate such a law even if one were the only person on earth. Such, according to Calvin, are the laws of the papacy, for they are promulgated with the understanding that they are per se necessary for eternal life.[32] "But thus the Kingdom of Christ is invaded; thus the freedom given by him to the consciences of believers is utterly oppressed and cast down."[33]

The binding of the consciences of believers by such human laws is mutually exclusive of the freedom believers have by faith in Jesus Christ, for only Christ is Lord and king of the consciences of the faithful.[34] Therefore, their consciences are freed from all human lawmakers. The consciences of believers are governed only by the Word of the Lord, the holy gospel of Jesus Christ; therefore, their consciences are freed from all laws arising from human opinion. The consciences of believers inherit the dominion over creation that was lost in Adam; therefore, their consciences are freed from all human laws that bind them vis-à-vis externals. "This is Paul's reasoning: 'Those who bring consciences into bondage do injury to Christ, and make void his death. For whatever is of human invention does not bind the conscience!' "[35]

The Proper Use of Freedom

The freedom of conscience that the faithful have in Jesus Christ is their inalienable possession before God, regardless of the attitude of other human beings or of their own external circumstances. The primary purpose of such freedom is to make us confident that all we intend to undertake is pleasing to God. The possession or enjoyment of this freedom of conscience, however, is not the same as the use of this freedom in the human community. "Liberty lies in the conscience and looks to God. Its use lies in externals and deals not only with God but also with men."[36] The freedom is ours before God in our consciences, even if we never manifest it in the human community. However,

30. Comm. Rom. 14:23, *Commentarius*, p. 304; C.N.T.C. 8:301–2.
31. *Inst.* III.xix.16; O.S. IV.296.11–13 (1:849).
32. Here Calvin, like Luther, seems to be thinking especially of the bull *Unam Sanctam* promulgated by Pope Innocent III.
33. *Inst.* IV.x.1; O.S. V.164.26–30 (2:1180).
34. *Inst.* IV.x.1; O.S. V.165.4–10 (2:1180).
35. Comm. Col. 2:22, C.O. 52:115; C.N.T.C. 11:342.
36. Comm. Gal. 5:13, C.O. 50:250; C.N.T.C. 11:100.

even though the freedom of the conscience is exclusive of any attempt to bind the conscience by laws, the use of the freedom of conscience is not indeterminately free, but is governed by certain rules.

In this context, Calvin can speak of conscience in the broad sense as well as the narrow. In the narrow sense, the conscience before the judgment seat of God looks only to the freedom procured for it by Jesus Christ and is bound by no necessity or law with regard to other human beings. In the broad sense, however, our consciences are under obligation to others. This obligation is not based on external actions that are in and of themselves necessary, but on external actions that are required because of their consequences. A law is binding on the conscience in the narrow sense when it is commanded in and of itself, regardless of the consequences, and in this sense the consciences of believers are bound only by the law of God and by the Lordship of Jesus Christ. However, a law may be observed by the conscience in the broad sense when it is not held to be necessary in and of itself, but is rather observed because of the good purposes or consequences that it entails.[37] The same God who frees our consciences from all externals in the narrow sense of conscience puts us under obligation to others in the broad sense of the conscience; however, it is an obligation that involves actions that are not necessary in and of themselves but that are commanded because of their consequences. The possession of our liberty is unbridled by any consideration of other human beings, for it lies in our conscience before the judgment seat of God; however, the use of our freedom is not indeterminate, but is governed by God according to certain general rules having to do with the consequences of the use of our freedom in the human community.[38]

Although Calvin designates four specific areas as being such consequential limitations on the use of our freedom of conscience in the human community, all of them could be said to be controlled by one governing principle: love.[39] Calvin is as concerned with the revocation of the liberty of conscience by the tyranny of human law as he is with the abusive and licentious abuse of freedom in the human community. Those who are free in their consciences before God are to use their freedom in the human community under the rule of love, with an eye toward actions that build up others. "In a word, if we serve one another through love, we shall always have regard to edification; so that we shall not grow wanton, but use the grace of God to His honour and the salvation of our neighbors."[40] In sum, inward freedom of conscience before God through faith is seen by Calvin as being oriented toward outward service of others through love.[41]

---

37. Comm. 1 Cor. 10:29, C.O. 49:470; C.N.T.C. 9:223.
38. See Harro Hoepfl, *The Christian Polity of John Calvin* (Cambridge: Cambridge University Press, 1982), pp. 38–39.
39. Comm. Gal. 5:13, C.O. 50:250; C.N.T.C. 11:100.
40. Ibid.
41. Thus Calvin clearly endorses the direction set forth by Luther in *The Freedom of the Christian*.

There are four general areas where the rule of love is specifically applied by the Word of God to the use of our freedom of conscience. The first has to do with the use of the good things given to us by God in creation. The freedom of the conscience in external things that are of themselves indifferent is based upon the fact that in Jesus Christ believers inherit the dominion over and proper use of creation lost in Adam. However, God does not allow believers to use creation as their own consciences see fit, but rather prescribes general rules in Scripture.[42] Yet these rules are not to be too narrowly and strictly conceived, because then consciences are constrained more than the Lord wishes them to be—as happened, according to Calvin, in the rules for the use of creation drawn up by the church fathers.[43] According to Calvin, the best way to avoid libertine abuse on the one hand, and excessive legalism on the other, is to look at the purpose for which God gave us the good things of creation; when we do so, we see that the Father gave them to us not only for our necessities but also for our delight and enjoyment. "Did he not, in short, render many things attractive to us, apart from their necessary use?"[44]

On this basis, Calvin develops four rules for the proper use of the good things of creation: first, that we ought to give thanks to God for the good things bestowed on us; second, that we should bear deprivation patiently; third, that we should remember we are stewards of creation who must render an account to God for our use of creation; and finally, that we should remain content in the calling or station of life in which the Lord has placed us. All of these specific rules might be seen under the one general rule of patient moderation. "And let them regard this as the law of Christian freedom; to have learned with Paul, in whatever state they are, to be content; to know how to be humble and exalted; to have been taught, in any and all circumstances, to be filled and to hunger, to abound and to suffer want [Phil. 4:12]."[45] Our use and enjoyment of the good things of creation with a free conscience are governed by the God-given law that such use and enjoyment conform to the purposes for which God gave us those good things; such a teleological law does not, therefore, create scruples of conscience or obliterate Christian freedom.

The second area in which the Lord teleologically regulates the use of our freedom among humanity is civil government. The relationship between obedience to the civil authorities and the freedom of the Christian conscience is made especially complex by Romans 13, in which Paul directly links such obedience to the conscience. "Therefore one must be subject, not only because of [God's] wrath but also because of conscience" (Rom. 13:5). In order to preserve the freedom of the conscience in God's sight (*coram Deo*), but also to do justice to this passage, Calvin uses the distinction between the broad

42. *Inst.* III.x.1; O.S. IV.178.7–10 (1:720).
43. *Inst.* III.x.1; O.S. IV.177.28–32 (1:720).
44. *Inst.* III.x.2; O.S. IV.178.32–34 (1:721).
45. *Inst.* III.xix.9; O.S. IV.289.20–24 (1:841–42).

and narrow sense of conscience. We are to obey the laws of the land and the governing authorities by obligation of conscience—that is, even if we could disobey them with civil impunity—but that does not mean that civil laws are binding on our consciences. "For even though individual laws may not apply to the conscience, we are still held by God's general command, which commends to us the authority of magistrates."[46]

Once again, the limitation of our freedom of conscience, this time by obedience to those in civil authority, does not entail the binding of conscience by laws that are per se necessary, but rather by laws that are to be followed because of their purposes. "For all obligation to observe laws looks to the general purpose, but does not consist in the things enjoined."[47] Civil laws are to be obeyed by the broad sense of conscience because through them God wishes to maintain the good of order in the human community.[48] The preservation of order in the human community is in itself an expression of the law of love, which is the general rule governing all particular rules that apply to the use of our freedom.[49]

Out of love for our neighbors and out of a concern that order and peace be maintained in the human community, the godly will limit the external use of their freedom by obeying the civil authorities, so long as those authorities make no laws either against the faith or binding on the conscience. Short of those qualifications, we must obey the government, even when it is tyrannical; not even a tyrant can extinguish the freedom we have in our consciences.[50] In this way, Calvin is in complete agreement with Luther that the freedom of the Christian is found in the conscience before God, and not in the flesh before humanity, so that "spiritual freedom can perfectly well exist along with civil bondage."[51] We obey the laws of the state out of love, with regard to the goal of peace and order in the human community, according to the will of God.

The third way in which the use of freedom of conscience is regulated by a general law of God is in church polity, which is closely related in Calvin's mind to civil polity. If civil law is instituted in order to preserve peace and order in the world, church polity is instituted so that "all things should be done decently and in order" (1 Cor. 14:40). Once again it can be seen that the rule governing the use of Christian freedom is teleological and not deontological: church polity is necessary for the maintenance of certain purposes and goals (such as decency and order), but church laws are not necessary in and of themselves, nor do they constitute the spiritual worship of God, and hence they are not binding on the conscience.[52] The consciences of Christians

46. *Inst.* IV.x.5; O.S. V.168.4–7 (2:1183–84).
47. *Inst.* IV.x.5; O.S. V.168.16–18 (2:1184).
48. Comm. Jer. 35:7, C.O. 39:105; C.T.S. 20:310.
49. Comm. Rom. 13:8, *Commentarius*, p. 286; C.N.T.C. 8:284.
50. Comm. Acts 15:1, C.O. 48:336; C.N.T.C. 7:22–23.
51. *Inst.* IV.xx.1; O.S. V.472.25–26 (2:1486).
52. Comm. 1 Cor. 14:40, C.O. 49:535; C.N.T.C. 9:310.

are not bound before God by the observance of church polity, as though their salvation depended on it, in contrast to the claims of Rome. However, God does not leave church polity up to our own free decision, but rather reveals the goal such polity is to serve and instructs us through the Word as to what shape that polity should take, "in such a way that it is only from His Word that we can make up our minds about what is right."[53]

Calvin is in complete agreement with Luther regarding the latter's rejection of Roman canon law; he agrees that no law governing externals can be binding on conscience (deontological), but rather must serve the goal of order and peace (teleological). The goal itself is not a human tradition subject to human decision and reason (including the state) or to the authority of the pope, but is rather something taught us by Jesus Christ himself in the Word.[54]

Calvin does not mean by this that each specific law governing church discipline and order must be decided from the Word of God; freedom is allowed in these specific laws given the special needs and concerns of the church in various times and places. The specific laws, therefore, are human; but the general rule that such laws are to serve—that all things be done decently and in order—is not human but divine. "It is of God in so far as it is part of that decorum whose care and observance the apostle has commended to us [1 Cor. 14:40]. But it is of men in so far as it specifically designates what had in general been suggested rather than explicitly stated."[55] The general rule of decency and order thus places believers under obligation in the broad sense of conscience, so that it would be disobedient to God to treat them with contempt; but the specific laws drafted to maintain church decency and order are not binding on conscience in the narrow sense, as though they were per se necessary.

The Word of the Lord thus sets before the church a twofold goal: that all things be done decently—that is, that the worship demonstrate an appropriate dignity and reverence—and that all things be done in order, meaning that the form of worship should be orderly and that discipline should be exercised in the church. "Thus all ecclesiastical constitutions which we accept as holy and salutary should be reckoned under two heads: the first type pertains to rites and ceremonies; the second, to discipline and peace."[56] Rites and ceremonies are performed decently when they not only exhibit our piety and reverence before God and other people, but also when they set forth Jesus Christ himself. "Now ceremonies, to be exercises of piety, ought to lead us straight to Christ."[57] Such decency includes kneeling during prayer, handling the Lord's Supper and baptism with dignity, and burying the dead decently.

53. Comm. 1 Cor. 14:40, C.O. 49:535–36; C.N.T.C. 9:310.
54. Comm. 1 Cor. 14:40, C.O. 49:536; C.N.T.C. 9:310.
55. *Inst.* IV.x.30; O.S. V.192.20–23 (2:1208). For the same interpretation of 1 Cor. 14:40 in Luther, see *Von den Konziliis und Kirchen,* 1539. W.A. 50.614.8-17; L.W. 41:131.
56. *Inst.* IV.x.29; O.S. V.192.6–9 (2:1207).
57. *Inst.* IV.x.29; O.S. V.191.22–24 (2:1207).

The church is governed in order not only when regular forms of worship are instituted and regular hours of worship set, but also when catechesis, discipline, and excommunication are properly maintained.[58]

Calvin's concern for church polity thus not only includes a concern for order and peace, in common with the purposes of civil law and in harmony with Luther's view of the matter; but it is primarily directed toward the goal of conforming the external rites, ceremonies, and behavior of the Christian community to its profession of faith in Jesus Christ. According to Calvin, the rites and ceremonies of the church should above all exhibit Christ, as should the lives of the people gathered together to worship. This reveals a fundamental difference between Luther and Calvin: namely, that Calvin insisted on the conformity between the inward faith of conscience and the external appearance of the church, both in terms of the ceremonies of the church and in terms of the lives of the believers.

This does not mean that Calvin makes sanctity of life a mark of the church, along with Word and sacraments; indeed, he rejects the zeal of those who take such a position. "When they do not see a quality of life corresponding to the doctrine of the gospel among those to whom it is announced, they immediately judge that no church exists in that place."[59] In contrast to such severity, Calvin agrees with Luther and Melanchthon that there are only two external marks of the church: "Wherever we see the Word of God purely preached and heard, and the sacraments administered according to Christ's institution, there, it is not to be doubted, a church of God exists [cf. Eph. 2:20]."[60]

However, even though Calvin rejects the correspondence of life to the gospel as a mark of the church, he reveals his basic sympathy for those who take such a position even as he criticizes their severity. "This is a very legitimate complaint, and we give all too much occasion for it in this miserable age. . . . Woe to us, then, who act with such dissolute and criminal license that weak consciences are wounded because of us."[61]

This is a theme that distinguishes Calvin from Luther: namely, that weak consciences are wounded as much by the example of lives that do not correspond to the gospel as they are by the exercise of freedom in things in themselves indifferent. Calvin reveals just how close he is to the position he rejects when he specifies what he means by a charitable judgment of others with regard to their membership in the visible church. "And, since assurance of faith was not necessary, he substituted for it a certain charitable judgment whereby we recognize as members of the church those who, by confession of faith, by *example of life*, and by partaking of the sacraments, profess the same God and Christ with us."[62]

58. *Inst.* IV.x.29; O.S. V.192.4–6 (2:1207).
59. *Inst.* IV.i.13; O.S. V.17.9–12 (2:1027).
60. *Inst.* IV.i.9; O.S. V.13.24–27 (2:1023).
61. *Inst.* IV.i.13; O.S. V.17.12–20 (2:1027).
62. *Inst.* IV.i.8; O.S. V.13.16–20 (2:1022–23), my emphasis.

Indeed, the same theme can be seen in Calvin's definition of the church: for although Calvin does not make a life corresponding to the gospel a third mark of the church, he implicitly includes it by qualifying Melanchthon's first mark of the church. Melanchthon says: "The church is the assembly of saints in which the Gospel is purely taught and the sacraments are administered rightly."[63] Calvin qualifies this significantly by saying, "Wherever we see the Word of God purely preached *and heard*, and the sacraments administered according to Christ's institution, there, it is not to be doubted, a church of God exists [cf. Eph. 2:20]."[64]

According to Calvin, therefore, both the preaching of the Word and the administration of the sacraments point in the direction of church discipline, in which believers are exhorted to demonstrate a correspondence between their profession of faith and their lives, while those who are unrepentant about the lack of such correspondence are excommunicated. Excommunication is only to be applied by the duly constituted authorities in the church to publicly manifested and chastised sins. It has three purposes, all of which focus on the importance of a life corresponding to our faith in Christ. The first goal is that those who lead filthy and infamous lives may not be called Christians, to the dishonor of God and the church. This applies not only to the pure hearing of the Word of God, but also to the proper administration of the sacraments. "And here we must also preserve the order of the Lord's Supper, that it may not be profaned by being administered indiscriminately."[65] The second goal is so that the good, especially the weak, may not be corrupted by the bad examples of the manifestly ungodly. The third is to lead the wicked to repentance by shaming them.[66]

Although discipline is not a third mark of the church, it is essentially related to the pure preaching of the gospel and the proper administration of the sacraments. The pastor, according to Calvin, has the authority and duty privately to warn and exhort all to whom he preaches if he sees they are not showing forth the preached gospel in their lives; and the assembly of elders has the authority to excommunicate those who refuse such warning and exhortation.[67]

However, it cannot be said that Calvin's emphasis on a life corresponding to the profession of faith is a disagreement with Luther. It rather constitutes, like the third use of the law, Calvin's explicit emphasis on a theme present in, but less strongly emphasized by, Luther. Luther, unlike Melanchthon, adds the proper response to the Word of God not only in profession of faith, but also in form of life, as being constitutive of the first "holy possession" of

---

63. *The Book of Concord*, ed. Theodore A. Tappert (Philadelphia: Fortress Press, 1959), p. 32.
64. *Inst.* IV.i.9; O.S. V.13.24–27 (2:1023), my emphasis.
65. *Inst.* IV.xii.5; O.S. V.215.20–21 (2:1232).
66. *Inst.* IV.xii.5; O.S. V.216 (2:1232–34).
67. *Inst.* IV.xii.2; O.S. V.213.10–33 (2:1230–31).

the church, namely the holy Word of God. "Now, wherever you hear or see this Word preached, believed, professed, *and lived*, do not doubt that the true *ecclesia sancta catholica*, 'a Christian holy people' must be there, even though their number is very small."[68] Luther also includes the exercise of discipline and excommunication in the proper administration of baptism and the Lord's Supper. Speaking of false and unbelieving Christians secretly among the true church, Luther says, "They, however, do not profane the people of God because they are not known; the church, or God's people, does not tolerate known sinners in its midst, but reproves them and also makes them holy. Or, if they refuse, it casts them out from the sanctuary by means of the ban and regards them as heathen, Matthew 18[:17]."[69]

The relationship of discipline to the sacraments becomes explicit when Luther makes the keys the fourth holy possession of the true church, for they include both public and private admonition. "That is, as Christ decrees in Matthew 18[:15-20], if a Christian sins, he should be reproved; and if he does not mend his ways, he should be bound in his sin and cast out. If he does mend his ways, he should be absolved. That is the office of the keys."[70] Luther himself exercised the keys in the form of the ban or excommunication by excommunicating the antinomians from the church.[71] Indeed, Luther concludes his discussion of the seven holy possessions of the church by stating, in fundamental agreement with Calvin, that the goal of all of these possessions is true holiness and sanctification by the Holy Spirit, on the basis of the forgiveness of sins.

> These are the true seven principal parts of the great holy possession whereby the Holy Spirit effects in us a daily sanctification and vivification in Christ, according to the first table of Moses. By this we obey it, albeit never as perfectly as Christ. But we constantly strive to attain this goal, under his redemption or remission of sin, until we too shall one day become perfectly holy and no longer stand in need of forgiveness. Everything is directed toward this goal.[72]

Thus Calvin's insistence on a life corresponding to our faith in Christ, reinforced by church discipline and excommunication, does not constitute in any sense a disagreement with Luther, but at most a difference of emphasis. Calvin does, however, differ with Luther over the status of church polity. Although he agrees with Luther that church polity is not strictly binding on conscience, he disagrees that it is only an external matter subject to regulation

68. *Von den Konziliis und Kirchen*, 1539. W.A. 50.629.28–31; L.W. 41:150, my emphasis.
69. Ibid. W.A. 50.631.31–35; L.W. 41:152–53.
70. Ibid. W.A. 50.632.17–20; L.W. 41:153.
71. Ibid. W.A. 50.632.17–20; L.W. 41:153.
72. Ibid. W.A. 50.642.32–36, 643.1–2; L.W. 41:166.

by human reason and the civil government. Instead, it must be governed by the "useful form" of worship and polity given to us in Scripture by God.[73]

The fourth area in which God has given us rules for the use of our freedom has to do with the problem of offending the weak in faith, those who are not yet assured in their consciences of their freedom before God in regard to external matters. Even though the strong in faith are confident that all things are free to them before God, they nonetheless ought to refrain from using that freedom if its use will offend a weaker sister or brother in the faith. The rule governing the use of freedom here is love, in that our actions ought to build up our neighbors and not cause them to stumble. "Nothing is plainer than this rule: that we should use our freedom if it results in the edification of our neighbor, but if it does not help our neighbor, then we should forgo it."[74] According to this rule of love, there are not only times when we ought to forgo using our freedom out of concern that we might offend the weak, but there are also times when we ought to use our freedom out of concern that the weak might have their freedom taken away by the proud. "Thus we shall so temper the use of our freedom as to allow for the ignorance of our weak brothers, but for the rigor of the Pharisees, not at all!"[75]

Therefore, they violate the rule of love who do not use their freedom when it is being illegitimately denied them by the proud, just as they do who use their freedom when its use unnecessarily offends the weak. In each case, the consequence of our use of freedom would not be edifying to our neighbors. We are bound by conscience in the broad sense to use our freedom under the rule of love, but how we are to use that freedom will vary depending on the consequences in various situations.

However, Calvin insists that just as the use of our freedom is governed by the rule of love, so the rule of love is subordinated to the rule of faith. Those who obey precepts or conform to ecclesiastical or civil behavior that is in itself impious and ungodly, out of a professed concern not to offend their weak neighbors, are building up the consciences of their neighbors, not in righteousness but in sin. "But those people are not to be listened to who, after making themselves leaders in a thousand sorts of wickedness, pretend that they must act so as not to cause offense to their neighbors [cf. 1 Cor. 8:9]; as if they were not in the meanwhile building up their neighbors' consciences into evil, especially when they ever stick fast in the same mud without hope of getting out."[76]

73. Comm. 1 Cor. 14:37, C.O. 49:535; C.N.T.C. 9:309. Here Calvin may in particular be thinking of the fourfold polity of the church that he claimed was set forth in Scripture—that is, pastors, teachers, elders, and deacons. However, even here Calvin is willing to exhibit latitude, allowing for the retention of bishops in Scotland and England, provided that they were godly bishops who preached the gospel and were concerned about proper discipline.

74. *Inst.* III.xix.12; O.S. IV.292.6–8 (1:845).

75. *Inst.* III.xix.11; O.S. IV.290.27–29 (1:843).

76. *Inst.* III.xix.13; O.S. IV.292.25–29 (1:845).

Our neighbors are edified not only when we abstain from indifferent things out of a concern that they be offended, but also when we manifest a correspondence between our actions and our profession of faith. We cannot, according to Calvin, forgo that conformity of life with faith out of concern that others be offended; for our outward conformity with impious behavior confirms our neighbors' consciences in the same impiety. "Hence it happens, that while they all profess to be withheld by fear of giving offense, but are, in fact, afraid of exciting indignation against themselves, no one begins to be distinguished from others by the sincerity and purity of his conduct."[77]

Over and above such conformity of life to our profession of faith, however, Calvin insists that impious ceremonies and actions are not external matters that are in and of themselves indifferent. Here Calvin has a serious disagreement with Luther. According to Luther, the inward faith of conscience was all that mattered; the external behavior in church ceremonies was indifferent, including both the mass and images. If we are convinced in our conscience that the mass is not a sacrifice, then it is not in fact a sacrifice, even if we were outwardly to profess that it were. "Where, however, such a conscience does not exist, there one does not sacrifice, even if one raised it above the heavens and the whole world shouted: Sacrifice, Sacrifice!"[78]

Luther applies the same disjunction between internal faith of conscience and external behavior to the issue of images in the church. According to Luther, the Word of God does not explicitly prohibit images, but the *worship* of images. Therefore, consciences must be instructed by the Word of God that images are not to be worshiped; after that, images are indifferent things and can either remain in or be removed from the church by the duly constituted governing authorities. "This means to instruct and enlighten the conscience that it is idolatry to worship them, or to trust in them, since one is to trust alone in Christ. *Beyond this let the external matters take their course.* God grant that they may be destroyed, become dilapidated, or that they remain. *It is all the same and makes no difference*, just as when the poison has been removed from a snake."[79] Luther insists on this disjunction between externals and the faith of conscience on two grounds: because of the theology of the cross, for that theology believes the truth of God in spite of the external appearance that contradicts it, whereas the theology of glory judges all things by their appearances; and also because of his doctrine of the two kingdoms, which subjects all external things to reason and thus to civil law.

Calvin disagrees with Luther on two grounds in this matter. To begin with, Calvin does not think that it is only the idolatry of the conscience that constitutes the poison of images, but that images are in and of themselves poison, because they directly contradict the Word of God.[80] Since images are per se

---

77. *De fugendis impiorum illicitis sacris, et puritate Christianae religionis observanda*, C.O. 5:273; *Tracts* 3:405–6.

78. *Wider die himmlischen Propheten*, 1525. W.A. 18.122.22–28; L.W. 40:140.

79. Ibid. W.A. 18.74.6–10; L.W. 91, my emphasis.

80. *Inst.* III.xix.13; O.S. IV.292.32–35 (1:845).

impious and ungodly, the conscience must not only be instructed that it is idolatry to worship them; images must be materially removed on the grounds of faith. "It is certain that the *idolomania* with which the minds of men are now fascinated, *cannot be cured otherwise than by removing the material cause of the infatuation.*"[81] The removal of images cannot be delayed even temporarily out of concern that the weak in faith be offended; for their very presence is a temptation for the weak to offend God. "They indeed avert offense from themselves, but they entice others, by their example, to offend God."[82]

Calvin considered the second commandment prohibiting the making and worshiping of images (Exod. 20:4-6; Deut. 5:8-10) to be binding not only on the Jews but also on Christians, since the prohibited practices directly contradict the infinite and spiritual essence of God (*qualis sit Deus*). Calvin therefore deploys his understanding of the second commandment against the carnal conceptions of God that are formed by human opinion on the basis of the taste of divinity that the ungodly attain from the powers of God manifested in the universe. According to Calvin, not only the worship but also the placing of images in the church is categorically prohibited by the deontologically binding Word of God, on the basis of God's infinite and spiritual nature and on the basis of Jesus Christ alone being the image of the invisible God.

Luther, on the other hand, did not hear the second commandment as the Word of God prohibiting the presence of images, but only their worship. "And if you reply: The text [Exod. 20:4] says, 'You shall not make any images,' then [our Roman opponents] say: It also says, 'You shall not worship them.' In the face of such uncertainty who would be so bold as to destroy the images? Not I."[83] Images may be present in churches, according to Luther, so long as they are not worshiped. For Calvin, their very presence signifies an intention to worship them, and hence both their presence and worship are prohibited by the second commandment.

Luther clarifies his position regarding the apparent prohibition of images by norming the Ten Commandments by the natural law of the conscience. "Therefore Moses' legislation about images and the Sabbath, and what else goes beyond the natural law, since it is not supported by the natural law, is free, null, and void, and is specifically given to the Jewish people alone."[84] On this basis, Luther omits any mention of the second commandment in all of his commentaries on the Ten Commandments (the *Sermon on Good Works*, and the Small and Large Catechisms). By doing so, Luther appears to be distorting the Word of God and also to be directly contradicting himself. With regard to every other issue, he insists that the conscience cannot norm the Word of God but must be taken captive by, and stand under the authority of,

81. *De necessitate reformandae ecclesiae*, C.O. 6:476; *Treatises*, p. 190, my emphasis.
82. C.O. 5:273; *Tracts* 3, p. 405.
83. *Invocavit Predigten*, 1522. W.A. 10(III).27.1-8; L.W. 51:82.
84. W.A. 18.81.7-10; L.W. 40:97-98.

the Word of God. Commenting on Deut. 4:2—"You must neither add anything to what I command you nor take away anything from it"—Luther categorically states: "In one short expression this passage condemns all human laws, and decrees that in a matter of conscience nothing but the Law and Word of God is valid. . . . Unless, therefore, God reveals His Law, by which He makes His will known to us (Ps. 103:7), there remains only that saying of ours: 'Every man is a liar; every man, vanity.' "[85]

Indeed, if the natural law norms the law of Moses, then not only the second and fourth, but also the tenth, commandments would be free, null, and void; for according to Luther, the natural law is utterly blind regarding the sin of concupiscence. The fact that Luther would violate the authority of the Word of God over the conscience in contradiction to his own theological principles, by norming the Ten Commandments by the natural law, and distort the Word of God by removing the second commandment from his teachings on the law of God, shows the extent to which Luther's theological concerns manifested in the theology of the cross kept him from associating in any way the faith of the conscience with externals like images and ceremonies.

Calvin agrees with Luther that faith is a matter of the conscience, but he insists, in contrast to Luther, that the worship of the Christian community conform with the nature and character of God revealed in the Word. Far from norming the Ten Commandments by the natural law—which for Calvin would entail the rejection not only of the second, but also of the first, third, fourth, and tenth commandments—in an attempt to relativize the second commandment, Calvin norms the natural law by the Ten Commandments. The natural law apprehended by conscience in a sense teaches the same thing as the law of Moses because it apprehends the spiritual majesty of God through its awareness of divine judgment, making us aware that there is a God who created us whom all ought to worship and adore, although it is utterly unable to bring itself to certain knowledge of who God is or what God is like. Instead, through their taste of God from creation, the ungodly offer carnal worship to their carnally conceived gods. The law of Moses, on the other hand, clearly portrays the spiritual nature and character of God; hence it is the norm of the natural law. Calvin does not ground the authority of the Ten Commandments in the natural law apprehended by the conscience, but in the character of God portrayed in the Decalogue. Calvin therefore deploys the second commandment against the carnal conceptions and superstitious worship of God common to all idolaters, not as a proof text, but as an exemplar of the spiritual nature and character of God to which our lives are to conform.

Just as the law of Moses norms the natural law, so the coming of Jesus norms the law of Moses. However, the coming of Jesus does not annul, but rather reinforces, the prohibition of images. Jesus teaches us that God is Spirit, to

---

85. *Deuteronomion Mosi cum annotationibus*, 1525. W.A. 14.585.15–16, 25–28; L.W. 9:50–51.

be worshiped in spirit and truth. And because Jesus Christ alone is the image of the invisible God, offered to us in the gospel and the sacraments, all other images of God are categorically prohibited. As the image of God, Jesus Christ is also the prime archetype or exemplar of God, fulfilling and transcending the law given to Moses. The resurrection of Jesus Christ fulfills the fourth commandment concerning the Sabbath in a spiritual manner, freeing Christians from its external observance; but the resurrection only reinforces the authority of the second commandment. Now that the image of the invisible God has been once for all revealed in Jesus Christ, we are prohibited from making any other images of God.[86]

The issue of images in particular, and external worship in general, reveals not only the two genuine disagreements between Luther and Calvin (with the possible exception of the definition of repentance), but also an internal contradiction in the theology of Luther itself. Against the scholastics, Luther insists on the truth of the Word of the law of God against all natural law of reason. "For since through the sin of Adam we are sunk in blindness, so that we are wholly ignorant of God in all His will and counsel, it is not only foolish but also impossible of ourselves to prepare a light and a way by which to approach God and find out what He would have us do."[87] Yet against Karlstadt and others (like Calvin) who wish to prohibit images on the basis of the Word of God in the second commandment, Luther also insists, in the very same lectures, "But since one must now affirm the liberty given by God, let us tell them that Moses in no way pertains to us in all his laws, but only to the Jews, except where he agrees with the natural law, which, as Paul teaches, is written in the hearts of the Gentiles (Rom. 2:15)."[88] Nor does Luther always equate the law that is binding on Christians with the natural law, but at times contrasts the natural law with the law of Christ, especially with regard to suffering injustice rather than fighting for one's rights.[89]

This leads to Calvin's second disagreement with Luther, namely that there cannot, under any circumstances nor under any pretext, be a disjunction, let alone a contradiction, between our inward faith of conscience and our external behavior. If we are convinced in our consciences that the mass and images

---

86. Comm. Col. 1:15, C.O. 52:86; C.N.T.C. 11:308.
87. W.A. 14.585.19–24; L.W. 9:51.
88. W.A. 14.621.39, 622.9–11; L.W. 9:81.
89. At places Luther states that the Sermon on the Mount is nothing more than an explication of the Ten Commandments, which themselves clearly portray the natural law; cf. W.A. 32.493–99. At other places Luther claims that the law of Christ teaches a way of life transcending and even contradicting the natural law; cf. *Ermahnung zum Frieden auf die zwoelf Artikel der Bauernschaft in Schwaben*, 1525. W.A. 18.291–334. Finally, at places Luther clearly distinguishes between the law of Christ as the following of Christ, the Ten Commandments, and the natural law of reason; cf. Parts I, IV, and V of *De votis monasticis Martini Lutheri iudicium*, 1521. W.A. 8.573–669. One way to make sense of this ambiguity or fluidity in Luther's appeal to the natural law is to see the natural law as applying to our relations with other people, for whom we seek justice from the governing authorities, whereas the law of Christ applies to our own person as a Christian, wherein we gladly suffer injustice in fellowship with Christ crucified.

are inherently idolatrous, then we cannot participate in them, according to Calvin. "What kind of person, pray, must he be, or rather where can the person possibly exist who, while his conscience inwardly declares to God that He alone ought to be adored, is able to frame his features and outward gestures so as to express adoration of an idol? . . . What do they gain by that secret confession, but just to accuse their outward idolatry before the divine tribunal, on the testimony of their own mind?"[90]

According to Calvin, such conformity of our behavior to our conscience extends not only to the mass and images, which are in and of themselves idolatrous, but also to ceremonies and other ecclesiastical rites. All of our actions are to set forth Jesus Christ and our faith in him. The ceremonies of the papacy do not set forth Christ but obscure him; hence they cannot be used under the pretext that they are in and of themselves indifferent. "Now, since it is plain that such ceremonies are neither veils nor sepulchres by which Christ is hidden, but rather stinking dunghills, by which sincere faith and religion are buried, those who make free and indiscriminate use of them, arrogate far more to the Pope than God grants in His law."[91]

Just as Luther's theology of the cross (*theologia crucis*) manifested his disjunction between inward faith and external appearances, so Calvin's theology of adoption allowed him to insist on a harmony and conformity between our inward faith in the conscience and our external behavior, especially in the worship of the Lord. "For we have been adopted as sons by the Lord with this one condition: that our life express Christ, the bond of our adoption."[92]

This is the most significant disagreement between Luther and Calvin regarding the testimony of the conscience. It is precisely here, and not in the relationship of justification and sanctification per se, that the fundamental difference between Luther and Calvin lies. For Luther, the essential issue is the faith or trust of the conscience; once that is based on the grace of God in Jesus Christ, and not on its own works, then all externals, including images, are indifferent. Otherwise, were externals made a matter of conscience for Christians, Luther was convinced that trust in them would again emerge, destroying faith in Christ.

For Calvin, the fundamental issue also is the faith of the conscience; but that faith cannot exist inwardly without being expressed outwardly in our behavior, so that images must be removed from all places of worship, as must all rites and ceremonies that do not express Christ. There are no rites or ceremonies of Christian worship that are in and of themselves indifferent. Some are inherently godless because they contradict the nature of God and of Christ (for example, images and the mass), and others must be teleologically rejected because they obscure Christ. Although Calvin agrees with Luther

---

90. C.O. 5:272; *Tracts* 3, p. 404.
91. Comm. Acts 16:3, C.O. 48:371; C.N.T.C. 7:65.
92. *Inst.* III.vi.3; O.S. IV.148.25–26 (1:687).

that rites and ceremonies are not necessary for our salvation, and hence are not binding on conscience, he disagrees with Luther when he insists that all rites and ceremonies must be judged by whether they clearly set forth Jesus Christ and correspond to the profession of faith in him.

However, one should not be left with the impression that Calvin saw his disagreement with Luther regarding images and ceremonies as church-divisive. In a letter Calvin wrote to Farel on 20 April 1539, he reveals that he had brought up his opinion about ceremonies with Melanchthon: "Of late, I have plainly told Philip to his face how much I disliked that overabounding of ceremonies; indeed, that it seemed to me the form which they observe was not far removed from Judaism."[93] Calvin is informed by Melanchthon that although Luther allowed the retention of such ceremonies because of the Canonists, he did not necessarily disapprove of the sparing use of ceremonies found among the Swiss. "But he made a small reservation, to the effect that the ceremonies which they had been compelled to retain were no more approved of by Luther than was our sparing use of them."[94]

Calvin then goes on to note that although Bucer came to the defense of Luther regarding these ceremonies, this does not mean that Bucer wishes to restore them in Strasbourg: "only he cannot endure that, on account of these trifling observances, we should be separated from Luther. *Neither, certainly do I consider them to be just causes of dissent.*"[95] Although Calvin tried as late as 1545 to come to an agreement with Luther and Melanchthon over the issue of images and ceremonies, he did not consider his disagreement sufficient to cause separation; neither, according to Melanchthon, did Luther.

---

93. C.O. 10:340; *Letters of John Calvin*, ed. Dr. Jules Bonnet (New York: Burt Franklin Reprints, 1972), vol. 1, p. 136.

94. Ibid.

95. Ibid., my emphasis.

CONCLUSION

IS GOD MERCIFUL ONLY TO
THOSE WHO BELIEVE
IN CHRIST?

At this point it is possible to summarize the similarities, differences, and genuine disagreements between Luther and Calvin regarding the assurance of faith, which is especially directed to the conscience of the believer. Luther roots the testimony of the conscience in the syllogistic process of practical reason, whereas Calvin bases it in the sense of divine judgment, giving the conscience an immediate awareness of the judgment of God that it does not have in Luther. Luther and Calvin both insist that the conscience apprehends enough of the law of God, especially the second table, to hold all sinners without excuse for their sin, as well as to provide the basis for all civil law. However, Luther claims that the natural law that remains in the consciences of all is in fact rightly apprehended only by a few, who are then both to teach and govern the many; whereas Calvin claims that the natural law makes the principles of human law available to all people, so that all may judge the laws of their land.

Luther understands all idolatry to be based in the phenomenon of the conscience, whereby the conscience imagines God to be a judge who is only gracious toward those who are aware of their righteousness. Calvin, in contrast, holds that the conscience is the sense of divinity within all people, which leads all to seek the knowledge of God from creation. Idolatry for Calvin is derived both from the sense of divinity in the conscience, and from the taste of divinity that is derived from the awareness of the powers of God in creation and distorted by blindness and ingratitude, leading to the formulation of carnal conceptions of God. Calvin therefore uses the knowledge of God the Creator as the first line of attack against idolatry, in conjunction with the Second Commandment; he holds that all carnal conceptions of God violate the Creator's infinite and spiritual essence and fail to acknowledge God as the author of every good perceived in the universe. Luther attacks idolatry solely by the preaching of the gospel, because for him all idolatry is rooted in the legal knowledge of God in the conscience and the subsequent trust of the conscience in its works. The knowledge of God the Creator as Father also gives Calvin a subsequent confirmation of faith that is not found in Luther.

Although both Luther and Calvin tend to speak of the testimony of the law before the testimony of the gospel, both also realize the limitations of that sequential position. Calvin seems increasingly to have spoken of knowing God as Father prior to knowing God as Lord, although he never completely broke with the older law-gospel model. Both Luther and Calvin claim that the testimony of the conscience can and must be brought into correspondence with the testimony of the law, so that our consciences themselves make us aware of our sinfulness as preparation for faith in Christ; both also speak of the necessity of the inner working of God along with the preaching of the law so that this correspondence might take place. However, Calvin is much more explicit than Luther regarding the necessity of the Holy Spirit in creating the awareness of our poverty and guilt in the conscience, and in insisting that there is no acknowledgment of guilt where there is not a prior awareness of the mercy of the Father.

Luther and Calvin agree that Christ is both the Redeemer and the true witness to redemption in the preaching of the gospel and in the sacraments. For Luther, the gospel offers us the promise of justification and the forgiveness of sins in the happy exchange, to be accepted by a faith that acknowledges the truth of God's Word. For Calvin, the gospel offers us Christ as the image of the invisible Father, the fountain of every good, in the wonderful exchange, to be accepted by a faith that engrafts us into Christ himself. Our participation in Christ takes away every evil that we have and gives us every good thing that we lack, especially the twofold grace of justification and sanctification.

Calvin's understanding of Christ as fountain means that Christ himself is the object of faith, and not justifying grace per se; and this allows him to discuss the twofold grace of Christ in either order, since both are received simultaneously when we are engrafted into Christ by faith. Luther, on the other hand, invariably speaks of faith in justification before speaking of newness of life, primarily because of the theology of the cross in light of the legal knowledge of the conscience.

Calvin disagrees with Luther's definition of repentance as the conscience terrified by the law and consoled by the gospel. Calvin defines repentance as the mortification of the old person and the vivification of the Spirit; he claims that repentance does not precede, but is born of, faith, although he is not entirely consistent about this position given his retention of the law-gospel sequence. However, what Calvin calls repentance Luther speaks of as sanctification—which he usually describes either as the gift of the Holy Spirit or as Christ in us. He agrees with Calvin that the gift of sanctification is inseparable from the grace of justification, although the theology of the cross usually leads Luther to subordinate sanctification to justification.

Both Luther and Calvin see a positive use of the law in the life of the sanctified, in teaching and exhorting them to do what God requires. For both theologians, the law in its teaching and exhorting mode is freed from the curse of God by faith in Christ; believers willingly obey because of the work of the Spirit within their hearts and wills, inspired by their confidence in God as a forgiving Father. Luther does not, however, call this the third use of the law, nor call it the principal and primary use of the law, as does Calvin; this point further illustrates Calvin's greater emphasis on obedience compared to Luther.

Luther and Calvin also agree that the faith of believers must be confirmed by the testimony of a good conscience that grows out of sanctification by Christ and the Holy Spirit, and that the lack of such confirming testimony falsifies any claim to faith. Both Luther and Calvin insist that the confirming testimony of the good conscience must be built upon the foundation of faith and assurance in the forgiveness of sins as attested to us in the gospel; while Calvin sees yet another foundation of assurance not found in Luther, that of the knowledge of Christ as the fountain of every good.

However, the distinction both theologians make between the foundation and confirmation of assurance is inherently unstable, given their combination of the universal reconciliation in Christ offered to all in the gospel with the individual reconciliation of the believer in faith limited by divine election. In light of universal reconciliation in Christ, the assurance of faith is grounded in the fact that God is gracious to sinners in Jesus Christ alone; and the terrified conscience before the judgment seat of God makes it necessary to seek assurance of the mercy of God not in ourselves but in the testimony of Christ to us in the gospel. In light of individual reconciliation by faith in Christ, the assurance of faith is qualified by the fact that God is gracious only toward those sinners who sincerely believe in Christ, making it necessary for believers to find confirmation of their assurance within themselves; and the testimony of a good conscience before the judgment seat of God confirms that we are the godly to whom God has promised to be merciful in Christ.

Given this combination of universal reconciliation with limited election, it is impossible for Luther and Calvin to make the distinction between the foundation of assurance in the testimony of the gospel, and its confirmation in the testimony of a good conscience, as stable as they wanted to make it. The possibility is left open that the foundation and confirmation of faith might be reversed, as in fact happened in Beza and Westminster (that is, since the grace of Christ only benefits the elect, then one must first assure oneself of one's election through the testimony of a good conscience before one can confidently believe in Christ). Such a reversal is in principle possible in both theologies, although it in fact appears in neither. Calvin does point to a promising resolution of this problem in his understanding of Christ as the image of the Father, in whom the Father has laid up all of the good things to be offered to sinners in the wonderful exchange. However, the one good thing the Father does not set forth in the wonderful exchange in Christ is election. Yet this makes election, along with Christ himself, the fountain of all grace, for Christ as the fountain of every good thing profits only those who believe in him. Calvin did not seem to be aware of the tension inherent in making both Christ and election the fountain of every good for sinners.

Finally, with regard to Christian freedom, both Luther and Calvin insist that neither church polity nor external matters of worship could be made matters of conscience. However, Calvin claims that church polity should follow the guidance of the Word of God, and that our worship must correspond with our profession of faith in Christ. For Luther, whatever is not expressly prohibited in the Word of God is allowed, including many of the rites and ceremonies from the papal church, whereas for Calvin the whole life of the church must be tested by its correspondence to Christ, necessitating the reformation or abolition of papal ceremonies that either obscure or deny Christ. Calvin also categorically prohibits images, both because of God's infinite and spiritual nature and because Jesus Christ alone is the image of the invisible God; he does not allow for any delay in abolishing the mass out of fear of offending the weak, contrary to Luther's policy in Wittenberg during 1522. For Luther, once the conscience is freed from externals by faith in Christ, all externals are a matter of indifference, and their use is governed only by the rule of love. For Calvin, even though faith frees the conscience from externals, the use of externals, especially in worship, must always correspond to the profession of faith in Christ, even as it is also governed by the rule of love.

All of these differences and disagreements regarding the testimony of the conscience and its role in the assurance of faith can only be understood in light of the overall framework of Luther and Calvin's thought. It is the theology of the cross, especially in light of the legal knowledge of God and tribulation (*Anfechtung*), that leads Luther to subordinate sanctification to justification and to make all externals a matter of indifference, to the point of norming the Ten Commandments by the natural law; for the inward faith is always contradicted by the external appearance. And it is his understanding of the Lord as our Father in Jesus Christ through the Holy Spirit that allows Calvin to distinguish between the knowledge of God the Creator and the knowledge of God the Redeemer, and to use both against idolatry; and to make Jesus Christ himself the object of faith, from whom flows the twofold grace of justification and sanctification, so that sanctification can be subordinated to justification regarding the basis of our adoption, whereas justification can be subordinated to sanctification regarding the goal of our adoption. These contexts not only account for the two theologians' different emphases even in cases where they fundamentally agree, as in the relationship of the testimony of the good conscience to the assurance of faith, but they also account for the place where they disagree, regarding the status of images and externals.

It is my sincere hope that this examination of the theologies of Luther and Calvin will lead to a fairer assessment of the strengths of both. I especially hope that this study will help lay to rest the commonplace but highly inaccurate contrast usually drawn between Luther and Calvin on the assurance of faith. On the one hand, Calvin shares with Luther an impressive focus on the centrality of the wonderful exchange in Jesus Christ as the once-for-all event of our reconciliation with God, attested to us in the gospel by Jesus Christ himself through the Holy Spirit; he also insists that God can only be for us in the gospel if we allow God to be against us in the law, because God justifies only those sinners who condemn themselves. On the other hand, Luther's theology shares with Calvin's certain unresolved problems, especially regarding the inherent instability of the law-gospel paradigm and the relationship between Christ and election. These problems arise precisely when the theologians depart from their focus on the revelation of God the Father in Jesus Christ, by distinguishing the law of God from the gospel of Christ, and by distinguishing the election of God from the happy exchange in Christ. Ironically, it was Calvin more than Luther who was increasingly aware of these problematic areas and who offered the most promising resolution of both in his doctrine of Christ as the image of the Father, although this doctrine was not consistently carried through in his theology.

BIBLIOGRAPHY

Primary Sources

Calvini, Ioannis. *Ioannis Calvini opera quae supersunt omnia.* Edited by William Baum, Edward Cunitz, and Edward Reuss. 59 vols. Brunsvigae: C. A. Schwetschke and Son (M. Bruhn), 1863–1900.

———. *Ioannis Calvini opera selecta.* Edited by Peter Barth, Wilhelm Niesel, and Dora Scheuner. 5 vols. Munich: Chr. Kaiser, 1926–1952.

Luther, Martin. *D. Martin Luthers Werke: Kritische Gesamtausgabe.* Weimar: Hermann Boehlau, 1883–1983.

———. *Dr. Martin Luthers Saemmtliche Schriften.* Edited by Johann Georg Walch. 23 vols. St. Louis: Concordia, 1881–1910.

Translations

Calvin, John. *Calvin: Institutes of the Christian Religion.* Edited by John T. McNeill and translated by Ford Lewis Battles. 2 vols. Philadelphia: Westminster Press, 1960.

———. *Calvin: Theological Treatises.* Edited by J. K. S. Reid. Philadelphia: Westminster Press, 1954.

———. *Calvin's New Testament Commentaries.* Edited by David W. Torrance and Thomas F. Torrance. 12 vols. Grand Rapids, Mich.: Wm. B. Eerdmans, 1959–1972.

———. *The Commentaries of John Calvin on the Old Testament.* 30 vols. Edinburgh: Calvin Translation Society, 1843–1848.

———. *Concerning the Eternal Predestination of God.* Translated by J. K. S. Reid. London: James Clarke and Co., Ltd., 1961.

———. *Concerning Scandals.* Translated by John W. Fraser. Grand Rapids, Mich.: Wm. B. Eerdmans, 1978.

———. *Institutes of the Christian Religion, 1536 Edition.* Translated by Ford Lewis Battles. Grand Rapids, Mich.: Wm. B. Eerdmans, 1986.

———. *John Calvin's Sermons on Ephesians.* Translated by Arthur Golding, Leslie Rawlinson, and S. M. Houghton. Edinburgh: Banner of Truth Trust, 1973.

———. *John Calvin's Sermons on the Ten Commandments.* Edited and translated by Benjamin W. Farley. Grand Rapids, Mich.: Baker Book House, 1980.

———. *Letters of John Calvin.* Edited by Dr. Jules Bonnet. 4 vols. Philadelphia: Presbyterian Board of Publication, 1858.

———. *Sermons from Job.* Translated by Leroy Nixon. Grand Rapids, Mich.: Baker Book House, 1979.

———. *Sermons on Isaiah's Prophecy of the Death and Passion of Christ.* Translated and edited by T. H. L. Parker. London: James Clarke and Co., 1956.

———. *Sermons on the Saving Work of Christ.* Translated by Leroy Nixon. Grand Rapids, Mich.: Baker Book House, 1980.

———. *Tracts and Treatises.* Translated by Henry Beveridge. 3 vols. Grand Rapids, Mich.: Wm. B. Eerdmans, 1958.

———. *Treatises Against the Anabaptists and Against the Libertines.* Translated and edited by Benjamin W. Farley. Grand Rapids, Mich.: Baker Book House, 1982.

———. "A Warning Against Judiciary Astrology and Other Prevalent Curiosities." Translated by Mary Potter. *Calvin Theological Journal* 18 (1983), 157–89.

Calvin, John, and Jacopo Sadoleto. *A Reformation Debate*. Edited by John C. Olin. Grand Rapids, Mich.: Baker Book House, 1976.

Luther, Martin. *Luther's Commentary on the First Twenty-two Psalms*. Edited by John Nicholas Lenker. Vol. 1. Sunbury, Pa.: Lutherans in All Lands, 1903.

————. *Luther's Works*. American edition. Edited by Jaroslav Pelikan and Helmut T. Lehman. 54 vols. St. Louis: Concordia Publishing House; Philadelphia: Fortress Press, 1955–1967.

————. *Sermons of Martin Luther*. Edited by John Nicholas Lenker. 8 vols. Grand Rapids, Mich.: Baker Book House, 1983.

Secondary Sources

Alanen, Yrjo J. E. *Das Gewissen bei Luther*. Annales Academiae Scientiarum Fennicae, Ser. B., Vol. 29/2. Helsinki, 1934.

Baylor, Michael G. *Action and Person. Conscience in Late Scholasticism and the Young Luther*. Leiden: E. J. Brill, 1977.

Beintker, Horst. "Das Gewissen in der Spannung zwischen Gesetz und Evangelium." *Lutherjahrbuch* 48 (1981): 115–47.

Bizer, Ernst. *Fides ex auditu*. 3d ed. Neukirchen, Germany: Moers, 1966.

Bohatec, Josef. *Calvin und das Recht*. Feudingen in Westfalen: Buchdruckerie v. Verlagsanstalt G.m.b.H., 1934.

Bornkamm, Heinrich. "Bindung und Freiheit in der Ordnung der Kirche." In *Das Jahrhundert der Reformation*. Goettingen: Vandenhoeck und Ruprecht, 1961, pp. 185–202.

————. "Christus und das 1. Gebot in der Anfechtung bei Luther." *Zeitschrift fur systematische Theologie* 5 (1927–28): 453–77.

————. "Zur Frage der Iustitia Dei beim jungen Luther." *Archiv fur Reformationsgeschichte* 52 (1961), 15–29; 53 (1962), 1–59.

Bouwsma, William J. *John Calvin: A Sixteenth Century Portrait*. Oxford and New York: Oxford University Press, 1988.

Bremi, Willi. *Was ist das Gewissen? Seine Beschreibung, seine metaphysische und religiose Deutung, seine Geschichte*. Zurich: Orell Fussli, 1934.

Brosche, Fredrik. "Luther on Predestination: The Antinomy and Unity Between Love and Wrath in Luther's Concept of God." Doctoral diss., Uppsala University, 1978.

Brunner, Emil. *Natural Theology*, including Barth's *Nein!* Translated by Peter Fraenkel. London: Centenary Press, 1946.

Brunner, Peter. "Das Problem der natuerlichen Theologie bei Calvin." *Theologische Existenz Heute* 18 (1935): 3–60.

Cochrane, Arthur C. "Natural law in Calvin." In *Church-State Relations in Ecumenical Perspective*. Edited by Elwyn A. Smith. Pittsburg: Duquenne University Press, 1966, pp. 176–217.

Cranz, F. Edward. *An Essay on the Development of Luther's Thought on Justice, Law, and Society*. Cambridge, Mass.: Harvard University Press, 1959.

Dowey, Edward A., Jr. *The Knowledge of God in Calvin's Theology*. New York and London: Columbia University Press, 1952.

Ebeling, Gerhard. *Luther: An Introduction to His Thought*. Translated by R. A. Wilson. Philadelphia: Fortress Press, 1972.

————. "Cognitio Dei et hominis." In *Lutherstudien I*. Tuebingen: Mohr (Paul Siebeck), 1971, pp. 221–72.

————. "Theologische Erwaegungen ueber das Gewissen." In *Wort und Glaube*. Tuebingen: Mohr, 1967, pp. 429–46.

Foxgrover, David Lee. "John Calvin's Understanding of Conscience." Ph.D. diss., Claremont School of Theology, 1978.

————. " 'Temporary Faith' and the Certainty of Election." *Calvin Theological Journal* 15 (1980): 220–32.

Gerrish, Brian A. *Grace and Reason*. Oxford: Oxford University Press, 1962.

Gessert, Robert A. "The Integrity of Faith: an Inquiry into the Meaning of Law in the Thought of John Calvin." *Scottish Journal of Theology* 13 (1960): 247–61.

Gloede, Guenter. *Theologia naturalis bei Calvin*. Stuttgart: Kohlhammer, 1935.

Grane, Leif. "Luthers Auslegung von Rom 2:12-15 in der Romerbrief-vorlesung." *Neue Zeitschrift fur systematische Theologie* 17 (1975): 22–32.

Grislis, E. "Calvin's use of Cicero in Inst. I.1–5: A Case Study in Theological Method." *Archiv fur Reformationsgeschichte* 62 (1971): 5–37.

Haile, H. G. "Algorithm and Epikeia: Martin Luther's Experience with Law." *Sound* 6 (1978): 500–514.

Heintze, Gerhard. *Luthers Predigt von Gesetz und Evangelium*. Munich: Chr. Kaiser Verlag, 1958.

Hesselink, I. John. *Calvin's Concept and Use of the Law*. Dissertation, Universitat Basel, 1961.

————. "Christ, the Law, and the Christian: An Unexplored Aspect of the Third Use of the Law in Calvin's Theology." In *Reformatio perennis*. Pittsburgh: Pickwick Press, 1981, pp. 11–26.

Hirsch, Emanuel. *Lutherstudien*. Vol. 1: *Drei Kapital zu Luthers Lehre vom Gewissen*. Gutersloh: C. Bertelsmann, 1954.

Hoepfl, Harro. *The Christian Polity of John Calvin*. Cambridge: Cambridge University Press, 1982.

Hoffmann, Heinrich. "Reformation und Gewissensfreiheit." *Archiv fur Reformations-geschichte* 37 (1940): 170–88.

Holl, Karl. *Gesammelte Aufsaetze zur Kirchengeschichte*. Vol. 1: *Luther*. 7th ed. Tuebingen: Mohr (Paul Siebeck), 1948.

————. *What Did Luther Understand by Religion?* Translated by Fred W. Meuser and Walter R. Wietzke. Philadelphia: Fortress Press, 1977.

Holmes, Arthur Baines. "Conscience as a Soteriological Battlefield: The Concept of Conscience Operative in Luther's Galatians Lectures of 1531." Ph.D. diss., Drew University, 1971.

Jacob, Guenter. *Der Gewissensbegriff in der Theologie Luthers, Bertraegezur histo-rischen Theologie*. Nendeln, Liechtenstein: Kraus, 1966.

Joest, Wilfried. *Gesetz und Freiheit. Das Problem des Tertius usus legis bei Luther und die neutestamentliche Paranaise*. 2d ed. Goettingen: Vandenhoeck und Ruprecht, 1961.

————. *Ontologie der Person bei Luther*. Goettingen: Vandenhoeck und Ruprecht, 1967.

Kelly, Robert Allen. "Free Conscience and Obedient Body: Martin Luther's Views on Authority in Church and State Analyzed in the Context of his Theology of the Cross." Ph.D. diss., Fuller Theological Seminary, 1981.

Lane, A. N. S. "Calvin's Doctrine of Assurance." *Vox Evangelica* 11 (1979), 32–54.

Loewenich, Walter von. *Luthers theologia crucis*. 5th ed. Wittenberg: Luther-Verlag, 1967.

Lohse, Bernhard. *Ratio und Fides. Eine Untersuchung ueber die ratio in der Theologie Luthers*. Goettingen: Vandenhoeck und Ruprecht, 1957.

————. "Conscience and Authority in Luther." In *Luther and the Dawn of the Modern Era*. Edited by Heiko A. Oberman. Leiden: E. J. Brill, 1974, pp. 158–83.

McGrath, Alister E. *Luther's Theology of the Cross*. Oxford: Basil Blackwell, 1985.

McIntyre, Russel Leonard. "Christian Freedom and Ethical Decision in the Theology of Martin Luther." Ph.D. diss., Toronto University, 1969.

McNeill, John T. "Natural Law in the Thought of Luther." *Church History* 10 (1941), 211–27.

————. "Natural Law in the Teaching of the Reformers." *Church History* 26 (1946): 168–82.

Mau, Rudolph. "Gebundenes und befreites Gewissen: zum Verstaendnis von conscientia in Luthers Auseinandersetzungen mit dem Moenchtum." *Theologische Versuche* 9 (1977): 177–89.

Meinhold, Peter. "Gewissen und Freiheit bei Luther." In *Pluralisme et oecumenisme en recherches Theologiques*. Gembloux: Duculot, 1976, pp. 51–56.

Muelhaupt, Erwin. "Schrift, Vernunft, Gewissen— die Parole von Worms." In *Luther in Worms—1971*. Worms: Stadtarchiv, 1973, pp. 73–84.

Neal, John Raymond. "Conscience in the Reformation Period." Ph.D. diss., Harvard University, 1972.

Niesel, Wilhelm. *The Theology of Calvin*. Translated by Harold Knight. Grand Rapids, Mich.: Baker Book House, 1980.

Oberman, Heiko A. "Headwaters of the Reformation: *Initia Lutheri—Initia Reformationis*." In *Luther and the Dawn of the Modern Era*. Edited by Heiko A. Oberman. Leiden: E. J. Brill, 1974, pp. 40–88.

————. "Simul Gemitus et Raptus." In *The Reformation in Medieval Perspective*. Edited by Steven E. Ozment. Chicago: Quadrangle, 1971, pp. 219–51.

Ozment, Steven E. *The Age of Reform, 1250–1550: An Intellectual and Religious History of Late Medieval and Reformation Europe*. New Haven and London: Yale University Press, 1980.

————. *Homo Spiritualis: A Comparative Study of the Anthropology of Johannes Tauler, Jean Gerson, and Martin Luther (1509–1516) in the Context of their Theological Thought*. Leiden: E. J. Brill, 1969.

Parker, T. H. L. *Calvin's Doctrine of the Knowledge of God: A Study in the Theology of John Calvin*. Edinburgh: Oliver & Boyd, 1969.

Pelikan, Jaroslav. *The Christian Tradition: A History of the Development of Doctrine*. Vol. 4: *Reformation of Church and Dogma (1300–1700)*. Chicago and London: University of Chicago Press, 1984.

Pelkonen, J. P. "The Teaching of John Calvin on the Nature and Function of the Conscience." *Lutheran Quarterly* 21 (1969): 74–88.

Pinomaa, Lennart. *Der existentielle Charakter der Theologie Luthers*. Annales Academiae Scientiarum Fennicae, Ser. B., Vol. 47/B. Helsinki, 1940.

Rupp, E. Gordon. *The Righteousness of God. Luther Studies*. London: Hodder and Stoughton, 1953.

Schott, Erdmann. *Fleisch und Geist nach Luthers Lehre*. Darmstadt: Wissenschaftliche Buchgesellschaft, 1969.

Seeberg, Reinhold. *The History of Doctrines*. Translated by Charles E. Hay. 2 vols. Grand Rapids, Mich.: Baker Book House, 1978.

Selge, Kurt-Victor. "Capta conscientia in verbis dei, Luthers Widerrufsverweigerung in Worms." In *Der Reichstag zu Worms von 1521: Reichspolitik und Luthersache*. Edited by Fritz Reuter. Worms: Norberg, 1971, pp. 155–207.

Siegfried, Theodor. *Luther und Kant; Ein geistesgeschichtlicher Vergleich im Anschluss an den Gewissensbegriff*. Giessen, **pub.?** 1930.

Stelzenberger, Johann. *Syneidesis, Conscientia, Gewissen*. Paderborn, Germany: Ferdinand Schoningh, 1963.

Stendahl, Krister. "The Apostle Paul and the Introspective Conscience of the West." *Harvard Theological Review* 55 (1963): 199–215.

Street, Thomas W. "John Calvin on Adiaphora: an Exposition and Appraisal of his Theory and Practice." Ph.D. diss., Union Theological Seminary, 1955.

Sundquist, Ralph Roger, Jr. *The Third Use of the Law in the Thought of John Calvin: an Interpretation and Evaluation*. Ph.D. diss., Columbia University, 1970.

Thomas, J. N. "The Place of Natural Theology in the Thought of John Calvin." *Journal of Religious Thought* 15 (1958): 107–36.

Torrance, T. F. *Calvin's Doctrine of Man*. Grand Rapids, Mich.: Wm. B. Eerdmans, 1957.

Trinkaus, Charles, and Oberman, Heiko A., eds. *The Pursuit of Holiness in Late Medieval and Renaissance Religion*. Leiden: E. J. Brill, 1974.

Troeltsch, Ernst. *The Social Teaching of the Christian Churches*. Translated by Olive Wyon. 2 vols. Chicago and London: University of Chicago Press, 1976.

Vercruysse, Jos. E. "Conscience and Authority in Luther's Explanation of the Fourth Commandment." *In Luther and the Dawn of the Modern Era*. Edited by Heiko A. Oberman. Leiden: E. J. Brill, 1974, pp. 184–94.

Verhey, Allen Dale. "Natural Law in Aquinas and Calvin." In *God and the Good. Essays in Honor of Henry Stob*. Edited by Clifton Orlebeke and Lewis Smedes. Grand Rapids, Mich.: Wm. B. Eerdmans, 1975, pp. 80–92.

Verkamp, Bernard J. "Limits Upon Adiaphoristic Freedom: Luther and Melanchthon." *Theological Studies* 36 (1975): 52–76.

Warfield, Benjamin B. "Calvin's Doctrine of the Knowledge of God." In *Calvin and Augustine*. Philadelphia: Presbyterian and Reformed Publishing Co., 1956, pp. 29–130.

Weber, Carl. "The Third Use of the Law and Luther's Lectures on Galatians (1535)." *American Benedictine Review* 17 (1966): 372–96.

Weber, Max. *The Protestant Ethic and the Spirit of Capitalism*. Translated by Talcott Parsons. New York: Charles Scribner's Sons, 1958.

Wicks, Jared. *Man Yearning for Grace: Luther's Early Spiritual Teaching*. Wiesbaden: Franz Steiner, 1969.

Willis, E. David. *Calvin's Catholic Christology*. Leiden: E. J. Brill, 1966.

Wilterdink, Garret. *Tyrant or Father? A Study of Calvin's Doctrine of God*. 2 vols. Bristol, Ind.: Wyndham Hall Press, 1985.

Wolf, Ernst. "Gewissen zwischen Gesetz und Evangelium." In *Peregrinatio II*. Munich: Kaiser, 1965, pp. 104–18.

———. "Vom Problem des Gewissens in reformatorischer Sicht." In Wolf's *Perigrinatio*. Munich: Kaiser, 1954, pp. 81–112.

———. "Zur Frage des Naturrechts bei Thomas und bei Luther." *Jahrbuch der Gesellschaft fuer die Geschichte des Protestantismus in Osterreich* 67 (1951): 186–204.

INDEX